MW01039054

Building New Deal Liberalism
The Political Economy of Public Works, 1933–1956

This book provides the first historical study of New Deal public works programs and their role in transforming the American economy, landscape, and political system during the twentieth century. Reconstructing the story of how reformers used public authority to reshape the nation, Jason Scott Smith argues that the New Deal produced a revolution in state-sponsored economic development. The scale and scope of this dramatic federal investment in infrastructure laid crucial foundations – sometimes literally – for postwar growth, presaging the national highways and the military-industrial complex. This impressive and exhaustively researched analysis underscores the importance of the New Deal in comprehending political and economic change in modern America by placing political economy at the center of the "new political history." Drawing on a remarkable range of sources, Smith provides a groundbreaking reinterpretation of the relationship between the New Deal's welfare state and American liberalism.

Jason Scott Smith is an assistant professor of history at the University of New Mexico. He previously held a Mellon Fellowship in American Studies at Cornell University, where he was a visiting assistant professor in the department of history and the department of government. In 2001–02 he was the Harvard-Newcomen Fellow at the Harvard Business School, where he taught courses on the history of capitalism. His work has appeared in a number of journals, including the *Journal of Social History*, *Pacific Historical Review*, *Reviews in American History*, and the *Journal of Interdisciplinary History*.

"Jason Scott Smith explores the very foundation of New Deal liberalism by examining the relationship among infrastructure, state authority, and durable partisan loyalty. Placing the political economy at the center of this story, *Building New Deal Liberalism* makes an important contribution to our understanding of American political development in this pivotal era."

– Brian Balogh, University of Virginia

"This book, which opens new pathways for understanding the significance of the New Deal, marks a major contribution to the literature concerned with the federal government's twentieth-century growth. Here, beautifully rendered by a master historical craftsman, are the nuts and bolts of the New Deal edifice."

– Edward D. Berkowitz, George Washington University

"A fine study brimming with insights about the New Deal state, expertise, and the political economy of public works in the middle decades of the twentieth century."

– Jessica Wang, *Technology and Culture*

Building New Deal Liberalism

The Political Economy of Public Works, 1933–1956

JASON SCOTT SMITH

University of New Mexico

CAMBRIDGE UNIVERSITY PRESS

CAMBRIDGE UNIVERSITY PRESS
Cambridge, New York, Melbourne, Madrid, Cape Town, Singapore,
São Paulo, Delhi, Dubai, Tokyo, Mexico City

Cambridge University Press
32 Avenue of the Americas, New York, NY 10013-2473, USA

www.cambridge.org
Information on this title: www.cambridge.org/9780521139939

First published 2006
First paperback edition 2009
Reprinted 2010

A catalog record for this publication is available from the British Library.

Library of Congress Cataloging in Publication Data

Smith, Jason Scott, 1970–
Building New Deal liberalism : the political economy of public works, 1933–1956 /
Jason Scott Smith.
    p.   cm.
Includes bibliographical references and index.
ISBN 0-521-82805-8 (hardback)
1. New Deal, 1933–1939.   2. United States – Economic policy – 1933–1945.
3. United States – Economic conditions – 1918–1945.   4. United States –
Politics and government – 1933–1945.   5. Liberalism – United States –
History – 20th century.   I. Title.
HC106.3.S537   2005
338.973'009'043 – dc22   2005006335

ISBN 978-0-521-82805-5 Hardback
ISBN 978-0-521-13993-9 Paperback

Cambridge University Press has no responsibility for the persistence or accuracy of URLs
for external or third-party Internet Web sites referred to in this publication and does not
guarantee that any content on such Web sites is, or will remain, accurate or appropriate.

Contents

List of Illustrations   *page* vi

Acknowledgments   ix

Common Abbreviations in Text and Notes   xiii

1   Reevaluating the New Deal State and the Public Works
    Revolution   1

2   Economic Development and Unemployment during the
    Early New Deal   21

3   Making a New Deal State: Patronage and the Public
    Works Administration   54

4   The Dilemma of New Deal Public Works: People or
    Projects?   85

5   "Boondoggling" and the Welfare State   135

6   Party Building and "Pernicious Political Activities":
    The Road to the Hatch Act   160

7   Public Works and New Deal Liberalism in Reorganization
    and War   190

8   Public Works and the Postwar World   232

9   Epilogue: Public Works and the Building of New
    Deal Liberalism   258

Sources   267

Index   273

Illustrations

1 Triborough Bridge, New York City   *page* 123
2 Water Purification Works, Cincinnati, Ohio   123
3 Alameda County Courthouse, Oakland, California   124
4 Reservoir and Water System, Los Angeles, California   124
5 O'Shaughnessy Dam, Hetch Hetchy Reservoir, California   125
6 Port of Oakland, California   125
7 State Capitol, Salem, Oregon   126
8 Coast Bridge, Oregon   126
9 Pierre S. DuPont High School, Wilmington, Delaware   127
10 Surgical Hospital Building, Hopemont, West Virginia   127
11 Overseas Highway, Florida   128
12 Cold Storage Plant, Mobile, Alabama   128
13 Administration Building, Municipal Airport, Fort Worth, Texas   129
14 Davidson County Courthouse, Nashville, Tennessee   129
15 Armory, Minneapolis, Minnesota   130
16 Allegheny County Bridge, Pennsylvania   130
17 Central Fire Station, Louisville, Kentucky   131
18 Surgical Operating and Ward Building, Boston, Massachusetts   131
19 Public Library, De Pere, Wisconsin   132
20 Grade School, Parco, Wyoming   132
21 Williamsburg Houses, Brooklyn, New York   133

22 U.S.S. *Yorktown*   133
23 Federal Trade Commission Building, Washington, D.C.   134
24 U.S. Bullion Depository, Fort Knox, Kentucky   134

Acknowledgments

I owe a great debt to many people and institutions for their support of this project. This book began as a dissertation in the history department at the University of California, Berkeley, and took shape over several years while I held postdoctoral fellowships at Harvard University and at Cornell University. At Berkeley, I owe more than I can say to Robin Einhorn, not only for her amazingly fast and perceptive readings of chapters, but more importantly for teaching me what history is all about. I cannot imagine a better adviser, nor a more steadfast friend and colleague as I navigated the academic job market. I am grateful to David Hollinger and to Kiren Chaudhry for their encouragement and guidance, both as they served on my committee and afterward. Jim Kettner always had time to offer his quiet blend of kindness and insight, and I am saddened he did not live to see this book completed. Paul Sabin, Phil Soffer, and Anne Woo-Sam provided counsel at an early stage, and Guian McKee, Monica Rico, Chad Bryant, J. P. Daughton, Brad Hunt, and Kaarin Michaelsen supplied advice on a number of the chapters. Randy Starn and Tina Gillis at the Doreen B. Townsend Center for the Humanities provided a fellowship and support while I began writing. Hee Ko, Mabel Lee, Chaela Pastore, Michelle Tusan, Diana Selig, Susanna Barrows, Yuri Slezkine, Dan Rolde, Robert Avila, Paul Romano, Nils Gilman, David Milnes, Judy Rummelsburg, Kevin Chen, Anthony De Ritis, and Stephen Cole helped in multiple ways.

At Harvard, I was fortunate to hold the Harvard-Newcomen fellowship at the Harvard Business School. This was a wonderful experience, in great part because it meant that I got to know Thomas McCraw. Tom's intelligence and encouragement have meant a great deal to me, and our conversations about the New Deal and capitalism helped to sharpen my arguments. At HBS, Walter Friedman read the entire manuscript with care and Yankee ingenuity. David Moss, Jeff Fear, Geoffrey Jones, Nancy Koehn, Richard Tedlow, Dan Wadhwani, and Stephen Mihm provided helpful insights and friendship. Margaret Willard edited the manuscript and saved me from many errors and infelicities. Across the Charles River, Sven Beckert proved a generous and thoughtful colleague, and the seminar on political economy that he directed at the Charles Warren Center was continually stimulating. Alice O'Connor generously commented on an early conference paper I presented at the Policy History Conference in St. Louis, and has been a friendly source of wisdom and insight, both during her time as a Fellow at the Warren Center and subsequently. I also learned much from presentations made by Paul Samuelson, at the Business History Seminar at HBS, and by John Kenneth Galbraith, in a forum arranged by Richard Parker at Harvard's Kennedy School of Government. Regina Abrami, Gunnar Trumbull, Meg Jacobs, Chris Capozzola, Anthony De Ritis, Veronica Ryback, and Jonathan Zatlin helped to make Cambridge and Boston feel like home.

Many comments and suggestions from audience members at various conference presentations have proven exceedingly helpful, and I apologize for not being able to acknowledge by name all of the people who asked such interesting questions. I am grateful to Catherine Collomp and Mark Meigs for an invitation to present my work at the Université de Paris VII, at the conference "Beyond the New Deal." Conversations there with Lizabeth Cohen, Allida Black, Marianne Debouzy, Cathy Turner, and Bob Cherny helped a great deal. At the International Planning History Society conference in Barcelona, I learned much from my co-panelists Kelly Quinn and Brad Hunt, and I thank Bob Breugmann for his incisive critiques of our papers. I want to thank Richard John for the opportunity to give a paper at the Technology, Politics, and Culture seminar at the Newberry Library in Chicago, as well as for his generous assistance on a number of matters. Brian Balogh thoughtfully located my work in the growing "new political history" in his comments on a paper I presented at the annual meeting of the American Historical Association, and conversations with a number of people at the Policy History Conference, including Bill Novak, Ajay Mehrotra, Gail Radford, Margaret O'Mara, and Michael Bernstein, helped me clarify what is at stake in examining the New Deal through the lens of historical political economy.

At Cornell, I am grateful to Larry Moore and Elizabeth Sanders for selecting me as a Mellon Fellow, and for the opportunity to serve as an assistant professor in the department of history and department of government. I have thus been able to complete this book while living in a remarkable community of scholars, and I have learned much from conversations with Bernadette Meyler, Sandra Greene, Val Bunce, Richard Bensel, Richard Polenberg, Fredrik Logevall, Ed Baptist, Derek Chang, Holly Case, Aaron Sachs, and, in Cornell's Mellon Humanities Seminar, Robert Frank, Harry Shaw, Ron Kline, and Michele Moody-Adams.

At the University of New Mexico, I thank Jane Slaughter, Virginia Scharff, Tim Moy, Andrew Sandoval-Strausz, Cathleen Cahill, and the members of the history department for their engagement with my work and for providing such a warm welcome to the Southwest. Lew Bateman and everyone at Cambridge University Press have been a tremendous help in the publication process, and I greatly appreciate their assistance. Mark Leff and Ed Berkowitz provided detailed advice as readers for Cambridge, and they subsequently took me out for a memorable lunch. I hope I can somehow repay their multiple investments in this project.

This book simply would not exist without the work done by many talented archivists and library staff, and I thank them all for helping me locate and gain access to so many obscure sources. The National Archives in Washington, D.C., and in College Park, Maryland, the manuscript division of the Library of Congress, and the Franklin D. Roosevelt Library in Hyde Park, New York, are terrific places to work. The helpful staff of these archives, and of the vast library systems of Berkeley, Harvard, and Cornell, was indispensable to me. I am also grateful to the University of California Press and the *Pacific Historical Review* for permission to draw upon aspects of my article, "New Deal Public Works at War: The WPA and Japanese American Internment." The University of California, Berkeley, department of history, the Mellon Foundation, the Franklin and Eleanor Roosevelt Institute, the Newcomen Society, and Harvard Business School's Division of Research provided financial support for this project. While all of these people and institutions have helped me, the ultimate responsibility for this book is mine.

Finally, I owe a great debt to my parents, Daniel and Yvonne. I thank them not only for their love and support, but also for giving me such a wonderful sister, Sarah.

Common Abbreviations in Text and Notes

Organizations

ACA	Advisory Committee on Allotments
AALL	American Association for Labor Legislation
AFL	American Federation of Labor
AGC	Associated General Contractors of America
CCC	Civilian Conservation Corps
CWA	Civil Works Administration
ERCA	Emergency Relief and Construction Act
FERA	Federal Emergency Relief Administration
FWA	Federal Works Agency
GSA	General Services Administration
NIRA	National Industrial Recovery Act
NPB	National Planning Board
NRA	National Recovery Administration
NRPB	National Resources Planning Board
PECE	President's Emergency Committee for Employment
PWA	Public Works Administration
PWR	Public Works Reserve
RFC	Reconstruction Finance Corporation
TVA	Tennessee Valley Authority
WRA	War Relocation Authority
WCCA	Wartime Civilian Control Administration
WPA	Works Progress Administration (after 1939, Work Projects Administration)

Archives

FDRL	Franklin D. Roosevelt Library
	OF Official File
	PPF President's Personal File
	PSF President's Secretary's File
JERS	Japanese American Evacuation and Resettlement Records
LC	Manuscript Division, Library of Congress
NA	National Archives, Washington, D.C.
NA–College Park	National Archives, College Park, Maryland
RG	Record Group

Building New Deal Liberalism

The Political Economy of Public Works, 1933–1956

I

Reevaluating the New Deal State and the Public Works Revolution

This is a history of how reformers built modern America during depression and war. Although I am indebted to the work of previous scholars, my goal with this book is to construct a new narrative. Using the interpretive lens of political economy, I seek to recast our understanding of the New Deal's significance through a fresh investigation of the archival record. The New Deal, I argue, revolutionized the priorities of the American state, radically transforming the physical landscape, political system, and economy of the United States.

We can begin to recover the scope of this transformation by looking directly at how the New Deal state spent its money.[1] On average, between 1933 and 1939 over two-thirds of federal emergency expenditures went toward funding public works programs.[2] These dollars, representing an increase in federal construction spending of 1,650 percent over the four years that preceded the Depression (1925–29), were allocated to

---

[1] In doing this, I follow the advice of economist Joseph Schumpeter. In his classic essay, "The Crisis of the Tax State," Schumpeter, borrowing the insights of sociologist Rudolf Goldscheid, declared, "The budget is the skeleton of the state, stripped of all misleading ideologies." See Joseph A. Schumpeter, "The Crisis of the Tax State," trans. W. F. Stolper and R. A. Musgrave, *American Economic Papers* 4 (1954): 5–38 (originally published in German in 1918); and Rudolf Goldscheid, "A Sociological Approach to Problems of Public Finance," in Richard A. Musgrave and Alan T. Peacock, eds., *Classics in the Theory of Public Finance* (London: Macmillan, 1964), 202–13.

[2] I have calculated this figure using *The Budget of the United States Government for the Fiscal Year Ending June 30, 1940* (Washington, D.C.: U.S. Government Printing Office, 1939), vii; and *The Budget of the United States Government for the Fiscal Year Ending June 30, 1941* (Washington, D.C.: U.S. Government Printing Office, 1940), xxi–xxii. Between 1933 and 1939 emergency spending averaged about 50 percent of all federal expenditures.

new agencies, such as the Public Works Administration (PWA), and later the Works Progress Administration (WPA). The PWA, created in 1933, received an initial appropriation of $3.3 billion (about $45.8 billion in 2002 dollars), which it mainly applied to heavy construction and large-scale building. To put this figure in context, this amount was just over 165 percent of the federal government's revenues in 1933, or 5.9 percent of the 1933 U.S. gross domestic product (GDP). Relying on private contractors, the PWA deployed its funds in 3,068 of the nation's 3,071 counties, while helping to pay for projects like the Tennessee Valley Authority and Boulder Dam. Created in 1935, the WPA did lighter construction work and avoided private contracting. Its initial appropriation of $4.88 billion (about $64 billion in 2002 dollars) was about 135 percent of the federal government's revenues in 1935, or about 6.7 percent of GDP in that year. Although primarily intended as a vast relief effort for employing the unskilled, the WPA built an impressive range of projects, including over 480 airports, 78,000 bridges, and nearly 40,000 public buildings. Both programs were the beneficiaries of the federal government's commitment to construction. During these years, the payrolls of the PWA and the WPA were among the largest in the nation, easily dwarfing those of the largest private enterprises. In carrying out their mandates, the two programs integrated a multitude of municipal construction experts, members of the Army Corps of Engineers, and civil engineers into the national state.[3]

By viewing the New Deal in this way, we can begin to see the outlines of a different interpretation. The terrific increase over pre–Depression

[3] Roger Daniels, "Public Works in the 1930s: A Preliminary Reconnaissance," in *The Relevancy of Public Works History: The 1930s – A Case Study* (Washington, D.C.: Public Works Historical Society, 1975), 5. See also Ellis L. Armstrong, ed., *History of Public Works in the United States, 1776–1976* (Chicago: American Public Works Association, 1976), 681. Throughout this study, I employ Armstrong's definition of public works: "The physical structures and facilities developed or acquired by public agencies to house governmental functions and provide water, waste disposal, power, transportation, and similar services to facilitate the achievement of common social and economic objectives." Armstrong, ed., *History of Public Works in the United States*, 1.
   The most important recent treatment of New Deal social policy provides an excellent account of the WPA's central place within the New Deal state but unfortunately neglects the economic and political dimensions of the actual public works produced under this program. See Edwin Amenta, *Bold Relief: Institutional Politics and the Origins of Modern American Social Policy* (Princeton: Princeton University Press, 1998); and Edwin Amenta, Ellen Benoit, Chris Bonastia, Nancy K. Cauthen, and Drew Halfmann, "Bring Back the WPA: Work, Relief, and the Origins of American Social Policy in Welfare Reform," *Studies in American Political Development* 12 (Spring 1998): 1–56.

spending on public construction that these programs represented, the far-reaching federal efforts invested in directing this money, and the long-run impact of the infrastructure itself form the components of the story of a public works revolution. This revolution helped justify the new role of the state in American life, legitimizing – intellectually and physically – what has come to be known as Keynesian management of the economy. By sponsoring this infrastructure, New Dealers remade the built environment that managed the movement of people, goods, electricity, water, and waste. Among the New Deal's projects were some of the largest and most significant structures ever built in human history.[4]

Although public works have had an undeniable impact on the nation, Americans have generally taken them for granted, often forgetting that government has long been central to constructing basic infrastructure. As early as 1776, economist Adam Smith observed that in a functioning economy it was the government's duty to build "those public works, which, though they may be in the highest degree advantageous to a great society, are, however, of such a nature, that the profit could never repay the expense to any individual or small number of individuals." In the nineteenth century, federal and state governments in the United States subsidized such projects as canals and railroads through a mixture of direct financing, land grants, and reliance on private enterprise. City governments, for their part, treated public works construction as their

---

[4] While economic historians have done a lot of work on problems of public finance at the federal, state, and local levels during the New Deal, they generally draw a distinction – unwarranted, in my view – between spending on "public works" done by the PWA and "work relief" performed by the WPA, neglecting the fact that both efforts produced substantial infrastructure throughout the nation. For a review of the best of this literature, see John Joseph Wallis, "The Political Economy of New Deal Spending Revisited, Again: With and without Nevada," *Explorations in Economic History* 35 (1998): 140–70; and see also Wallis and Wallace E. Oates, "The Impact of the New Deal on American Federalism," in Michael D. Bordo, Claudia Goldin, and Eugene N. White, eds., *The Defining Moment: The Great Depression and the American Economy in the Twentieth Century* (Chicago: University of Chicago Press, 1998), 155–80; Wallis, "The Political Economy of New Deal Fiscal Federalism," *Economic Inquiry* 29 (July 1991): 510–24; Wallis, "The Birth of the Old Federalism: Financing the New Deal, 1932–1940," *Journal of Economic History* 44 (March 1984): 139–59; Wallis, "Work Relief and Unemployment in the 1930s" (Ph.D. diss., University of Washington, 1981); Gavin Wright, "The Political Economy of New Deal Spending: An Econometric Analysis," *Review of Economics and Statistics* 56 (Feb. 1974): 30–38; Don C. Reading, "New Deal Activity and the States, 1933 to 1939," *Journal of Economic History* 33 (December 1973): 792–810; Leonard J. Arrington, "The New Deal in the West: A Preliminary Statistical Inquiry," *Pacific Historical Review* 38 (August 1969): 311–16; and, still worth reading, E. Cary Brown, "Fiscal Policy in the Thirties: A Reappraisal," *American Economic Review* 46 (December 1956): 857–79.

primary activity. The economic upheavals of the twentieth century, however, brought into focus an increasing need for more public investment.[5]

In reconstructing this story, I argue that public works programs are critical to our understanding of New Deal liberalism. I reexamine the role that
these government agencies played in the creation of the modern American
welfare state, breaking sharply from previous accounts that dismiss them
simply as temporary efforts that failed to solve the crisis of the Great
Depression. Instead, I look at them as important, wide-ranging investments in national infrastructure, rich in significance for understanding
the many changes that occurred in government policy, business interests,
and organized labor during this period. Redefining the New Deal through
an examination of its expenditures on public works allows for new questions to be asked, and for older questions to be asked again in new ways.
How, seen through the perspective of the public works programs, do we
view the expansion and growth of the federal government that took place
between 1933 and World War II? Despite their documented failures as
unemployment relief measures, were these programs successful in laying
the structural foundations for postwar economic development and prosperity? Does the fact that New Deal spending priorities were directed
toward these massive construction programs clarify what one historian
has recently termed "the ambiguity of New Deal economics?"[6] In light
of all of this, can we better understand the successes and failures of New
Deal liberalism as an episode in modern American politics?

In carrying out this study, I have greatly benefited from the insights of
a number of scholars. I have relied on an older literature that clarifies the

[5] Adam Smith, *An Inquiry into the Nature and Causes of the Wealth of Nations*, ed.
Edwin Cannan (Chicago: University of Chicago Press, 1976), 2:244; George Rogers
Taylor, *The Transportation Revolution, 1815–1860* (New York: Harper and Row, 1951);
Jon C. Teaford, *The Unheralded Triumph: City Government in America, 1870–1900*
(Baltimore: Johns Hopkins University Press, 1984); R. Rudy Higgens-Evenson, *The Price
of Progress: Public Services, Taxation, and the American Corporate State, 1877–1929*
(Baltimore: Johns Hopkins University Press, 2003); Alfred D. Chandler, *The Visible Hand:
The Managerial Revolution in American Business* (Cambridge: Harvard University Press,
1977); Thomas J. Misa, *A Nation of Steel: The Making of Modern America, 1865–1925*
(Baltimore: Johns Hopkins University Press, 1995); and Thomas P. Hughes, *American
Genesis: A Century of Invention and Technological Enthusiasm, 1870–1970* (New York:
Viking, 1989). For a wide-ranging and provocative account of the relationship between
government and the economy, see Peter H. Lindert, *Growing Public: Social Spending and
Economic Growth Since the Eighteenth Century*, vol. 1: *The Story* (Cambridge: Cambridge
University Press, 2004).
[6] Robert M. Collins, *More: The Politics of Economic Growth in Postwar America* (New
York: Oxford University Press, 2000), 1–16.

historical relationship between government and the economy, while incorporating the insights of more recent scholarly attention to the contingent growth and development of structures of public finance, public works, and political economy.[7] This interpretive focus restores the New Deal public works programs to the broader narrative of American economic development, a narrative that acknowledges the importance of World War II government contracts to American business and highlights the central role played by government spending in the subsequent growth of the postwar period, but has comparatively neglected the events of the New Deal years.[8]

Public works were a crucial element of government policy making, from the Great Depression to the Cold War. During these years, changing rationales justified their use: from economic development (via the PWA) to social welfare (through the WPA) during the Depression, and back to economic development (by means of the Federal Works Agency, defense

---

[7] On government and the economy, see Oscar Handlin and Mary Flug Handlin, *Commonwealth: A Study of the Role of Government in the American Economy: Massachusetts, 1774–1861* (Cambridge: Harvard University Press, 1947); Louis Hartz, *Economic Policy and Democratic Thought: Pennsylvania, 1776–1860* (Cambridge: Harvard University Press, 1948); Taylor, *Transportation Revolution*; and James Willard Hurst, *Law and the Conditions of Freedom in the Nineteenth-Century United States* (Madison: University of Wisconsin Press, 1956). The best study of economic thought and government policy during the New Deal remains Ellis W. Hawley, *The New Deal and the Problem of Monopoly: A Study in Economic Ambivalence* (Princeton: Princeton University Press, 1966). For important recent work in historical political economy, see, e.g., David Moss, *When All Else Fails: Government as the Ultimate Risk Manager* (Cambridge: Harvard University Press, 2002); William Novak, *The People's Welfare: Law and Regulation in Nineteenth-Century America* (Chapel Hill: University of North Carolina Press, 1996); Sven Beckert, *The Monied Metropolis: New York City and the Consolidation of the American Bourgeoisie, 1850–1896* (Cambridge: Cambridge University Press, 2001); and Robin L. Einhorn, *Property Rules: Political Economy in Chicago, 1833–1872*, 2d ed. (Chicago: University of Chicago Press, 2001).

[8] See, e.g., John Morton Blum, *V was for Victory: Politics and Culture During World War II* (New York: Harcourt Brace Jovanovich, 1976), 117–46; Bruce J. Schulman, *From Cotton Belt to Sunbelt: Federal Policy, Economic Development, and the Transformation of the South, 1938–1980* (Durham: Duke University Press, 1995); David M. Kennedy, *Freedom From Fear: The American People in Depression and War, 1929–1945* (New York: Oxford University Press, 1999); James T. Patterson, *Grand Expectations: The United States, 1945–1974* (New York: Oxford University Press, 1996); related scholarship on twentieth-century government and public finance is covered in W. Elliot Brownlee, ed., *Funding the Modern American State, 1941–1995: The Rise and Fall of the Era of Easy Finance* (Cambridge: Cambridge University Press, 1996). For a key exception to my generalization about the history of twentieth-century economic development and the New Deal literature, see my discussion of Jordan A. Schwarz's work, below.

spending, and the postwar highway movement) during World War II and the early Cold War. These programs helped to shape the relations between economic development, state building, and party building at the federal, state, and local levels. The first head of the WPA, Harry Hopkins, claimed that the New Deal was a political project that could "tax and tax, spend and spend, and elect and elect." This boast points to the qualities that made New Deal liberalism so powerful and so controversial: The taxing and spending functions of government could remake the political, as well as the physical, landscape of the nation. Before turning to these larger issues, however, let me first step back in order to address a straightforward question: Why have historians failed to tell the full story of the New Deal's public works?

PUBLIC WORKS IN NEW DEAL HISTORIOGRAPHY: LIBERAL AND NEW LEFT APPROACHES

Even before President Franklin Roosevelt's first 100 days in office came to an end, Americans struggled to comprehend the nature and limits of the New Deal order.[9] In the years since then, historians have argued over whether the New Deal was "America's Third Revolution," or if it is better viewed as a "halfway revolution" that left much undone.[10] Whether portrayed as a new departure in the trajectory of a reforming impulse that stretched back to William Jennings Bryan or as a high point in a generation's rendezvous with destiny, the New Deal is viewed by most interpretative traditions as a fundamentally liberal and progressive political event.[11] This reading has been qualified by a variety of scholars who have, in different ways, presented the New Deal as a historical moment that signaled

---

[9] For the concept of the "New Deal order," see Steven Fraser and Gary Gerstle's introduction in Steven Fraser and Gary Gerstle, eds., *The Rise and Fall of the New Deal Order, 1930–1980* (Princeton: Princeton University Press, 1989).

[10] Carl Degler, *Out of Our Past: The Forces that Shaped Modern America*, 3d ed. (New York: Harper and Row, 1984), ch. 13; and William E. Leuchtenburg, *Franklin D. Roosevelt and the New Deal* (New York: Harper and Row, 1963), 347.

[11] Richard Hofstadter, *The Age of Reform: From Bryan to F.D.R.* (New York: Vintage, 1955); and Eric F. Goldman, *Rendezvous with Destiny: A History of Modern American Reform*, rev. ed. (New York: Vintage, 1977). Other analyses of the links between the New Deal and earlier generations of reformers include Otis L. Graham, Jr., *An Encore for Reform: The Old Progressives and the New Deal* (New York: Oxford University Press, 1967), and, more recently, Daniel T. Rodgers, *Atlantic Crossings: Social Politics in a Progressive Age* (Cambridge, MA: Harvard University Press, 1998), especially 409–84.

the end of reform.[12] Where the older work of liberal historians presents these years as the Age of Roosevelt, dominated by the dashing president who soaked the rich and mobilized the state against economic royalists on behalf of the "forgotten man," the work of subsequent scholars is, on balance, much more skeptical.[13] They argue that high federal income tax rates did not actually generate much revenue and served mainly as a smoke screen to distract the public from heavy sales taxes levied on consumers.[14] The new regulations enacted by the state, they claim, in fact reflected the interests of business.[15] Where earlier historians believed that organized labor had at last found its "Magna Charta" in New Deal labor law, their successors have asserted that this guarantee of collective bargaining functioned merely as a "counterfeit liberty."[16] In searching for ways to understand the New Deal, some scholars have recently employed a "new" institutional approach that studies the capacities of the state to shape society.[17]

While historians have not fully grasped the far-reaching impact of the New Deal's public works programs, it is clear that they have not ignored them. Discussions of public works find their place in the very first chronicles of the New Deal, written by the New Dealers themselves. In 1935 Harold Ickes, the Interior Secretary and head of the Public Works

[12] Alan Brinkley, *The End of Reform: New Deal Liberalism in Recession and War* (New York: Alfred A. Knopf, 1995). Others who have questioned the commitment of the New Deal to reform include Howard Zinn, Paul Conkin, Barton Bernstein, Ronald Radosh, Gabriel Kolko, and Colin Gordon.

[13] For the classic liberal account, see Arthur M. Schlesinger, Jr., *The Age of Roosevelt*, 3 vols. (Boston: Houghton Mifflin, 1957–60).

[14] Mark H. Leff, *The Limits of Symbolic Reform: The New Deal and Taxation, 1933–1939* (Cambridge: Cambridge University Press, 1984).

[15] Colin Gordon, *New Deals: Business, Labor, and Politics in America, 1920–1935* (Cambridge: Cambridge University Press, 1994).

[16] AFL President William Green called Section 7(a) the "Magna Charta of Labor of the United States." Quoted in Irving Bernstein, *Turbulent Years: A History of the American Worker, 1933–1941* (Boston: Houghton Mifflin, 1970), 349. For a recent analysis of New Deal labor historiography, see David Brody, *Workers in Industrial America: Essays on the Twentieth Century Struggle*, 2d ed. (New York: Oxford University Press, 1993), especially 82–156. For other studies of industrial relations during the 1930s and 1940s, see Milton Derber and Edwin Young, eds., *Labor and the New Deal* (Madison: University of Wisconsin Press, 1957), especially Selig Perlman, "Labor and the New Deal in Historical Perspective," 361–70. For the "counterfeit liberty" reading of the history of labor law, see Christopher L. Tomlins, *The State and the Unions: Labor Relations, Law, and the Organized Labor Movement in America, 1880–1960* (Cambridge: Cambridge University Press, 1985), 326–28.

[17] Kenneth Finegold and Theda Skocpol, *State and Party in America's New Deal* (Madison: University of Wisconsin Press, 1995).

Administration, set the tone for future liberal interpretations of federal public works in his celebratory history of the PWA, *Back to Work*.[18] The PWA was "an emergency agency born of the crisis," designed to help the nation recover from the Depression. "The government embarked on the public works program," wrote Ickes, "because of the timidity of private capital to come out from under the bed."

> Something had to be done about the depression if we were ever to shake it off. And fortunately the great majority of the people wanted to do something about it. They wanted to march out and meet the enemy in hand-to-hand conflict. President Roosevelt had the same impulse, and immediately after his inauguration he set out to engage in mortal combat as insidious and as relentless a foe as a champion has ever faced.[19]

In short, the enemy was unemployment, and the weapon used to fight it was public works. If the overall purpose of the New Deal was to bring about relief, recovery, and reform, the public works programs were understood to focus on these first two tasks. According to these initial versions of the story, then, thanks to federally funded public works the nation was moving again, money was being pumped into the economy, and people were going back to work.

The creators of the New Deal had originally conceived of public works as a temporary recovery measure. The PWA, after all, was enacted as Title II of the National Industrial Recovery Act, passed as part of the emergency legislation signed into law by Roosevelt during the first 100 days of his first term. This conception of the New Deal public works organizations as temporary programs, designed to relieve the short-term effects of unemployment, quickly became entrenched in histories of the New Deal. Subsequent accounts have thus treated New Deal public works solely as a remedy for the unemployment question, concluding, not surprisingly, that programs such as the PWA and the WPA were stop-gap measures to combat joblessness and help the nation recover from the Depression.

Among the most influential of these accounts are the histories of Arthur Schlesinger, Jr. *The Age of Roosevelt*, Schlesinger's trilogy, is a classic work of political history, with the interwar years' politicians, labor leaders, businessmen, and events set in relief against an interpretation of American history as cycles of conservative reaction and progressive reform.[20] While grounded in a variety of sources, Schlesinger's

---

[18] Harold L. Ickes, *Back to Work: The Story of PWA* (New York: Macmillan, 1935).

[19] Ibid., 229, 233.

[20] For more on the interpretive significance of Schlesinger's work, see Alan Brinkley, "Prosperity, Depression, and War, 1920–1945," in Eric Foner, ed., *The New American History*, rev. ed. (Philadelphia: Temple University Press, 1997), 134–37.

account of the New Deal echoed the sentiments of New Dealers such as Ickes and Hopkins in its treatment of public works. The PWA was, for Schlesinger, "an emergency program," part of a two-pronged strategy of recovery that presented the National Recovery Administration (NRA) and the PWA working in concert.[21] The industrial codes of the NRA would restrict harmful competition, raising wages and reducing hours, while the PWA would inject cash into the economy. Schlesinger's exposition of the PWA and the WPA emphasizes the administrative issues and personality conflicts that occupied Roosevelt and the members of his cabinet who were concerned with economic matters: fiscally conservative director of the budget, Lewis Douglas, NRA head, Hugh Johnson, Ickes, and Hopkins.

If to Hugh Johnson the object of public works was to stimulate the heavy industries, and if to Harry Hopkins its object was to provide relief and re-employment, to Ickes its object was to beautify the national estate through the honest building of durable public monuments. To Lewis Douglas, it had no object at all. These various conceptions clashed at the meetings of the Public Works Board during the sweltering summer of 1933, its members sitting, coats off, on leather-cushioned chairs around the polished oval table in Ickes' office.[22]

In Schlesinger's view, then, these New Dealers jostled for political advantage and for Roosevelt's ear, each eager to advance his vision for public works in a political climate characterized by economic crisis. Schlesinger's work is essential for understanding the political debates and personalities that surrounded the New Deal, at the same time also providing much insight into the backstage workings of policy making. In echoing the heroic, liberal view of the New Deal that was first put forward by the New Dealers themselves, however, Schlesinger treats public works programs only as short-term relief and recovery measures, as political chips to be tossed around polished oval tables. Schlesinger and his liberal colleagues in the historical profession applauded FDR for finally "trying something," viewing the public works programs as the epitome of the spirit of pragmatic experimentation that they felt permeated the New Deal. This point of view is invariably reflected in the story line attached to the public works programs in histories like Schlesinger's, whose narrative unfolds as follows: Dr. New Deal made a bold attempt to end widespread unemployment and place the nation on a course toward recovery. Although the temporary programs he set up did not accomplish these goals, they provided

---

[21] Arthur Schlesinger, Jr., *The Coming of the New Deal*, vol. 2 of *Age of Roosevelt* (Boston: Houghton Mifflin, 1958), 108.
[22] Ibid., 284.

much-needed welfare for the jobless; when the European conflict erupted, Dr. Win-the-War took over, effectively ending the Depression while his predecessor's short-lived remedies were quietly phased out.[23]

The slow process of the historical revision of this interpretation can be dated back to William E. Leuchtenburg's influential 1963 synthesis, *Franklin D. Roosevelt and the New Deal*. Indeed, in much the same way that Schlesinger's *Age of Roosevelt* determined the boundaries of debate for an earlier generation of historians, Leuchtenburg's book was a turning point in our understanding of the legacy of the New Deal. Leuchtenburg, like Schlesinger, approached the New Deal from a sympathetic, liberal perspective. Departing from the untempered optimism of earlier interpretations, however, Leuchtenburg advanced what historian James T. Patterson has termed a "cautiously positive interpretation of Roosevelt," paying more attention to the limits of the New Deal, its inability to solve the puzzle of the Depression, its failure to restructure the economic order, and its mixed record on racial equality.[24]

With respect to public works programs, though, Leuchtenburg does not move beyond the analyses of previous scholars. He notes that FDR was initially opposed to large amounts of federal spending on public works programs, with Secretary of Labor Frances Perkins, adviser Hopkins, and Senators Robert Wagner, Robert La Follette, Jr., and Edward P. Costigan having to convince the president to support federal public works spending in 1933.[25] In his treatment of the impact of public works on the economy, Leuchtenburg recapitulates the standard criticism of Ickes: that he was too slow and cautious in spending the PWA appropriations, barely holding the line in the fight against the Depression when he could have made significant strides against it. Leuchtenburg, however, does observe that even

[23] The work of the two most influential biographers of FDR generally follows this interpretation. See Frank Freidel, *Franklin D. Roosevelt*, 4 vols. (Boston: Little, Brown, 1952–73); Freidel, *Franklin D. Roosevelt: A Rendezvous with Destiny* (Boston: Little, Brown, 1990); James MacGregor Burns, *Roosevelt: The Lion and the Fox* (New York: Harcourt, Brace, 1956); and Burns, *Roosevelt: The Soldier of Freedom* (New York: Harcourt Brace Jovanovich, 1970).

[24] James T. Patterson, "United States History since 1920," in Mary Beth Norton, ed., *The American Historical Association's Guide to Historical Literature*, 3d ed. (New York: Oxford University Press, 1995), 2:1455; and Patterson, "Americans and the Writing of Twentieth-Century United States History," in Anthony Molho and Gordon S. Wood, eds., *Imagined Histories: American Historians Interpret the Past* (Princeton: Princeton University Press, 1998), 185–205. See also Brinkley, "Prosperity, Depression, and War," 143–44.

[25] Leuchtenburg, *FDR and the New Deal*, 52–53.

though the WPA and the PWA were unable to provide aid to everyone, when measured against pre-1932 spending, "Roosevelt's works program marked a bold departure," adding, "By any standard, it was an impressive achievement."[26] Leuchtenburg termed Ickes "a builder to rival Cheops," citing the PWA's ability to place bridges over rivers; roads between cities, schools, and hospitals in rural communities; and new ports and airports around the nation.[27]

Leuchtenburg's judicious, even-handed synthesis foreshadowed the subsequent revisionist efforts of New Left scholars such as Howard Zinn, Barton Bernstein, and Ronald Radosh.[28] In drawing a distinction between "liberal" and "New Left" scholarship, though, I do not mean to imply that the New Leftists were the first to question the liberal interpretation of the New Deal. Far from it. For example, one of the profession's leading "consensus" historians, Richard Hofstadter, published a book chapter on FDR in the late 1940s that was far from laudatory.[29] Hofstadter subsequently produced a synthetic treatment that, in the words of one critic, emphasized the "amoral, instrumental character of New Deal reform."[30] While Hofstadter is perhaps best considered as *sui generis*, the harshest critiques of the New Deal (excepting those constructed by the Right) were found not among the New Left, but rather among the Old.[31] As Leuchtenburg himself observes:

There is no basic distinction between the New Left and the Old Left in interpreting the New Deal. All of us who were raised in the Roosevelt era and lived through the intellectual arguments of the 1940s grappled with the Marxist critique of the

[26] Ibid., 129–30.
[27] Ibid., 133.
[28] For a review of the literature that suggests that the range and subtlety of Leuchtenburg's work was one of the reasons why the New Left never really developed a sustained critique of the New Deal, see Brinkley, "Prosperity, Depression, and War," 143–44.
[29] Richard Hofstadter, "Franklin D. Roosevelt: The Patrician as Opportunist," *The American Political Tradition and the Men Who Made It* (New York: Alfred A. Knopf, 1948), 409–56.
[30] The synthetic treatment is, of course, *The Age of Reform*; the critic is Gary Gerstle, "The Protean Character of American Liberalism," *American Historical Review* 99 (Oct. 1994): 1043. For a more detailed assessment, see Alan Brinkley, "Richard Hofstadter's The Age of Reform: A Reconsideration," *Reviews in American History* 13 (September 1985): 462–80.
[31] Conservative assessments of the New Deal are rare; for the key work, see Edgar E. Robinson, *The Roosevelt Leadership, 1933–1945* (Philadelphia: J.B. Lippincott, 1955). More recently, see Gary Dean Best, *Pride, Prejudice, and Politics: Roosevelt versus Recovery, 1933–1938* (New York: Praeger, 1991); and Gene Smiley, *Rethinking the Great Depression* (Chicago: Ivan Dee, 2002).

New Deal. . . . No New Left critic has damned the New Deal with more abandon than the old Marxists.[32]

   While the New Leftists were not the first to unravel the New Deal, they did, however, perform a vital task within a critical tradition that itself has a long history.[33] In the introductory essay to his 1966 document anthology, *New Deal Thought*, Howard Zinn took the first step in reapplying this critical tradition to the New Deal, responding directly to the claims of Hofstadter, Schlesinger, and Leuchtenburg.[34] Zinn revisits the New Deal years not to bury them, but instead to find a usable past that could speak to the concerns of intellectuals in the 1960s. Zinn begins this reexamination with the definition of New Deal ideology provided by Hofstadter in *Age of Reform*. Hofstadter had argued that the works of New Deal antitrust expert Thurman Arnold epitomized the essence of the New Deal, for in them, Hofstadter wrote, "[W]e find a sharp and sustained attack upon ideologies, rational principles, and moralism in politics. We find, in short, the theoretical equivalent of FDR's opportunistic virtuosity in practical politics – a theory that attacks theories."[35] Zinn presses this definition of New Deal ideology further than Hofstadter, pointing out the darker consequences of emphasizing method over substance and focusing on the millions of people who, in his words, "still awaited a genuine 'new deal.'"[36] While Zinn acknowledges the New Deal's accomplishments, he presents its public works programs as falling victim to Roosevelt's "experimental, shifting, and opportunistic" temperament.[37] Zinn assesses the public works programs succinctly, observing that the "TVA, a brief golden period of federal theater, a thin spread of public housing, and a public works program called into play only at times of desperation, represented the New Deal's ideological and emotional limits in the creation of public enterprise."[38]

---

[32] William E. Leuchtenburg, "The Great Depression and the New Deal," in William E. Leuchtenburg, *The FDR Years: On Roosevelt and His Legacy* (New York: Columbia University Press, 1995), 232.

[33] For an opinionated, but very useful, assessment of the connection between the Old and New Left, see John Patrick Diggins, *The Rise and Fall of the American Left* (New York: W. W. Norton, 1992).

[34] This essay has been republished as "The Limits of the New Deal," in Howard Zinn, *The Politics of History*, 2d ed. (Urbana: University of Illinois Press, 1990), 118–36.

[35] Hofstadter, *Age of Reform*, 319.

[36] Zinn, "Limits of the New Deal," 125.

[37] Ibid., 133.

[38] Ibid., 134.

Other revisionist accounts of the New Deal come to similar conclusions regarding public works. Relying on the assumptions that underwrite most "corporate liberal" interpretations of U.S. history, historian Barton Bernstein argues that "the liberal reforms of the New Deal did not transform the American system; they conserved and protected American capitalism, occasionally by absorbing parts of threatening programs."[39] Bernstein treats the public works organizations solely as welfare programs, faulting the government for spending too slowly and cautiously, tersely noting that after six years of the New Deal, "In most of America, starvation was no longer possible. Perhaps that was the most humane achievement of the New Deal."[40] Because the New Deal's achievements were ultimately so limited, people who joined the New Deal political coalition were evidence of "one of the crueler ironies of liberal politics, that the marginal men trapped in hopelessness were seduced by rhetoric, by the style and movement, by the symbolism of efforts seldom reaching beyond words."[41] To the extent that public works programs achieved anything, in Bernstein's view, they were part of a larger enterprise that created a sort of false consciousness, capable only of duping the masses into voting for FDR.

Ronald Radosh, in his essay, "The Myth of the New Deal," provides some perspective on the efforts of his fellow New Left historians to study the New Deal.[42] Asserting that the NRA was "meant to be a conservative prop to the existing order," Radosh conceives of the public works programs, ironically, much in the same way as Schlesinger, basing his discussion on the assumption that the industrial codes of the NRA were

[39] Barton J. Bernstein, "The New Deal: The Conservative Achievements of Liberal Reform," in Bernstein, ed., *Towards a New Past: Dissenting Essays in American History* (New York: Vintage, 1967), 264. The intellectual genealogy of corporate liberalism can be traced through William Appleman Williams, *The Contours of American History* (New York: New Viewpoints, 1973), esp. 439–69; Gabriel Kolko, *The Triumph of Conservatism: A Reinterpretation of American History, 1900–1916* (New York: Free Press, 1963); James Weinstein, *The Corporate Ideal in the Liberal State* (Boston: Beacon Press, 1968); Gabriel Kolko, *Main Currents in Modern American History* (New York: Harper and Row, 1976), esp. 111–57; and Martin J. Sklar, *The Corporate Reconstruction of American Capitalism, 1890–1916: The Market, the Law, and Politics* (Cambridge: Cambridge University Press, 1988). See also R. Jeffrey Lustig, *Corporate Liberalism: The Origins of Modern American Political Theory, 1890–1920* (Berkeley: University of California Press, 1982).

[40] Bernstein, "The New Deal," 278.

[41] Ibid., 281.

[42] Ronald Radosh, "The Myth of the New Deal," in Ronald Radosh and Murray N. Rothbard, eds., *A New History of Leviathan: Essays on the Rise of the American Corporate State* (New York: E. P. Dutton, 1972), 146–87.

originally intended to work in concert with the PWA.[43] Radosh argues, though, that the main role of public works programs was not just to garner the support of the business community for the idea of industrial codes, but rather to win support from liberals.

Of all the New Deal reforms, public works seemed to most people to have the aura of "socialism" or at least of an attack on private interests. To the hungry and unemployed, it symbolized a direct concern by the government for their plight.... That the New Deal's public works was of a limited nature and did not interfere with private business prerogatives went unnoticed. In the area in which public-works development was most needed, housing, the New Deal program was hardly successful and in many ways a total failure. All this was ignored. The name "public works" and the PWA itself produced a sympathetic response from the populace, the "liberal" political groups, and the organized political left.[44]

Radosh's analysis reflects the interest of most New Left critics in the role the New Deal played in channeling or limiting participatory democracy, and while his eagerness to portray public works as a sop to the Left leaves little room for complexity, Radosh does at least perform the valuable service of taking these programs seriously.[45] Despite subsequent work by others in the corporate liberal tradition – culminating in Colin Gordon's *New Deals,* a bold attempt to recast the National Industrial Recovery Act, the Wagner Act, and the Social Security Act as measures that somehow reflected the interests of a disorganized, yet very powerful, business community – Radosh's exceedingly brief treatment of the New Deal public works programs remains the fullest that we have from a New Left perspective. While Gordon's *New Deals* surveys much fresh ground, presenting itself as "the first major reinterpretation of the New Deal in almost thirty years," its discussion of the public works programs appears only in a footnote. Here, Gordon acknowledges that his study will "only touch upon [the New Deal's] provisions for public works."[46]

Historians, I propose, ought to do more than just "touch upon" public works programs when they think about the New Deal. While liberal historians presented the public works programs as well-intentioned welfare programs that failed to end unemployment, and subsequent critics

[43] Ibid., 169.
[44] Ibid., 170.
[45] For a more recent account, demonstrating the ways the state responded to and ultimately contained broad-based political and social movements, see Alan Dawley, *Struggles for Justice: Social Responsibility and the Liberal State* (Cambridge: Harvard University Press, 1991).
[46] Gordon, *New Deals,* 166, n. 1.

dismissed them as underfunded measures that served only to prop up the existing order, blinding people to the limits of the New Deal, both sides neglect the fact that public works programs were the New Deal's central enterprise. By paying close attention to these visible functions of the state, this book builds upon and advances the work of the only scholar to view the New Deal as "a massive governmental recapitalization for purposes of economic development," Jordan A. Schwarz. While Schwarz develops this theory through a brilliant series of personal portraits of such characters as David Lilienthal, Sam Rayburn, and Lyndon B. Johnson, he recognizes that the philosophy of this political undertaking reached far beyond individuals. Schwarz's account allows us to view the New Deal as a political project that "sought to create long-term markets by building an infrastructure in undeveloped regions."[47]

In recapturing the New Deal's focus on the construction of public works projects, my study also provides important evidence supporting recent accounts that have emphasized the gendered and racial boundaries of the American welfare state. In basing their welfare state on the building of public works projects, New Dealers reinforced these boundaries. By directing so much attention to construction, they supported an economic sector (the construction industry and building trades) long noted as a bastion of white male employment and discrimination against African Americans and women.[48] The creation of public works programs during the New Deal reinforced these biases, largely bypassing the maternalist legacies of Progressive Era public policy. Although women such as Hilda Worthington Smith, Sue Shelton White, and Ellen Woodward were important players in the development of New Deal social-welfare policy, theirs was a very abbreviated moment. As Susan Ware has argued, for all the influence that these women wielded, their institutional power began to fade away as early as 1936.[49]

---

[47] Jordan A. Schwarz, *The New Dealers: Power Politics in the Age of Roosevelt* (New York: Alfred A. Knopf, 1993), xi.

[48] Michael Kazin, *Barons of Labor: The San Francisco Building Trades and Union Power in the Progressive Era* (Urbana: University of Illinois Press, 1989); and Robert A. Christie, *Empire in Wood: A History of the Carpenter's Union* (Ithaca: Cornell University Press, 1956) make this point effectively.

[49] Susan Ware, *Beyond Suffrage: Women in the New Deal* (Cambridge: Harvard University Press, 1981), esp. 116–31. On the maternalist legacies, see Landon R. Y. Storrs, *Civilizing Capitalism: The National Consumers' League, Women's Activism, and Labor Standards in the New Deal Era* (Chapel Hill: University of North Carolina Press, 2000); and Kathryn Kish Sklar, "Two Political Cultures in the Progressive Era: The National Consumers' League and the American Association for Labor Legislation," in Linda K.

By exploring the workings of the federal government and its agencies, I am of course also drawing upon and contributing to the research program commonly flagged (and occasionally flogged) by the phrase "bringing the state back in."[50] While this program has evolved over time, it has consistently underwritten much scholarly investigation by vigorously promoting the notion that states and institutions are subjects worthy of research. This "new institutionalist" focus on the state, however, has at times discounted factors such as ideology and politics, and generally pays less attention to the significance of broader social forces, such as urbanization and industrialization.[51] With the history of the American state now attracting much scholarly interest, political historians, in the words of one recent observer, ought not to adopt the "dense, internal analysis of state imperatives" advocated by the new institutionalists "as a complete model" for their investigations.[52] Instead, by defining political history as a

Kerber, Alice Kessler-Harris, and Kathryn Kish Sklar, eds., *U.S. History as Women's History: New Feminist Essays* (Chapel Hill: University of North Carolina Press, 1995), 36–62. See also Theda Skocpol, *Protecting Soldiers and Mothers: The Political Origins of Social Policy in the United States* (Cambridge: Harvard University Press, 1992); Linda Gordon, *Pitied But Not Entitled: Single Mothers and the History of Welfare, 1890–1935* (Cambridge: Harvard University Press, 1994); Suzanne Mettler, *Dividing Citizens: Gender and Federalism in New Deal Public Policy* (Ithaca: Cornell University Press, 1998); Nancy E. Rose, *Workfare or Fair Work: Women, Welfare, and Government Work Programs* (New Brunswick: Rutgers University Press, 1995); and Jill Quadagno, "From Old-Age Assistance to Supplemental Security Income: The Political Economy of Relief in the South, 1935–1972," in Margaret Weir, Ann Shola Orloff, and Theda Skocpol, eds., *The Politics of Social Policy in the United States* (Princeton: Princeton University Press, 1988), 235–63.

50 Even an incomplete list of works that fit under this rubric would take up too much space. Key texts include Stephen Skowronek, *Building a New American State: The Expansion of National Administrative Capacities, 1877–1920* (Cambridge: Cambridge University Press, 1982); Peter R. Evans, Dietrich Rueschemeyer, and Theda Skocpol, eds., *Bringing the State Back In* (Cambridge: Cambridge University Press, 1985); Weir, Orloff, and Skocpol, eds., *Politics of Social Policy*; and Finegold and Skocpol, *State and Party in America's New Deal.*

51 Compare the treatment of agricultural interests in Theda Skocpol and Kenneth Finegold, "State Capacity and Economic Intervention in the Early New Deal," *Political Science Quarterly* 97 (Summer 1982): 255–78, with Grant McConnell's classic, *The Decline of Agrarian Democracy* (Berkeley: University of California Press, 1953). See also two useful assessments of institutionally oriented scholarship: Terrence J. McDonald, "Building the Impossible State: Toward an Institutional Analysis of Statebuilding in America, 1820–1930," in John E. Jackson, ed., *Institutions in American Society: Essays in Market, Political, and Social Organizations* (Ann Arbor: University of Michigan Press, 1990), 217–39; and David Brian Robertson, "The Return to History and the New Institutionalism in American Political Science," *Social Science History* 17 (Spring 1993): 1–36.

52 Mark H. Leff, "Revisioning U.S. Political History," *American Historical Review* 100 (June 1995): 850.

field that "deals with the development and impact of governmental institutions, along with the proximate influences on their actions," political
historians have the opportunity to capitalize on a growing methodological
overlap among political, social, and cultural history.[53] My study follows
this broad-minded definition, drawing upon the scholarly return to institutions in its focus on the state, yet remaining sensitive to the analytic
importance of society.

Chapter 2 examines the politics of economic development and unemployment during the early New Deal, concentrating on the years 1933
through 1935. My concern is with the New Deal's first public works
program, the Public Works Administration, which conceived of public
works not simply as a remedy for unemployment, but primarily as part
of a strategy of economic development and resource management, echoing the approach of Herbert Hoover's Reconstruction Finance Corporation to public works. I explore how New Dealers and other progressives
conceived of the relationship among government construction, economic
development, and unemployment during Roosevelt's first term.

In Chapter 3, I evaluate the success of these state-building efforts, using
the records of the PWA's division of investigation. These extraordinarily
detailed records provide an insider's account of what was at stake in the
constructing of the New Deal state. The New Deal's own investigators created a remarkable day-by-day record of the many difficulties confronting
the PWA as it transformed the physical infrastructure of the nation. In
the course of their work, investigators interviewed PWA staffers, private contractors, laborers, and citizens across the country. The division
of investigation scrutinized and recorded the daily problems the PWA
grappled with as it attempted to pacify job seekers, congressmen, senators, state and local officials, contractors, labor unions, and civic boosters. Despite being beset by overstaffed and often incompetent divisions of
engineering, finance, and legal affairs, the PWA generated a wealth of new
infrastructure.

Chapter 4 turns to this infrastructure, examining the projects built
by the PWA and looking at how they elucidate the political and economic dimensions of New Deal liberalism. This construction represented

[53] Leff, "Revisioning U.S. Political History," 829. For more on the advantages of an interdisciplinary approach to political history, see Byron E. Shafer and Anthony J. Badger, eds.,
Contesting Democracy: Substance and Structure in American Political History, 1775–
2000 (Lawrence: University Press of Kansas, 2001); and Meg Jacobs, William J. Novak,
and Julian E. Zelizer, eds., *The Democratic Experiment: New Directions in American*
Political History (Princeton: Princeton University Press, 2003).

an enormous leap forward in state-funded public works projects, realizing on a much larger scale the public works philosophy of the Hoover administration. It also, however, contained important implications, both for the kind of public construction that was performed by the Works Progress Administration (addressed in Chapters 5 and 6), and for the direction that public construction later took during and after World War II (covered in Chapters 7 and 8).

New Deal public works programs facilitated the twin goals of state building and party building. Chapter 6 examines how the 1938 elections and FDR's attempt to purge the Democratic Party of its conservative elements helped lead to the passage of the Hatch Act, restricting the role that the PWA and the WPA could play in the political process. While the WPA paid more attention to the problem of unemployment than did the PWA, by 1939 both programs were placed within the Federal Works Agency during the reorganization of the executive branch of the federal government. Rather than quietly accept that war and a more conservative Congress meant the curtailment of public works projects, various New Dealers attempted successfully to synthesize their social concerns with the emergency presented by wartime. These liberals quickly realized that justifying expenditures for public works as "necessary wartime emergency spending" provided a powerful rationale for continuing to spend money on programs that were becoming increasingly unpopular.

In fact, with the outbreak of World War II New Dealers no longer had to rely upon the mere "analogue" of war when building a case for further reforms. They could now point to war itself.[54] While the architects of the reorganized New Deal public works programs did succeed in using the war to justify their continued existence, this victory came at a significant price, as I discuss in Chapter 7. Nowhere can this price be better measured than by the yardstick of the most socially progressive of the New Deal's works programs, the WPA. With the building of wartime public works, the WPA increasingly discarded its standard

---

[54] For the classic account of the widespread use of wartime metaphors by New Dealers, see William Leuchtenburg's essay, "The New Deal and the Analogue of War," revised and reprinted in William E. Leuchtenburg, *The FDR Years: On Roosevelt and His Legacy* (New York: Columbia University Press, 1995), 35–75. For an important recent treatment of state building during World War I, see Mark Allen Eisner, *From Warfare State to Welfare State: World War I, Compensatory State Building, and the Limits of the Modern Order* (University Park: Pennsylvania State University Press, 2000).

method of construction, "force account," whereby the WPA put people to work directly in order to reduce unemployment, in favor of cost-plus contracting, which emphasized timely production and willingness to set aside the goal of reducing unemployment in order to get the job done. More notably, however, New Dealers within the WPA demonstrated the extent to which they were willing to cast aside social concerns in the name of wartime emergency when they played a crucial role in carrying out Executive Order 9066, interning Japanese Americans in relocation camps on the West Coast.

Chapter 8 traces the postwar legacy of New Deal public works, exploring their influence on the development of federal highway policy up to the 1956 Federal-Aid Highway Act. While the Federal Works Agency continued to function until 1949, at this point the federal government again reorganized its public works bureaucracy. Under the recommendation of a commission headed by a retired president, Herbert Hoover, the federal government folded the responsibilities of the Federal Works Agency into the General Services Administration. The creation of the GSA formalized the return of federal public works to an ideal of efficiency and economy, an ideal first epitomized by the public works promoted by the Reconstruction Finance Corporation when Hoover was president. In reconstructing these events, Chapter 8 lays the groundwork for understanding how politicians such as Lyndon Johnson came to believe in exporting a Keynesian vision of economic development to Southeast Asia, calling for projects like the Tennessee Valley Authority to be built on the Mekong Delta. This internationalization of the New Deal can also be traced through the postwar activities of such construction firms as Kaiser, Bechtel, Brown & Root, and Morrison-Knudsen.

In sum, this book argues that New Deal public works programs were not simply employment measures that failed due to insufficient state capacities. Instead, they were an extraordinarily successful method of state-sponsored economic development. In his first inaugural address as president, FDR established the central role that public works would play in his administration. Although remembered today primarily for the statement that "the only thing we have to fear is fear itself," this speech contained Roosevelt's brief for the New Deal. "Our greatest primary task is to put people to work," he declared. "This is no unsolvable problem if we face it wisely and courageously." But FDR did not simply call for the government to create employment for employment's sake. Rather, he argued that this employment must have a greater purpose. It must be tied to "accomplishing greatly needed projects to stimulate and reorganize the use of our natural resources."[55] In short, it would be through its public works programs – through the accomplishment of greatly needed projects – that the New Deal would attempt to grapple with the problem of mass unemployment. In the following chapters, I take these accomplishments seriously. By reevaluating the New Deal state and its public works, I provide a new account of the building of New Deal liberalism.

[55] Samuel I. Rosenman, ed., *The Public Papers and Addresses of Franklin D. Roosevelt* (New York: Random House, 1938). 2:11, 13.

2

Economic Development and Unemployment during the Early New Deal

Facing a set of violent transformations in the late nineteenth and early twentieth centuries, Americans struggled to bring order to the social and economic upheaval that increasingly characterized their lives. No longer a nation of isolated "island communities," the United States was becoming a fully modern country. While a more integrated global economy brought waves of immigrants across national borders, American businesses busily exported goods to foreign markets. At home, however, the limitations of the nation's infrastructure were beginning to show. In 1900, for example, only a few hundred miles of the nation's 2.4 million miles of roadway were paved with hard surfaces. While the 1916 Federal-Aid Road Act addressed this infrastructure deficit by initiating a national road system, the program was barely underway before it had to be put on hold when the nation entered World War I. This left the business of road building to the state governments that chose to take up the task. Although some attempts were made to plan for economic development after the war ended, the potential for the federal government to remake the nation's roads remained largely unfulfilled.[1]

---

[1] This and the following paragraph draw on Robert Weibe, *The Search for Order, 1877–1920* (New York: Hill and Wang, 1967); Alan Dawley, *Struggles for Justice: Social Responsibility and the Liberal State* (Cambridge: Harvard University Press, 1991); Emily S. Rosenberg, *Financial Missionaries to the World: The Politics and Culture of Dollar Diplomacy, 1900–1930* (Cambridge: Harvard University Press, 1999); Andrew Wender Cohen, *The Racketeer's Progress: Chicago and the Struggle for the Modern American Economy, 1900–1940* (Cambridge: Cambridge University Press, 2004); and Ellis L. Armstrong, ed., *History of Public Works in the United States, 1776–1976* (Chicago: American Public Works Association, 1976). For examples of state-level public works building during the 1920s, see R. Rudy Higgens-Evenson, *The Price of Progress: Public*

This road-building story could be repeated for a great range and variety of public works projects. By the time the Great Depression arrived, America's highways, waterways, urban mass transportation, airports, flood-control and drainage systems, irrigation systems, electric-power facilities, sewage-treatment plants, public buildings, schools, housing, parks and recreational facilities, and military installations all cried out for improvement. New Dealers responded to the Depression by using the federal government – the power of the public – to employ citizens in building useful public works.

New Deal public works programs are better understood not as unsuccessful state-employment measures, but rather as a strikingly effective method of state-sponsored economic development. The origins of this policy emerged at the intersection of economic development and unemployment during the early New Deal. Between 1933 and 1935, the New Deal's first public works program, the Public Works Administration (PWA), conceived of public works not simply as an employment measure but as part of a larger strategy of economic development and resource management. Supervised by a former Bull Moose Republican, Secretary of the Interior Harold L. Ickes, this program built upon earlier public works programs initiated under Herbert Hoover's Reconstruction Finance Corporation. With the creation of the PWA, New Dealers and other progressives transcended these previous efforts and reconciled the relations between government construction, economic development, and unemployment.

In so doing, Ickes and the PWA drew upon the thinking of a generation of engineers and economists in embracing the capacity of public works to provide needed municipal improvements, employment on work sites, and indirect employment in related industries. Throughout the 1930s and 1940s, New Dealers conducted a running debate with the construction industry over whether the government should cooperate with, regulate, or provide a state-supervised alternative to the private building market.[2] In the years before public works became the central enterprise of the New

---

  Services, Taxation, and the American Corporate State, 1877–1929 (Baltimore: Johns
   Hopkins University Press, 2003); and Michael R. Fein, "Public Works: New York Road
   Building and the American State, 1880–1956" (Ph.D. diss., Brandeis University, 2003).
[2] For the importance of the construction industry to the American economy, see William
   Haber, *Industrial Relations in the Building Industry* (Cambridge: Harvard University
   Press, 1930); Alexander J. Field, "Uncontrolled Land Development and the Duration of
   the Depression in the United States," *Journal of Economic History* 52 (December 1992):
   785–805; and for the severity of the Depression's economic impact across different sectors,
   see Michael A. Bernstein, *The Great Depression: Delayed Recovery and Economic Change
   in America, 1929–1939* (Cambridge: Cambridge University Press, 1987), 48–102.

Deal, political, business, intellectual, and labor communities developed a range of arguments about the proper role that public works policy could play in American society. A brief examination of these previous policy communities illuminates the variety of positions held early on by New Deal reformers, revealing that these approaches did not simply appear in 1933 as a fully formed philosophy, but, rather, that they had deep and at times complicated roots.

A "PREHISTORY" OF PUBLIC WORKS POLICY

While the Great Depression and the New Deal are rightly viewed as pivotal events in United States history, too often the big bang that they represent in the growth of the American state obscures what one historian has called the prehistory of public works policy before the New Deal. Indeed, the idea of using government-funded construction to counter the effects of unemployment dates as far back as the economic downturns of the 1830s, the 1850s, and the 1870s. In 1855, for example, immigration officials in New York put the unemployed to work on enlarging the Erie Canal. With the financial panic of 1893, cities and smaller towns began to perceive periods of unemployment as opportunities to hire inexpensive labor for constructing the public works that they needed. These programs, though, were too scattered and too small to have any noticeable impact. As historian Herbert Gutman observed, throughout the Gilded Age "nothing better illustrated the differences between the small town and large city than attitudes toward public works for the unemployed," as urban Americans responded to the clamor for work relief with "surprise, ridicule, contempt, and genuine fear." With the unemployment rate soaring as high as 20 percent, populist leader Jacob S. Coxey captured the nation's horrified attention in 1894 when he led a "living petition" of jobless workers – "Coxey's Army" – from Massilon, Ohio, to Washington, D.C., demanding that the government employ them on public works. For many Americans, this was like watching the traumatic events of Edward Bellamy's popular novel, *Looking Backward*, leap off the page and spring to life.[3]

---

[3] Udo Sautter, "Government and Unemployment: The Use of Public Works before the New Deal," *Journal of American History* 73 (June 1986): 59; and Sautter, *Three Cheers for the Unemployed: Government and Unemployment before the New Deal* (Cambridge: Cambridge University Press, 1991). Also see Don D. Lescohier, "Working Conditions," in John R. Commons et al., *History of Labor in the United States, 1896–1932* (New York: Macmillan, 1918–35), 3:164–78; Arthur D. Gayer, *Public Works in Prosperity and*

While efforts like Coxey's fell short of success, a growing number of progressive intellectuals, journalists, and politicians began to consider seriously the construction of public works as a way to combat unemployment. The founding of the American Association for Labor Legislation (AALL) in 1906 marked an important watershed, as it soon became the central organization for translating concerns over unemployment into concrete policy measures. With funding from men such as John D. Rockefeller and Elbert H. Gary, and, it should be noted, with tepid support from organized labor, the AALL attracted progressives such as Richard T. Ely, Henry Rogers Seager, Henry Farnam, John R. Commons, John B. Andrews, Irene Osgood, Jane Addams, and Charles Henderson. In 1914, this organization published a four-point plan, proposing: "(1) the establishment of public employment exchanges; (2) the systematic distribution of public work; (3) the regularization of industry; and (4) unemployment insurance."[4]

While the AALL's plan, entitled "A Practical Program for the Prevention of Unemployment in America," was reprinted several times, public works advocates achieved only occasional legislative success at the state level before the 1930s. Nevertheless, the debate over the merits of using publicly funded construction to ease mass unemployment continued to grow. At the close of World War I, Congress created a new division of the Department of Labor, the Division of Public Work and Construction Development, intended to prod states and cities into conducting public

Depression (New York: National Bureau of Economic Research, 1935); Armstrong, ed., *History of Public Works in the United States, 1776–1976*; Herbert Gutman, "The Workers' Search for Power: Labor in the Gilded Age," in Ira Berlin, ed., *Power and Culture: Essays on the American Working Class* (New York: New Press, 1987), 86–7; and see Edward Bellamy, *Looking Backward: 2000–1887*, ed. Daniel H. Borus (New York: Bedford Books, 1995), 147–48.

4 For a brief account of the AALL's history, see Kathryn Kish Sklar, "Two Political Cultures in the Progressive Era: The National Consumers' League and the American Association for Labor Legislation," in Linda K. Kerber, Alice Kessler-Harris, and Kathryn Kish Sklar, eds., *U.S. History as Women's History: New Feminist Essays* (Chapel Hill: University of North Carolina Press, 1995), 36–62; and Theda Skocpol, *Protecting Soldiers and Mothers: The Political Origins of Social Policy in the United States* (Cambridge: Harvard University Press, 1992), 176–204. For a more extensive treatment, see David A. Moss, *Socializing Security: Progressive-Era Economists and the Origins of American Social Policy* (Cambridge: Harvard University Press, 1996).
      In 1915, Samuel Gompers resigned from the AALL and stated that it ought to be named the "American Association for the Assassination of Labor Legislation." Moss, *Socializing Security*, 32; and see James Weinstein, *The Corporate Ideal in the Liberal State: 1900–1918* (Boston: Beacon Press, 1968), 48. For the AALL's plan, see Sautter, "Government and Unemployment," 60–61.

works projects. AALL member Otto T. Mallery headed the division, but his efforts – consisting mostly of bulletins of uplifting pronouncements sent to various mayors – must be seen in the context of prevailing attitudes toward the role of government in the return to a peacetime economy. The government could not determine the shape of the postwar reconversion, President Woodrow Wilson stated to Congress, "any better than it [the reconversion] will direct itself." While some members of Congress – most notably, Senator William S. Kenyon of Iowa – pushed for the creation of a federal board to supervise public works construction, Congress agreed with Wilson's assessment of the federal government's limitations and declined to act.[5]

Government attitudes began to shift slightly with President Warren Harding's 1921 conference on unemployment. Although Harding and Commerce Secretary Herbert Hoover stressed that private charity was far more desirable than public assistance, the conference participants, after hearing from Mallery, recommended that the nation plan for "future cyclical periods of depression and unemployment by a system of public works," even advocating that federal loans be advanced to municipalities during periods of depression. While this recommendation led in the short run only to several bills in the House that failed to attract enough support to pass, it did help to shape the boundaries of the debate over the idea of federal government intervention.[6]

Public works thus began to receive explicit consideration as more than a measure to combat unemployment, as a growing number of policy makers began calling for planned public works projects to be built during periods of depression to stabilize the economy. Washington Senator Wesley L. Jones's 1928 proposal for a "prosperity reserve" of federal public works, for example, viewed federal construction as a macroeconomic tool.[7] Other students of government policy took notice of this activity and

[5] Wilson quoted in Sautter, "Government and Unemployment," 66. See also Gayer, *Public Works in Prosperity and Depression*, 11; and Jack P. Isakoff, *The Public Works Administration* (Urbana: University of Illinois Press, 1938), 11–12.

[6] Sautter, "Government and Unemployment," 67–68; Joseph Dorfman, *The Economic Mind in American Civilization*, 5 vols. (New York: Viking Press, 1946–59), 4:35–36. On Hoover, see Joan Hoff-Wilson, *Herbert Hoover: Forgotten Progressive* (New York: HarperCollins, 1975), 90–93; and Ellis W. Hawley, "Herbert Hoover, the Commerce Secretariat, and the Vision of an 'Associative State,' 1921–1928," *Journal of American History* 61 (June 1974): 116–40.

[7] Gayer, *Public Works in Prosperity and Depression*, 12. For more on Jones's belief in using public works to advance economic development, see Jordan A. Schwarz, *The New Dealers: Power Politics in the Age of Roosevelt* (New York: Alfred A. Knopf, 1993), 48–49.

linked the concept of the "business cycle" with public works programs. They argued that government construction contained the potential to minimize the cycle's depth.[8] A generation of businessmen and politicians soon came to associate public works spending with economic stabilization and economic growth. Wilsonians such as William Gibbs McAdoo, Herbert Hoover, and Bernard Baruch helped combine a southern prodevelopment heritage with a western desire for infrastructure and growth. This view of federal construction helped the southern and western factions of the Democratic Party unite behind a shared desire for public works.[9] While politicians, businessmen, and civic boosters advocated permanent improvements to public infrastructure, reform-minded organizations, such as the National Unemployment League and the AALL, also continued to press for nationally planned public works, making the case for their effectiveness as relief measures.

This pressure took on fresh urgency with the stock-market crash of 1929. President Hoover moved in early 1930 to increase public road building by $75 million (about $807 million in 2002 dollars) in order to counter the economic downturn, using planned public works to minimize the downward turn of the business cycle. When this had little effect, Hoover asked Congress to appropriate $150 million (about $1.6 billion in 2002 dollars) for emergency construction projects and created the President's Emergency Committee for Employment (PECE). These increases in federal construction, however, were not sufficient to offset the enormous decline in state and local construction caused by the collapse of revenue sources such as the property tax. PECE chair Arthur Woods responded by advocating more spending on construction than Hoover wanted, eventually resigning in April 1931 to indicate his dissatisfaction with the administration.[10] Progressive senators, most notably New York's Robert Wagner, Wisconsin's Robert La Follette, Jr., and

---

[8] Isakoff, *Public Works Administration*, 12–16; Gayer, *Public Works in Prosperity and Depression*, 7–13; and Otto T. Mallery, "The Long-Range Planning of Public Works," *Business Cycles and Unemployment* (New York: National Bureau of Economic Research, 1923), ch. 13.

[9] Schwarz, *New Dealers*, 43. For an important account that establishes the political activism of farmers in the peripheral regions of the South and Midwest, and emphasizes the political legacies of agrarian populism within the Democratic Party in the creation of an activist central state, see Elizabeth Sanders, *Roots of Reform: Farmers, Workers, and the American State, 1877–1917* (Chicago: University of Chicago Press, 1999), esp. 13–29; 148–72.

[10] Sautter, "Government and Unemployment," 79; Joseph Dorfman, *The Economic Mind in American Civilization*, 5 vols. (New York: Viking Press, 1946–59), 5:616–17; and Gayer, *Public Works in Prosperity and Depression*, 203.

Colorado's Edward P. Costigan, along with publishing magnate William Randolph Hearst, led renewed demands for increased spending on public works. State governors, such as Franklin D. Roosevelt in New York, enacted their own relief programs. La Follette and Wagner, in particular, pressed these issues in Senate debates, championing public works measures, employment stabilization, and increased funding for the gathering of labor statistics.[11]

With the creation of the Reconstruction Finance Corporation and the signing of the Emergency Relief and Construction Act (ERCA) in 1932, Hoover seemed to be strengthening his campaign against the Depression. In doing so, Hoover not only called on his legacy as the "great humanitarian" who directed relief to Europe after World War I. He also drew on his experience during the 1927 Mississippi River flood. This disaster had been an important moment in Hoover's career, as he took the thankless task of coordinating the battle against the flood and turned it into a potent political platform upon which he began his run for the presidency in 1928.[12] By 1932, though, three political realities had pushed Hoover toward embracing the RFC and the ERCA: the extreme character of the Depression and the collapse in local revenues; the congressional drive for a more activist response to relief through public works programs; and the presidential election scheduled for later that year. Modeled after the War Finance Corporation of World War I, the RFC provided loans to banks and railroads. Sarcastically termed a "millionaire's dole" by New York congressman Fiorello La Guardia, the RFC was roundly criticized for its conservative and narrowly focused lending practices during the first half of 1932.[13]

Produced by a compromise between Hoover, Wagner, and Texas Congressman (and, eventually, FDR running mate) John Nance Garner, the

[11] Isakoff, *Public Works Administration*, 13; Gayer, *Public Works in Prosperity and Depression*, 12–13; Jordan A. Schwarz, *The Interregnum of Despair: Hoover, Congress, and the Depression* (Urbana: University of Illinois Press, 1970), 23–44; Irving Bernstein, *The Lean Years: A History of the American Worker, 1920–1933* (Boston: Houghton Mifflin, 1960), 262–68; and J. Joseph Huthmacher, *Senator Robert F. Wagner and the Rise of Urban Liberalism* (New York: Atheneum, 1968), 60–3; 71–86.

[12] Hoff-Wilson, *Herbert Hoover*, 114–17; and John M. Barry, *Rising Tide: The Great Mississippi Flood of 1927 and How it Changed America* (New York: Simon & Schuster, 1997), 261–89; 363–95.

[13] Sautter, "Government and Unemployment," 82–83; Schwarz, *Interregnum of Despair*, 91–96; 162–78; Bernstein, *Lean Years*, 467–69; Howard Zinn, *La Guardia in Congress* (Ithaca: Cornell University Press, 1958), 209; James Stuart Olson, *Herbert Hoover and the Reconstruction Finance Corporation* (Ames: Iowa State University Press, 1977); and Olson, *Saving Capitalism: The Reconstruction Finance Corporation and the New Deal, 1933–1940* (Princeton: Princeton University Press, 1988).

ERCA merits attention not because it was a rousing success – indeed, it was not – but rather because it provided the legislative blueprint for the New Deal's Public Works Administration. The ERCA broadened the powers of the RFC, providing, with its first title, for federal loans of $300 million (about $4 billion in 2002 dollars) to the states for direct and work relief at 3 percent interest, which they would repay out of future federal highway allotments. Title II made $1.5 billion (about $20 billion in 2002 dollars) available to the states as loans for self-liquidating public works projects, such as dams, bridges, and roads, with the potential to generate revenues that would cover the costs of their construction. The third title appropriated $322 million (roughly $4.3 billion in 2002 dollars) for national public works projects, such as the Hoover Dam, hospitals, military airports and bases, and other public buildings, bridges, and utilities, in order to stimulate the heavy construction industry. Although the $300 million from Title I was distributed to the states for relief, the second title's strict self-liquidating requirement and higher interest rates resulted in only $147 million in projects approved (and of that, only $15.7 million spent) by the end of December 1932. Title III was even less successful than Title II, resulting in scarcely $6 million being spent on public works. Contractors and the construction industry nevertheless applauded this small level of spending and pushed for even more. Despite its shortcomings, the ERCA established an important precedent by demonstrating alternative uses of the state's capacity to influence society. The RFC had created a new division to supervise the construction of self-liquidating public works, forging direct financial relationships between the federal government and state and local political subdivisions. The PWA would soon expand and nourish these relationships.[14]

THE FIRST HUNDRED DAYS: NATIONAL RECOVERY AND A NEW DEAL FOR PUBLIC WORKS

During the 1932 presidential campaign, Franklin D. Roosevelt followed an electoral front-runner's customary strategy of keeping statements that

[14] J. Kerwin Williams, *Grants-In-Aid Under the Public Works Administration: A Study in Federal-State-Local Relations* (New York: Columbia University Press, 1939), 24–31; Isakoff, *Public Works Administration*, 14–16; Gayer, *Public Works in Prosperity and Depression*, 87–88; Sautter, "Government and Unemployment," 83–86; H. P. Gillette, "Why Many Toll Bridges Should Be Built Now," *Roads and Streets* 76 (January 1933): 18; and Gail Radford, "From Municipal Socialism to Public Authorities: Institutional Factors in the Shaping of American Public Enterprise," *Journal of American History* 90 (December 2003): 863–90.

might be construed as controversial to a minimum. Thus, Roosevelt said nothing about the potential of public works to serve as a relief or recovery measure. FDR, however, did gain the support of Republican senators who had actively supported the use of public works, including La Follette, Costigan, Bronson Cutting, Hiram Johnson, and George Norris. In fact, Costigan and La Follette, together with Robert Wagner, were known as the "three musketeers" in the fight for public works spending. Private contracting organizations, such as the American Road Builders Association, also joined in this fight, calling for the creation of a federal department of public works. The president of the Portland Cement Association urged his fellow contractors "to sell construction to the public, to build business for the industry, to create demand for construction work." The American Federation of Labor's building trades unions echoed these calls, lobbying the government to undertake the widespread construction of public works projects. Unlike many economic sectors, the construction industry had long enjoyed relative cooperation between contractors and labor at the local level, and both parties welcomed the idea of more government-sponsored works.[15]

The first 100 days of Roosevelt's first term, one of the most creative periods of governance in United States history, have assumed almost mythic status. The new president's brain trust of advisers hammered out fifteen legislative measures which were quickly passed by Congress. The Agricultural Adjustment Act, the Securities and Exchange Commission, banking reform and the Federal Deposit Insurance Corporation, and the Federal Emergency Relief Administration were just several of their more important initiatives. The centerpiece of this legislative outpouring, however, was the National Industrial Recovery Act. Title I of the NIRA suspended antitrust laws and called for industries to draw up codes of industrial production, in order to guard against the dangers of competition. This title also provided labor with the right to organize and bargain collectively with employers. Title II of the NIRA called for the creation of

---

[15] Harold L. Ickes, *Back to Work: The Story of PWA* (New York: Macmillan, 1935), 12; William E. Leuchtenburg, *Franklin D. Roosevelt and the New Deal* (New York: Harper & Row, 1963), 12–13; Frank Freidel, *Franklin D. Roosevelt: The Triumph* (Boston: Little, Brown, 1956), 323–71; "Resolutions Adopted by Highway and Building Conference," *Roads and Streets* 76 (February 1933): 73; Edward J. Mehren, "Selling Construction to Public Through a United Industry," *Roads and Streets* 76 (March 1933): 114; "Wide-Spread Relief Projects," *American Federationist* 40 (June 1933): 622–26; "A Normal Program for Public Works Construction to Stimulate Trade Recovery and Revive Employment," *Bulletin of the General Contractors Association* 23 (May 1932): 97–100; and Cohen, *Racketeer's Progress.*

a Federal Emergency Agency for Public Works, or as it soon came to be known, the PWA. Both Labor Secretary Frances Perkins and Senator Wagner supported the legislative separation of the codes from the public works program, a decision that was later to preserve the PWA's existence, when in 1935 the Supreme Court ruled Title I of the NIRA unconstitutional in *Schechter Poultry v. U.S.* In Roosevelt's opinion, the NIRA was "the most important and far-reaching legislation ever enacted by the American Congress."[16]

The National Recovery Administration's production codes reflected an uneasy mixture of policy ideas. As historian Ellis Hawley put it in his classic treatment, the NRA codes drew upon a conservative, "associative ideal" of a rationalized "business commonwealth," melded with a progressive notion of collectively planned democracy and an older "competitive ideal" of an "atomistic economy." Hawley's assessment of the NRA is similar to that of New Dealer Rexford Tugwell, who argued that "there was a good deal more in the proposed National Recovery Act [*sic*] than met the eye," for "converging in it were several streams of thought developed by individuals or groups who hoped to serve one or another interest, not all of which were by any means public."[17]

Although little noticed by historians, the NIRA's public works title similarly drew support from a range of interests. From the construction industry, one of the sectors hit hardest by the Depression, professional building contractors welcomed a chance to go back to work on government contracts. Organized labor – especially the building trades, the "citadel" of the American Federation of Labor (AFL) – similarly looked forward to a return to employment. Progressive organizations, such as the National Unemployment League, the United Relief Program, the National Conference of Catholic Charities, and the Joint Committee on Unemployment, also supported public works, anticipating that these projects would alleviate unemployment. The differing expectations of these various constituencies planted the seeds of conflict within the PWA over its eventual goals.[18]

---

[16] Frances Perkins, *The Roosevelt I Knew* (New York: Viking Press, 1947), 272; Reeves, "The Politics of Public Works," 9–12; FDR quoted in Ellis W. Hawley, *The New Deal and the Problem of Monopoly: A Study in Economic Ambivalence* (Princeton: Princeton University Press, 1966), 19.

[17] Hawley, *New Deal and the Problem of Monopoly* 35–52; and Rexford G. Tugwell, *The Democratic Roosevelt* (Garden City, NJ: Doubleday, 1957), 280.

[18] Robert D. Kohn to Louis Howe, March 10, 1933; and Dwight L. Hoopingarner, "Memorandum on Public Works," May 9, 1933; both in "[Official File] OF 140 Public Works"

FDR resisted public demands for a huge $5 billion appropriation, telling the press, "Do not write stories about five or six billion dollars of public works. That is wild." Wild or not, however, the very drafting of the NIRA legislation reflected the pressures of the moment. Even the final amount appropriated by Title II for public works, $3.3 billion (about 5.9 percent of 1933 GDP), resulted from a misunderstanding between Wagner and his aide, Simon Rifkind. Surrounded by a crowd while reviewing the final draft of the bill in his office, Wagner supposedly asked Rifkind, "Does the three billion for public works include the three hundred million for New York?" Rifkind replied that he had put it in, but Wagner thought he heard Rifkind say, "Put it in." Wagner struck out the $3 billion figure from the text and replaced it with $3.3 billion. Within the president's cabinet, Frances Perkins and Harold Ickes championed the creation of the PWA for different reasons: the former, for its potential to relieve unemployment while the latter welcomed its promised ability to improve the nation's infrastructure.[19]

Donald Richberg, a former law partner of Ickes who had joined the Roosevelt administration to help hammer out the details of the NIRA, observed approvingly that the PWA was included in the recovery plan as part of a broader scheme to satisfy different political constituencies. The PWA's works projects would create employment and attract public support, he thought, while the less popular production codes of the NRA would stabilize the economy. In Richberg's view, "If industrial control leads off, with public works as a secondary, incidental part of the program, it will be difficult to avoid violent opposition from those now clamoring for public works who might swallow a somewhat 'fascist' proposal to get

folder, box 1, OF 140, F.D.R. Papers, F.D.R. Library; Corrington Gill, "The Effectiveness of Public Works in Stabilizing the Construction Industry," *Proceedings of the American Statistical Association*, n.s., 28, suppl. (March 1933): 196–200; Reeves, "Politics of Public Works," 11–12; Stephen B. Adams, *Mr. Kaiser Goes to Washington: The Rise of a Government Entrepreneur* (Chapel Hill: University of North Carolina Press, 1997), 33–62; Booth Mooney, *Builders for Progress: The Story of the Associated General Contractors of America* (New York: McGraw-Hill, 1965); Mark Perlman, "Labor in Eclipse," in John Braeman, Robert H. Bremner, and David Brody, eds., *Change and Continuity in Twentieth-Century America: The 1920s* (Columbus: Ohio State University Press, 1968), 112; Christopher L. Tomlins, "AFL Unions in the 1930s: Their Performance in Historical Perspective," *Journal of American History* 65 (March 1979): 1021–42; and William Green, "Employment is Essential for Business Recovery," *Engineering News-Record*, (May 18, 1933), 611–12.
[19] Samuel I. Rosenman, ed., *The Public Papers and Addresses of Franklin D. Roosevelt* (New York: Russell & Russell, 1938), 2:140–41; Ickes, *Back to Work*, 14.

their 'democratic' measure of relief."[20] While the titles of the legislation
were in fact eventually reversed, with the result that the sweet syrup of
public works (Title II) followed the bitter pill of industrial codes (Title I),
Richberg was correct to sense the many different political trajectories
running through the public works program of the early New Deal. These
concerns persisted, and were soon taken up by the Special Board for Public
Works.

Created by FDR to expedite the allocation of funds for public works
projects, the Special Board was composed of Ickes, temporary administrator Donald Sawyer, and a number of cabinet officers (the attorney general,
the secretaries of war, agriculture, commerce, and labor, and the director
of the budget).[21] The records of its meetings document, in explicit detail,
the political world inhabited by Ickes and his fellow board members,
such as Frances Perkins and Rexford Tugwell, during the early days of
the New Deal.[22] These New Dealers argued strenuously over a number
of problems: how to guard against graft and waste; how to accommodate those who were eager to benefit from government largess, including
organized labor, private contractors, and politicians; how to provide useful public works projects across the nation; and how to put people back
to work. Not least, they had to figure out how to do all this swiftly
while carefully spending $3.3 billion. Within the PWA, New Dealers first
gathered and explored the potential for the federal government to relieve
unemployment and remake the nation's landscape and built environment.

INITIAL CONCERNS: PROJECTS, PROBITY, STRUCTURE,
AND SPENDING

From their initial meetings, members of the Special Board were highly
attuned to potential public reception of their decisions. Although they
drew on the earlier work of the Reconstruction Finance Corporation's
division for self-liquidating public works, and did immediately adopt

---

[20] Undated memorandum, "1933, Undated" folder, box 1, Donald R. Richberg Papers,
Manuscript Division, Library of Congress. For more on the links between NIRA's Title I
and II, see Raymond Moley, *After Seven Years* (New York: Harper & Brothers, 1939),
172–75.

[21] Ickes, *Back to Work*, 20–21.

[22] Ickes himself reprinted several excerpts from the Special Board minutes in his *Back to
Work*. The only historian to make sustained use of this source is William D. Reeves,
"PWA and Competitive Administration in the New Deal," *Journal of American History*
60 (September 1973): 357–72; and "The Politics of Public Works, 1933–1935" (Ph.D.
diss., Tulane University, 1968).

many of the plans formulated by RFC personnel, these New Dealers still had much work ahead: They had to build a new organization from scratch, determine their priorities, and overcome obstacles to public construction, such as city-charter and state-constitutional provisions against carrying excessive debt. In order to accomplish its agenda quickly, the PWA, like other New Deal public works programs, chose to appoint to its staff civil and military engineers who were skilled at construction, instead of hiring social workers who were experienced in dealing with the unemployed. Ickes summed up the daunting enormity of the task ahead, writing, "It helped me to estimate [the appropriation's] size by figuring that if we had it all in currency and should load it into trucks we could set out with it from Washington for the Pacific Coast, shovel off one million dollars at every milepost and still have enough left to build a fleet of battleships."[23]

From the beginning, Ickes and the members of the Special Board anticipated that a positive public image was crucial. Attorney General Homer Cummings realized what was at stake. "They will say: 'Why in hell do you do that? that is a crazy project.' . . . [U]nless we have got some well-defined principles by which we are going to proceed, we are going to be in trouble." Secretary of Commerce Dan Roper concurred with Cummings, but with a caveat. Roper wanted the Special Board to develop a long-term policy that would extend beyond the immediate emergency. More bluntly, though, Roper agreed that the PWA had to grasp the importance of "knowing how to sell to the American people the wisdom of our procedure."[24]

In addition to developing a coherent policy and shaping its political justification, the Special Board grappled with the closely related issue of openness and honesty in executing the PWA's mandate. Roper cautioned that the PWA had to avoid the taint of graft. He warned, "Don't let the fellow who wants a contract think he can send someone down to Washington who is a Democrat who has all influence here and who can take somebody out to lunch and fix him." While the members of the Special Board shared Roper's larger concerns about public appearances, Secretary of War George Dern drew their attention to the specific problems presented by the PWA's appropriation. "This program contains a lot of camouflage," Dern warned. "This is not $3,500,000,000 for new works."

---

[23] Ickes, *Back to Work*, 56.
[24] Minutes of the meetings of the Special Board for Public Works, 1933–1935, 1:22–24, June 19, 1933, entry 1, "Minutes of Meetings of the Special Board for Public Works, 1933–1935," Records of the Public Works Administration, Record Group 135, National Archives, Washington, D.C. (Each day's minutes were individually paginated.)

Rather, he pointed out, substantial portions of the PWA appropriation were already slated for other government departments. "We are trying to fool the American people with a program of $3,500,000,000 when we haven't got it." The PWA's earmarked spending particularly benefited the armed forces, especially the Navy, which was due to receive more than $200 million for shipbuilding.[25]

The Special Board thus began its work with a substantial amount of the PWA's $3.3 billion appropriation already parceled out. The question of transferring PWA funds to other government departments – what one student of the PWA has termed "budget substitution" – would continue to bedevil the PWA throughout its existence.[26] As it first convened, then, the central question for the Special Board was how to reconcile these "substitutions" with plans for spending the PWA's money. Should it allocate further monies to established federal departments, such as the Army and the Navy, or should it attempt to fund "nonfederal projects," as they were called in PWA parlance. Frances Perkins consistently supported the construction of nonfederal projects, arguing that local projects would generate more widespread benefits. Solicitor General James C. Biggs, however, warned his colleagues that many government departments – the Army and Navy, especially – viewed the PWA as an opportunity to get money for construction projects that Congress had previously blocked. The Army, for example, was already lobbying for $500 million from the PWA to spend on river and harbor improvements.[27]

To Ickes and most of the Special Board, though, it seemed only logical that the established departments of the federal government would be able to get projects underway in a timely fashion. This still left the question of what kinds of projects the PWA would distribute across the nation. Lawrence W. Robert, Jr., the assistant treasury secretary in charge of public buildings, spoke for many when he commented, "Ultimately, what we want is quick action. Major projects are impossible to get underway and complete quickly. If big flood control projects or big irrigation projects, like Boulder Dam, are to be taken into consideration, we are spending a vast amount of money." Robert acknowledged the merits of Perkins's position. In addition to quick action, he observed, "What we

[25] Special Board Minutes, 1:23–27, June 19, 1933, RG 135, NA; and Ickes, *Back to Work*, 20–21; 37–38.
[26] Special Board Minutes, 1:50, June 21, 1933, RG 135, NA; Isakoff, *Public Works Administration*, 18; and for "budget substitution," see Reeves, "PWA and Competitive Administration," and "Politics of Public Works."
[27] Special Board Minutes, 4:52, June 29, 1933, RG 135, NA.

want is to have, as near as possible, small projects spread over the country, just exactly like we are doing on this highway work. We want to try to work in 75 percent of all counties and all states. That should be our object." Donald Sawyer, the temporary administrator of the PWA, added that, regardless of where the work was located, increases in construction would stimulate the economy of states that were home to construction-related industries, such as California, Illinois, Indiana, New York, Ohio, and Pennsylvania.[28]

Following this initial discussion of PWA policy and project distribution, the Special Board turned to three related issues: the assembly of state advisory boards; the formal regional organization of the nation's public works projects; and the prioritizing of fund allocation. Lawrence Robert proposed that each state ought to have a full-time state administrator, an advisory board of three to be appointed by the president, and a chief technical officer to mediate between the board and the state administrator. Once these people were named, the PWA could bring them directly to Washington for consultation. The gatekeeping role of the engineers would be particularly crucial, Robert thought. "Each one of these engineers is going to be told that we are depending on him to weed out the bad projects and only send the good ones up here."[29] Turning to the organization of the nation's PWA projects, the Special Board provisionally agreed, without any debate, to adapt a thirty-year-old system used by the Treasury Department, dividing the country into seven zones. Despite this decision, in the following days the Special Board did consider whether the PWA should adopt an organization based on the federal-reserve districts. A regional approach would facilitate the PWA's ability to gather information and organize it in a way that was compatible with the records of other governmental agencies and bodies. This issue was left unresolved, after much debate.[30] Finally, the Special Board considered a report from their Subcommittee on Policy regarding how the PWA would choose projects for financing. This memorandum recommended that the PWA weigh two questions in selecting projects: Would the project provide immediate unemployment relief, and what was the social usefulness of the project over time? While these yardsticks seemingly put "people"

[28] Ickes, *Back to Work*, 24–25; and Special Board Minutes, 1:53, June 21, 1933, RG 135, NA.
[29] Special Board Minutes, 1:72, 73, June 21, 1933, RG 135, NA.
[30] Special Board Minutes, 1:85–86, June 21, 1933; and 3:45, June 28, 1933; both in RG 135, NA.

above "projects," in reality, the members of the Special Board, Ickes, and FDR – during his weekly meeting with Ickes to review PWA allotments – did not hesitate to ignore this guideline. (Not incidentally, these meetings with FDR provided Ickes with a terrific opportunity to lobby the president on a variety of issues, an arrangement that Ickes's successor termed "a good one, especially for the [PWA] Administrator.")[31] Once it had drafted a funding policy and begun to assemble the necessary administrative personnel, the Special Board turned to the specifics of launching public works.

Despite uncertainty over the merits of distributing its funds through federal departments, the PWA quickly began to do just that. Indeed, one week into the Special Board's existence, the PWA was working almost entirely through existing federal departments. Sawyer reported to the Special Board that $1.25 billion of the $3.3 billion had already been allocated, in some cases explicitly, according to the terms of the NIRA's Title II. Outside of the $450 million for roads and the $238 million for naval ships, an additional $350 million was earmarked for federal construction to be conducted by the Army, the Navy, and about eighty other government departments, including $50 million for the newly established Tennessee Valley Authority and $25 million for subsistence homesteads. During a meeting at his Hyde Park residence later that summer, FDR assured Ickes that the government would fund these major projects via the PWA appropriation.[32]

CONTRACTORS, WORKERS, AND CEMENT

The PWA was not at a loss for projects to consider. The Construction League of the United States, for example, had submitted a list of various

[31] John M. Carmody to Colette and Nell Cummiskey, December 5, 1962, "PWA Catherine" folder, box 261, John M. Carmody Papers, FDR Library [hereafter FDRL]; T. H. Watkins, *Righteous Pilgrim: The Life and Times of Harold L. Ickes* (New York: Henry Holt, 1990), 370.
[32] Special Board Minutes, 4:54, June 29, 1933, RG 135, NA; for the text of Title II of the National Industrial Recovery Act, see *Principal Acts and Executive Orders Pertaining to Public Works Administration*, compiled by Minnie Wiener (Washington, D.C.: U.S. Government Printing Office, 1938), no folder, box 14, entry 49, "Records of the Projects Control Division, Research Materials, 1935–1940," RG 135, NA; Ickes, *Back to Work*, 235–55; and "August 27, 1933, at Hyde Park, Franklin D. Roosevelt-HLI," August 27, 1933, attached to Ickes to Waite, September 3, 1933, "Public Works 2 1933 September 1–15" folder, box 248, Harold L. Ickes Papers, Manuscript Division, Library of Congress.

projects worth $2 billion to be considered by the PWA's Special Board. Perkins, though, was deeply concerned about the response of organized labor to such developments, and she raised the question of creating a labor advisory committee that would report to Ickes or to the Special Board. Perkins suggested that the PWA could create a "business advisory committee" to give the appearance, at least, of balancing concern with labor issues with solicitude for the problems of the business community. The development that most preoccupied organized labor, Perkins reported, was the creation of a government-run employment service. Such a bureaucracy, she declared, "alarmed" organized labor "for fear that, in the employment of skilled men, the United States Public Employment Service would supplant the Union headquarters." In her dealings with the AFL building trades, Perkins noted that private acknowledgment of labor's concerns would not suffice. "If we do it behind closed doors," she told her colleagues on the Special Board, "even if we do it to their satisfaction, they will not be satisfied."[33]

Perkins's reasoning persuaded Ickes, and Perkins's assistant, economist Isador Lubin, was put in charge of the PWA's labor advisory board, which eventually forged a compromise on hiring policy with building-trades leaders such as the plumbers' John Coefield, the bricklayers' Richard J. Gray, the carpenters' George H. Lakey, the electricians' Charles L. Read, and the head of the AFL's building trades, Michael J. McDonough. They agreed that union hiring halls would have forty-eight hours to provide skilled labor requested by a contractor; after that the revived United States Employment Service (USES) would fill the request from its rolls. USES would also provide all nonunion labor to project sites.[34]

After workers were hired, how many hours could they work? While this was seemingly a straightforward question, the Special Board's debates over this issue reveal the tension between fostering economic development and relieving unemployment that permeated the establishment of public works during the early New Deal. Despite their commitment to executing public works via private contracting, Special Board members expressed deep ambivalence toward both the construction industry and private contracting in general. Initially, the Board considered allowing PWA workers to labor eight hours a day, six days a week, instead of being restricted to the maximum of thirty hours a week stipulated under the National Recovery Act. This would allow contractors on rural road projects to

[33] Special Board Minutes, 4:79–83, June 29, 1933, RG 135, NA.
[34] Ickes, *Back to Work*, 32–33.

build smaller camps at their work sites to accommodate the small construction gangs working more hours. The Board soon arrived at a consensus to hold the PWA to the thirty-hour-week provision, championed by Alabama Senator Hugo Black. During the Board's discussion of this topic, Rexford Tugwell, sitting in at a meeting for Agriculture Secretary Henry Wallace, observed that Thomas H. MacDonald, head of the Bureau of Public Roads, had told him that "there is a social reason" for permitting rural road laborers to work a higher number of hours. Assistant Treasury Secretary Lawrence Robert clarified MacDonald's position for the Special Board, remarking, "If you have a bunch of Negroes working thirty hours a week up in a mountain camp, and there are a number of women around there, with all that time left for leaving there will be a real social problem." Although both Ickes and Tugwell were progressive thinkers on race, Robert's remark passed without any recorded comment by either man. This lapse perhaps indicated both their grasp of political realities and the limits of their outlook on race. Subsequently, though, Ickes did champion the inclusion of African Americans on the PWA's work rolls, instituting hiring quotas to ensure that they benefited from public works construction. This use of quotas, while limited, was one of the first systemized government efforts to reshape a labor market characterized by racial discrimination.[35]

As the PWA began allocating money and making funding decisions, Secretary of Labor Perkins conferred with a delegation of AFL building trades unionists, reporting back to Ickes and the Special Board on organized labor's reactions to the PWA's decisions. This group was led by the AFL building trades president, Michael McDonough, and included the heads of electric, plumbers and steamfitters, bridge and iron workers, bricklayers and plasterers, and carpenters and joiners unions. Perkins stressed the ability of public works projects to alleviate the high percentage of unemployment in the building trades, while the delegation of labor leaders advocated the construction of schools, hospitals, community centers, and other municipal, state, and federal projects to improve the nation's infrastructure. That these improvements would also benefit

---

[35] Special Board Minutes, 2:84, June 22, 1933, RG 135, NA; the PWA had difficulty enforcing these quotas in the South. See Mark W. Kruman, "Quotas for Blacks: The PWA and the Black Construction Worker," *Labor History* 16 (Winter 1975): 37–51; and Harvard Sitkoff, *A New Deal for Blacks: The Emergence of Civil Rights as a National Issue – The Depression Decade* (New York: Oxford University Press, 1978), 68–69.

the skilled building trades workers was a fact not lost on these union officers.[36]

Isador Lubin spearheaded the efforts of the PWA's Labor Advisory Board to devise a stabilized wage scale, in consultation with the AFL. The agreement on this wage scale rested upon Lubin's proposal to reconcile wage disparities among various regions and urban and rural locations by dividing the nation into three zones: North, Central, and South. The agreement also fixed different rates for skilled and unskilled labor, reflecting the AFL's desire that members of building trades unions, while not receiving union rates, would at least be better paid than unskilled recruits. Some contractors were unsure about the benefits of increased government involvement in the construction industry. One trade journal at first hailed the "great accomplishment" of the NRA's construction code, only to declare subsequently that the PWA's wage agreement "made more certain" the likelihood of labor's disrupting the progress of construction.[37]

As part of these negotiations about wages, the PWA proposed the creation of a tripartite Board of Labor Review, which would deal with grievances that came up under contracts financed by PWA funds. This Board was to be composed of three members appointed by the president: one for labor, one for contractors, and one for the PWA. Labor leaders, including McDonough, president of the AFL building trades department, and Henry W. Blumenberg of the carpenters and joiners signed on to this proposal. McDonough heralded the Board's creation at the AFL building trades convention scarcely one month later.[38] While it is difficult to glean much from the surviving records of the Board of Labor Review, one contemporary student of the PWA, J. Kerwin Williams, argued that "the Board undoubtedly helped to obviate the need for resort to the courts, but it was never called upon to play an important direct role." After speaking with several AFL officials in Washington, D.C., Williams concluded,

---

[36] July 15, 1933, Department of Labor Press Release, in Special Board Minutes, 5:7–9, July 17, 1933, RG 135, NA.

[37] Special Board Minutes, 6:2, August 10, 1933; and 6:8–10, August 15, 1933; both RG 135, NA; "Wide-Spread Relief Projects," *American Federationist* 40 (June 1933): 623; "The Construction Code," *Engineering News-Record*, August 3, 1933, 236; and "Wage and Labor Confusion," *Engineering News-Record*, August 31, 1933, 269.

[38] Special Board Minutes, 6:8–10, August 15, 1933, RG 135, NA; and *Report of Proceedings of the Twenty-Seventh Annual Convention of the Building Trades Department, American Federation of Labor* (Washington, D.C.: American Federation of Labor, 1933), 54–58.

"While there has been some criticism from organized labor that the PWA mediator has in some instances weakened labor's side in a dispute by dealing with the particular small union directly concerned rather than with the stronger national and international unions, it is safe to say that grave injustice has been avoided."[39]

Ickes was determined to limit the amount of PWA work (particularly road construction) that was supervised by the government directly, an arrangement termed "force account" construction. At the same time, Ickes was not enthusiastic about the alternative of working through private contractors. Tugwell also balked at the use of private contractors for road building, asserting that "in some States contractors have to add at least 20 percent to costs for graft." Indeed, Ickes observed, relying on contractors had implications that stretched beyond the economic arena and into the political realm. "I know in every municipal campaign in Chicago," Ickes offered, "the backbone of the enormous campaign funds that were raised came from the contractors." Direct employment of workers by the government, Ickes recalled, was discussed in building Hoover – or as Ickes, no fan of Hoover, renamed it, Boulder Dam. Lawrence Robert, however, was not convinced that it was at all feasible to ramp up the necessary state capacities to supervise so many workers directly. Contracting organizations, for the most part, were eager to show Ickes and the PWA that they were capable of getting the job done, but they balanced this goal with a concerted effort to combat "those who desire to dominate our branch of the industry by rules and exorbitant high wage rates."[40]

In seeking a possible alternative to the use of private contracts for carrying out their public works program, the Special Board debated the notion of conducting one PWA project with direct government employment of labor, simply as a test of a different approach. Troubled by the idea, Robert noted that the only qualified people the PWA could turn to in order to try out this plan "would necessarily be the men who had experience. They would be contractors to start with." Conceding the overwhelming nature

[39] Williams, *Grants-in-Aid under the Public Works Administration*, 209, n. 87, 214; the extant Board of Labor Review records can be found in box 1, entry 22, "Decisions Rendered by the Board of Labor Review, 1934–1936," RG 135, NA. See also Lindsay Rogers, "The Independent Regulatory Commissions," *Political Science Quarterly* 52 (March 1937): 1–17.

[40] Special Board Minutes, 2:91 and 2:93–94, June 22, 1933, RG 135, NA; and "Contractors Stress Necessity for United Action to Secure Fair Code for the Industry," *Bulletin of the General Contractors Association* 24 (September 1933): 153.

of the challenge, he concluded, "It is a monumental proposition." The next best thing, the Special Board speculated, would be for the PWA to purchase all the raw materials necessary for its projects while the contractors bid to carry out the actual construction. "I think it would be a distinct public service to show these burglars up," Ickes said of the contractors.[41]

In concurring with the idea that the federal government should be put in charge of purchasing of construction materials, Ickes was drawing on his recent experience with the cement contract for Boulder Dam. "The trade papers all through the country pounded me, telling me what kind of a fool I was, but after rejecting the bids twice they did come down, with the result that we saved $52,000 on 400,000 barrels," Ickes recalled. His feelings on this subject shaped the initial draft of his address to the Associated General Contractors of America in February 1934. In an entry to his diary that he subsequently withheld from publication, Ickes recorded that the speech he planned to make to the contractors "is a pretty stiff dose and I may decide not to accept the invitation," adding, "One thing is certain. If I do accept the invitation I am going to talk cold turkey to them." Ickes did speak to the AGC, talking frankly about the dangers posed to the public trust by contractors' collusive bidding, by their "skimping" on building materials, and by their extortion of kickbacks in wages from their workers. If contractors would not police themselves, Ickes warned, "the great force of inspectors and investigators that we are building up in connection with our Public Works Administration" would be on the watch against corruption. "This is what 'The New Deal' means to me," Ickes declared, "an era of acute social consciousness and realization of mutual responsibility, a time of reciprocal helpfulness, of greater understanding and willingness to work together for the good of all." This New Deal, Ickes continued, "is already being translated into reality" through the allocation and spending of PWA funds.[42]

[41] Special Board Minutes, 2:95; 2:97, June 22, 1933, RG 135, NA.
[42] Special Board Minutes, 2:99–100, June 22, 1933, RG 135, NA; Harold L. Ickes Diary, 414, Jan. 15, 1934, "Diary Nov. 1, 1933–Feb. 28, 1934. Pp. 350–452" folder, box 1, Ickes Papers, LC; and January 31, 1934, speech of Harold L. Ickes to the Associated General Contractors of America, in *The Public Speeches and Statements of Secretary of the Interior Harold L. Ickes*, vol. 1, box 1, entry 26, "Public Speeches and Statements of Harold L. Ickes, 1934–1939," RG 135, NA; and see also Ickes's recollection in Harold L. Ickes, *The Secret Diary of Harold L. Ickes: The Inside Struggle, 1936–1939* (New York: Simon & Schuster, 1954), 2:78.

EXPERTISE POLITICIZED

As the Special Board went about planning the PWA's organizational structure, Ickes was struck by the intense concern that various political interests showed in the process. In order to appoint an advisory committee of three people in each state, for instance, Ickes sent out letters to the governor, senators, and chambers of commerce to solicit suggestions. This elicited quite a reaction. As Ickes put it, "Hell is popping all over the place." Ickes was deluged with personal visits, phone calls, and letters. "There is pulling and hauling, and a lot of people are smelling the frying bacon, and want to get in with their plates and get theirs," Ickes complained to the Special Board. The demands for patronage quickly led the Board to restrict the number of candidates the governor and senators from each state could recommend to one.[43]

By early July 1933, despite its earlier debates, the PWA had still not settled on a plan of organization. At this point FDR stepped in, declaring that the PWA would be a regional – rather than a state – organization, and that each state would have an advisory committee of three, to be appointed by the president. This tactic, though, did not remove political concerns from the organization. Later that year, Ickes reported to the United States Conference of Mayors, "We wanted to keep these [state advisory committees and regional adviser positions] out of politics." He observed, "The pressure to appoint men for partisan reasons or for sinister purposes can be imagined." While Ickes asserted that the appointments "were generally acclaimed throughout the country as appointments of a high order," this caveat was no doubt offered for public consumption. In fact, a number of the advisory boards were probably appointed only to satisfy the senators and governors from their states, as the board members subsequently complained of being ignored entirely by the PWA's Washington headquarters.[44]

Political concerns also entered into decisions about hiring technical advisers and engineers. Assistant Secretary of Labor Turner Battle argued that these specialized personnel should come from outside the state in

[43] Special Board Minutes, 3:44, June 28, 1933, and 4:30–31, June 29, 1933, RG 135, NA.
[44] Special Board Minutes, 5:6, July 8, 1933; September 23, 1933, speech of Harold L. Ickes to the U.S. Conference of Mayors, in *The Public Speeches and Statements of Secretary of the Interior Harold L. Ickes*, vol. 1, box 1, entry 26, "Public Speeches and Statements of Harold L. Ickes, 1934–1939"; and "Report of Regional Conference Federal Emergency Administration of Public Works called by Colonel H. M. Waite, Deputy Administrator," February 14–March 1, 1934, in "Feb. 14–Mar. 1, 1934" folder, box 1, entry 23, "Minutes and Reports of Conferences of the PWA, 1934–1941," all in RG 135, NA.

which they were to work, to minimize the potential for corruption charges arising from connections to contractors and others in their localities. Robert informed his colleagues that FDR "thought it an excellent idea" to import engineers and other technical advisers from outside the state, in order to minimize the appearance of impropriety. Others on the Special Board, though, anticipated similar dangers in selecting technical advisers who were unfamiliar with the legal and economic conditions of the particular region they were assigned to supervise.[45] These concerns, as we shall see in the following chapter, would soon be overshadowed by the political stakes of staffing a new national bureaucracy.

The central question – whether recovery would be stimulated by increases or reductions in spending – that haunted the early New Deal policy debates also dominated the debates of the Special Board. The arguments intensified when the members were considering what interest rate to set on PWA loans to states and localities. The heated debates finally pushed the Board to take up the fundamental task of defining its approach to funding public works. While each project would be funded with a grant amounting to 30 percent of the project's cost, the rest would be covered by a loan from the PWA. Rexford Tugwell suggested starting with an interest rate of 3.5 percent, and, as recovery got underway, adjusting this rate to as high as 5 percent. Budget Director Lewis Douglas, perhaps the strongest voice for economy in the administration, strenuously objected to Tugwell's low initial rate. Concerned about estimates that put county and municipal debt for the following year at approximately $6 million, Douglas worried that charging 3.5 percent interest on PWA loans would soon threaten the credibility of the federal government. As Douglas wrote in a memo to FDR, when public works "are continued over a long period of time they cease to become primers of the pump, and to the extent to which they pile up expenditures beyond the borrowing capacity of the government to meet, they cause infinitely more harm through the consequent paper inflation than any amount of good which might flow from them." To avoid this potential nightmare, Douglas argued, the PWA should loan its money at a constant rate of 4.5 percent.[46]

[45] Special Board Minutes, 6:3–4, August 3, 1933, RG 135, NA.

[46] Julian E. Zelizer, "The Forgotten Legacy of the New Deal: Fiscal Conservatism and the Roosevelt Administration, 1933–1938," *Presidential Studies Quarterly* 30 (June 2000): 331–61; Williams, *Grants-in-Aid under the Public Works Administration*, 104–8; 119–22; Isakoff, *Public Works Administration*, 20–21; Special Board Minutes, 3:1–8, July 1, 1933, RG 135, NA; and Lewis Douglas to FDR, December 30, 1933, "Bureau of the Budget 1933–34" folder, OF 79, FDR Papers, FDRL.

Attorney General Cummings tried to mediate between these two positions, favoring 3.75 percent as a compromise. Regardless of what interest rate the PWA charged, Cummings argued, "We must get this money out. We must carry out the [National Industrial Recovery] Act in good faith." Ickes later noted that the Special Board chose to compromise among Tugwell, his subcommittee, and Douglas, by setting the interest rate for loans at 4 percent, because "this charge would not be low enough to attract cities with good financial standing, who could borrow from the usual sources at a lower rate" and "would not be so high as to deter borrowers and still assure the Federal Government a fair return on its investment."[47]

As the Special Board hammered out these policy details, Ickes, in an interview broadcast on NBC radio, told the listening public that the PWA aimed to provide employment to the unemployed, to "prime the pump of business revival," to build projects of "lasting benefit," and to encourage economic recovery. Echoing the homespun language of FDR, Ickes described the workings of the PWA as "much like priming an old-fashioned pump. In cold weather you can work the pump handle up and down until you are tired and still not a drop of water will come. But if you will pour warm water down that pump then you can get all the water you want." The PWA, Ickes argued, "will have this same effect. By pouring money down the pump to prime it we will start the returning flow which will mean better times and greater prosperity." To safeguard labor, Ickes declared, "We will do everything possible to hold contractors down to a legitimate profit." He added, "We will seek to safeguard all public works undertaken by us from corruption or graft. We will see to it that works are carefully inspected during their progress so that the taxpayers of the United States who are so generously contributing this vast fund for the common good may be assured that every dollar spent represents a dollar of value." Speaking later over the phone to an audience gathered in Indianapolis, Ickes stressed that the PWA's projects represented a wise use of money. "Public works represent capital investments," Ickes said. "They include buildings, bridges, schools, sewage disposal plants, water works, municipal electric light plants, reclamation projects, flood control, river and harbor work, shipbuilding, road building and a great variety of other enterprises."[48]

[47] Special Board Minutes, 3:18, July 1, 1933, RG 135, NA; and Ickes, *Back to Work*, 27.
[48] July 2, 1933, Harold L. Ickes interview on NBC radio; and August 21, 1933, Harold L. Ickes telephone speech, both in *The Public Speeches and Statements of Secretary of*

Managing these capital investments promised to be a difficult challenge, given the fragile condition of state and local finances throughout the nation. The Special Board was eager to fund worthy public improvements and speed recovery, yet at the same time the members also wanted to insure that states and localities would be able to repay their PWA loans. Many states convened special legislative sessions to rescind their constitutionally imposed debt limits, and governors consulted directly with Ickes about finding ways to maximize their ability to attract PWA funds.[49] The Board was itself not certain how to handle the questions surrounding state debt limits, a task made more difficult by the different interpretations of its enabling legislation. Specifically, Section 203(d) of the NIRA's Title II caused much confusion. It stated, "The President, in his discretion, and under such terms as he may describe, may extend any of the benefits of this title to any State, county, or municipality notwithstanding any constitutional or legal restriction or limitation on the right or power of such State, county, or municipality to borrow money or incur indebtedness."[50]

Section 203(d) was added to Title II by Georgia Democratic Senator Richard Russell to, in his words, "enable a considerable number of political subdivisions to obtain very necessary assistance in addition to the highway funds, and create work for the unemployed." Lawrence Robert interpreted this clause to mean that FDR could use his judgment to "grant anything he wants to" to any state or locality that was unable to carry any more debt. While Secretary of War Dern suggested the option of organizing private corporations to borrow on behalf of indebted states and localities, Robert felt that this would cause too much of a delay in the federal government's ability to move funds out of Washington and into the nation. The PWA, Robert argued, needed to find a balance between giving money away and "trying to find a reasonable excuse to say that we are lending it to the community. We are not looking for an iron-bound, RFC self-liquidating loan by any means. If we were, we might just as well quit operating now and just devote ourselves to Federal projects and let these others alone."[51]

the Interior Harold L. Ickes, vol. 1, box 1, entry 26, "Public Speeches and Statements of Harold L. Ickes, 1934–1939," RG 135, NA.
[49] See, for example, Utah Governor Henry H. Blood to Ickes, July 2, 1933, in Special Board Minutes, 5:25–26, July 6, 1933, RG 135, NA.
[50] For the complete text of the act, see Ickes, *Back to Work*, 235–55.
[51] Special Board Minutes, 5:29–34, July 6, 1933, RG 135, NA; Russell quoted in Williams, *Grants-in-Aid under the Public Works Administration*, 229.

Speaking two weeks later over NBC radio, though, Ickes proclaimed that the PWA would be cautious in extending loans. He declared, "We would be failing in our duty to the people of the Nation as a whole if we should not insist, where necessary, upon a prudent and businesslike management of the affairs of any applicant for a loan." By October 1933, the PWA's assistant counsel, E. H. Foley, Jr., reported to the Special Board that, in cases where state constitutions still restricted debt and borrowing, the Board's interpretation of Section 203(d) had rendered the PWA "helpless" to assist them further. While its reading of the law potentially empowered the PWA to provide funds to debt-strapped states and communities, the Board's final decision to interpret Section 203(d) narrowly added to the difficulties confronting the PWA.[52]

UNEMPLOYMENT OR DEVELOPMENT?

While the PWA struggled with decisions about how to begin distributing funds to the states and localities, from its inception the organization made a robust commitment to large-scale public works construction. The hydroelectric projects funded by the PWA epitomized the organization's difficulty in reconciling Ickes's desire to develop national resources and build lasting infrastructure with the need to alleviate unemployment. These projects were also of particular interest to FDR, as he checked regularly with Ickes for detailed updates on the Casper–Alcova Project in Wyoming, Montana's Fort Peck Project, the Kaw River Project, the Upper Mississippi River Project, and the Columbia River Project. Within the Special Board, members debated the merits of the PWA's approach. Pointing to the Casper–Alcova project, Assistant Labor Secretary Turner Battle objected that not enough of the money allocated to its construction was going to relieve unemployment directly. However, Elwood Mead, the head of the Bureau of Reclamation, responded that public works, such as the Casper–Alcova project and Colorado's Boulder Dam, had important and overlooked repercussions. The indirect employment stimulated by such projects was equally, if not more, important than the employment required to complete the project itself. Direct employment,

---

[52] July 18, 1933, speech of Harold L. Ickes over NBC radio, in *The Public Speeches and Statements of Secretary of the Interior Harold L. Ickes*, vol. 1, box 1, entry 26, "Public Speeches and Statements of Harold L. Ickes, 1934–1939"; and October 19, 1933, PWA Press Release, vol. 4, box 1, entry 24, "Press Releases, 1933–1939," both in RG 135, NA.

Mead asserted, "is a very small part of the contribution that development has made to the need of the unemployed." Although many of the hydro-electric projects were located in sparsely populated western states, Mead pointed out, "We have contracts today in Pittsburgh and Detroit, in Wilmington...[and] 40 percent of the money that is being spent out there is being spent east of the Mississippi River and is being spent to keep factories open that would otherwise be closed."[53]

As the Special Board reviewed its allotments, however, it became clear that certain states were benefiting more than others. Or, as Solicitor General Biggs pointedly asked, "Is there any limit to the amount we give to California?" Ickes retorted that "California is way behind a lot of the other States," including Washington, Idaho, Arizona, and New Mexico. This debate was prompted in part by a lengthy article from the *Chicago Tribune*, reprinted in the *Washington Star*, which reported that "California and New York were receiving 25% of all federal funds."[54] At the end of November 1933, the Special Board took stock of the progress of the PWA. Thirty-four states were below their quota for PWA funding. Many of these underfunded states had legal and financial constraints that, thanks to the Special Board's reading of Section 203(d), had prevented projects from getting underway.[55] These delays gave the Special Board good cause to be concerned about reactions from Congress. Turner Battle reported to Ickes and his colleagues that the Labor Department had met with the House Appropriations Committee, which had strenuously protested the PWA's refusal to allocate money for projects already approved by Congress and threatened to withhold future appropriations unless the PWA acted more swiftly. While the Special Board continued to argue over the merits of various approaches, it was becoming clear that a public works policy that favored development over unemployment did not benefit just hydroelectric projects. The big winner in such a policy was national defense, a fact that Ickes and other New Dealers would embrace in the 1940s.[56]

By October, the Navy Department had already spent $188 million of its $256 million PWA allotment, while the War Department had spent

[53] Special Board Minutes, 6:6–8, July 24, 1933, RG 135, NA.
[54] Special Board Minutes, 10:26–27, October. 19, 1933, RG 135, NA. The scholarly consensus on the regional distribution of New Deal funds is that western states received more than southern states because they were electoral swing states. John Joseph Wallis, "The Political Economy of New Deal Spending Revisited, Again: With and without Nevada," *Explorations in Economic History* 35(1998): 140–70.
[55] Special Board Minutes, 14:59, November 29, 1933, RG 135, NA.
[56] Special Board Minutes, 15:10, December 7, 1933, RG 135, NA.

$51 million of its $259 million PWA apportionment, representing a total of $239 million, an amount that dwarfed the $83 million spent by nonmilitary departments of the federal government. Between 1933 and 1935, in fact, the Army and Navy received over 45 percent of the PWA money spent on federal projects. This amount was larger than the total sum of money spent on nonfederal PWA projects sponsored by states, municipalities, and other public bodies. Agriculture, Commerce, Interior, Justice, Labor, Post Office, State, Treasury, and other federal departments and agencies moved far more slowly in spending their PWA funds. By October 1933, they had started work on about $83 million worth of projects out of roughly $660 million allotted.[57]

Secretary of War George Dern reported to the Special Board that his War Department was swiftly running through PWA funds, having invested $6 million in fortifications for Hawaii and Panama, $6 million for ammunition, and $7 million for military-related flood control on the lower Mississippi River, in addition to increasing the amounts spent on housing for the Army, motorizing antiaircraft artillery, and modernizing various equipment. Dern argued that these projects "would furnish employment to factories located in the great centers of unemployment and will keep men employed during the winter months when outdoor work must be suspended and when unemployment is usually at its peak."[58]

While this spending suggests a windfall for workers employed on military projects, in fact it was not. In April 1934, for example, Turner Battle told the Special Board of a recent meeting he had attended of the PWA's Labor Advisory Board, where the United Electrical Workers Union complained that the federal government's departments were, in his words, "among the most flagrant violators in the paying of Public Works scale of wages." Battle noted that in a number of cases the worst offenders were the Navy and the Army. These cases included a naval hospital in Philadelphia, army construction at West Point, and a number of airfields throughout the rest of the nation. By July 1934, Ickes was moved to observe that "the Navy has more Public Works money tied up than anyone else," adding,

[57] Special Board Minutes, 8:2–3, October 5, 1933, RG 135, NA; Gayer, *Public Works in Prosperity and Depression*, 102; and Samuel Grafton, "The New Deal Woos the Army," *American Mercury* 33 (December 1934): 436–43. Ickes urged FDR to send letters to each member of the cabinet, asking them to use their PWA money "in getting men to work at the earliest possible moment." Ickes to FDR, September 25, 1933, "OF 466b PWA Aug–Sept" folder, box 13, OF 466b, FDR Papers, FDRL.

[58] Special Board Minutes, 7:6–7, August 24, 1933, RG 135, NA.

"There isn't enough money in the United States Treasury to satisfy the Navy."[59]

Ickes voiced his concerns about the Navy's use of PWA funds to FDR himself, but his complaints had little impact on the military division's former assistant secretary. Indicative of the military's hunger for PWA funds were the gales of laughter that Ickes elicited from Special Board members when he confided, "Just between us, if we gave the Navy and the Army all they asked for..." leaving his punch line unspoken yet clear to all. Admiral Christian Peoples tried to defend the spending practices of the Navy, offering the opinion, "It is distinctly to the advantage of the national defense of the country to build up reserve stocks of ammunition." Ickes, though, again drew chuckles from the Special Board when he replied, "I move you convince the building trades on that score," following up with the remark, "I do not know how permanent ammunition is, but I do know that public buildings have at least an equal claim to permanency."[60]

GROWING CRITICISM OF THE PWA

Ickes was perplexed when criticisms of the PWA began to appear in the press as soon as late August and early September of 1933. The criticism focused on the fact that men were not being put back to work quickly enough. As one trade journal bleakly noted, "The spirit of quick and hearty cooperation on which the success of any such great undertaking as that of the Public Works Administration depends has been destroyed." Ickes, however, was at a loss to explain what the Special Board could do to alleviate unemployment once it had consigned PWA funds to a project, and he was convinced that PWA allocations "had been done regularly and as expeditiously as possible." Ickes blamed the delays on state and municipal bodies, commenting that they were just too slow in proposing projects to the PWA for consideration.[61]

After reading an article by John T. Flynn in the *New Republic*, Ickes and Commerce Secretary Daniel Roper instructed the PWA to engage in "interpretative publicity" on behalf of the organization. Flynn's article posed the question, "Who's Holding Back Public Works?" He answered

[59] Special Board Minutes, 22:9, April 4, 1934; and 31:9, July 5, 1934, RG 135, NA.
[60] Memo of Ickes phone call, August 24, 1933, "OF 466b PWA Aug–Sept" folder, box 13, OF 466b, FDR Papers, FDRL; and Special Board Minutes, 39:6–7, September 12, 1934, RG 135, NA.
[61] "Codes and Public Works," *Engineering News-Record*, August 24, 1933, 237; and Special Board Minutes, 7:1–2, September 5, 1933, RG 135, NA.

his own query by blaming Roosevelt for failing to push the works program forward quickly enough. Flynn, however, also pointed to Lewis Douglas's influence in convincing FDR to halt all other government construction while the PWA was getting underway. In so doing, the government, Flynn wrote, "not only did nothing, but undid all that the Democratic House of Representatives had forced from the unwilling Hoover."[62]

Benjamin Cohen, the PWA's associate general counsel, agreed with Flynn's analysis, reporting to his mentor Felix Frankfurter that Flynn's criticisms were solid. "On the other hand," he wrote, "I do not think the alternative to the present program is . . . the doling out of funds indiscriminately to states and municipalities for worthless projects." Rather, Cohen paraphrased the assessment of Lewis Mumford, who reacted to Flynn's article by underscoring "the dangers of a permanent Public Works program being irreparably damaged if our first venture results in the dotting of the country from coast to coast with monstrous and ill-planned monuments." In any event, Cohen concluded that there was little he could do to influence policy making at the PWA. (Soon enough, however, Cohen would exert a great deal of influence on policy making by helping to draft a number of important laws, including the Securities Exchange Act of 1934.)[63]

The severe delays in the PWA's public works program that Flynn criticized, particularly in road construction, prompted Ickes to propose that the PWA threaten to revoke allotted monies from states that were not spending quickly enough. While states that were tardy in deploying the PWA's money were the targets of this threat, this did not mean that things were going smoothly in states where the money was being spent. "Will the Public-Works Program Fail?" worried the *Engineering News-Record*. The Colorado Association of Highway Contractors protested that PWA funds were being spent on "day labor" road construction. This method, the highway contractors complained, was contrary to the NRA's goals of economic recovery and, further, was a "wasteful procedure which results in county political machines at the sacrifice of good highways." More to

[62] Special Board Minutes, 8:6, September 19, 1933, RG 135, NA; and John T. Flynn, "Who's Holding Back Public Works?" *New Republic*, September 20, 1933, 145–48; quote from 146.
[63] Benjamin V. Cohen to Felix Frankfurter, October 9, 1933, "Special Correspondence. Oxford Correspondence. Cohen, Ben V. 1933–34 & undated" folder, reel 70, Felix Frankfurter Papers, Manuscript Division, Library of Congress; and Thomas K. McCraw, *Prophets of Regulation: Charles Francis Adams, Louis D. Brandeis, James M. Landis, Alfred E. Kahn* (Cambridge: Harvard University Press, 1984), 169–81.

the point, however, was the fact that day labor put a lot of unskilled peo-ple to work, while contractors and their equipment sat unused. "Please insist," the highway contractors asked the PWA, "on contract method which results in immediate employment and recovery of industry and satisfactory construction and honest values."[64]

Despite these problems and complaints, Ickes tried to put the best face on the PWA's beginnings. In January 1934, he summed up the initial efforts made by the Special Board and the PWA as a whole. "We have undoubt-edly made mistakes," Ickes acknowledged. "There have been errors of judgment, unavoidably so. But by and large I am prepared to assert and to prove that the Public Works Administration has written a new page in civil administration." While the PWA would continue to supervise the expen-diture of the $3.3 billion it had already allotted, Ickes sadly noted that "there are many hundreds of worthy projects still pending with no money to be allotted to them unless Congress should make a further appropria-tion."[65] Nevertheless, he found encouragement when Roosevelt assured him that the PWA had a secure place in his administration. "I think the President has a different notion about Public Works now," Ickes told the Special Board, "not going on such a scale as we have been, but having a permanent Public Works Bureau."[66] The Special Board agreed that it could safely assume the Congress would appropriate more money for PWA, and thus it continued to review projects and earmark funds.

Perhaps sensing Roosevelt's inclination to place social worker Harry Hopkins in charge of all the New Deal's public works, Ickes took his case to the nation's most important social-work organization, Survey Asso-ciates. Addressing directly the question of whether Congress would con-tinue to fund the PWA, Ickes set out to justify the PWA's mission. This time, however, he did not emphasize infrastructure or economic develop-ment, as he had in his speech to the Conference of Mayors. "In carry-ing out this Public Works program," Ickes declared, "the Government is once more acting as a social agency and not merely as a tax-collector, a

[64] "Will the Public-Works Program Fail?" *Engineering News-Record*, October 5, 1933, 419; Charles H. Moorefield, "Public Works and National Economic Stability," *Roads and Streets* 76 (December 1933): 427–29; Special Board Minutes, 8:10, September 28, 1933, RG 135, NA; and Colorado Association of Highway Contractors to Oscar L. Chapman, October 2, 1933, in Special Board Minutes, 8:5–6, October 3, 1933, RG 135, NA.
[65] January 8, 1934, speech of Harold L. Ickes over NBC radio, in *The Public Speeches and Statements of Secretary of the Interior Harold L. Ickes*, vol. 1, box 1, entry 26, "Public Speeches and Statements of Harold L. Ickes, 1934–1939," RG 135, NA.
[66] Special Board Minutes, 16:6, January 9, 1934, RG 135, NA.

policeman, or an arbitrator. People were out of work; they were cold; they were hungry; they were rapidly losing their morale." The government, he went on,

lost no time in quibbling over technicalities or worrying about precedents. An acute problem had to be solved. A social crisis must be met. President Roosevelt, recognizing his grave responsibility, met this crisis. Later, with winter approaching and millions of men still out of work, in spite of the desperate effort that had been made to start the Public Works program at top speed, the President turned over hundreds of millions of dollars to the brilliant and able Federal Relief Administrator, Harry L. Hopkins, with instructions to put men back to work over the winter instead of carry them on relief rolls. The effect of this bold stroke on the morale of the country has been marvelous. Thanks to the fine and humane work of Mr. Hopkins, we are coming through the winter of 1933–34 as a people in the best physical and spiritual condition since the crash that brought us to our knees in September of 1929.[67]

Thus, in one rhetorical stroke, Ickes tried to justify PWA as a social-welfare program and attempted to subsume the achievements of Harry Hopkins's Civil Works Administration (CWA) under the umbrella of PWA sponsorship. (While the PWA had provided the $400 million spent by the CWA during the winter of 1933–34, thus requiring the CWA to adhere to PWA standards for wages and hours, Hopkins had been put in charge of the CWA's operating details.) Interestingly, though, neither Ickes nor Hopkins won more than lukewarm support from the professional social-work community. In no small measure, this was due to the fact that engineering experts from the Army Corps of Engineers and private engineering firms made up the core of the administrative personnel for both the CWA and the PWA.[68]

In its first months of existence, as we have seen, the Special Board confronted a number of obstacles in putting together the PWA. Ickes and his colleagues had to come up with plans for projects, guard against graft and waste, and weigh the pros and cons of distributing their appropriations either through the states and municipalities or through the federal departments. They had to hire nonpartisan personnel, overcome the fiscal collapse in cities and states, work with organized labor, and counter the

[67] February 9, 1934, speech of Harold L. Ickes to Survey Associates, in *The Public Speeches and Statements of Secretary of the Interior Harold L. Ickes*, vol. 1, box 1, entry 26, "Public Speeches and Statements of Harold L. Ickes, 1934–1939," RG 135, NA.

[68] Bonnie Fox Schwartz, *The Civil Works Administration, 1933–1934: The Business of Emergency Employment in the New Deal* (Princeton: Princeton University Press, 1984), 39–71.

growing impression that the PWA's money was going exclusively to western hydroelectric projects and various military endeavors. While the PWA was not entirely successful on all these fronts, it was ultimately successful in building projects throughout the United States, as it spent money in all but three of the nation's counties. During the early years of the New Deal, however, the PWA was slow to get underway. While the Special Board for Public Works had allocated $3.3 billion by January 1934, at that point only about $2 billion of this amount had been spent.[69]

Within the PWA, New Dealers explored the potential for remaking the nation's landscape through government construction. This New Deal construction realized on a much larger scale the public works philosophy of the Hoover administration. It also established a template for the sorts of public construction that were later undertaken during World War II. While this policy led to a great wealth of infrastructure, it also had certain costs. Most notably, an emergency organization that was part of a series of acts designed to fight an economic depression was spending money through the military and funding giant dams in the South and the Northwest. Struggling with the difficult process of actually building the New Deal state, the PWA found itself facing a choice between projects and people. This choice held important implications for how New Dealers would conceive of the relationship between "public works" and "work relief" in the years to come.

[69] Special Board Minutes, 16:9, January 2, 1934; and Table A-50, November 17, 1937, "Aug 31, 1937" folder, box 11, entry 61, "Statistical Materials Relating to PWA Projects, 1934–1942," both in RG 135, NA.

3

Making a New Deal State

Patronage and the Public Works Administration

To build public works projects in practically every county in the nation, Harold Ickes, Rexford Tugwell, Frances Perkins, and the other members of the PWA's Special Board for Public Works confronted a perplexing dilemma. They had to figure out how to assemble and supervise a new bureaucracy. Lawyers, accountants, engineers, inspectors, and investigators had to be trained and instructed in the ways of government service. In addition to finding qualified personnel, the PWA had to reckon with the desire of the Democratic Party to fill many of these new government positions, created outside of the civil-service structure, with patronage appointments. The public pronouncements of the New Dealers themselves have often shaped the history of these aspects of the New Deal. "To undertake this gigantic task we had no machinery at hand and no precedent to guide us," Ickes wrote in his celebratory history of the PWA, *Back to Work*. "The seas were uncharted. If there was any works plan in existence anywhere, we were not informed of it. We had to find projects upon which we could expend public funds within the limitations imposed by Congress, and we had to develop an administrative technique that could effectuate the object we had in view."[1]

Developing the "administrative technique" of the New Deal, however, was much more difficult than Ickes's brief summary of the challenge indicates. While some scholars have emphasized the importance of looking beyond the nation's capital to understand how the New Deal was constructed, suggesting that the program's "impact should be measured less by the lasting accomplishments of its reforms and more by the attitudinal

---

[1] Harold L. Ickes, *Back to Work: The Story of PWA* (New York: Macmillan, 1935), 51.

changes it produced," I argue in this chapter that the consequences of the dramatic, unprecedented expansion of the U.S. government that occurred before 1940 can be better understood by reexamining national state structures and looking directly at the New Deal's accomplishments.[2]

Despite many obstacles, the PWA managed to put in place the development-oriented foundations of the early New Deal state. The PWA overcame the national mistrust of bureaucracy and carved out a space within the New Deal state for engineers and lawyers to introduce and carry forward new kinds of "economic knowledge." The PWA carefully spent an initial appropriation of $3.3 billion, generating a wealth of infrastructure and forging a new political order. Staffed with experts who were concerned more with efficiency than with redistribution, the PWA set in motion a vast organization that had more in common with the development-minded Tennessee Valley Authority than it did with the economist-dominated National Resources Planning Board, or with welfare-oriented organizations such as the National Consumers' League. National in scope, the PWA promulgated the New Deal's case that segmented, weak governmental authorities had to be replaced if shared resources were to be developed through public works projects.[3]

The division of investigation was one of the first parts of the new bureaucracy. The PWA's investigation division became a key component of the New Deal public works programs, as it not only scrutinized the Public

[2] Lizabeth Cohen, *Making a New Deal: Industrial Workers in Chicago, 1919–1939* (Cambridge: Cambridge University Press, 1990), 289.

[3] Philip Selznick, *TVA and the Grass Roots: A Study in the Sociology of Formal Organization* (Berkeley: University of California Press, 1953); Patrick D. Reagan, *Designing a New America: The Origins of New Deal Planning, 1890–1943* (Amherst: University of Massachusetts Press, 1999); John M. Jordan, *Machine-Age Ideology: Social Engineering and American Liberalism, 1911–1939* (Chapel Hill: University of North Carolina Press, 1994); Landon R.Y. Storrs, *Civilizing Capitalism: The National Consumers' League, Women's Activism, and Labor Standards in the New Deal Era* (Chapel Hill: University of North Carolina Press, 2000); Kathryn Kish Sklar, "Two Political Cultures in the Progressive Era: The National Consumers' League and the American Association for Labor Legislation," in Linda K. Kerber, Alice Kessler-Harris, and Kathryn Kish Sklar, eds., *U.S. History as Women's History: New Feminist Essays* (Chapel Hill: University of North Carolina Press, 1995); and Robyn Muncy, *Creating a Female Dominion in American Reform, 1890–1935* (New York: Oxford University Press, 1991). For a classic account of how the authority of the New Deal state brought about regional development, see William E. Leuchtenburg, *Flood Control Politics: The Connecticut River Valley Problem, 1927–1950* (Cambridge: Harvard University Press, 1953); for more on "economic knowledge" see Mary O. Furner and Barry Supple, eds., *The State and Economic Knowledge: The American and British Experiences* (Cambridge: Cambridge University Press, 1990).

Works Administration and Harry Hopkins's Civil Works Administration but also provided the precedent for the Works Progress Administration's own investigative staff.[4] In their work, the PWA's own investigators generated a remarkable day-by-day record of the many difficulties confronting the agency as it transformed the physical infrastructure of the nation. Investigators interviewed PWA staffers, private contractors, laborers, and citizens across the country. They scrutinized and recorded the PWA's attempts to satisfy job seekers, congressmen, senators, state and local officials, contractors, labor unions, and civic boosters.

Ickes initially took considerable satisfaction and pride in the division of investigation's work and in the judgment of its director, Louis Glavis. Felix Frankfurter and Nathan Margold had first recommended Glavis to Ickes in March 1933 as Ickes looked for someone to investigate the relationship between the Army Corps of Engineers and private power companies at Muscle Shoals in Alabama.[5] For progressive Republicans like Ickes and Senator George Norris, much was at stake. If Norris's dream of a Tennessee Valley Authority was to be realized, the rapids at Muscle Shoals, where the Tennessee River plummeted 134 feet over 37 miles, were an ideal site for harnessing the river's potential.[6]

Glavis's work at Muscle Shoals, which demonstrated that only a new agency, such as the TVA, could resist the influence of private interests, pleased Ickes greatly. Many years earlier, in 1909, Glavis had been dismissed from the Department of Interior's General Land Office by President William Howard Taft, a casualty of the celebrated Ballinger–Pinchot controversy. (Glavis was the source of charges that Secretary of the Interior Richard Ballinger had abused his authority by allowing private interests to exploit public resources.) During the ensuing years, Glavis served on the California Conservation and Water Power Commission, was chief investigator for the Senate Indian Affairs Committee, and worked for

---

[4] For the CWA's dependence on the PWA's division of investigation, see PWA Press Release #474, vol. 11, box 3, entry 24, "Press Releases, 1933–1939," Records of the Public Works Administration, Record Group 135, National Archives, Washington, D.C.

[5] Ickes to Felix Frankfurter, March 25, 1933; Nathan Margold telegram to Frankfurter, March 27, 1933; both in "Subject File. Interior Department. 1933–38. Ickes, Harold L. Margold, Nathan R.," folder, reel 94, Felix Frankfurter Papers, Manuscript Division, Library of Congress; and Ickes, *The Secret Diary of Harold L. Ickes* (New York: Simon & Schuster, 1953), 1:550.

[6] For more on the TVA's origins, see Erwin C. Hargrove, *Prisoners of Myth: The Leadership of the Tennessee Valley Authority, 1933–1990* (Princeton: Princeton University Press, 1994), 19–41; and Thomas K. McCraw, *TVA and the Power Fight, 1933–1939* (Philadelphia: J.B. Lippincott Company, 1971), 34–36.

William Randolph Hearst's publications.[7] With his reinstatement into government service on April 27, 1933, Ickes wrote, Glavis and his staff were "entrusted the duty of protecting the vast system of public works from the grafter, the exploiter, the chiseler, the cheating contractor, and the crooked politician." While their work sometimes drew "a howl of surprise and anguish from some political or business crook, accustomed to the easy pickings of past public works programs," the public generally "applaud[ed] our relentless war on graft and corruption."[8] Restoring Glavis to civil-service status in government meshed perfectly with Ickes's view of his job as a historic opportunity to reverse the scandal-ridden heritage of the Interior Department. Rexford Tugwell agreed with Ickes on the need for constant and thorough investigation of the PWA, telling him, "I would rather expend any amount of money on this than to have a $10 scandal anywhere."[9]

Glavis divided the nation into ten regions, placing a special agent in charge of each area and selecting an investigating staff. The agents' background varied, but generally Glavis selected engineers with construction experience, legal investigators, and accountants to work for him.[10] In the division's first internal circular, Glavis gave his agents frank instructions:

Public Works, by their very nature, open the door to every type of political favor and graft, and, in the past, as you know, they have often resulted in no end of scandals. By vigorous contact with all projects in your region before the contracts actually go into effect, you will unearth and prevent many loose and dishonest methods and serve notice on the parties involved that you not only know your business as well as your specific duty, but that you mean to enforce rugged honesty in their relations with the Government.

The Director of Investigations assumed, in appointing you, that your engineering training and experience were such as to qualify you for your present position. Do not burden this office with lengthy discussions; but give us the facts completely, tersely and to the point, together with your specific recommendations. There is no room for pussyfooting in this work. State your convictions clearly and get them to us at once. You may rest assured that if you are right, you may strike hard and often, no matter what influence the wrong-doer may claim to have.

---

7 Information drawn from "Louis R. Glavis" memo, February 1, 1937, "Departmental File Interior: 1936–39" folder, box 54, President's Secretary's File, F.D.R. Papers, F.D.R. Library.

8 Ickes, *Back to Work*, 60, 78.

9 T. H. Watkins, *Righteous Pilgrim: The Life and Times of Harold L. Ickes* (New York: Henry Holt, 1990), 332–33; and Special Board Minutes, 4:46, June 29, 1933, entry 1, "Minutes of Meetings of the Special Board for Public Works, 1933–1935," RG 135, NA.

10 Ickes, *Back to Work*, 77.

Set your mind in the direction that these public works funds are partially your funds and guard the expenditures even more conscientiously than if they were your own. The man who succeeds in this work has got to have sufficient backbone to weather criticism, as the greater his success the more he will be criticized.[11]

Ickes echoed this internal circular in his own public pronouncements, declaring that Glavis's investigators "are veterans, picked for personal probity, as well as for ability," and that their "surveillance" of the public works program "is necessary only because there are traitors in even the finest army."[12] Initially, Glavis employed 150 agents, but this number grew to 225 by May 1936, and eventually almost reached 400.[13] Glavis had sole authority in selecting his staff, and he told Ickes that he planned "to use as far as possible the services, by detail from the Navy Department," choosing these investigators from the officers and civilians who "were members of the cost inspection and accounting forces of the Navy Department" during World War I.[14] At least one Democrat complained, however, that the people Glavis was recruiting were "red hot Republican Old Liners."[15]

Glavis and his force of investigators worked hard to keep the PWA free of graft and corruption, and they provided Ickes with an extensive record of bureaucratic problems within the PWA itself. In August 1935 Glavis reported to Ickes that the number of investigative reports produced by his

---

[11] PWA Division of Investigations *Circular No. 1*, August 1, 1933, "PWA – Miscellaneous. Division of Investigations releases" folder, box 1, entry 103, "Miscellaneous Issuances, 1933–1938," RG 135, NA.

[12] Harold L. Ickes, "Spending Three Billions of Your Money!" clipping from *The American Magazine*, October 1933, "Articles 'Spending Three Billions of Your Money' October 1933 [corres. Aug.–Oct. 1933]" folder, box 170, Ickes Papers, LC.

[13] For the figure of 225 investigators, see "Accomplishments of the Federal Emergency Administration of Public Works, from July 8, 1933 to May 18, 1936," "Public Works Administration Miscellaneous" folder, box 1, entry 51, "Miscellaneous Publications, 1936–1941. Projects Control Division," RG 135, NA. For the figure of 400 investigators, see Jack Alexander, "Reformer in the Promised Land," *Saturday Evening Post*, July 22, 1939.

[14] Glavis to Ickes, July 7, 1933, no folder, box 11, entry 766, "Records of Interior Department Officials. Records of Secretary Harold L. Ickes. General Subject File, 1933–42," RG 48, NA–College Park. For Glavis's authority in building the division of investigation, see the testimony of E.K. Burlew in U.S. Congress, Senate, Committee on Public Lands and Surveys, *Hearings on the Nomination of Ebert K. Burlew to be First Assistant Secretary of the Interior*, 75th Cong., 3d sess., Part I (Washington, D.C.: U.S. Government Printing Office, 1938), 18.

[15] L. E. Bottom to James A. Farley, October 23, 1933, "Patronage Matters, Misc." folder, box 96, Emil E. Hurja Papers, FDRL.

division during the first half of 1935 had gone up 132 percent, compared with the same period in 1934.[16] The division of investigation categorized its reports as administrative, project, bid-opening, and criminal, labeling each one as "favorable" or "adverse." For a category to be labeled "adverse," agents were instructed, a report must show "a violation of law or applicable regulations"; it must conclude with a recommendation for administrative action or, in the case of personnel investigations, advise against appointment or suggest that the employee be terminated, transferred, or reprimanded; or demonstrate that a project has defects in construction or has departed from previously approved specifications. Otherwise, a report was to be labeled "favorable."[17] While the PWA's extant records are incomplete, we know that in 1934 the PWA finished the year with 164 special agents on staff. The division of investigation spent $628,000 on salaries, transportation, automobile purchases and maintenance, office supplies, and upkeep. Out of 9,361 cases closed, 6,780 were classified as favorable and 2,581 as adverse, while 400 cases were pending. The PWA referred 300 cases to the Department of Justice for prosecution, and, of these, 40 were prosecuted by the year's close.[18] These records provide a detailed portrait of the political maneuvering behind the construction of a public works program.

MAKING A NEW DEAL: THE POLITICS OF STATE CAPACITY

In forming a new governmental agency, the PWA relied heavily upon the staff of the Reconstruction Finance Corporation's self-liquidating public works division. The PWA hired a number of people directly from the RFC and turned to the RFC's files of public works plans to find worthwhile projects. Ickes also looked to the nation's cities as progressive laboratories for public works, drawing particularly on Cincinnati's civil servants, who were recommended by reformers such as Charles Merriam and Louis Brownlow. The PWA's chief legal counsel, Henry T. Hunt, had served as Cincinnati's mayor in 1911, presiding over an

[16] Glavis to Ickes, August 2, 1935, in "AF 341" folder, box 10, entry 85, "Case Files Relating to Investigations of Personnel, 1933–1941," RG 135, NA.
[17] "Public Works Administration. Division of Investigations. Manual of Instructions," February 1, 1936, entry 95, "Records of Projects. Records of the Division of Investigation. Manual of Instructions, 1936," box 1, RG 135, NA.
[18] Glavis to Ickes, January 28, 1935, "AF 221" folder, box 7, entry 85, "Case Files Relating to Investigations of Personnel, 1933–1941," RG 135, NA.

impressive program of municipal public works. Hunt's chief engineer in Cincinnati, Colonel Henry M. Waite, subsequently became the PWA's deputy administrator.[19]

While the PWA grappled with the difficulties in assembling a staff, from its very beginning the creators of the New Deal had to reckon with the Democratic office seekers who descended upon Washington after so many years of exile from the executive branch of government. James Farley, the chair of the Democratic Party's National Committee and the new postmaster general, controlled patronage in the new administration. As Ickes began to build the PWA, Farley requested that FDR clear the names of candidates for public works positions with him before making any decisions about appointments. Farley passed along approved lists of office seekers to FDR adviser Louis Howe, and he wrote to New Dealers, such as Ickes and Harry Hopkins, to ensure their cooperation in making politically sensitive appointments. Before taking on anyone from Vice President John Garner's home state of Texas, for example, Farley asked that they first secure Garner's approval.[20]

State congressional delegations made it a point to stop by the PWA's offices, to ensure that their states cornered their share of the PWA's $3.3 billion appropriation. For example, the entire delegation from Utah descended on Colonel Henry M. Waite, the PWA deputy director. Utah's representatives arrived, an exasperated Waite reported to Ickes, "in full force, sat in my office this morning and went over the same old arguments for the same old projects in the same old interminable way." Soon afterward, North Dakota Senator Gerald Nye implored Ickes to meet with twenty prominent North Dakotans, including Democratic National Committeemen and women, to discuss PWA spending in their state. A Louisiana congressman pressed for information about flood-control work on the Mississippi River; the Secretary of the Navy inquired about a

[19] PWA Press Release #12 [undated, but between July 14 and July 18, 1933], vol. 1, box 1, entry 24, "Press Releases, 1933–1939," RG 135, NA; Ickes, *Back to Work*, 17–18; and see the discussion of Cincinnati's public works construction in Arthur D. Gayer, *Public Works in Prosperity and Depression* (New York: National Bureau of Economic Research, 1935), 178–82.

[20] James A. Farley, *Behind the Ballots* (New York: Harcourt, Brace and Company, 1938), 223–38; Stephen Early to FDR, confidential memo, June 29, 1933, "Post Office Dept. 1933" folder, box 1, OF 19, F.D.R. Papers, FDRL; James A. Farley to Louis Howe, June 17, 1933; and Farley to Harold L. Ickes, June 22, 1933; both in "Harold L. Ickes Secretary of Interior File, Political, 2) 1933 June–July" folder, box 227, Harold L. Ickes Papers, Library of Congress; and Farley to Harry L. Hopkins, June 22, 1933, "Farley, James A." folder, box 37, Harry L. Hopkins Papers, FDRL.

Marine Hospital in Philadelphia; Texas senators urged FDR to approve the construction of post offices in San Antonio, Waco, and Austin, and asked about improvements of the Corpus Christi harbor.[21]

While the PWA struggled to satisfy all of these requests, one of its biggest obstacles to starting construction was a shortage of qualified lawyers to review public works contracts. One of the first things Interior Department solicitor Nathan Margold did was to consult with his mentor, Felix Frankfurter, for personnel recommendations. Margold asked Frankfurter to sound out law school deans in the West and Southwest for suggestions (historically, these regions were important constituencies for the Interior Department), and solicited his advice about which members of Congress might prove helpful. Frankfurter suggested that Margold contact the law school deans at the universities of Wisconsin, Colorado, and California, and he thought that Senators Costigan, La Follette, Cutting, Norris, Borah, Wheeler, and Hiram Johnson "ought to understand the rigorous necessity for high professional standards in the enforcement of social aims of the administration." Frankfurter also praised Harry Slattery, Gardner Jackson, and Alger Hiss, assuring Margold of their potential worth as employees in the Interior Department. As the PWA began to take shape, PWA counsel Henry T. Hunt also contacted Frankfurter for assistance in finding lawyers who specialized in bond issues. Hunt wanted men with "liberal views" who were "capable of providing solutions rather than obstacles."[22]

Ickes complained to one Illinois PWA advisor about "our inability to build up a sufficient staff of competent lawyers." Even after obtaining qualified personnel, Ickes grumbled, congressional pressure made it difficult to get things done. "You can't imagine the precious hours that we have to give clamorous members of Congress who come singly, in pairs, in trios

---

[21] Henry M. Waite to Ickes, October 28, 1933; and Gerald Nye to Ickes, October 30, 1933; both in "Harold L. Ickes Secretary of Interior File, Political, 2) 1933 June–July" folder, box 227, Ickes Papers, LC; Ickes to Waite, August 23, 1933; and FDR to Ickes, August 19, 1933; both in no folder, box 11, entry 766, "Records of Interior Department Officials. Records of Secretary Harold L. Ickes. General Subject File, 1933–42," Records of the Department of the Interior, RG 48, NA, College Park, Maryland.

[22] Nathan Margold to Felix Frankfurter, March 27, 1933; and Frankfurter to Margold, March 30, 1933; both in "Subject File. Interior Department. 1933–38. Ickes, Harold L. Margold, Nathan R." folder, reel 94, Felix Frankfurter Papers, Library of Congress. For more on the Margold–Frankfurter relationship, see Peter H. Irons, *The New Deal Lawyers* (Princeton: Princeton University Press, 1982), 60–68. Henry T. Hunt to Frankfurter, June 10, 1933, "Subject File. National Recovery Act. 1933–36" folder, reel 102, Frankfurter Papers, LC.

and in droves, dinning the same speeches into your ears and demanding
that their projects be approved whether they are meritorious or not, and
not only approved, but they they [*sic*] be given preference over everyone's
else [*sic*] projects." These obstacles led the PWA's lawyers to acquire the
reputation of slow-moving fact checkers, derisively labeled "semi-colon
boys" by New York Mayor Fiorello La Guardia.[23]

The conflict between the need to approve necessary public works
projects quickly and put people back to work, on the one hand, and Ickes's
desire to run a nonpolitical, graft-free operation, on the other, affected the
organization on many levels. Ickes put the PWA's investigation division
to work checking up on his staff. At one point, he assigned 150 agents
to spend the night going through desks in the PWA offices to check for
irregularities. After receiving reports of drawers filled with unanswered
correspondence, Ickes fired off a memo, ordering that every letter must
be acknowledged within twenty-four hours of receipt, and for good measure instructing PWA employees not to use the telephone for personal use.
Ickes reprimanded the PWA housing division for taking long lunches and
rebuked its staff for too much socializing. In the finance division, however,
Ickes approved a rather confused division of labor: A South Carolinian
supervised the Dakotas and the Northwest, while a northerner who had
never been south of Washington, D.C., handled projects for Virginia and
the Carolinas. While this neatly exemplifies Ickes's inability to see the big
picture due to his preoccupation with details, it also indicates his desire
to ensure neutrality in the administration of PWA.[24]

This desire, though, was tempered by an awareness of political realities.
In fact, Ickes initially favored a flexible policy that allowed for administrative discretion in permitting technical advisers to work on their home
state. With fellow Special Board members Rexford Tugwell, Commerce

[23] Ickes to Lawrence Houghteling, October 28, 1933, "Harold L. Ickes Secretary of Interior
File, Political, 2) 1933 June–July" folder, box 227, Ickes Papers, LC. Thomas Kessner,
Fiorello H. La Guardia and the Making of Modern New York (New York: McGraw-Hill,
1989), 300; for the PWA's response, see PWA Press Release #1746 [undated], vol. 40,
box 8, entry 24, "Press Releases, 1933–1939," RG 135, NA.
[24] Raymond Clapper diary, March 2, 1934, "Diaries Jan–May, 1934" folder, box 8,
Raymond Clapper Papers, LC; Division of Investigation report, May 28, 1934, "AF 6"
folder, box 1, entry 85, "Case Files Relating to Investigations of Personnel, 1933–1941,"
RG 135, NA. Ickes was also known for taking the doors off the stalls in the men's room
to cut down on newspaper reading, and for locking the doors to the Interior Department
building shortly after the workday began to encourage promptness. See Katie Louchheim,
ed., *The Making of the New Deal: The Insiders Speak* (Cambridge: Harvard University
Press, 1983), 248–49.

Secretary Daniel Roper, and Assistant Secretary of Labor Turner Battle, Ickes argued that in certain cases familiarity with a particular state's laws and conditions could be an asset that outweighed the potential "embarrassment," as Battle put it, of connections to state contractors and special interests.[25] This need for expert knowledge, in practice, often overrode concerns over impartiality. In Ohio, for example, despite accusations that L. A. Boulay, the PWA state engineer, was purchasing a high proportion of equipment for PWA projects from his brother-in-law's equipment company, these suspect dealings did not result in his removal from his PWA position.[26] In general, though, Ickes hewed to the position he articulated to FDR, that "it is frequently of great benefit to the public service to have some one from outside the state rather than to have to take some one from within the state."[27]

Concerns over impartiality, however, too often took priority over the need to start construction on projects. Charles Merriam, a political science professor at the University of Chicago and member of the newly created National Planning Board (NPB), noted in June 1933 that this tension could prove problematic. "It would be easy," Merriam wrote to Ickes, his long-time friend, "to make a mess of the expenditure of the vast sum of money contemplated – a scandal which would rock the party, the nation and in fact the whole world." Ickes, in reply, cited the need for caution, complaining, "It has been a delicate matter trying to unravel the mixup caused by General [Hugh] Johnson when he impetuously proceeded to set up an organization under his own authority to administer the public works."[28]

---

[25] Minutes of the Meetings of the Special Board for Public Works, 1933–1935, 6:3–4, August 3, 1933, entry 1, "Minutes of Meetings of the Special Board for Public Works, 1933–1935," RG 135, NA.

[26] Glavis to E. K. Burlew, July 26, 1934, "AF 93" folder, box 4, entry 85, "Case Files Relating to Investigations of Personnel, 1933–1941," RG 135, NA. Boulay later became PWA state director in Ohio; for his résumé, see Ickes to FDR, March 30, 1936, "OF 466b PWA Jan–Mar 1936" folder, OF 466b, FDR Papers, FDRL.

[27] Ickes to FDR, April 22, 1933, OF 2, FDRL.

[28] Charles E. Merriam to Ickes, June 24, 1933; and Ickes to Merriam, June 27, 1933; both in "Interior File Public Works 1) 1933 June–August" folder, box 248, Ickes Papers, L.C. For more on Ickes and Merriam's friendship and experience in Chicago progressive politics, see Watkins *Righteous Pilgrim*, 90–94; 103–109; and Barry D. Karl, *Charles E. Merriam and the Study of Politics* (Chicago: University of Chicago Press, 1974), 226–59; for the planning board see Patrick D. Reagan, *Designing a New America: The Origins of New Deal Planning, 1890–1943* (Amherst: University of Massachusetts Press, 1999); and Marion Clawson, *New Deal Planning: The National Resources Planning Board* (Baltimore: Johns Hopkins University Press, 1981).

By October 1933, Merriam and fellow National Planning Board member Frederic Delano had done an about-face: Each wrote to Ickes to express his distress over the way the PWA was proceeding. Merriam pointed out to "Honest Harold" the costs of his cautious approach, worrying that "the whole idea [of public works] may be discredited in a panicky impulse such as may readily sweep over us in a period of discontent such as this." Merriam urged Ickes to take dramatic measures to speed up the public works program. He recommended the creation of a new official, an "accelerator," to monitor progress on federal and non-federal projects funded by PWA. Merriam also advised Ickes to accept the suggestions of state boards for projects costing less than $100,000 as final (thus eliminating a time-consuming review process), to bring in his NPB colleague Louis Brownlow to consult on improving administrative organization, and to increase legal advice to state boards, thus reducing the time spent parsing legal technicalities. In short, Ickes should delegate his authority, rather than obsess over details. Most important, Merriam thought it vital that the PWA eliminate the delay between allocation of funds and the actual signing of contracts to begin construction. Merriam argued, "My whole proposition comes down to this. Spending more funds for overhead administration. Reorganization in such a way as to remove detail from the Secretary [of Interior]. Speeding up the whole tempo of the organization. Getting actual 'work hours.'"[29] PWA state engineers confirmed these delays, repeatedly telling Washington that appointments of personnel, such as project inspectors, were taking far too long. A further complaint was that once these appointments were finally made, the personnel would often start work without even reporting to the office of the state engineer or familiarizing themselves with their job duties.[30]

Frederic Delano, for his part, echoed many of the points made by Merriam. Delano pointed out to Ickes the advantages of following the recommendations of the state advisory boards, especially for smaller projects. This would address the perception that the complex bureaucratic structure in Washington served mainly to block and delay projects. "There are

---

[29] Merriam to Ickes, October 2, 1933, "Interior File, Friends, Charles Merriam, 1933–45" folder, box 162, Ickes Papers, LC.

[30] "Report of Regional Conference Federal Emergency Administration of Public Works called by Colonel H. M. Waite, Deputy Administrator," February 14–March 1, 1934, in "Feb. 14–Mar. 1, 1934" folder, box 1, entry 23, "Minutes and Reports of Conferences of the PWA, 1934–1941," RG 135, NA. This report summarizes the proceedings of PWA conferences held in New York, Boston, Detroit, St. Paul, Atlanta, Portland, Los Angeles, Little Rock, and Fort Worth.

many obstacles," Delano noted, "so much so that if a local project has a strong backing, a committee of leading citizens, including some politicians, is sent to Washington to exert pressure upon the Administration or its staff. There is a feeling that only in that way are projects reasonably certain of approval." Delano also recommended that the PWA permit force-account and cost-plus contracts to be let, but only with reliable contractors.[31]

Ickes disagreed sharply with Merriam and Delano, countering that it was not the PWA that was holding things up. Indeed, Ickes had already begun to urge federal departments to move more quickly to start public works construction. Ickes thought that the PWA's engineering and financial divisions were functioning well, and that any delays on the PWA's part were to be blamed on their shortage of lawyers. He vigorously took exception to the charge that he was failing to delegate work to others.[32] Subsequently, though, Ickes refused to grant more authority or responsibility to his deputy administrator, Colonel Waite, forcing his resignation in August 1934.[33]

Criticism of the PWA's delays continued to frustrate Ickes, particularly when the criticism was public. When, for example, Assistant Secretary of the Interior Oscar Chapman told newspaper reporters, "There has been some conflict between the legal and finance divisions of the administration" of the PWA, Ickes let Chapman know he was not pleased.[34] Jim Farley noted that Ickes's organization was in such disarray that there was "a feeling of suspicion around his Department to such an extent that not one person trusts the other; the impression prevailing that everybody is being spied upon."[35] Ickes did little to build the morale of his legal staff when he inserted quotations from *Alice in Wonderland* into public works contracts and sent them to be reviewed by the PWA's attorneys.

[31] Frederic Delano to Ickes, October 6, 1933, "Political 4, 1933, October 2–15" folder, box 248, Ickes Papers, LC.
[32] Ickes to Merriam, October 4, 1933, "Interior File, Friends, Charles Merriam, 1933–45" folder, box 162, Ickes Papers, LC; for Ickes's efforts to spur federal departments to accelerate their construction, see Ickes to FDR, September 25, 1933, "OF 466b PWA Aug–Sept" folder, box 13, Official File 466b, FDRL.
[33] PWA Press Release #859 [undated], vol. 21, box 4, entry 24, "Press Releases, 1933–1939," RG 135, NA; and Ickes, *Secret Diary*, 1:141–42; 193–94.
[34] Chapman quoted in the July 16, 1934, issue of the *Rocky Mountain News*; Chapman to Ickes, July 16, 1934; and Ickes to Chapman, July 20, 1934; all in "Political 8) 1934, June–August" folder, box 227, Ickes Papers, LC.
[35] James A. Farley diary, December 20, 1934, "Private File, 1934 Oct.–Dec." folder, box 37, James A. Farley Papers, LC.

When the contracts came back to his desk with seven approvals, Ickes called a staff conference, announced that he could confidently sign anything that they had approved, and then picked up the test contracts and read them aloud. In addition to such stunts, Ickes further hurt his staff's morale by firing legal proofreaders for taking too much sick leave.[36]

The chief administrator of the PWA's finance division, Fred R. Deaton, presented Ickes with a more serious problem. Deaton regularly handed out confidential information and internal PWA reports to contractors and politicians, and he arranged for projects that his friends supported to be funded exclusively by grants, rather than by the usual mix of grants and loans. Deaton, a Texan, wrote to his contact in Dallas, advising him to write to him only at Deaton's home, as "every letter that comes into the Interior building, if it is not marked 'Personal' and some that are, is opened and a summary made of the contents so that practically every official from Secretary Ickes on down knows the contents of the letters received. As you can see, this often proves embarrassing."[37]

Over at the PWA's accounting division, in order to advance his own career, division head George H. Parker commonly welcomed staff members who owed their appointments to the intercession of influential people. William Bowers, one of these accountants, noted that Parker was glad to hire him because he came recommended by Ickes's former law partner, New Dealer Donald Richberg. Parker, Bowers wrote Ickes, "welcomed my appointment because he thought that my appointment would help him in his relationships with you and possibly with Mr. Richberg. He has continually favored me in various matters, I feel because he expected my being in his Division would assist him in indirect ways." Bowers observed "that Mr. Parker appears to favor appointment in his Division of individuals [such] as Mr. James Schneider, a Senator Guffy protégé and Colonel R. G. Wooton, a Senator Bilbo protégé, also Mr. Don C. Fithian, said to be a protégé of Mr. Burlew," a personal assistant to Ickes who had been employed in Interior since 1923. Bowers initially refused to accept any of these men into his section, but eventually, he wrote, "practically

[36] Clapper diary, March 12, 1934, "Diaries Jan–May, 1934," folder, box 8, Clapper Papers, LC; and Division of Investigation Report, August 29, 1935, "AF 366" folder, box 11, entry 85, "Case Files Relating to Investigations of Personnel, 1933–1941," RG 135, NA.

[37] Fred R. Deaton to George L. Simpson, quoted in Division of Investigation Report, August 6, 1934, "AF 82" folder, box 3, entry 85, "Case Files Relating to Investigations of Personnel, 1933–1941," RG 135, NA.

on an ultimatum from Mr. Parker, I accepted Colonel Wooton and Mr. Schneider."[38]

While Bowers considered Parker an excellent administrator who produced first-class work, his laudatory opinion was undermined, in Ickes's view, by the warning he issued that Parker "had the personal habit of drinking too much which left him with hangovers and interferred [*sic*] with his work." Indeed, on a train trip from Washington to Chicago for an auditors' conference, Parker and approximately eighteen PWA employees drank between four and six cases of whiskey and, Bower related to Ickes, "In the midst of this [drinking] Mr. Parker asked me to write you a letter for his signature asking that the salaries of all the officials of the Accounting Division be greatly increased. For the next day and a half I was hounded by Mr. Parker and his drinking associates on the preparation of this letter." Parker was eventually fired for falsifying his travel vouchers. His dismissal, however, did not turn the PWA accounting division into an efficient, nonpolitical bureau. By May 1935, PWA accountants so routinely invoked their political connections in attempts to improve their salaries and workloads that Charles Maxcy, the new chief of the accounting division, was forced to announce that he would no longer consider any request that was based on "political pressure."[39]

The problems of the PWA's finance and accounting divisions paled next to the difficulties confronting the PWA's engineering division. The division was strikingly inefficient, thrown together with 133 examiners and 72 stenographers and clerks. Its role of reviewing projects sent in by PWA state engineers for approval soon made it a magnet for politicians, contractors, and local boosters, all lobbying to have projects approved. Interestingly, though, this new bureaucracy was supposed to compensate for the Army Corps of Engineers' perceived relationships with private interests. As Ickes later wrote to one young historian, his own investigations in the summer of 1933 had disclosed that there was a "close camaraderie between the Army Engineers and the private utilities."[40] Indeed,

---

[38] William Bowers to Ickes, December 18, 1934, "AF 186" folder, box 6, entry 85, "Case Files Relating to Investigations of Personnel, 1933–1941," RG 135, NA.

[39] Ibid.; and "AF 183" folder, box 5, entry 85, "Case Files Relating to Investigations of Personnel, 1933–1941," RG 135, NA. See also Accounting Division Order #7, May 1935, "ACCOUNTING DIVISION ORDERS 1–41 inclusive," folder, box 1, entry 104, "Orders Issued by the Accounting Division, 1935–1939," RG 135, NA.

[40] Ickes to William E. Leuchtenburg, July 21, 1950, "General Correspondence 1946–1952. Leuchtenburg, William E. July 21, 1950–Jan 20, 1951" folder, box 71, Ickes Papers, LC.

Ickes's first assignment for Louis Glavis was to investigate the relationship between the Army Corps of Engineers and these private interests.

Ickes sent Glavis to examine the management of the Wilson Dam power plant at Muscle Shoals, Alabama. FDR had toured the site with Senator George Norris in January 1933 when he was contemplating the creation of the Tennessee Valley Authority. Glavis reported that the systems of the Alabama Power Company and the Tennessee Power Company had been connected at Muscle Shoals, with the full knowledge of the Army Corps of Engineers operating at Wilson Dam. Glavis showed that the federal government was losing revenue from this secret arrangement and revealed that the power companies and the Corps of Engineers cooperated in hiding their relationship from FDR.[41] This state of affairs impelled Ickes to build a separate engineering staff, independent of the Corps of Engineers. Although this tactic allowed Ickes to avoid the pitfalls that might have befallen the PWA had it worked through the Corps, the PWA division of engineering could hardly be termed a success.

The primary task of the engineering division was to check over the state engineers' reports and project applications. The PWA's engineers, however, were simply recopying, verbatim, the state engineers' evaluations into their reports, rather than doing their own original analysis. Moreover, the detailed report that the PWA engineers produced was subsequently never used by any other PWA division. This relationship turned the state engineers into mere "office boys," as the PWA's engineering division in Washington kept them "groping in the dark at all times for information." A typical state engineer faced "a constant pecking away" at his authority, investigators found, "with the result that his morale had become seriously affected, thereby destroying the prestige of the state engineer in the community, and concentrating the attention of the applicant on Washington rather than on the local state engineer's office." The state engineer who supervised Maine, New Hampshire, and Vermont concurred with this assessment, observing of the PWA engineering division that it is in "the nature of the beast" to hamper the functions of the state engineers.

Clarence McDonough, the head of the PWA engineering division, claimed that the state engineers' reports were shoddy and that "they were subject to politics and above all" oversight was needed because

---

[41] Louis Glavis to Ickes, in "The Glavis Report," April 12, 1933, "Glavis-Thompson Tennessee Valley Authority 1933–34" folder; and see also "Statements of Maj. Gen. Lytle Brown, Mr. Carl H. Giroux, Lt. Col. Edmund L. Daley, Major Robert R. Neyland, Captain H. D. W. Riley," "Glavis-Thompson Invest. Tennessee Valley Authority 1934" folder, all in OF 42, FDRL; and Ickes, *Secret Diary*, 1:17–18.

the state engineers blindly "approved all projects." If this was the case, though, the PWA engineering division was not an effective check. In 1934, for example, only 103 projects out of approximately 9,800 projects submitted by state engineers were disapproved by engineering examiners in Washington. McDonough employed eleven of his former colleagues in his division, and three of the division's four section heads had worked with him in private industry. McDonough never clarified exactly what the engineering-division staff was supposed to do, leaving all control to the section heads and keeping himself secluded in his sixth-floor office.[42]

The staff of the engineering division often exceeded their responsibilities by considering questions of economic soundness when reviewing project plans. They not only duplicated the work done by the finance division, but they also were not as efficient as the financial staff in reviewing the plans submitted by state engineers. This sort of internal confusion led to much back-and-forth discussion between Ickes and his assistants. Ickes argued that the finance division should properly handle these questions, tersely ordering that "in the future, members of the engineering staff should confine their attention to engineering questions."[43] The engineering staff, for their part, were still faced with a mountain of forms, correspondence, and paperwork. One engineer observed, "We can't keep a record of all conversations [about public works projects]. Christ, we haven't enough stenographic help here now to get our letters out."[44]

Despite Ickes's instructions to use extreme care when approving exemptions to the usual PWA practice of relying on private contractors to build public works, the engineering division apparently employed a very free hand in permitting public works to be executed by "force account," a category of construction that was built directly by the government. The PWA's projects division was described by investigators as "a floundering unit," one that was "serving no one and without any definite goal." Nominally, the projects division was in charge of summarizing the reports of

[42] "Engineering Division Etc. The Report," [unpaginated] n.d., no folder, box 1, entry 93, "Records Relating to the Investigation of the Engineering Division, 1934," RG 135, NA; and see also, "An Engineer in Wonderland: The PWA Washington Office," *Engineering News-Record*, September 6, 1934, 293–94.

[43] Ickes to Major Fleming, January 14, 1935, "Public Works 23) 1935 Jan.–Feb." folder, box 252, Ickes Papers, LC; and see Glavis to Harry Slattery, January 10, 1935, and Slattery to Ickes, January 11, 1935, both in "Public Works 23) 1935 Jan.–Feb." folder, box 252, Ickes Papers, LC.

[44] Transcript of PWA Division of Investigation interview with Henry J. Sullivan and Arthur J. Bulger, January 21, 1935, "AF 266" folder, box 8, entry 85, "Case Files Relating to Investigations of Personnel, 1933–1941," RG 135, NA.

other PWA divisions and noting when they disapproved of any projects, which made them ineligible for funding. One PWA employee, though, stated that in reality the projects division was "like a large snake with its head cut off – writhing here and there without any particular direction." The PWA's technical board of review, originally intended as a forum for appeals from state engineers, instead became a helpless "sixth finger," serving only to delay progress on public works.[45]

Notwithstanding their lackluster performance, these engineers left a valuable record of how the PWA functioned during the early New Deal. Private interests often intersected with public works. For example, A. L. Sherman, chief engineering examiner in charge of sewer, water, and irrigation projects, once reprimanded another PWA engineer, E. B. Besselievre, for acting simultaneously as an engineer for the PWA and as a salesman for the Dorr Company. Sherman did not want Besselievre to give out confidential information regarding a $21 million Washington, D.C., sewage project to Dorr, but his disapproval was not based on ethics. Rather, Sherman was concerned that Besselievre might accidentally undo the "gentleman's agreement" by which the project was already awarded to another group of engineers friendly with District of Columbia commissioners. In the midst of blithely relating this incident to two PWA investigators, Sherman asked, "This is only among we three, isn't it?" Informed that Ickes would be told of the interview, he remarked, "Well, I'll shut up then." The remainder of the interview proceeded in a clearly restrained fashion. Sherman and his colleagues, however, continued to meet with private contractors and local officials interested in getting PWA approval for their projects, occasionally using private rooms at the Hotel Powhattan in Washington.[46]

Andrew B. Lail, the PWA engineer examiner in charge of preparing resolutions and summary memoranda for the PWA Special Board, was described by one coworker as "a snake in the grass" who "has no business in the [PWA] organization at all." Lail regularly phoned congressmen to pass along confidential information and was working with a number of

[45] "Engineering Division Etc. The Report," [unpaginated] n.d., no folder, box 1, entry 93, "Records Relating to the Investigation of the Engineering Division, 1934," RG 135, NA. For the PWA technical board of review, see PWA, *Circular No. 1*, 10. Jack P. Isakoff, *The Public Works Administration* (Urbana: University of Illinois Press, 1938), 43–44.

[46] Division of Investigation report, September 25, 1934, "AF 137" folder, box 5; Glavis to Ickes, January 16, 1935, "AF 265" folder, box 8; and I. J. Canton to Glavis, March 30, 1935, "AF 211" folder, box 6, all in entry 85, "Case Files Relating to Investigations of Personnel, 1933–1941," RG 135, NA.

large private engineering firms, hoping eventually to secure other employment. Lail told investigators that there was nothing wrong with one of these firms, Remington and Goff, "except that they are normal municipal engineers." Asked what this meant, Lail replied, "It means that – I will not say in every case, but the majority of your municipal contracts, you get them through political pull." Lail added this clarification:

What I meant was that it required politics. For instance, if you were acquainted with the right kind of political party and worked with the administration on this particular municipality – I do not mean graft if that is what you mean. I will say that I have been in the engineering business a long time now and I have never seen any graft. There are isolated cases, of course. When I say political pull I do not mean anything like that. When I say political pull I mean if you were a municipal engineer and wanted to, you could go to, say, Philadelphia to get a contract. Your only chance of getting that contract would be if you were a good democrat or good party man. That would be the only chance you have of getting it. If you have one of your friends who has influence in that community to go in and speak for you. That is what I mean. I do not mean this idea of so much graft in engineering and Public Works. I have never run across it. There are only isolated cases.[47]

While the head of the engineering division, Clarence McDonough, tried to argue that the PWA was not subjected to lobbying from contractors or from members of Congress, the investigative agents asked McDonough, incredulously, "How then does it appear that the Congressmen from the various districts where projects were being propounded would make representations by telephone, letter, or in person?" McDonough tried to dodge this issue, stating, "That influence never exerted any pressure on our opinion." Investigators returned to this question, however, pressing McDonough, who finally acknowledged the influence of interested politicians. Laughing heartily, McDonough conceded to the investigators that when push came to shove, "There is no way of keeping a Congressman from seeing an examiner."[48]

While some engineers readily entertained project applicants and congressmen, others used their position to advance their own interests more directly. Investigators discovered that George F. Hurt, an engineer

[47] G. H. Hurley, "Memorandum for the File," March 4, 1936; and transcript of interview between PWA Special Agent Russell MacDonald and Andrew B. Lail, Engineering Division, PWA, May 25, 1936; both in "AF 494" folder, box 15, entry 85, "Case Files Relating to Investigations of Personnel, 1933–1941"; and "Engineering Division Etc. The Report," [unpaginated] n.d., no folder, box 1, entry 93, "Records Relating to the Investigation of the Engineering Division, 1934"; all in RG 135, NA.
[48] "Engineering Division Etc. The Report," [unpaginated] n.d., no folder, box 1, entry 93, "Records Relating to the Investigation of the Engineering Division, 1934," RG 135, NA.

examiner who worked on power projects, was engaged in a "sinis-ter" attempt to gather information regarding public works projects that required incinerators while he was involved in patenting his own inciner-ator design. Hurt gave information about PWA projects to private con-tractors, and in exchange the contractors would use his patented design.[49] Clarence Rose, a former engineer examiner, and Benjamin F. Thomas, Jr., an engineer examiner who worked with Hurt in the power section, con-firmed the report on Hurt's actions. Hurt had his private mail brought by messenger to him each morning, so he could easily hide the fact that he was corresponding with construction companies while they were bidding on PWA projects. Another group of engineers, who were assigned to review power projects, had been hired by the PWA after long careers with pri-vate utilities. Philosophically opposed to municipally owned power plants, these engineers regularly convened over scotch and soda to denounce FDR and the New Deal and were slow to approve applications to develop pub-licly owned power plants.[50]

Despite these many obstacles to building public works projects, the PWA managed to persevere. McDonough left the PWA to join the Lower Colorado River Authority and was replaced as director of the engineer-ing division by Jabez G. Gholston in October 1935. Before joining the PWA, Gholston had worked in Central and South America as an engineer for a variety of railroads, oil companies, and large ship-and-dock compa-nies. At the PWA, however, Gholston failed to distinguish himself. By the summer of 1936, he was reassigned as director of the PWA's inspection division. Here, Gholston was responsible for monitoring the execution of PWA construction, making certain that the plans and specifications approved by the PWA were in fact carried out in the field. While this lat-eral move does not directly condemn Gholston's performance as director of the engineering division, the circumstances surrounding his departure from the PWA in 1937 indicate the scope of opportunities in the private sector that were available to PWA administrators.[51]

---

[49] "Engineering Division Etc. The Report," [unpaginated] n.d., no folder, box 1, entry 93, "Records Relating to the Investigation of the Engineering Division, 1934"; and Glavis to Ickes, January 26, 1935, "AF 258" folder, box 8, entry 85, "Case Files Relating to Investigations of Personnel, 1933–1941," both in RG 135, NA.

[50] Glavis to Ickes, January 26, 1935, "AF 258" folder, box 8; Division of Investigation report, January 14, 1936, "AF 468" folder, box 15, both in entry 85, "Case Files Relating to Investigations of Personnel, 1933–1941," RG 135, NA.

[51] PWA Press Release #1648, October 1935, vol. 38, box 8; and PWA Press Release #2019, circa May–July 1936, vol. 42, box 9, both in entry 24, "Press Releases, 1933–1939,"

After refusing to resign, following charges of improper lobbying before Congress, Gholston was fired from the PWA. Ickes informed FDR that he was drafting a statement "in line with your suggestion that it might be well to circulate something of this kind throughout the Government service" to discourage activity along these lines, enclosing with his memo a copy of the dismissal letter sent to Gholston.[52] By April 1938, though, Gholston was reemployed as an engineering consultant by Ickes's office, and by July he was again receiving a salary of $6,000 per year from the PWA. In February 1939, Gholston decided to capitalize on his PWA contacts. He wrote to G. L. Rounds, an assistant PWA director in Michigan, that he was going to enter the insurance business, since "I have friends among the contractors, engineers, and architects in the country who will give me a hand. Many influential friends have encouraged me to make such a hook-up for some time in order to cash in on the Nation wide contacts that I have." Gholston was blunt in explaining his plans to Rounds. "After we get our offices in Washington set up and going we can write bonds and insurance for anybody in the United States in our office. I am giving you this confidential information for this reason; I know that you have confidential friends in Illinois, who, by simple suggestion, can throw bond and insurance business our way."

If Gholston thought that any of his ventures constituted the crossing of ethical boundaries, he did not say so to Rounds. Rather, in his view, setting himself up in the insurance business for contractors while continuing to work for the PWA was a simple matter of common sense. Gholston informed Rounds, "I know I do not have to explain to you that I am even suggesting that you do anything unethical. The simple fact of the whole thing is that somebody will get the business, if we can get it without placing ourselves in an unethical position it is nobody's business." Indeed, Gholston thought, Rounds himself ought to realize that "no one is in a better position than yourself to know how the necessary contacts could be set up and you might just as well have something out of that knowledge as some of the big shots in Washington who have all kinds of outside relationships. I have found out a lot about how they make their money and have decided to give some of them a little competition."[53] Gholston's

RG 135, NA. On the PWA inspection division see Isakoff, *Public Works Administration*, 48–49.

[52] Ickes to FDR, September 14, 1937, "OF 466b PWA May–Aug 1937" folder, box 15, OF 466b, FDRL.

[53] J. G. Gholston to G. L. Rounds, February 10, 1939, in "AF 652" folder, box 28, entry 85, "Case Files Relating to Investigations of Personnel, 1933–1941," RG 135, NA.

letter was obtained by the PWA division of investigation. Five days after sending it, he quietly submitted his resignation to the PWA. He left as his forwarding address an office in the Normandy Building, located on K Street, a neighborhood that is still familiar to the Washington lobbying community.

PUBLIC WORKS AND PATRONAGE

Speaking of the occasionally nightmarish logistics of passing New Deal legislation, Virginia Senator Carter Glass once quipped that the road to hell was often lined with post offices. While the complexities inherent in building a new organization led to many delays in getting public works construction underway, the PWA's bureaucracy and its projects, once functioning, did play a key role in building and solidifying the Democratic Party at federal, state, and local levels of government. Central to brokering this relationship between government and party was Emil E. Hurja, who coordinated patronage during the early stages of the PWA. Hurja was in charge of distributing patronage appointments for the Democratic Party, placing people not only in Ickes's Interior Department and the PWA, but also consulting with Postmaster General James Farley and New Dealer Rexford G. Tugwell about appointments in Tugwell's Resettlement Administration. Although Hurja is little remembered today, in 1935 one journalist observed that he was "as much a product of the New Deal as Rex Tugwell ... an actuarial antidote to the nonpolitically minded and impractical brain trusters and reformers." While this statement contrasts Hurja with a stereotypical view of Tugwell, the general point about Hurja's importance is well taken.[54]

Michigan born, Hurja was the son of immigrants from Finland. Following his graduation from the University of Washington, he served in the Army in World War I, owned a newspaper in Texas, and worked on Wall Street, analyzing mining and oil stocks. After working for James Farley and the Democratic Party during the 1932 campaign, Hurja became one of Ickes's two administrative assistants at the PWA; E. K. Burlew, a career official in the Department of Interior, was the other. Hurja's official job duties were described as "Coordination between Federal State

---

[54] Glass quoted in Anthony J. Badger, *The New Deal: The Depression Years, 1933–1940* (New York: Hill and Wang, 1989), 275; Farley diary, July 17, 1935, "Private File 1935 July 1–18," box 38, Farley Papers, LC; and Ray Tucker, "Chart and Graph Man," *Collier's* (January 12, 1935), in "Reference File Hurja Emil" folder, box 153, Clapper Papers, LC.

Representatives, Regional Offices, State officials & Public Bodies – & the Public Works Administration."[55]

While the PWA created new ties between the federal government and localities by distributing federal grants and loans, the large number of appointments required by the PWA led to a silent upheaval in the distribution of patronage by the Democratic Party.[56] The task of staffing the PWA was suffused with political considerations. While Postmaster General Farley approved all state-level appointments to the PWA, party pollster Hurja correlated job offers by congressional district, past election returns, and the loyalty of the applicant's congressman to Roosevelt. In the opinion of his biographer, Melvin Holli, Hurja was thus able "to transform spoilsmanship into a quasi-scientific exercise in personnel management." Relying on Hurja's careful statistical calculations and Farley's political power, Democrats steered government relief funds toward states that might be leaning against them in upcoming elections. The influx of money into Louisiana after Huey Long's death, for example, was dubbed the "Second Louisiana Purchase," a reference to the local Democratic Party's use of federal relief dollars to solidify its political machine. While it is logical to assume that FDR and the Democrats expected to reap political benefits from New Deal programs, previous research on this question has indicated that, whatever his intentions, FDR's spending strategy probably did not succeed directly in influencing the fortunes of Democrats at the ballot box.[57]

[55] Hurja quoted in Tucker, "Chart and Graph Man"; see also Paul Mallon, "Right-Hand Man," *Today* (November 3, 1934); and "Political Notes," *Time* (March 2, 1936); both in "Reference File Hurja Emil" folder, box 153, Clapper Papers, LC. Hurja's job duties listed in October 1933 organization chart, entry 28, "Organization Charts, 1933–1934," RG 135, NA.

[56] For more on the history of federal-state-local relationships, see J. Kerwin Williams, *Grants-in-Aid Under the Public Works Administration: A Study in Federal-State-Local Relations* (New York: Columbia University Press, 1939); James T. Patterson, *The New Deal and the States: Federalism in Transition* (Princeton: Princeton University Press, 1969); and see also John Joseph Wallis and Wallace E. Oates, "The Impact of the New Deal on American Federalism," in Michael D. Bordo, Claudia Goldin, and Eugene N. White, eds., *The Defining Moment: The Great Depression and the American Economy in the Twentieth Century* (Chicago: University of Chicago Press, 1998), 155–80. Ickes, *Back to Work*, 63.

[57] Melvin G. Holli, *The Wizard of Washington: Emil Hurja, Franklin Roosevelt, and the Birth of Public Opinion Polling* (New York: Palgrave, 2002), 59; see also William D. Reeves, "PWA and Competitive Administration in the New Deal," *Journal of American History* 60 (September 1973): 367–68. For Louisiana, see Douglas L. Smith, *The New Deal in the Urban South* (Baton Rouge: Louisiana State University Press, 1988), 111–12; a lucid summary of the impact of New Deal spending on the Democratic Party can be

Hurja kept records of the distribution of PWA funds for federal and nonfederal projects by state, displaying them in carefully drawn bar charts. Hurja also tracked the number of PWA employees in Washington, D.C., tallying their home states and recording whether they had been "endorsed" by a home-state congressman or senator. Hurja, in fact, began filling jobs in the PWA while he was still working as a special assistant in the Reconstruction Finance Corporation. The RFC, a precursor to the PWA as the central clearing house for approval of federal public works projects, also set an important precedent in the dispensing of patronage. Hurja mailed lists of engineers directly to Major Philip B. Fleming of the Army Corps of Engineers, who worked for the PWA for many years and eventually ran the Federal Works Agency from 1941 to 1949. After reviewing the list of prescreened candidates, Fleming contacted Hurja to confirm or reject appointments from the list of recommended engineers.

Hurja, in his own records, wrote down each engineer's name, home state, work experience, and political endorsements. In addition to help-ing staff the PWA Washington headquarters, Hurja kept copious records of state engineering appointments for the PWA, noting the senators and congressmen who had approved the candidates and recording items of interest, such as whether a candidate supported FDR before the Chicago nominating convention. After Ickes sent his list of candidates to Hurja and Joseph O'Mahoney, the first assistant postmaster general, for review and approval, Hurja and O'Mahoney returned "a substitute list based on [their] investigations." The two men contacted senators, congressmen, and state party chairmen, summarizing their thoughts in a final list made up of two columns, one labeled "Ickes List" and the other "Hurja List."[58]

Engineering-division director Clarence McDonough recalled how Hurja directed the hiring of his personnel: "Mr. Hurja brought over a

found in Jeremy Atack and Peter Passell, *A New Economic View of American History: From Colonial Times to 1940*, 2d ed. (New York: W.W. Norton, 1994), 645–46; the essential treatment of this issue is John Joseph Wallis, "The Political Economy of New Deal Spending Revisited, Again: With and without Nevada," *Explorations in Economic History* 35 (1998): 140–70.

[58] "Public Works Administration Funds Allotted (Confidential)" and "Number of Washing-ton PWA Employees as of January 15, 1934" bar charts; Hurja's Administrative Assistant to Philip B. Fleming, July 14, 1933; and "Engineers' Applications Submitted to Major Fleming by E. E. Hurja, Special Assistant to the Directors, Reconstruction Finance Corp," all in "Patronage Matters, Misc." folder, box 96, Hurja Papers, FDRL. See also Ickes to Joseph O'Mahoney, August 4, 1933; O'Mahoney to Ickes, August 4, 1933; and unlabeled and undated notes; all in "Public Wks State Engrs" folder, box 96, Hurja Papers, FDRL. For more patronage-related materials, see also notes and documents in boxes 90–95, Hurja Papers, FDRL.

bunch of applications that came from (pause) the personnel office (pause) that was – Hurja's office." McDonough cursorily interviewed these candidates, skimming their employment history, and "if they had enough on their applications to show who they worked for, I would have believed it." This practice quickly led to the hiring and overpaying of many marginally qualified, if personally and politically connected, engineering inspectors.[59]

By January 1934, however, journalists in Washington were reporting that Hurja was planning to leave the PWA, "after an unhappy five months as 'patronage man' in the Interior Department." Hurja was rumored to be considering running for a Michigan senate seat; others reported that he desired to be appointed envoy to Finland. Ickes and E. K. Burlew were said to be blocking Hurja in what one reporter termed "his efforts to find jobs for worthy Democrats." Although Ickes no longer wanted Hurja to be in the PWA, Farley was more than happy to welcome him and his political expertise back to the Democratic National Committee. Hurja's vast circle of acquaintances and his personal relationships with virtually every senator and congressman made him the ideal candidate to take over much of Farley's detailed preparations for the upcoming 1934 congressional elections. With Hurja's return, Thomas Corcoran wrote to Felix Frankfurter that Hurja was "now the real head of the Democratic National Committee."[60] By 1936 the *Saturday Evening Post* agreed with Corcoran, proclaiming Hurja "the New Deal's Political Doctor." Hurja's careful record keeping, the *Post* reported, showed "not only how the vital organs of the New Deal are doing but how each muscle, nerve and cell is getting along."[61]

While Emil Hurja played an important role in Washington, D.C., connecting the PWA's bureaucracy and projects to the larger task of building and solidifying the Democratic Party at the federal, state, and local levels of government, much of the hard work of party building took place away

[59] "Engineering Division Etc. The Report," [unpaginated] n.d., no folder, box 1, entry 93, "Records Relating to the Investigation of the Engineering Division, 1934," RG 135, NA.
[60] Newspaper clipping (source unknown), January 17, 1934, and *New York Times* clipping, no date (probably January 3, 1934), both in "Reference File Hurja, Emil" folder, box 153, Clapper Papers, LC; Farley diary, March 5, 1934, "James A. Farley Private File 1934 March–April" folder, box 37, Farley Papers, LC; Press Release #588, March 15, 1934, vol. 13, box 3, entry 24, "Press Releases, 1933–1939," RG 135, NA; and Thomas G. Corcoran to Felix Frankfurter, April 22, 1934, "Special Correspondence. Oxford Correspondence. Corcoran, Thomas G. 1933–34 & undated" folder, reel 70, Frankfurter Papers, LC.
[61] Alva Johnston, "'Prof.' Hurja, The New Deal's Political Doctor," *Saturday Evening Post* (June 13, 1936), in "Reference File Hurja Emil" folder, box 153, Clapper Papers, LC.

from the nation's capital. The growing involvement between these different levels of government led National Planning Board member Louis Brownlow (himself a former city manager) to observe that if the early New Deal was a period in which "it has been said that the federal government has discovered the cities, it is equally true that the cities have discovered the federal government."[62]

The nation's mayors were especially interested in the PWA's potential to aid the cities, banding together in 1933 to form the United States Conference of Mayors. This development, one political scientist has declared, made 1933 "the most eventful [year] for municipal affairs in the twentieth century."[63] On September 23, 1933, Ickes traveled to Chicago to address the mayors at their national meeting. In his speech, he confronted their charges that the PWA was holding up the distribution of public works funding, arguing that the cities were failing to send Washington their plans for fiscally sound projects in a timely fashion. Interestingly, even with one-quarter of the nation out of work, Ickes did not justify the PWA as an unemployment relief program to the assembled mayors. Rather, he announced that the PWA "offers the greatest opportunity for municipal improvements in the history of any country." He added, "Here is an opportunity to build necessary and desirable public works on more favorable terms than you have ever had before or than you may ever have again. Do you need new water works, or an extension of your present plant? Do you want a new or improved sewage system? Do you require bridges or viaducts or public buildings or roads or new schools? These things and others you may have on unbelievably generous terms."[64]

Although the PWA was instrumental in creating jobs, Ickes emphasized the agency's pivotal role in increasing "indirect" employment. He argued, "For every hundred thousand men at work on public works projects there are at least an equal number at work back of the lines in saw mills, in steel mills, in factories, in quarries, and on railroads, producing materials and performing services necessary to supply the men on actual projects with what they need for their work."[65] Ickes's emphasis on the twin abilities of

---

[62] Brownlow quoted in Mark I. Gelfand, *A Nation of Cities: The Federal Government and Urban America, 1933–1965* (New York: Oxford University Press, 1975), 37.

[63] Leonard D. White quoted in Gelfand, *Nation of Cities*, 66–67.

[64] September 23, 1933 speech of Harold L. Ickes to the U.S. Conference of Mayors, in *The Public Speeches and Statements of Secretary of the Interior Harold L. Ickes*, vol. 1, box 1, entry 26, "Public Speeches and Statements of Harold L. Ickes, 1934–1939," RG 135, NA.

[65] Ibid.

public works to provide needed municipal improvements and to stimulate indirect employment in related industries echoed a generation of thinking by engineers and economists like Otto T. Mallery, Leo Wolman, Arthur D. Gayer, and John Kenneth Galbraith.[66]

The mayors, however, were less interested in Ickes's thoughts on indirect employment than they were in the PWA's plans to eliminate delays in processing their applications for proceeding with construction. Ickes temporarily defused the mayors' anger by inviting them to send a subcommittee to Washington to see the PWA in action and to make suggestions for streamlining the application process. After reviewing the PWA's workings, Mayors T. Seems Walmsley (New Orleans), Daniel W. Hoan (Milwaukee), James M. Curley (Boston), Oscar Holcombe (Houston), C. Nelson Sparks (Akron), and Secretary of the U.S. Conference of Mayors Paul V. Betters declared that while Ickes's basic bureaucratic plan was sound, he lacked the personnel necessary for expediting applications.[67] Ickes remained unconvinced, however, that the PWA was at fault in any way. Despite efforts to address delays, in February and March 1934 the PWA again heard repeated complaints about bureaucratic slowness from state and local PWA officials in New York, Boston, Detroit, St. Paul, Atlanta, Portland, Los Angeles, Little Rock, and Fort Worth.[68]

Local and state politicians also looked to federal public works funds to advance their own interests. In Chicago, for example, local politicians seized upon the PWA as a chance to improve the Democratic Party's fortunes. There had been a precedent for this kind of opportunism in a number of scandals that had beset the Civil Works Administration, most notably a kickback scheme involving truck rentals in Chicago. While both

---

[66] Otto T. Mallery, "The Long-Range Planning of Public Works," *Business Cycles and Unemployment* (New York: National Bureau of Economic Research, 1923), ch. 14; President's Conference on Unemployment, Report of the Committee on Recent Economic Changes, *Planning and Control of Public Works, Including the Report of Leo Wolman* (New York: National Bureau of Economic Research, 1931); Gayer, *Public Works in Prosperity and Depression*; J. K. Galbraith, assisted by G. G. Johnson, Jr., *The Economic Effects of the Federal Public Works Expenditures, 1933–1938* (Washington, D.C.: U.S. Government Printing Office, 1940); and see also Edwin T. Layton, *The Revolt of the Engineers: Social Responsibility and the American Engineering Profession* (Baltimore: Johns Hopkins University Press, 1986).

[67] PWA Press Release #171, September 29, 1933, vol. 3, box 1, entry 24, "Press Releases, 1933–1939," RG 135, NA.

[68] "Report of Regional Conference Federal Emergency Administration of Public Works called by Colonel H. M. Waite, Deputy Administrator," February 14–March 1, 1934, in "Feb. 14–Mar. 1, 1934" folder, box 1, entry 23, "Minutes and Reports of Conferences of the PWA, 1934–1941," RG 135, NA.

Ickes and Harry Hopkins often brought in presumably nonpartisan army officers from the Army Corps of Engineers to oversee problematic relief and public works programs, just as often the PWA and the CWA were content to turn projects over to local political machines, both Democratic and Republican, so long as major scandals were avoided.[69]

The absence of major scandals, however, did not indicate that New Deal public works program were free from politics. The Democratic Party in Chicago, for example, called on PWA employees and the personnel in other local agencies, such as the Chicago Sanitary District, to raise party funds. As one of several overlapping governmental authorities in Chicago, the Sanitary District served as a public body separate from city government, borrowing money and supervising projects such as canal construction. All but three of the Sanitary District's twenty-seven engineers regularly paid dues to various local Democratic organizations.

A secretary to Chicago congressman Adolph Sabath directly approached one PWA engineering inspector, Myles S. Tomaska, suggesting that he stop by the local Democratic Party headquarters. Upon doing so, Tomaska was informed that since his job was "a political job," he was required to pay 2 percent of his monthly salary, or $9.50, to his Democratic precinct captain, Joseph Hines, every month. Later that week, Hines told Tomaska that since he did not live in the ward where he worked, Tomaska needed to pay an additional $10 a month. "While I was at the Democratic Headquarters," Tomaska later recalled, "I was told that if I did not pay the money that they asked, my position would be in jeopardy, and that I could lose my job," even though "at no time did I have any knowledge of owing any dues to this organization, nor have I been a member of this organization prior to this time."[70] Despite Sabath's active encouragement of these traditional patronage arrangements, Tomaska was blamed for his predicament. A letter written by his supervisor and sent to Washington

---

[69] For the CWA in Chicago, see Roger Biles, *Big City Boss in Depression and War: Mayor Edward J. Kelly of Chicago* (DeKalb: Northern Illinois University Press, 1984), 34; for CWA personnel, see Bonnie Fox Schwartz, *The Civil Works Administration, 1933–1934: The Business of Emergency Employment in the New Deal* (Princeton: Princeton University Press, 1984), 72–101; and for the experience of cities during the New Deal, helpful works include Gelfand, *Nation of Cities*; Bruce M. Stave, *The New Deal and the Last Hurrah: Pittsburgh Machine Politics* (Pittsburgh: University of Pittsburgh Press, 1970); Lyle W. Dorsett, *Franklin D. Roosevelt and the City Bosses* (Port Washington, N.Y.: Kennikat Press Corp., 1977); Biles, *Big City Boss in Depression and War*; and Jo Ann Argersinger, *Toward a New Deal in Baltimore: People and Government in the Great Depression* (Chapel Hill: University of North Carolina Press, 1988), 57–92.

[70] Affidavit of Myles S. Tomaska, February 26, 1935, in "AF 250" folder, box 7, entry 85, "Case Files Relating to Investigations of Personnel, 1933–1941," RG 135, NA.

complained, "If I had my way about this matter I would immediately dismiss the man [Tomaska] for ignorance. . . . If he shows such stupidity as to pay for his job, he most certainly is not the kind of a man we should have in our organization."[71]

This encounter between the Chicago Sanitary District, Congressman Sabath, and PWA engineer inspector Myles Tomaska was not an isolated occurrence. Rather, many similar incidents were recorded by the PWA division of investigation, in many parts of the nation. As we shall see in Chapter 5, both the Public Works Administration and the Works Progress Administration played a critical part in shaping arenas for local political struggles. While the local impact of New Deal spending has been noted by historians, the significance of their findings has not transcended a narrowly focused debate on the relationship between the New Deal and the fate of urban-boss rule. To be sure, as FDR pointed out, the New Deal "never had a teapot dome scandal." But the New Deal's works programs did reshape the nation's political landscape, affecting the political possibilities that were available to local interests at the precinct level.

THE COSTS OF SURVEILLANCE

While Glavis began his job as head of the PWA's division of investigation with Ickes's full backing, he soon began to overstep his authority. The head of PWA's investigation division, one Department of the Interior report observed, had "gathered around him a small coterie of special agents who were little more than personal retainers."[72] Ickes later told his immediate circle of aides that he had initially given Glavis "very extraordinary powers," because the PWA staff had been assembled so quickly that it was impossible to tell "whom I could trust and whom I could not trust." But once Ickes had figured this out, and once Glavis began to investigate the PWA too closely, relations between the two soured.[73]

Glavis's investigation into bidding practices on the construction of a New York City post office annex led to his undoing. The procurement

[71] Burton A. Boxerman, "Adolph Joachim Sabath in Congress: The Roosevelt and Truman Years," *Journal of the Illinois State Historical Society* 66 (Winter 1973): 430; C. H. Bauer to H. A. Gray, February 25, 1935; and Report of PWA Special Agent J. F. O'Connell, May 24, 1935; both in "AF 391" folder, box 12, entry 85, "Case Files Relating to Investigations of Personnel, 1933–1941," RG 135, NA.

[72] "Louis R. Glavis" memo, February 1, 1937, "Departmental File Interior: 1936–39" folder, box 54, PSF, FDRL.

[73] Minutes of Staff Meeting, May 11, 1938, "Interior File. Friends. Charles West, 1937–42" folder, box 164, Ickes Papers, LC.

division of the Treasury Department, which was letting this contract with PWA funds, had three times rejected bids for construction on the post-office annex in New York City until, Glavis reported to Ickes, "its favored company underbid competitors, whereupon it was promptly awarded the contract."[74] This favored company, James Stewart & Company, was not just any preferred business. Fred Driscoll told PWA investigators that the failure of his firm, Driscoll and Company, to win the contract, could in part be explained by the fact that Postmaster General Jim Farley, an owner of the General Builders Supply Company of New York City, wanted the contract to go to the James Stewart Company. Farley's company would then sell building materials to the Stewart Company. Driscoll added that Assistant Secretary of the Treasury Lawrence "Chip" Robert also had links to Stewart. Robert, a Democrat and friend of Farley, was in charge of the Treasury's procurement division. PWA agents confirmed that Robert was "known to be very friendly with officers of the James Stewart Company" and "has been entertained by the Stewarts in New York rather extensively."[75]

After getting wind that the Treasury Department seemed to be involved in a scheme to funnel PWA contracts to construction companies with direct links to party leaders such as Farley, Louisiana Senator Huey Long blasted Farley and the Roosevelt administration on the Senate floor, calling for an inquiry. The Senate quickly passed a resolution, requesting from the PWA all materials mentioning the Stewart Company and Farley, while, for his part, Farley repeatedly denied the substance of Long's charges. FDR instructed Ickes to gather all the facts on the case and prepare a summary to be sent to the Senate only after FDR, Treasury Secretary Henry Morgenthau, Jr., Ickes, and Farley had collectively reviewed it. FDR made a point of telling Ickes to talk to Glavis, Farley recalled, and to order him to "stay in his own back yard."[76]

74 Glavis to Ickes, December 21, 1934, no folder, box 1, entry 25 (unidentified entry), "Records Relating to Investigation of New York Post Office Annex and Courthouse. Division of Investigation," RG 135, NA.
75 PWA Special Agent Thomas J. Dodd to PWA Special Agent A. D. Bailey, Jr., Re: Interview of Fred Driscoll, February 19, 1935, "AF 245" folder, box 7, entry 85, "Case Files Relating to Investigations of Personnel, 1933–1941," RG 135, NA. For Robert's denials of these allegations, see Admiral Christian Peoples to Glavis, February 27, 1935, "AF 249" folder, in ibid.
76 T. Harry Williams, *Huey Long* (New York: Vintage, 1981), 806–10; Ickes, *Secret Diary*, 1:294–300; John Morton Blum, *From the Morgenthau Diaries: Years of Crisis, 1928–1938* (Boston: Houghton Mifflin, 1959), 87–91; Typed Notes "Dictated 3/1/35 En Route" and Farley diary, February 18, 1935, both in "Private File 1935 Jan.–April" folder, box 37,

While Long continued to draw attention to himself with his vigorous promotion of his "share-the-wealth" plan, Ickes and NRA head Hugh Johnson struck back. In a nationally broadcast speech, Johnson famously proclaimed that, thanks to Long and his fellow pied piper, Detroit priest and radio broadcaster Father Charles Coughlin, "this country was never under a greater menace." Ickes threatened to revoke federal funds for Louisiana unless Long stopped trying to impose state authority over these moneys. "No public works money is going to build up any share-the-wealth machine," Ickes declared. After Long declared that Ickes could go "slambang to hell," Ickes rejoined that the Kingfish had "halitosis of the intellect."[77]

Although Glavis survived in his post until July 1936, several incidents following the Farley–Long episode further hurt his relationship with Ickes. When Glavis and the division of investigation used thin evidence to suspend two engineer examiners and the PWA acting director for Rhode Island and Connecticut, Ickes reversed his action and reprimanded Glavis for overstepping his bounds. Glavis's assistant, B. W. McLaughlin, then infuriated Ickes by criticizing him for too often disregarding the division of investigation's findings. Exasperated, Ickes finally eased Glavis out of his post, allowing him to save face through a transfer to the staff of the Senate's campaign expenditures investigating committee. Troubled by this series of events, Ickes reexamined his entire view of Glavis's life history, even going all the way back to the Ballinger–Pinchot affair for another look at Glavis's involvement. The fresh scrutiny led to a reversal of his initial assessment of Ballinger's guilt and Glavis's innocence. In the division of investigation, Glavis had "raised up a veritable Frankenstein's monster" within the Public Works Administration, Ickes concluded. The investigators whom Ickes had previously so trusted had become "persecutors, man hunters, and they are just as eager to hunt and drag down members of my staff as they are lobbyists and crooked contractors against whom we are trying to protect the Department and PWA."[78]

Farley Papers, LC; and see also Farley, *Behind the Ballots*, 247; Minutes of PWA Staff Meetings, February 19 and February 26, 1935, both in "PWA Staff Meetings" folder, box 2922, entry 749B, "Office of the Secretary. Central Classified Files, 1937–53," RG 48, NA–College Park; and PWA Special Agent Wharton Green to Glavis, February 26, 1935; PWA Special Agent L. W. Morrissey to Green, February 26, 1935; and PWA Special Agent Maxwell B. Bruce to Green, February 26, 1935; all enclosed in Farley to Ickes, March 1, 1935, "Interior File Post Office Dept. 1933–1935" folder, box 242, Ickes Papers, LC.

[77] Williams, *Huey Long*, 808–13.

[78] Glavis to Ickes, November 9, 1935, in "AF 443" folder, box 14, entry 85, "Case Files Relating to Investigations of Personnel, 1933–1941," RG 135, NA; PWA Press Release

CONCLUSION

In building the New Deal state, the PWA created overstaffed and often incompetent divisions of engineering, finance, and legal affairs and built up an overly zealous division of investigation. Despite these mistakes and many other obstacles, the New Deal's first public works program still succeeded in building a tremendous variety of necessary infrastructure during the depths of the Great Depression. The PWA satisfied a range of interested parties, from contractors to local politicians, from civic boosters to organized labor. Treating public works projects as a key element of public investment, the PWA brought into the New Deal state a veritable army of engineers and lawyers, creating a bureaucratic culture distinct from other parts of the federal government. In organizing the early New Deal around the principle of public works, Ickes became a builder "to rival Cheops."[79]

The next chapter turns directly to a consideration of this infrastructure built by the PWA under Ickes's leadership, comparing it to the public works built by Harry Hopkins's Works Progress Administration, and looking at the significance of this building for comprehending the changing shape of New Deal liberalism.

#1775 [undated, but between November 1, 1935 and January 31, 1936], volume 40, box 8, entry 24, "Press Releases, 1933–1939," RG 135, NA; Ickes to Glavis, April 9, 1936, in "Louis R. Glavis" memo, February 1, 1937, "Departmental File Interior: 1936–39" folder, box 54, PSF, FDR Papers, FDRL; and Ickes, *Secret Diary*, 1:549–51, 641, for Ickes's continued interest in Glavis's role in the Ballinger–Pinchot affair, see Harold L. Ickes, *Not Guilty: An Official Inquiry Into the Charges Made by Glavis and Pinchot Against Richard A. Ballinger, Secretary of the Interior, 1909–1911* (Washington, D.C.: U.S. Government Printing Office, 1940); and Ickes, "Not Guilty! Richard A. Ballinger – An American Dreyfus," *Saturday Evening Post*, May 25, 1940.

79 William E. Leuchtenburg, *Franklin D. Roosevelt and the New Deal* (New York: Harper & Row, 1963), 133.

4

The Dilemma of New Deal Public Works

People or Projects?

In carrying out the agenda of the Public Works Administration, Harold Ickes and other New Dealers had to ponder a stark question: Were they, in fact, sending people back to work by adhering to a philosophy of selecting "worthwhile" public works projects? This philosophy was not new to the New Deal. The notion that government construction should be "worthwhile" was rooted in the assumption that public works should be self-liquidating. Earlier progressives like Herbert Hoover believed that public works projects should make back the cost of their construction by generating revenue. A dam, for example, could produce revenue by selling the electricity it generates. The Hoover administration, in choosing and funding public works through the Reconstruction Finance Corporation (RFC), followed this approach.[1]

However, as economist and public works advocate Otto T. Mallery pointed out in a candid moment, the RFC defined "self-liquidating" in such a limited way that it came to mean, in effect, "a first-class business proposition in which the government can't lose and which will not be paid

---

[1] For more on the history of public works financing, see V. A. Mund, "Prosperity Reserves of Public Works," *Annals of the American Academy of Political and Social Science* 149, Part II (May 1930): 1–9; Arthur D. Gayer, *Public Works in Prosperity and Depression* (New York: National Bureau of Economic Research, 1935), 268–332; Jack P. Isakoff, *The Public Works Administration* (Urbana: University of Illinois Press, 1938), 11–17; J. Kerwin Williams, *Grants-in-Aid Under the Public Works Administration: A Study in Federal-State-Local Relations* (New York: Columbia University Press, 1939), 1–40; and Roger Daniels, "Public Works in the 1930s: A Preliminary Reconnaissance," in *The Relevancy of Public Works History: The 1930s – A Case Study* (Washington, D.C.: Public Works Historical Society, 1975), 2–17.

for in any part out of the proceeds of taxation."[2] Self-liquidation produced valuable public works in a financially prudent manner, but during the Depression this strategy had its limitations: It did not seem to put the public to work. Despite this drawback, Hoover's programs represented an important shift in public works policy. For the first time, the federal government was undertaking large-scale national planning and coordination of public construction. Because of their restrictions, though, the RFC's public works did not do much to alleviate the Depression, and when compared to the relatively well-funded New Deal agencies these programs represented only the proverbial drop in the bucket.[3]

Although Ickes and the PWA relaxed the Hoover-era requirement that public works be self-liquidating, the change was made only on paper. The PWA proclaimed that projects would be chosen based on their social and economic "desirability," their fit with preexisting plans, their engineering and technical "soundness," the financial stability of the applicant, and the "legal enforceability" of any securities bought by the federal government in order to fund the project.[4] In fact, however, only the last three factors – engineering, legal, and financial soundness – were formally measured and reviewed by the PWA, as its administrators assumed that any project that reached it was perforce socially and economically desirable.[5]

This ideology of self-liquidation shaped the way that New Dealers like Ickes and Harry Hopkins defined the proper role of public works in addressing the crisis of the Depression. Despite having to create a new federal bureaucracy and remake the fiscal ties that joined local, state, and federal levels of government, the PWA eventually succeeded in deploying its funds in all but three of the nation's counties, building an impressive amount of infrastructure. By 1935, however, the PWA's apparent slowness

[2] Joseph Dorfman, *The Economic Mind in American Civilization*, 5 vols. (New York: Viking Press, 1946–59), 5:619; Udo Sautter, "Government and Unemployment: The Use of Public Works before the New Deal," *Journal of American History* 73 (June 1986): 83–84; for a more detailed account see Udo Sautter, *Three Cheers for the Unemployed: Government and Unemployment before the New Deal* (Cambridge: Cambridge University Press, 1991). For the RFC, see James Stuart Olson, *Herbert Hoover and the Reconstruction Finance Corporation, 1931–1933* (Ames: Iowa State University Press, 1977) and Olson, *Saving Capitalism: The Reconstruction Finance Corporation and the New Deal, 1933–1940* (Princeton: Princeton University Press, 1988).
[3] Nancy E. Rose, *Put to Work: Relief Programs in the Great Depression* (New York: Cornerstone Books, 1994), 24.
[4] Federal Emergency Administration of Public Works, *Circular No. 1. The Purposes, Policies, Functioning and Organization of the Emergency Administration. The Rules Prescribed by the President* (Washington, D.C.: U.S. Government Printing Office, 1933), 7–8.
[5] Williams, *Grants-in-Aid Under the Public Works Administration*, 122–23.

in taking people off the unemployment rolls propelled Roosevelt and his advisers into taking a new tack. They created a new works program, the Works Progress Administration, committing $4.88 billion (about 6.7 percent of the 1935 GDP, or $64 billion in 2002 dollars) to public works.

Although the WPA is best remembered today for the assistance it provided to artists, actors, musicians, and writers, this impression does not reflect the WPA's actual priorities during the Depression. William Stott, in his landmark study, *Documentary Expression and Thirties America*, noted that the WPA in many ways symbolized the New Deal itself. Stott observed, "The WPA's monuments are all about: highways and streets, small dams, sewers, parks, power flumes, hospitals, airports, libraries, schools . . . [but] they are not why WPA captures the imagination." Rather, "WPA looms large in our thinking of the thirties thanks to projects that cost less than 7 per cent of its budget . . . the arts projects."[6] Stott's emphasis on the cultural significance of these arts projects, first published in 1973, has profoundly shaped subsequent historical inquiries.[7] While we now know much, for example, about the murals painted by WPA artists on the interiors of WPA buildings, plays performed under the auspices of the Federal Theater Project, and travel guides written by employees of the Federal Writers Project, we have not yet taken account of the fact that the WPA's central achievement was the large-scale production of public works projects. In fact, 75 percent of WPA employment and 75 percent of WPA expenditures went to highways, streets, public buildings, airports, public utilities, and recreational facilities. The creation of Harry Hopkins's WPA resolved a fierce debate among New Dealers over the benefits of direct and indirect employment created by public works.

While the WPA spent its funds on "work relief" and the PWA spent its funds on "public works," both efforts in fact produced substantial infrastructure throughout the nation. During this period, the federal government worked with labor and industry to use public works spending – what we today call "public investment" – to revive the construction sector, and through it, to try to pull the economy out of the Depression. New Dealers, though, never attempted or seriously contemplated the use of public works projects to effect radical structural reform of American capitalism. New Dealers did not propose that the federal government

[6] William Stott, *Documentary Expression and Thirties America* (Chicago: University of Chicago Press, 1986), 102–3.

[7] Karal Ann Marling, *Wall-to-Wall America: A Cultural History of Post-Office Murals in the Great Depression* (Minneapolis: University of Minnesota Press, 1982); and Bruce I. Bustard, *A New Deal for the Arts* (Seattle: University of Washington Press, 1997).

nationalize the investment functions of the economy, for example. Rather, public works spending took its place as an important component in the policy-making toolkit of mixed economies. During the Depression, public works programs helped to promote a series of striking innovations and technical changes in such fields as civil and structural engineering, transportation, distribution, machine production, electric-power generation, and aeronautics. These programs played a key part in advancing U.S. economic productivity in a variety of sectors, setting the stage for postwar economic growth.[8]

THE TRIUMPH OF PWA INFRASTRUCTURE AND THE "FAILURE" OF PWA EMPLOYMENT

A closer look at what the PWA built makes it clear that as far as infrastructure was concerned, the PWA was a resounding, and nationwide, success. By March 1939 the PWA had authorized the construction of 34,508 projects costing over $6 billion, completing 34,448 of them. All but three of the nation's 3,071 counties had received PWA dollars, as the agency funded 17,831 projects costing $1.9 billion that were built by federal agencies, and 16,677 costing $4.2 billion that were sponsored by nonfederal bodies.[9]

---

[8] Alan Brinkley, *The End of Reform: New Deal Liberalism in Recession and War* (New York: Alfred A. Knopf, 1995); Thomas K. McCraw, "The New Deal and the Mixed Economy," in Harvard Sitkoff, ed., *Fifty Years Later: The New Deal Evaluated* (New York: Alfred A. Knopf, 1985), 37–67; Alexander J. Field, "The Most Technologically Progressive Decade of the Century," *The American Economic Review* 93 (September 2003): 1399–1413; Field, "Uncontrolled Land Development and the Duration of the Depression in the United States," *Journal of Economic History* 52 (December 1992): 785–805; David C. Mowery and Nathan Rosenberg, "Twentieth Century Technological Change," in Stanley Engerman and Robert Gallman, eds., *The Cambridge Economic History of the United States* (Cambridge: Cambridge University Press, 2000), 3:803–926; Robert M. Solow, "Technical Change and the Aggregate Production Function," *Review of Economics and Statistics* 39 (August 1957): 312–20; and see also John Joseph Wallis, "The Political Economy of New Deal Spending Revisited, Again: With and without Nevada," *Explorations in Economic History* 35 (1998): 140–70.
[9] It is difficult to pin down which counties did not receive PWA funds. Internal correspondence among PWA officials indicates that these counties were Ohio county (Indiana), Trimble county (Kentucky), and Kennedy county (Texas). All other counties in the United States received PWA funds: 3,035 counties received them in the form of projects, while 36 counties were the site of PWA spending through the Forest Service, the Coast and Geodetic Survey, geological surveys, entomology and plant quarantines, the Weather Bureau, or fishery related projects. See N. O. Wood, Jr., to Dan H. Wheeler, March 10, 1939, "Counties in Which No Projects Are Definitely Located" folder, box 8, entry 30, "Records of the Project Control Division, Subject Files, 1933–1940," Records of the Public Works Administration, RG 135, NA, Washington, D.C. In 1936, however, a

Streets and highways were the most common PWA projects, as 11,428 road projects, or 33 percent of all PWA projects, accounted for over 15 percent of total PWA spending. Educational buildings were the next most common project (7,488, or 22 percent of all PWA projects), composing about 14 percent of PWA spending. By July 1936, one or more PWA school projects had been built in nearly half (47 percent) of the nation's counties.[10] The PWA explicitly targeted some of its school (and several of its hospital) projects for African Americans, building these in twenty-four of the forty-eight states and concentrating its efforts in North Carolina, Alabama, Georgia, Florida, Missouri, and Tennessee.[11] Flood-control and reclamation projects, while making up only 1.4 percent of PWA projects, accounted for 10.4 percent of all PWA spending. Public buildings, along with sewer and water projects, were also a favored target of PWA funds; taken together, they comprised 25.3 percent of PWA projects and 20.3 percent of PWA spending.[12] During the period from 1933 to 1940, the PWA made possible about 80 percent of all sewer construction in the nation, allotting funds for more than 1,500 projects costing nearly half a billion dollars.[13]

Which projects were losers under the PWA? Clearly, despite all the attention they have gathered – from New Dealers, their critics, and subsequent historians – it is immediately evident that public housing under the PWA was nearly nonexistent. (See Table 4.1) The seven limited-dividend federal housing projects built by the PWA accounted for 0.02 percent of all PWA projects and 0.2 percent of total PWA spending, while the fifty-one

glossy promotional pamphlet published by the PWA claimed that Union and White counties in Georgia, along with Putnam county in Missouri, were the only counties in the nation where the PWA had built no projects. See *The Story of PWA in Pictures* (Washington, D.C.: U.S. Government Printing Office, 1936), unpaginated.

[10] "Educational Buildings and Facilities Provided by PWA Allotments under the National Industrial Recovery Act of 1933 and the Emergency Relief Appropriation Act of 1935," July 1, 1936, no folder, box 3, entry 50, "Publications of the Division, 1936–1939. Projects Control Division," RG 135, NA.

[11] "PWA Non-Federal Allotments: Educational Institutions for Negroes," undated [after March 1, 1939], no folder, box 11, entry 50, "Publications of the Division, 1936–1939. Projects Control Division"; and "Summary of PWA Allotments for Non-Federal Projects for Negroes, By State," September 30, 1937, "Negro Facilities (Correspondence)" folder, box 12, entry 30, "Records of the Project Control Division, Subject Files, 1933–1940," both in RG 135, NA.

[12] *America Builds: The Record of PWA* (Washington, D.C.: U.S. Government Printing Office, 1939), 264; 291, table 21.

[13] See materials in "Public Work Reserve" folder, box 3, entry 746, "Division of Information. Publications of the Federal Works Agency and Subordinate Agencies, 1936–1942," Records of the Works Progress Administration, Record Group 69, National Archives, Washington, D.C.

TABLE 4.1. *Federal Projects, Nonfederal Projects, and Federal Low-Cost Housing Projects Sponsored by the PWA (Through March 1, 1939)*

Type of Project	All PWA Projects (%)	All PWA Funds (%)
Educational buildings	22.0	14.0
Hospitals	2.0	4.1
Public buildings	12.4	9.1
Sewer systems	5.4	7.1
Water systems	7.5	4.1
Electric power	1.0	1.8
Streets and highways	33.0	15.7
Engineering structures	1.9	6.9
Flood-control/Reclamation	1.4	10.4
Limited-dividend housing	0.02	0.2
Federal low-cost housing	0.15	3.2
Railroads	0.09	4.7
Vessels	0.75	6.4
All others	12.0	12.2

Note: Column two (% of all PWA Funds) includes both loans and grants made by the PWA. No. = 34,508. Percentages reflect rounding.
Source: America Builds: The Record of PWA (Washington, D.C.: U.S. Government Printing Office, 1939), 291, table 21.

federal low-cost-housing projects sponsored by the PWA comprised 0.15 percent of all projects and 3.2 percent of all spending. This raises obvious questions about the validity of using PWA public housing as any kind of "test case" for examining New Deal public policy, except to point out the truly marginal status of housing within the PWA program.[14] Indeed, one might point to the more intriguing cases of PWA naval spending (0.75 percent of all projects accounted for an impressive 6.4 percent of PWA funds) and the PWA's modernization program for the nation's railroads (0.09 percent of all projects comprised 4.7 percent of PWA funds) when examining where the PWA's money and attention went. Overall, however, the projects most favored by the PWA were streets, highways, roads, and bridges; schools; and public buildings such as courthouses, post offices, auditoriums, armories, city halls, prisons, community centers, and government office buildings.[15]

[14] For an important and thoughtful treatment of the PWA's housing program, however, see Gail Radford, *Modern Housing for America: Policy Struggles in the New Deal Era* (Chicago: University of Chicago Press, 1996).
[15] *America Builds*, 291, table 21.

The eastern and midwestern parts of the United States benefited the most from the PWA's 16,645 nonfederal projects. Region one received 3,090 projects and allotments of $685 million and region two received 3,419 projects and allotments of $445 million. Out of these two regions, Ohio, Illinois, Pennsylvania, and New York received the most projects, but the greatest amount of PWA funds went to New York, Illinois, Pennsylvania, and Ohio. In the other PWA regions, Texas and California were clear winners. The Lone Star State received 912 projects and allotments of $109 million, while the Golden State was the recipient of 807 projects and allotments totaling $103 million. In an attempt to address criticism of unfair distribution of funds, the PWA compared New York and Pennsylvania with the southern states, looking at their population and at the number of people gainfully employed in the building trades. The PWA found that the percentage of PWA nonfederal projects in New York and Pennsylvania was close to the percentage of people gainfully employed in the building industry in each state. The southern states' share of PWA nonfederal projects, for the most part, exceeded the percentage of the building industry active in each state.[16]

In addition to providing direct employment on project sites, the PWA's projects generated over $2.1 billion in orders for construction materials between 1933 and 1939. Stone, clay, and glass products, such as brick, cement, concrete, marble, and tile, made up 28 percent of the total value. Sharing the lead with stone, clay, and glass were items made from iron and steel, such as nails, rails, pipes, and structural steel, also accounting for 28 percent of the total value of PWA material orders. Coming in at third place was machinery such as elevators, turbines, meters and gas generators, electric machinery, and refrigeration equipment, making up slightly over 16 percent of the total value. Miscellaneous items (electric wiring, furniture, unclassified paving, petroleum products, and unclassified plumbing supplies) followed closely in fourth place, at 14 percent of total value. Forest products such as lumber did not even make up 7 percent of PWA materials. Air, land, and water transportation equipment such as locomotives, airplanes, trucks, and boats comprised a little over 4 percent of the value of material orders. Bringing up the rear were nonferrous metals (aluminum, copper, lead, and zinc products), at 0.9 percent; chemicals (mostly paint and explosives), at 0.9 percent; and

---

[16] L. N. Beeker to M. L. Devine, January 18, 1939, "Non-Federal Projects, Accomplishments of the PWA, Review of PW Study, Looking into the Future, History of Time Limitations on PWA Program" folder, box 4, entry 49, "Records of the Projects Control Division, Research Materials, 1935–1940," RG 135, NA.

TABLE 4.2. *PWA Nonfederal Projects, by Region and State (Through March 1, 1939)*

Region and State	Number of Projects	Total PWA Loan and Grant Allotment (in Millions $)
Total	16,645	2,135
Region #1		
Connecticut	261	28
Delaware	43	3
Maine	84	4
Maryland	142	32
Massachusetts	392	50
New Hampshire	112	7
New Jersey	319	58
New York	762	358
Pennsylvania	784	125
Rhode Island	87	15
Vermont	104	3
Total for Region	**3,090**	**685**
Region #2		
Illinois	808	181
Indiana	477	44
Michigan	461	63
Ohio	1,061	103
West Virginia	150	20
Wisconsin	462	35
Total for Region	**3,419**	**445**
Region #3		
Alabama	330	32
Florida	232	32
Georgia	518	20
Kentucky	298	26
Mississippi	231	34
North Carolina	352	38
South Carolina	243	62
Tennessee	278	36
Virginia	350	31
Total for region	**2,832**	**311**
Region #4		
Iowa	598	24
Minnesota	564	35
Missouri	562	47

Region and State	Number of Projects	Total PWA Loan and Grant Allotment (in Millions $)
Montana	161	20
Nebraska	307	73
North Dakota	193	6
South Dakota	168	7
Wyoming	58	5
Total for Region	**2,611**	**217**
Region #5		
Arkansas	236	23
Colorado	206	21
Kansas	450	27
Louisiana	228	24
New Mexico	96	8
Oklahoma	302	39
Texas	912	109
Total for Region	**2,430**	**249**
Region #6		
Arizona	122	12
California	807	103
Nevada	42	2
Utah	182	9
Total for Region	**1,153**	**126**
Region #7		
Idaho	157	6
Oregon	291	17
Washington	496	34
Alaska	33	2
Total for Region	**977**	**59**
District of Columbia and Territories	n.a.	n.a.
District of Columbia	14	25
Hawaii	57	5
Puerto Rico	59	15
Virgin Islands	3	.1

Note: Dollar figures reflect rounding.

Source: America Builds: The Record of PWA (Washington, D.C.: U.S. Government Printing Office, 1939), 284–85, table 16.

textiles such as awnings, carpets, linoleum, and various cotton goods at
0.2 percent of materials used on PWA projects.[17]

The PWA was responsible for playing a pioneering role in funding
nonfederal and federal hydroelectric projects. These nonfederal projects
included, most notably, California's Hetch Hetchy and Imperial hydroelectric projects, South Carolina's Santee-Cooper project, the Grand River
Dam in Oklahoma, the sprawling Lower Colorado River Authority,
as well as projects ranging from Arizona, Idaho, Illinois, Maine, and
Michigan to Nebraska, Oregon, Utah, Virginia, and Washington. Federal projects included California's huge Shasta Dam, Montana's Fort Peck
Dam, the Bonneville Dam project, covering Washington and Oregon, the
Grand Coulee Dam in Washington, and the Tennessee Valley Authority, among others.[18] In 1937, the PWA estimated that seventeen western
states received approximately $268 million in federal money for irriga-
tion, power, and other water projects.[19]

Projects related to public health, such as sewers, waterworks, and
hospitals, received direct support from the PWA. The construction of
sewers and other waterworks projects received a substantial boost from
the PWA. The PWA funded 60 percent of all new sewer systems built in
the nation in 1934, increasing this support to 70 percent of 1935 projects,
81 percent of 1936 projects, and 80 percent of 1937 projects. The PWA
sponsored 37 percent of new waterworks projects built in 1934, 50 percent of those built in 1935, 77 percent of 1936 projects, and 37 percent of
1937 projects. By March 1939 the PWA had contributed to the building
of 1,527 sewer projects in the country.[20] At this point, the PWA was also
responsible for the construction of 762 hospitals, including insane asy-
lums, schools for the "feeble-minded," accommodations for victims of
epilepsy and tuberculosis, old-age homes, and general hospital facilities,
at an estimated cost of roughly $330 million.[21]

[17] *America Builds*, 273–74, table 2.
[18] Ibid., 277–78, table 7.
[19] Unsigned memo, Re: "Allotment and Estimated Cost of All PWA Federal and Non-
   Federal Projects Involving Irrigation, Irrigation and Power, and Other Water Conservation 17 Western States," July 22, 1937, "Flood Control, Reclamation and Related
   Projects" folder, box 12, entry 30, "Records of the Project Control Division, Subject
   Files, 1933–1940," RG 135, NA. For more on the connections between the PWA and
   the TVA, see Steven M. Neuse, *David E. Lilienthal: The Journey of an American Liberal*
   (Knoxville: University of Tennessee Press, 1996), 84; and Erwin C. Hargrove, *Prisoners of Myth: The Leadership of the Tennessee Valley Authority, 1933–1990* (Princeton:
   Princeton University Press, 1994), 44, 105.
[20] *America Builds*, 279, table 9 and table 10.
[21] Ibid., 280, table 12.

Between 1933 and 1939, the PWA invested in transportation projects and in city, county, and state government buildings. In the realm of transportation, the PWA built 11,159 federal projects at an estimated cost of about $761 million, and erected 2,080 nonfederal projects with about $687 million in PWA grants and loans. Streets, roads, and highways claimed the bulk of PWA transportation spending and projects. PWA federal and nonfederal street, road, and highway projects accounted for 11,428 of the 13,239 total transportation projects undertaken, at a total cost of about $1.3 billion in money loaned and granted by PWA.[22] In addition to other miscellaneous projects, the PWA spent over $200 million of its nonfederal funds, loaning this money to thirty-two railroad modernization projects. In doing this, Ickes argued, the PWA "will be able to finance such purchases with reasonable interest and in this way recall a great number of men to jobs in the fabrication of steel rails and other equipment and to aid the heavy industries in furthering reemployment in large centers of unemployment."[23]

Most of the roughly $142 million the PWA spent on government buildings for cities, counties, and states went to city and town halls, courthouses, and other administrative office buildings (a total of about $68 million), although jails, prisons, and warehouses were also recipients of about $17 million in PWA loans and grants.[24] The PWA engaged in high-profile projects in the nation's capital, for example undertaking a thorough cleaning and renovation of the Washington Monument so it might "look down without shame on the dazzlingly white Lincoln Memorial."[25]

All these different public works, distributed in counties across the nation, represented Ickes's vision for the nation: better streets and highways, schools, flood control and reclamation projects, public buildings, sewer and waterworks projects, and hydroelectric plants, to name but several of the PWA's project categories. Ickes put this vision of public works into words at the annual Associated Press luncheon in 1935. He argued that public works, when planned in advance and geared to fluctuations in unemployment, "would be as nearly perfect a regulator of the balance between the capital and consumption industries as is practically possible under our economic system." While in 1933, Ickes claimed that, "we had

---

[22] Ibid., 281–82, table 13.
[23] PWA Press Release 267, no date (between October and November 1933), vol. 5, box 1, entry 24, "Press Releases, 1933–1939," RG 135, NA.
[24] *America Builds*, 283, table 14.
[25] PWA Press Release 695, May 20, 1934, vol. 16, box 4, entry 24, "Press Releases, 1933–1939," RG 135, NA.

no tradition of public works," the United States did have "a hampering tradition of the pork barrel."

One of the most fundamental tasks we have undertaken in these two years has been to make over the unsavory tradition of the pork barrel into a tradition of Federal works executed as efficiently and honestly and intelligently in the public interest as private builders would build for their own account. We have been furiously attacked, as we have insisted on this transformation, for being "over-suspicious," "over-legal," "over-cautious." But we have held on because we were building for the future as well as for today.[26]

In arguing in favor of the PWA's public works program, however, Ickes neglected to mention the Achilles' heel of self-liquidation: its difficulties in generating direct employment. This distinction between direct and indirect employment long occupied many New Dealers. In a 1940 report he prepared for the National Resources Planning Board, economist John Kenneth Galbraith presented a clear definition of these two concepts:

The main purpose of work relief is to provide the maximum of direct, or on-site, employment to needy unemployed; usually this work is done by force account [directly supervised by the federal government] and not by contract. Public works place less emphasis on on-site employment; much of the expenditure is for materials which provides a considerable volume of off-site employment; a considerable volume of heavy construction is undertaken, and, typically, the work is done under contract. These differences are not too sharply defined, but the broad purposes of public works and work relief, as well as the different cost ratios and procedures, make such a distinction necessary.[27]

Indeed, these "different cost ratios and procedures" were at the heart of FDR's misgivings over the performance of the PWA, and they were a pivotal factor in his subsequent embrace of Harry Hopkins's WPA in 1935. As economist Herbert Stein noted, in comparing the PWA with the WPA, Roosevelt "could not get over the fact that, per dollar, the WPA program put about four times as many men to work *directly* as did the public-works program [i.e., the PWA]." But, in coming to this conclusion, what Roosevelt refused to grasp was the extent of indirect employment generated by the PWA. As Harold Ickes put it, "No one has been able to mention indirect employment to the President for a long time. He simply has no patience with the thought." The PWA estimated that

[26] Ickes speech at the Associated Press Annual Luncheon, April 22, 1935," "OF 466b PWA Jan–May 1935" folder, box 13, OF 466b, FDRL. Ickes was fond of contrasting the "pork barrel tradition" with the "intelligent public works tradition" inaugurated by the PWA; see PWA Press Release 1051, October 3, 1934, vol. 27, entry 24, "Press Releases, 1933–1939," RG 135, NA.
[27] Galbraith, *Economic Effects of the Federal Public Works Expenditures*, 107.

every two hours of on-site construction work it created resulted in five hours of work in various manufacturing and shipping industries. Straight work-relief programs, on the other hand, did not create any measurable amount of indirect employment, because of the lower wages they paid and the restricted range of building materials they used. If off-site employment was included in calculating the effectiveness of the PWA, John Kenneth Galbraith concluded that, contrary to conventional wisdom, the PWA stood up quite well to the WPA's record of creating jobs. "Total off-site and on-site employment resulting from PWA, Federal projects under the Works Program [FERA], RFC, and regular Federal construction averaged 1,177,000 men from 1934–38," Galbraith reported, "and the employment resulting from all work relief construction averaged 1,642,000 men." The PWA easily outpaced the WPA in generating material orders, spending a little over $2 billion compared with the other's $920 million. FDR, however, not only mistrusted data like these, but (just as Hoover had) he also refused to increase funding to the Census Bureau, fearing that more accurate employment figures would demonstrate that government relief efforts were insufficient.[28]

Despite the misgivings of FDR, Ickes and supporters of the PWA pointed to the public's support of the program, noting the willingness of localities to supplement the grants the PWA supplied to their projects.

---

[28] Jonathan R. Kesselman, "Work Relief Programs in the Great Depression," in John L. Palmer, ed., *Creating Jobs: Public Employment Programs and Wage Subsidies* (Washington, D.C.: Brookings Institution, 1978), 166, n. 40; 186–87; and Herbert Stein, *The Fiscal Revolution in America* (Chicago: University of Chicago Press, 1969), 50–51; 57–58. Emphasis in original. Ickes quoted in Stein, *Fiscal Revolution*, 57. For estimates of indirect and direct employment, see *America Builds*, 28–29; Isakoff, *Public Works Administration*, 138–39; and Horatio B. Hackett to Congressman Alfred F. Beiter, March 4, 1936, "Original Write-Ups on Direct & Indirect Labor" folder, box 17, entry 49, "Records of the Projects Control Division, Research Materials, 1935–1940"; and *PWA and Industry: A Four-Year Study of Regenerative Employment* (75th Congress, 3d Session – House Document No. 605), no folder, box 6, entry 21 (unidentified entry), "Published Reports on Non-Federal Projects, 1934–41. Projects Control Division," both in RG 135, NA. For more on the accomplishments of the PWA, see C. W. Short and R. Stanley-Brown, *Public Buildings: A Survey of Architecture of Projects Constructed by Federal and Other Governmental Bodies Between the Years 1933 and 1939 with the Assistance of the Public Works Administration* (Washington, D.C.: U.S. Government Printing Office, 1939); Galbraith, *Economic Effects of the Federal Public Works Expenditures*, 55; 23; see also David M. Polak to Acting Director, Projects and Statistics Division, "Review of Mr. Galbraith's Report on 'Economics of Public Works,'" January 23, 1940, no folder, box 6, entry 49, "Records of the Projects Control Division, Research Materials, 1935–1940," RG 135, NA. For FDR and Hoover's attitudes towards unemployment data, see Margo J. Anderson, *The American Census: A Social History* (New Haven: Yale University Press, 1988), 177 and Richard J. Jensen, "The Causes and Cures of Unemployment in the Great Depression," *Journal of Interdisciplinary History* 19 (Spring 1989): 564–65, n. 17.

Communities often voted, in special elections, to issue bonds to support public works projects. In 2,613 local elections, localities voted 83 percent of the time to make direct contributions to their public works. One concerned resident of Chula Vista, California, wrote of his community's willingness to provide more than $100,000 for a PWA street-paving project, expressing himself in words that would have pleased Ickes. To obtain a PWA grant, the residents of Chula Vista "went to the polls and voted to bond themselves in the amount of $107,000 to enter into the spirit of the New Deal."[29] For Chula Vista, the spirit of the New Deal meant the improvement of local streets by private contractors employing a combination of skilled labor and workers taken from the relief rolls, funded by a mixture of federal grants, loans, and locally issued bonds. This broad range of support for federal public works spending at the local level suggests that portraits of New Deal political culture that emphasize such features of daily life as taxpayer resistance or the role of mass culture in mediating the growing acceptance of the welfare state by ethnic workers are incomplete.[30] Through the PWA's public works, the New Deal won the support of native-born white property owners, too. Although the PWA's approach to public works would soon give way, for a time, to a revised approach to public works embodied in Harry Hopkins's Works Progress Administration, the public works built by the PWA epitomized this spirit – the spirit of self-liquidation.

FROM PWA TO WPA: PUBLIC WORKS, EMPLOYMENT, AND THE ECONOMY

Soon after Ickes had become director of the PWA, *Business Week* published an evaluation of the two programs created by the National

---

[29] "Accomplishments of the Federal Emergency Administration of Public Works," "Public Works Administration Miscellaneous" folder, box 1, entry 51, "Miscellaneous Publications, 1936–1941. Projects Control Division"; "Handbook of Pertinent Information Relative to Public Works Programs," May 1, 1936, no folder, box 2, entry 50, "Publications of the Division, 1936–1939. Projects Control Division"; and Howard D. Sutliff to James A. Farley, October 23, 1935, "8000-8499" folder, box 2, entry 70 "Records of the Engineering Division. Records Relating to Equipment to be Used on Certain PWA Projects, 1935–1938. #1,000-4,999," all in RG 135, NA. See also Louis Brownlow, "The Citizen as a Stockholder in Public Facilities," *Engineering News-Record*, May 18, 1933, pp. 628–31; and Leo Wolman, "Financial Aspects of Budgeting Public-Works Construction," ibid., pp. 659–60.

[30] David T. Beito, *Taxpayers in Revolt: Tax Resistance during the Great Depression* (Chapel Hill: University of North Carolina Press, 1989); and Lizabeth Cohen, *Making a New Deal: Industrial Workers in Chicago, 1919–1939* (Cambridge: Cambridge University Press, 1990).

Industrial Recovery Act – the National Recovery Administration and the PWA – entitled "The Three-Legged Stool." Ickes, the magazine editorialized, "has approached the public works program with the determination that there shall be 'no smell of pork,' that there shall be no graft, that loans shall be sound. All this is highly commendable – to a certain point, or under normal conditions." However, given the extended economic depression, *Business Week* clamored for quick spending on public works projects that would immediately put people back to work. "Mr. Ickes," the editorial concluded, "is running a fire department on the principles of a good, sound bond house." If economic recovery were to occur, New Dealers needed to realize that the recovery plan was like a three-legged stool: "[W]e can balance precariously on two legs for a little while, but unless the third soon is driven into place, we shall have a nasty fall." As one newspaper put it, "Let us get busy. Give the blue eagle [symbolizing the NRA] a running mate, a bird, say, with a shovel in one claw and a pickax in the other."[31]

Ickes responded to these criticisms, claiming that the PWA was trying to put men back to work quickly, and outlining the indirect benefits of the PWA for the economy. While "thousands of men are going back to work every day, on the roads of every state, along the inland rivers, in the shipyards on the coasts," Ickes also stressed that "back of these thousands are still other thousands who are resuming work in cement plants, quarries, asphalt refineries, steel mills, engine works, manufacturing, and in bringing to the men on public construction the materials they must have for their work." As these men received their paychecks, their "increased purchasing power leads to the employment of thousands of others. The benefits spread out through the community in an ever-widening circle." The PWA, despite evidence to the contrary, was "not a huge, impersonal thing of bridges and dams and battleships." Rather, "it is an intensely human, personal effort, which will mean a great deal to your neighbors and to yourself."[32]

By January 1935, however, David Cushman Coyle, a member of the PWA technical board of review, had rejected Ickes's position and had embraced the view put forth by *Business Week*. While the PWA was

---

[31] *Business Week*, August 26, 1933, clipping, "Editorials I" folder, box 157; "What About Public Works, Secretary Ickes?" clipping from the *St. Louis Post-Dispatch*, August 25, 1933, "Editorials I 1933–1935" folder; both in box 157, Harold L. Ickes Papers, LC.

[32] Ickes, "Spending Three Billions of Your Money!" clipping from *The American Magazine*, October 1933, "Articles 'Spending Three Billions of Your Money' October 1933 [corres. August–October 1933]" folder, box 170, Ickes Papers, LC.

generating worthwhile public works, Coyle dryly observed that "the big
gun that was going to blast the Depression out of the landscape finally
went off with a pop that was not heard round the world." The blame for
this failure, Coyle thought, lay in the philosophy of self-liquidating public
works that the PWA had inherited from Hoover's RFC. This approach,
Coyle wrote, "is one that is so arranged that charges can be laid directly
upon the consumer, so that no expense will fall on the Federal treasury
(and the income tax)."[33] Coyle had stumbled onto a point that other
proto–Keynesians, such as Harry Hopkins, economist Lauchlin Currie,
and Federal Reserve chairman Marriner Eccles, would amplify over the
next several years: If recovery were to occur, the federal government could
not simply produce public works. Rather, it had to produce public works
while injecting money into the economy, or, at a minimum, the government
had to produce public works without placing demands for construction
funds on those who could least afford it.[34]

To make this point, Coyle employed the image most often used in
discussions of public works: that of priming a pump. Coyle declared that
a truly effective public works program "would be like a pump that forces
the circulation of water by sucking the water out of one place and driving it
into another. . . . The function of an effective public works program would
be to draw off some of this unspendable surplus and spend it, forcing it
back into circulation. . . ." A public works program that hewed too closely
to a philosophy of self-liquidation, however, "is a means of connecting
the outgoing pipe back to the pump, so that the pump will not have to
draw from surplus incomes. The result is that a fine healthy current of
buying power goes out into the business world for a short distance and
then is cut back to the pump without making the full circuit." The policy
of self-liquidation, in Coyle's analysis, focused too narrowly on achieving
a return on investment in "worthwhile" public works, absorbing some
of the funds that, in a truly recovery-oriented program of public works,
should have been injected into the economy. "'Sound, self-liquidating'
public works, and 'sound' methods of doing the financing," argued Coyle,
"are clever ways of putting the suction end of the pump into the same
bucket as the discharge end, so that we may be allowed to splash happily

---

[33] David Cushman Coyle, "What About Public Works?" *Harper's Monthly*, January 1935,
147.
[34] For more on the growth of Keynesianism among the New Dealers, see Brinkley, *End of
Reform*; on the New Deal's sources of revenue, the key work is Mark H. Leff, *The Limits
of Symbolic Reform: The New Deal and Taxation, 1933–1939* (Cambridge: Cambridge
University Press, 1984).

without dampening the good old business cycle and the gentlemen who live by the same."[35]

If the New Deal's public works were to achieve economic recovery, Coyle concluded, it would "have to be correct in all the ways that the orthodox financial authorities do not like. It will have to be made up of non-self-liquidating Federal projects or grants-in-aid, adequate in volume and speed, temporarily financed by bonds sold only to banks, and ultimately validated by taxes on the upper brackets."[36] In other words, cautious public works projects, in conjunction with the recovery codes of the NRA, would not suffice. Rather, public works must be fully incorporated into a rethinking of the American economic system.

After keeping the Public Works Administration as the centerpiece of New Deal public works programs for nearly two years, FDR shifted tactics. Public works would remain the central focus of the New Deal, but a new administrator and a new organization would prosecute these projects. The PWA continued as a functioning agency, and its method of handling public works would again become important during World War II. Harry Hopkins's Works Progress Administration, however, would come to epitomize a different approach to labor, contractors, and construction.

THE ORIGINS OF THE WORKS PROGRESS ADMINISTRATION

The establishment of the WPA by Executive Order 7034 on May 6, 1935, grew out of the Roosevelt administration's experience in dealing with unemployment. In 1933, FDR had put Harry Hopkins in charge of the Federal Emergency Relief Administration (FERA) and, when it looked as if special measures were needed to combat the unemployment situation during the bitterly cold winter of 1933–34, gave him the task of running the Civil Works Administration (CWA). Both organizations tried to ease the burdens of unemployment by putting people to work on public works projects. Hopkins, a social worker from Iowa who had administered relief in New York State when FDR was governor, possessed both idealistic fervor and a keen sense of political realism. As Joseph E. Davies famously put it, Hopkins "had the purity of St. Francis of Assisi combined with the sharp shrewdness of a race track tout."[37]

[35] Coyle, "What About Public Works?," 148, 158.
[36] Ibid., 158.
[37] Davies quoted in Searle F. Charles, *Minister of Relief: Harry Hopkins and the Depression* (Syracuse: Syracuse University Press, 1963), 24. My account of the WPA's origins relies

Following large electoral victories for the Democrats in 1934, Hopkins and other New Dealers made the case to FDR for strengthening the federal government's commitment to work relief in place of a simple dole. In response to FDR's January 4, 1935, message to Congress, the House and Senate passed the 1935 Emergency Relief Appropriation (ERA) Act, totaling $4.88 billion. Hopkins and Harold Ickes immediately set to work lobbying FDR, each seeking to be put in charge of this new works program. By April, Roosevelt accommodated their rivalry by creating a new layer of bureaucracy. Frank C. Walker, a Democratic lawyer with a talent for soothing egos, was placed in charge of a new Division of Application and Information. Walker's DAI screened project applications and sent them to the Advisory Committee on Allotments, chaired by Ickes, which reviewed them and passed its recommendation along to FDR. Hopkins's Works Progress Administration would then be in charge of expediting selected projects and running smaller public works projects directly. FDR's desire to reduce unemployment through public works, however, led him to favor Hopkins's WPA and to slight Ickes.[38]

The WPA built on the organization of the FERA and the CWA, drawing on much of the same administrative personnel. The WPA was federally administered and organized by region and state, with a separate organization for New York City. The Senate confirmed WPA officials, generally state administrators, who were paid more than $5,000 a year. The WPA contained divisions in charge of engineering and construction, service projects, finance, employment, management, statistics, research, investigation, information, and legal matters. Hopkins's key aides included Aubrey Williams, who also ran the National Youth Administration, Ellen S. Woodward, Florence Kerr, Corrington Gill, Jacob Baker, Lawrence Westbrook, Howard O. Hunter, Alan Johnstone, and David K. Niles.

on Charles, *Minister of Relief*; Federal Works Agency, *Final Report on the WPA Program, 1935–1943* (Washington, D.C.: U.S. Government Printing Office, 1947); Donald S. Howard, *The WPA and Federal Relief Policy* (New York: Russell Sage Foundation, 1943); Arthur W. MacMahon, John D. Millett, and Gladys Ogden, *The Administration of Federal Work Relief* (Chicago: Public Administration Service, 1941); and George McJimsey, *Harry Hopkins: Ally of the Poor and Defender of Democracy* (Cambridge: Harvard University Press, 1987).
38 FDR, "Annual Message to the Congress," January 4, 1935, in Samuel I. Rosenman, ed., *The Public Papers and Addresses of Franklin D. Roosevelt* (New York: Random House, 1938) 4:15–25; and *Final Report on the WPA*, 7. For Walker's remembrances of this period, see Robert H. Ferrell, ed., *FDR's Quiet Confidant: The Autobiography of Frank C. Walker* (Niwot: University Press of Colorado, 1997), 98–101.

Hopkins also drew on engineering expertise, particularly relying on Army Corps of Engineers Colonel Francis C. Harrington, who would replace Hopkins as the head of the WPA at the end of 1938. Although hesitant initially, Hopkins soon embraced the notion of using army engineers in the WPA. They had the technical know-how to speed the execution of public works projects, and their air of military and scientific authority helped quiet charges of political favoritism in the WPA. The WPA in New York City and Los Angeles, for example, was run by officers of the Army Corps of Engineers.

Although Ickes always maintained that Hopkins intentionally selected the initials "WPA" in order to spark confusion with his PWA, Hopkins argued otherwise. On one occasion, Hopkins told a group of WPA officials in New York City that FDR aide Louis Howe came up with the name "Works Progress Administration" while reviewing government flow charts with Hopkins at the White House. Ill and dying, Howe reportedly made Hopkins promise to stop fighting with Ickes, and to ensure that Congress pass legislation establishing the WPA, name and all. Hopkins claimed that he still had the yellow sheet of notepaper inscribed with Howe's deathbed request.[39]

Although the Advisory Committee on Allotments was soon superseded by the growing influence of Hopkins and the WPA, the minutes of the ACA provide crucial evidence of the tensions that had been building among the New Dealers since 1933 over the nature and goals of public works. Within the ACA, the questions of employment versus indirect employment, "make work" over infrastructure, private contracting versus directly supervised government construction ("force account" work), and economic recovery versus economic development, were heatedly revisited and refought. The ACA contained a wide range of cabinet officers, New Dealers, and business executives, reflecting a variation on the "associationalism" between government and the private sector often ascribed to Hoover.[40] The director of the Treasury Department's public buildings division, the acting director of the budget, the head of the Army Corps of

---

[39] Harry Hopkins, untitled address, November 16, 1938, "Hopkins" folder, box 3, entry 737, "Division of Information. Administrative Speeches, 1933–1942," RG 69, NA.

[40] The classic statement on associationalism is Ellis W. Hawley, "Herbert Hoover, the Commerce Secretariat, and the Vision of an 'Associative State,' 1921–1928," *Journal of American History* 61 (June 1974): 116–40; an important reassessment is David M. Hart, "Herbert Hoover's Last Laugh: The Enduring Significance of the 'Associative State' in the United States," *Journal of Policy History* 10 (1998): 419–44.

Engineers, the commissioner of the Reclamation Division, the director of the Soil Erosion Service, the chief of the Forest Service, the heads of the Civilian Conservation Corps, Resettlement Administration, Rural Electrification Administration, and the National Youth Administration, and the head of the PWA's housing division joined such members of the Business Advisory Council as Sears, Roebuck president Robert Wood and Singer Sewing Machine Company president Robert Elbert, and other notables such as Frederic Delano, vice chairman of the National Resources Board, George Berry of the National Recovery Administration, Edward O'Neal of the American Farm Bureau Federation, Julien Hill representing the American Bankers' Association, and New York City Mayor Fiorello La Guardia, representing the U.S. Conference of Mayors.

FDR, speaking at the ACA's first meeting, placed the problem of providing work for the unemployed in front of the Committee as its "first task." FDR's skepticism about the PWA's efforts on this front were immediately evident. "Now, nobody knows what that total [employed] would be," he said. "Some experts say that we would employ indirectly two people by giving one man a job; others hold more than two; nobody seems to know."[41] Out of the 3.5 million people on relief that the administration classified as "employable" (excluding the elderly and children), 478,000 were in the building and construction trades, 524,000 were white-collar workers, 205,000 were skilled in trades other than construction, and 1 million were unskilled workers. Of the 3,022,000 workers who were not in construction, 2.5 million were men and 964,000 were women.[42]

At this first meeting, the ACA resolved to allot some of the $4.88 billion to specific projects: $400 million to roads and highways; $250 million to rural rehabilitation and conservation; $50 million to rural electrification; $225 million to housing; $150 million to white-collar jobs; $300 million to the Civilian Conservation Corps; $450 million to nonfederal self-liquidating public works; and $175 million for sanitation, prevention of soil erosion, flood control, and river and harbor projects.[43]

Fiorello La Guardia stressed the importance of presenting the new works program to the public in such a way that it reached beyond the relief of unemployment. The New York mayor observed, "we have a class

[41] Proceedings of the Advisory Committee on Allotments, 1:1–3, May 7, 1935, entry 32, "Minutes of Meetings of the Advisory Committee on Allotments," RG 135, NA.
[42] ACA Proceedings, 1:12, May 7, 1935.
[43] ACA Proceedings, 1:12–24, May 7, 1935.

of people in this country that just cannot understand anything spoken in humane terms, but they will understand you when you speak to them in terms of tons of steel, thousands of brick, and so forth; and that is the language in which we will have to talk with them." La Guardia argued that materials ordered for public works projects should be distributed widely. "Instead of giving an order for all the steel to one man we could distribute these orders to several manufacturers, or we can obtain permission to purchase these materials, provided the prices are favorable, of course, from the mills and factories throughout the country, and in that way we may obtain assurances from these various mills and factories that more men would be put to work." In addition to distributing these funds across industries, La Guardia also pushed for the WPA to earmark funds for each city in the nation.[44]

Hopkins stressed to his staff the importance of working with mayors and governors. "We would have been awful damned fools," he bluntly said, "if we thought for a minute that we have either the power or the ability to go out and set up 100,000 work projects as we are going to have to do, probably 200,000 before the year is over, without the complete cooperation of local and state officials. We couldn't do it if we wanted to." Indeed, Hopkins argued, the work the WPA does "in the main is work not on Federal property but on city and county and state property, it is work that is going to be of interest to the local taxpayers and local people, and we couldn't if we wanted to develop these projects, organize them or prosecute them for that matter, without bringing the cities and the counties and states into a complete partnership with us." Hopkins urged his staff to take care in selecting administrative personnel, stating that, in its reliance on the quality of its administrators, the WPA resembled no other organization except for the university. "A university depends on its faculty and on nothing else," Hopkins stated. "A university that had a great reputation twenty years ago is second-rate now. Why? Because the faculty have gone, some other university got the great teachers. Ninety per cent of this depends on the people we have to run it."[45]

[44] ACA Proceedings, 1:25, May 7, 1935; and ACA Proceedings 2:4, May 16, 1935.
[45] "Proceedings Staff Conference, Works Progress Administration," June 16, 1935, "100 May–Sept 35" folder, box 67, "Central Files: General 1935–1944. 100 Administration," Record Group 69, Records of the Works Progress Administration, National Archives, Washington, D.C. For more on the role of local constraints and the New Deal, see James T. Patterson, *The New Deal and the States: Federalism in Transition* (Princeton: Princeton University Press, 1969); Anthony J. Badger, "The New Deal and the Localities," in Rhodri

With administrative expertise, Hopkins thought, the WPA could avoid charges that they were playing politics. "We are going to be charged with buying the election," Hopkins told his staff. "We have already been charged with it, and boy, wait until this starts next fall and next spring." Hopkins, though, was skeptical of notions that federal spending on public works had a direct correlation on the voting of relief recipients. "If anybody thinks you can buy an election through giving relief, or even work relief jobs, I think it is the silliest thing in the world. I have been in this game now for two years, and if there is one way not to do it, it is by giving relief, because none of the clients like you. They all think you're terrible, and you are not going to buy any elections that way."[46] The WPA did believe in publicizing its program, however. During the summer of 1936, for example, the WPA broadcast 15-minute radio programs on 54,000 occasions, over 475 stations. Between August and December 1936, about ten million people saw twenty motion pictures produced by the WPA. David K. Niles, the director of the WPA's information service, urged the WPA to "proclaim from the housetops what you are doing for the underprivileged in your community."[47]

WPA AND LABOR

In trying to address the problem of direct employment, the ACA revisited the difficulty of trying to build public works, on the one hand, and trying to employ the maximum amount of workers off the relief rolls, on the other. Harry Hopkins asked James McEntee, the assistant director of the Civilian Conservation Corps, about using labor from the relief rolls in building camps for the CCC. McEntee reported that they had no difficulties drawing unskilled labor from people on relief, but that finding skilled labor was an entirely different matter. McEntee told Hopkins that

Jeffreys-Jones and Bruce Collins, eds., *The Growth of Federal Power in American History* (DeKalb: Northern Illinois University Press, 1983), 102–115; Badger, *New Deal*; the essays collected in John Braeman, Robert H. Bremner, and David Brody, eds., *The New Deal: The State and Local Levels* (Columbus: Ohio State University Press, 1975); and, more recently, Douglas Carl Abrams, *Conservative Constraints: North Carolina and the New Deal* (Jackson: University Press of Mississippi, 1992).

[46] "Proceedings Conference of State Administrators. Works Progress Administration," June 17–19, 1935, "100 May–Sept 35" folder, box 67, "Central Files: General 1935–1944. 100 Administration," RG 69, NA.

[47] "Proceedings Conference of State Administrators. Works Progress Administration," February 12–13, 1937, "100 Jan–Feb 37" folder, box 69, "Central Files: General 1935–1944. 100 Administration," RG 69, NA.

"building trades mechanics do not register there [with the various relief agencies]. That dates back to the PWA. They may be in distress and badly in need of work but because of the system of employment in the building trades – industry is something different – building trades mechanics do not register under these agencies."[48]

FDR himself held forth at a subsequent meeting of the ACA on this issue, summarizing an extended debate he had carried on with Ickes, Hopkins, Walker, and Treasury Secretary Morgenthau. FDR attempted to "paint the picture in its actual terms," arguing that the WPA had to spend its appropriation to put roughly 3.5 million people to work via direct employment.[49] Champions of projects that relied more on skilled labor, such as Edward Markham of the Army Corps of Engineers, objected to FDR's reasoning. "I think it would be wise and well," Markham said, "for others than those representing the construction agencies to make some remarks on the subject since it seems to me we are dealing with the impossible. If the direct and indirect [employment figures] are included in such matters, it begins to bring the figure to the levels that are preferred." FDR, however, offered this rebuttal to Markham: "I have said not once but two or three times there is no use mentioning indirect labor in these discussions. Indirect labor does not count in our figures. We have a figure of direct labor, three and one-half million people. We hope it will put another three and one-half million people on indirect labor but it does not enter into the consideration of our projects."[50] Between July 1935 and July 1943, the WPA employed a total of 8.5 million people, reaching a peak of about 3.3 million in late 1938.[51]

Hopkins echoed FDR's stance on direct employment while conferring with his staff ten days later. "When I talk about employment," Hopkins declared, "I am talking entirely about direct employment on the job, and I think tomorrow we will have to make it perfectly clear to the State Administrators that we are not discussing now indirect employment in any way. All of us know there will be indirect employment; none of us know how much. The guesses will run from 1:1 to 1:5, depending on who is doing the guessing." Instead of guessing, Hopkins focused on specifics: "We are talking about 3,500,000 particular men whose names and addresses we now know, who are going to move from the relief

[48] ACA Proceedings, 2:42–43, May 16, 1935.
[49] ACA Proceedings, 4:32–34, June 3, 1935.
[50] ACA Proceedings, 4:37, June 6, 1935.
[51] *Final Report on the WPA*, 28–30.

rolls to direct employment on these particular jobs, not the men on the relief rolls that may get jobs in other ways but these particular 3,500,000 jobs."[52]

Roads and highways provided about half of the WPA's employment on construction projects. Taken together, public utilities, such as water and sewer construction, public buildings, and parks and recreational facilities, accounted for one-third of WPA employment. Unskilled workers were employed in great numbers on WPA projects: Over 75 percent of road project workers were unskilled. While 60 to 70 percent of other construction-project workers were unskilled, this figure excludes public-building construction, which generally relied more on skilled workers. About 30 percent of public-building workers were skilled laborers; unskilled workers accounted for under 50 percent of the workforce on public buildings constructed by the WPA.[53]

PRIVATE CONTRACTING OR GOVERNMENT-RUN CONSTRUCTION?

While the WPA put people to work directly, by means of force-account labor, the PWA relied on contractors to build its projects. In the opinion of the PWA's administrators, its projects – built via contracts given to privately held construction firms – were erected at the same level of efficiency and fiscal responsibility as any that were sponsored exclusively by the private sector. After polling project sponsors, examining an independent survey of New York State schools, reviewing instances of duplicate bid taking, and scrutinizing other data in their files, one PWA official concluded that there was only a 1- to 3-percent increase in the costs of certain projects, and no increase at all in other projects. "Contractors who have expressed themselves on this subject – as well as engineers and architects engaged in the construction business," this PWA official wrote, "have asserted that there is no real basis" for claiming that the PWA's construction was unduly expensive or inefficient. "Any expense that might be involved in operating under conditions imposed by PWA is offset by the certainty that the payments to the contractor will be made in accordance with the definite terms of the contract." While the PWA wage scale also

[52] "Proceedings Staff Conference, Works Progress Administration," June 16, 1935, "100 May–Sept 35" folder, box 67, "Central Files: General 1935–1944. 100 Administration," RG 69, NA.
[53] *Final Report on the WPA,* 47–48.

TABLE 4.3. *Number of Contractors Used in PWA Nonfederal Projects, by State and Territory, as of November 1937*

Alabama	29	New Hampshire	8
Arizona	18	New Jersey	97
Arkansas	17	New Mexico	11
California	372	New York	592
Colorado	55	North Carolina	62
Connecticut	36	North Dakota	9
Delaware	3	Ohio	255
Florida	36	Oklahoma	26
Georgia	22	Oregon	9
Idaho	3	Pennsylvania	269
Illinois	438	Rhode Island	67
Indiana	99	South Carolina	16
Iowa	54	South Dakota	17
Kansas	16	Tennessee	76
Kentucky	53	Texas	242
Louisiana	47	Utah	27
Maine	16	Vermont	1
Maryland	74	Virginia	62
Massachusetts	93	Washington	46
Michigan	97	West Virginia	55
Minnesota	42	Wisconsin	105
Mississippi	100	Wyoming	3
Missouri	260	Washington, D.C.	18
Montana	29	Alaska	2
Nebraska	40	Hawaii	4
		Puerto Rico	11

Source: Dan H. Wheeler to H. N. Gillman, Jr., November 6, 1937, "Contractors (Receiving PWA Contracts)" folder, box 5, entry 30, "Records of the Project Control Division, Subject Files, 1933–40," RG 135, NA.

helped ensure cost certainty, PWA inspections were responsible for setting "higher standards of planning and execution" on PWA projects.[54]

The PWA's nonfederal program of public works relied on private contractors throughout the nation. (See Table 4.3) In the East, Massachusetts, New York, New Jersey, and Pennsylvania employed a great number of construction firms, while in the Midwest, Illinois, Missouri, Ohio, Wisconsin, Michigan, and Indiana did a similar job of spreading PWA employment among a variety of businesses. In the South, only

[54] Undated and anonymous confidential "Memorandum on PWA Construction Costs," "1939, Binder 1" folder, box 6, entry 6, "Materials Prepared for Congressional Hearings on PWA Appropriations, 1936–1941," RG 135, NA.

Texas and Mississippi equaled or exceeded the mark of 100 contractors
employed, and in the West, only California. On a per capita basis, it is
difficult not to be impressed by the number of contracting firms employed
in Washington, D.C. (eighteen), or, for that matter, in Montana (twenty-
nine), Utah (twenty-seven), Arizona (eighteen), South Dakota (seventeen),
or Puerto Rico (eleven). The PWA kept close track of contractors it had
banned from eligibility for PWA contracts. By 1939, however, the PWA
slightly relaxed its rules on employing banned contractors. Instead of
declaring these contractors completely out of bounds, the agency required
local PWA directors to request special approval from Washington in order
to sign the contractors for jobs sponsored by the PWA. Not until 1940 did
the PWA finish collecting comprehensive data about contractors working
on PWA nonfederal projects and become willing to make this information
public. Through July 23, 1940, the PWA had awarded 54,637 nonfederal contracts to 20,006 contractors, excluding material and equipment
contracts.[55]

The PWA took pains to publicize its viewpoint on the advantages of
working through private construction firms, for example broadcasting
a series of discussions about the PWA on the radio over several nights
in 1937. One discussion featured a PWA state director and an architect
discussing the support for PWA in the construction trades. In response
to the allegation that projects built under the PWA cost more because of
markups by the contractors, the architect called the claim "foolish, and
every contractor in this business knows it is."

When you start a Public Works Administration job, you know you're going to get
your money when you're supposed to get it. You know that nobody's going to
come around chiseling you, either. That's one of the best things about the PWA.
Its' [sic] stopped cheating. It kept out the fly-by-night contractors who skinned a
job, and took them away from legitimate contractors by cheating their workmen
and letting their sub-contractors hold the bag for them on financing. We have
had to do more paper work and keep better records than heretofore but we have
considered the expense we were put to in this connection as money spent for a
good education. We are keeping closer tract [sic] of jobs than we used to and
this applies to contractors as well; especially contractors who had been used to
keeping records on the back of envelopes, small notebooks stuffed in their pockets
and other inefficient methods.[56]

[55] E. W. Clark to Chief, Research and Statistics Division, PWA, September 5, 1940, "FWA"
folder, box 1, entry 34, "Records of the Projects Control Division. File of Lloyd N. Beeker,
Assistant Director of the Projects Control Division, 1936–1941," RG 135, NA.
[56] "Fifth Night–Radio Series" transcript, no date (probably after February 11, 1937),
"Addresses" folder, box 2, entry 34, "Records of the Projects Control Division. File

Jobs under the PWA, this architect and the PWA official agreed, were subject to close inspections and safety regulations and were executed efficiently. While clearly staged to drum up support for the PWA, the discussion concluded with the architect issuing a ringing endorsement of the program:

The PWA saved the contractors and the whole construction business. I have been working at architectural designs since 1920. When I had a job with Wells and Hudson as an architectural designer I never saw construction hit as it was hit in this Depression. From 1931 to 1933 we all sat tight with nothing to do. Many contractors had millions of dollars worth of equipment sitting idle and rusting away. If you do not believe this, go look up the building permits for this period and see for yourself. Many companies spent thousands of dollars in overhead and in trying to keep a nucleus of a force together, while not one nickel came in. The PWA was created in 1933 and a great many architects and contractors went back to work.[57]

Although it carried out its work by force account, relying on the federal government to supervise public works construction directly, the WPA seriously contemplated following the PWA's example of constructing its projects under contracts. Army engineer Francis P. Harrington recalled that the issue of contracting WPA work "was one of the first things which I had to deal with when I came with the WPA" in 1935. Contracting, however, did not present the WPA with the flexibility it needed to maximize the use of relief labor. Perhaps more important, contractors did not like to employ relief workers. "Some of them will do it," Harrington observed, "but those who don't want to just don't do it and that is that."[58]

Not surprisingly, contractors objected to being cut out of the WPA's construction process. One trade journal titled its profile of Hopkins, "The High Prophet of No Profits." Hopkins's approach to public works, it opined, was "the negative one. He doesn't believe in contractors, contractors' organizations, or contractors' profits. He is the high prophet of no profits, indeed, for the entire industry, and his day labor activities are of the sort that tend to dig themselves into the governmental system, deeper

---

of Lloyd N. Beeker, Assistant Director of the Projects Control Division, 1936–1941," RG 135, NA.
[57] Ibid.
[58] "Proceedings Conference of State Administrators. Works Progress Administration," February 12–13, 1937, "100 Jan–Feb 37" folder, box 69, "Central Files: General 1935–1944. 100 Administration," RG 69, NA.

and deeper."[59] Another contractor complained to New Mexico Senator Bronson Cutting, "When you consider the part contractors have taken in the development of these United States, it hardly seems square to wipe us off the map." Supporting contractors were the building-trades workers, who lobbied senators and congressmen as they considered the $4.8 billion 1935 Emergency Relief Appropriation. One head of a plumbers' union wrote that the bill "will work a great hardship on private enterprise if the government enters the plumbing industry by direct purchase of materials, and employs all labor, disregarding the plumbing dealer, now struggling in each community to carry on business."[60]

Despite the complaints of the contractors, though, they did much better under Roosevelt than they had under the preceding, Republican, administrations. As John Kenneth Galbraith observed, while federal public works spending accounted for 21.6 percent of total construction between 1925 and 1929, thanks to increases under the New Deal (and, not least, the collapse of state, local, and private construction), this figure grew to more than 50 percent during each year between 1933 and 1939, with the exception of 1937.[61]

A "DILEMMA" AFTER ALL? THE WPA AND INFRASTRUCTURE

The PWA often tried to portray itself as the agency of serious construction, contrasting itself to an image of the WPA as an agency that only incidentally did things while handing money out to the unemployed on the relief rolls. Many, including New Dealers, participated in constructing these impressions of both programs. In 1939, one PWA official summed up what he considered to be "the difference" between the two agencies, terming the WPA a "work-relief agency" that provides direct employment through providing make-work, while describing the PWA as a "reemployment agency" that generates direct and indirect employment while building substantial infrastructure.[62]

59 "The High Prophet of No Profits," in *The Central Constructor*, May 7, 1936, "Hopkins Biographical Material" folder, box 2, entry 746, "Division of Information. Publications of the Federal Works Agency and Subordinate Agencies, 1936–1942," RG 69, NA.
60 W. G. Ransom to Senator Bronson Cutting, January 28, 1935, and John Strumquist to Cutting, January 29, 1935, both in "'Public Works Act' and Unemployment Relief Jan–Apr. 1935" folder, box 37, Bronson Cutting Papers, Manuscript Division, LC.
61 Galbraith, *Economic Effects of the Federal Public Works Expenditures*, 36–37.
62 "The Difference Between WPA and PWA," January 10, 1939, "090–Public Works Administration" folder, box 3, entry 746, "Division of Information. Publications of the Federal Works Agency and Subordinate Agencies, 1936–1942," RG 69, NA.

But was the central dilemma of New Deal public works truly a choice
between employing people and constructing projects? The WPA, in fact,
made significant contributions to the national estate, although few recognized this fact at the time. By 1941, WPA chief engineer Perry Fellows
told the WPA's regional chief engineers that "the average man in the
street, even the average Congressman, little realizes how excellent the
WPA program is and what strides we are making in honest-to-goodness
employment on projects that are so far above the so-called standard of
excellence on which contractors operate that there is no comparison."
For this state of ignorance, Fellows blamed WPA engineers for not doing
a better job of explaining the program to the press, and he blamed the
press for neglecting to report the "story" of good work being well done.[63]

The WPA's division of engineering and construction solicited plans
from local and state sponsors, reviewed them, and either approved the
projects or returned the plans to their sponsors for revision. For larger
or more complex projects, the WPA consulted with the Public Health
Service, the Corps of Engineers, the Civil Aeronautics Administration,
the Department of Agriculture, and the Public Roads Administration.
The WPA classified its construction projects into six categories: municipal engineering projects, airports, public buildings, highway and road
projects, conservation projects, and engineering surveys. Municipal engineering projects were traditionally associated with public works carried
out at the state and local levels. The WPA built over 67,000 miles of city
streets. Roughly 30,000 of these miles were paved with what the WPA
termed "high-type surface," composed of concrete, bituminous, or some
other hard substance. Next to these streets, the WPA added 24,000 miles
of new sidewalk while repairing 7,000 more; the WPA also built 25,000
miles of curb while repairing 3,000 other miles. During winter months
the WPA built water- and sewage-treatment plants, building or improving about 500 water-treatment facilities, 1,800 pumping stations, and
over 19,700 miles of water mains and distribution lines that connected
to over 880,000 consumer outlets. In rural areas, the WPA added 4,000
new water wells, repaired 2,000 more, and added or improved 3,700
storage tanks and reservoirs. WPA workers built or improved over 1,500
sewage-treatment plants and 200 incinerators. These workers built over
24,000 miles of storm and sanitary sewer lines; they also improved 3,000
miles of sewers. The WPA also built or repaired hundreds of thousands

[63] "Excerpt from Minutes of Conference Chief Regional Engineers Work Projects Administration," May 15, 1941, "F. H. Dryden" folder, box 1, entry 737, "Division of Information. Administrative Speeches, 1933–1942," RG 69, NA.

of manholes and catch basins, and built over 2.3 million sanitary privies. The WPA was responsible for improvements to approximately 8,000 parks. Its work ranged from landscaping and tree planting to the construction of swimming pools and even stadiums. Under WPA auspices, about 3,300 stadiums, grandstands, and bleachers were built, and roughly 12,800 playgrounds were constructed or improved.[64]

The WPA's airport program built new airports and upgraded older ones. The large amount of grading, drainage, paving, and other ground improvements called for in airport work allowed the WPA to put large numbers of unskilled workers to work quickly on these projects. While this factor made airports an appealing project for the WPA, the work was done in consultation with the Civil Aeronautics Administration, and later with the War and Navy Departments. Almost 1,200 new buildings were constructed at airports, and 2,800 were improved or rebuilt. The WPA built 350 new landing fields and enlarged or improved almost 700 others, adding to the nation's runways, taxi strips, aprons, and turning circles. All told, the WPA built more than 480 airports and improved 470 others.[65]

The WPA built a wide variety of public buildings, including state, county, and city government facilities, schools and recreational buildings, hospitals, prisons, and military and naval facilities. During the Depression, following a period of years during which the military was neglected, the WPA was responsible for "prompt, extensive, and continuous construction, reconstruction, rehabilitation, repair, and improvement work ... at almost every regular army post and naval establishment in the country."[66] The *Army and Navy Register* reinforced this point, stating, "In the years 1935 to 1939, when regular appropriations were so meager, it was the WPA worker who saved many army posts and naval stations from literal obsolescence."[67]

The WPA built almost 40,000 public buildings and made improvements on over 85,000 other buildings. Public schools benefited from WPA work: Almost 6,000 new schools were built, 2,170 additions built on to older schools, and 31,000 schools modernized. Over 1,000 libraries were built or improved. The WPA built over 9,300 auditoriums and gymnasiums, and it improved 5,800 other buildings. Over 226 hospitals were

---

[64] *Final Report on the WPA*, 49–50.
[65] Ibid., 51; 85. For more on New Deal public works during World War II, see Chapter 7.
[66] Ibid., 52.
[67] Ibid., 85.

built, and 156 hospitals improved, by the WPA. WPA workers also built 6,400 office buildings, over 7,000 dormitories, 6,000 storage buildings, 900 armories, 2,700 firehouses, 760 buildings at various penal institutions, as well as a variety of other structures.

The WPA built and improved streets and roads in urban and rural areas. The WPA built roughly 572,000 miles of rural roads; 57,000 of these miles were constructed of such materials as concrete, bituminous, or macadam. The WPA constructed 78,000 new bridges and viaducts while improving over 46,000 structures. WPA workers also built more than 1,000 new tunnels. The WPA contributed a number of conservation projects to the nation, including projects dealing with water conservation, erosion control, and the sealing of abandoned coal mines. WPA workers also conducted a number of engineering surveys, improving the quality of maps and compiling data on boundaries, streams, and underground structures.[68]

Considered on a per capita basis, it is clear that sparsely populated western states that were the sites of substantial PWA construction, such as Montana, Nevada, and Wyoming, benefited more from PWA spending than from WPA funds. Previous analyses of New Deal spending have concurred that this imbalance most likely stemmed from political advantages (Nevada Senator Key Pittman, for example, was president pro tempore of the Senate). More directly, though, these western states were swing states in a political universe where other regions were known quantities. As such, the West could be wooed with a small amount of absolute funds that, per capita, turned out to be quite large indeed. Nevada, for example, ranked forty-sixth in the absolute allocation of funds, but first in per capita allocation.[69] Heavily populated states with large populations of the unemployed, such as New York, Illinois, Michigan, and Ohio, however, benefited more from Hopkins's WPA than from Ickes's PWA. Interestingly, however, several southern states emerge as rather unlikely per capita beneficiaries of PWA spending, in comparison to the WPA. (See Table 4.4) In states like Mississippi, North Carolina, South Carolina, and Virginia, PWA per capita spending nearly equaled or exceeded WPA per capita spending.

The South has generally been characterized, in the words of FDR, as "the Nation's No. 1 economic problem," reluctant to accept federal funds

[68] Ibid., 53–54.
[69] Reading, "New Deal Activity and the States," 794; and Wallis, "The Political Economy of New Deal Spending Revisited."

TABLE 4.4. *Per Capita Expenditures of the WPA and PWA, 1933–1941, in Dollars (States Listed by PWA Region)*

State	WPA	PWA (total)	PWA (federal)	PWA (nonfederal)
Region #1				
Connecticut	46	29	12	17
Delaware	30	42	20	22
Maine	27	35	29	6
Maryland	24	52	22	30
Massachusetts	75	25	12	13
New Hampshire	46	24	6	18
New Jersey	65	35	17	18
New York	82	36	7	29
Pennsylvania	74	29	8	21
Rhode Island	6	37	14	23
Vermont	32	21	11	10
Region #2				
Illinois	58	32	7	25
Indiana	20	25	6	19
Michigan	59	18	5	13
Ohio	78	26	10	16
West Virginia	56	31	16	15
Wisconsin	60	23	10	13
Region #3				
Alabama	29	18	5	13
Florida	50	40	18	22
Georgia	28	15	8	7
Kentucky	39	18	8	10
Mississippi	29	28	10	18
North Carolina	19	20	8	12
South Carolina	32	48	12	35
Tennessee	26	19	6	13
Virginia	20	48	35	13
Region #4				
Iowa	28	20	10	10
Minnesota	64	24	10	14
Missouri	6	25	11	14
Montana	88	170	132	38
Nebraska	45	68	15	53
North Dakota	59	22	12	10
South Dakota	66	26	15	11
Wyoming	49	112	91	21

State	WPA	PWA (total)	PWA (federal)	PWA (nonfederal)
Region #5				
Arkansas	36	24	12	12
Colorado	73	43	22	21
Kansas	45	25	11	14
Louisiana	40	25	13	12
New Mexico	64	68	50	18
Oklahoma	48	25	9	16
Texas	26	30	11	19
Region #6				
Arizona	58	133	105	28
California	60	35	16	19
Nevada	66	352	325	27
Utah	58	53	35	18
Region #7				
Idaho	51	46	34	12
Oregon	60	71	53	18
Washington	64	72	50	22
District of Columbia and Territories				
Washington, D.C.	–	254	191	63
Alaska	–	101	73	28
Hawaii	–	58	45	13
Puerto Rico	–	11	2	9
Virgin Islands	–	205	198	7

Sources: PWA figures calculated from Table A-40, July 1, 1941, "July 1 1941" folder, box 2, entry 61, "Statistical Materials Relating to PWA Projects, 1934–1942"; and Table SP-1369, December 19, 1939, "Quota Studies (Population and Distribution)" folder, box 3, entry 30, "Records of the Project Control Division, Subject Files, 1933–1940"; both in RG 135, NA. WPA figures taken from Leonard Arrington, "The New Deal in the West: A Preliminary Statistical Inquiry," *Pacific Historical Review* 38 (Aug. 1969): 315–16. Note: WPA figures run through 1939; PWA federal figures run through July 1941; PWA nonfederal figures run through December 19, 1939. Spending per capita calculated using population figures from the 1930 census.

and the threat to local control these funds implied.[70] When considering the full range of government expenditures, historian Jordan Schwarz

[70] FDR quoted in Bruce J. Schulman, *From Cotton Belt to Sunbelt: Federal Policy, Economic Development, and the Transformation of the South, 1938–1980* (Durham: Duke University Press, 1994), 3.

concluded that during the New Deal, even with "a sympathetic President and control in Congress, the South missed an opportunity to feed at the federal trough."[71] Comparing just the WPA and PWA, however, indicates that some southern states had a marked preference for Ickes's public works program, even though that program maintained quotas for black employment on PWA contracts.[72] In 1956, William Faulkner declared of the South, "Our economy is no longer agricultural. Our economy is the federal government."[73] As early as the 1930s, however, in the realm of public works, the federal government was already making important inroads into the South.[74]

A PUBLIC WORKS REVOLUTION

As the WPA and PWA built public works across the nation, transforming the physical landscape of the nation and making the case for the New Deal in cement, mortar, and steel, New Dealers underscored this revolution with their words. Few did it as eloquently as Jerome Frank. Frank, a brilliant lawyer educated at the University of Chicago, served as general counsel to the Agricultural Adjustment Agency, worked as an adviser to Ickes and the PWA on legal matters, and then took over as head of the Securities and Exchange Commission when FDR appointed William O. Douglas to the Supreme Court.[75] In a speech he made to the Harvard Business Club at the close of 1938, Frank demonstrated the central place of public works programs to the New Dealers' interpretation of history, and to their sense of the New Deal's existence as a political undertaking. Nineteenth-century America, Frank proclaimed, was "an era of the most stupendous pump-priming in the history of the modern world. Our continent was developed by individual private initiative – but that private initiative was stimulated and aided, and its exploits were made possible, by billions and billions of dollars of gifts from the government of these United States." By comparison, Frank argued, "the pump-priming of the

---

[71] Schwarz, *New Dealers*, 321.

[72] Marc W. Kruman, "Quotas for Blacks: The Public Works Administration and the Black Construction Worker," *Labor History* 16 (Winter 1975): 37–51.

[73] William Faulkner, "On Fear," in James B. Meriwether, ed., *Essays, Speeches and Public Letters by William Faulkner* (New York: Random House, 1965), 98.

[74] For more on the relationship between the South and the federal government in the twentieth century, the key work is Schulman, *From Cotton Belt to Sunbelt*.

[75] For more on Frank, see Schwarz, *New Dealers*, 177–94.

last few years is trifling." During the nineteenth century, he continued, public lands, forests, oil wells, and mines were transferred to private hands, spurring the construction of railroads and the growth of domestic industry. "Surely," Frank declared, "a country whose amazing development was based on Nineteenth Century pump-priming – on Nineteenth Century gigantic government aid to private enterprise – will not arrest its present development, and stifle its amazing potential future growth, merely because governmental aid to private enterprise must now take on a new form. What has mockingly been dubbed 'spending our way to prosperity' via government aid, is nothing new. It was the technique of Nineteenth Century America." Driving the point home, Frank concluded that this pump-priming "was essentially sound and conservative then, and it is sound and conservative now."[76]

Frank rallied New Dealers to a program of government investment and economic development, including the construction of low-cost housing, express highways, parks and playgrounds, schools and hospitals, reforestation to prevent floods and erosion, railroad modernization, the development of the South "and other parts of our 'internal frontier,'" among other items. "Such projects," Frank argued, "call for many billions of dollars of legitimate government investment over a period of many years, yielding us lasting physical improvements of the highest economic and social value, and unquestionably supplying us with that needed stimulus to private initiative which spells national prosperity." Referring to the dangers of fascism and communism, Frank stated that a program of public works construction, "sustaining our kind of civilization, is the intelligent alternative to dictatorship."[77] Indeed, the apparent success experienced by Hitler's Germany in using public works programs to address mass unemployment, especially between 1933 and 1936, reminded New Dealers of the high stakes of their moment.[78]

---

[76] Jerome Frank, Address before the Harvard Business Club, December 8, 1938, "Special Files. New Deal Era. Speeches & Writings Files. Speech File. Frank, Jerome N. 1938–1940" folder, box 218, Thomas G. Corcoran Papers, Manuscript Division, LC.

[77] Ibid.

[78] Dan P. Silverman, *Hitler's Economy: Nazi Work Creation Programs, 1933–1936* (Cambridge: Harvard University Press, 1998); Harold James, *The German Slump: Politics and Economics, 1924–1936* (New York: Oxford University Press, 1986); and R. J. Overy, *War and Economy in the Third Reich* (New York: Oxford University Press, 1994). For comparative treatments of the U.S. and Germany, see, e.g., Alan Dawley, *Struggles for Justice: Social Responsibility and the Liberal State* (Cambridge: Harvard University Press, 1991);

Frank's emphasis on creating a "usable past" for the New Deal and its public works was echoed by a range of New Dealers.[79] Given the ability of programs like the PWA and WPA to provide public works to the western and southern regions of the nation, however, it should not come as a surprise to find that politicians from these regions shared an affection for economic development. In addressing Virginia's Jeffersonian Democratic Club in 1940, Washington Senator Lewis Schwellenbach outlined for his audience "the philosophy of the democracy of the far West," so that "you good folks in Virginia can find some profit in understanding our political background on the Pacific Coast and why, in that area, there exists such substantial and enthusiastic support for the New Deal Administration of President Roosevelt." The animating spirit of the New Deal, Schwellenbach argued, was "the spirit of the Pioneer."[80] Anticipating objection to this claim, Schwellenbach continued, in a passage he often inserted into his speeches, "I know that right here the doubters and the scoffers will rise up and say that these pioneers had no governmental assistance. They did not get PWA grants. They had not CCC boys to build their trails. There were not any WPA jobs. They could not collect wheat checks

and John A. Garraty, "The New Deal, National Socialism, and the Great Depression," *American Historical Review* 78 (October 1973): 907–44.

[79] Historians, too, helped forge this usable past, enlisting Andrew Jackson and Thomas Jefferson into the pantheon of New Deal predecessors. For Jackson, see of course Arthur Schlesinger, Jr., *The Age of Jackson* (Boston: Little, Brown, 1945); and Schlesinger's acknowledgment that in many ways "*The Age of Jackson* voted for Franklin Delano Roosevelt," in his memoir, *A Life in the 20th Century: Innocent Beginnings, 1917–1950* (Boston: Houghton Mifflin, 2000), 360–63; for a revealing discussion of the creation of the New Deal's relationship to Jefferson see Merrill D. Peterson, *The Jefferson Image in the American Mind* (Charlottesville: University of Virginia Press, 1998), 330–458.

Similarly, during these years the Social Science Research Counsel sponsored a number of investigations into the history of the relationship between government and the economy, producing accounts that presented a precedent for the New Deal. See, for example, Oscar Handlin and Mary Flug Handlin, *Commonwealth: A Study of the Role of Government in the American Economy: Massachusetts, 1774–1861* (Cambridge: Harvard University Press, 1947); and Louis Hartz, *Economic Policy and Democratic Thought: Pennsylvania, 1776–1860* (Cambridge: Harvard University Press, 1948). For an excellent review of this literature, see Harry N. Scheiber, "Government and the Economy: Studies of the 'Commonwealth' Policy in Nineteenth-Century America," *Journal of Interdisciplinary History* 3 (Summer 1972): 135–51.

[80] Lewis Schwellenbach, Address before the Jeffersonian Democratic Club, May 4, 1940, "1940" folder, box 3, Lewis B. Schwellenbach Papers, Manuscript Division, LC.

or old age pensions. That is absolutely true." However, Schwellenbach argued:

Don't let anyone tell you that government bounties were not being given in those days. The difference was that the real pioneers who grubbed and slaved and really developed the country got none of them. The railroads got their sections of land in each township to encourage their efforts. Vast tracts of timber lands were made available for spoilation [*sic*] by the timber operators. The mineral and oil resources were quickly acquired by a greedy few. A protective tariff system was maintained by which hidden taxes were removed from the pockets of everyone who labored in industry or agriculture. A system of financial control was fostered and protected which resulted in increased cost on everything which was purchased or sold. Government did not bother business in those days. It couldn't. Why? For the simple reason that business wouldn't let it. In those days, business ran government. There were bounties galore. But the people who worked, and who bought and consumed our products never got in on them.[81]

New Dealers, then, framed the public works of the PWA and WPA – as well as the entire New Deal, itself – as following in a long history of using government to foster economic development, with the key difference being that this time "the people" rather than "the interests" would benefit. Focused as they have been on the question of employment, however, historians have concluded that the public works programs came up short, leaving the promise of the New Deal unrealized. Judging these programs by what they accomplished, however, rather than by what they failed to do, it is clear that these agencies performed impressively, bringing roads, schools, courthouses, post offices, airports, and other improvements to almost every county in the nation. They helped to spur dramatic advances in economic productivity, carving out a middle way between advocates of laissez-faire and proponents of national ownership of industry. Instead of recognizing these far-reaching achievements, historians such as Arthur Schlesinger, Jr., have fixed on the deep and bitter personality conflict between Harold Ickes and Harry Hopkins, portraying the PWA and WPA as pawns in a "battle for relief," rather than as programs that remade the nation.[82] These programs were not simply the backdrop to a clash of

---

[81] Lewis Schwellenbach speech, July 15, 1938, "Speeches & Writings File. 1938" folder, box 3, Schwellenbach Papers, LC. For a recent historical treatment that has much in common with Schwellenbach's analysis, see Elizabeth Sanders, *Roots of Reform: Farmers, Workers, and the American State, 1877–1919* (Chicago: University of Chicago Press, 1999).

[82] Arthur Schlesinger, Jr., *The Politics of Upheaval* (Boston: Houghton Mifflin, 1960), 343–61. For a dissent from Schlesinger's account, see Felix Frankfurter to Arthur

egos, nor were they, as another historian recently suggested of the WPA, simply Prozac that improved the deflated morale of Americans.[83] The public works programs of the New Deal were more than this: They built a public works revolution in the United States.

Schlesinger, Jr., June 18, 1963, in reel 62, Felix Frankfurter Papers, LC. Washington, D.C.

[83] June Hopkins, "The American Way to Welfare: Harry Hopkins and New Deal Work Relief," in Byron W. Daynes, William D. Pederson, and Michael P. Riccards, eds., *The New Deal and Public Policy* (New York: St. Martin's Press, 1996), 241, n. 45. A number of historians have stressed the WPA's role in uplifting morale; see, for example, Barbara Blumberg, *The New Deal and the Unemployed: The View from New York City* (Lewisburg, PA: Bucknell University Press, 1979), 302.

FIGURE 1. The Triborough Bridge connected the New York City boroughs of Queens, Manhattan, and the Bronx. One of 388 bridges and viaducts built or improved by the PWA; the WPA also built 78,000 bridge and viaduct projects and improved 46,000 others.

FIGURE 2. This water purification works, built in Cincinnati, Ohio, is one of 2,419 waterworks projects built by the PWA. The WPA constructed over 1,500 such projects.

FIGURE 3. The Alameda County Courthouse, in Oakland, California, is one of 295 courthouses built by the PWA.

FIGURE 4. Built in the Hollywood Hills by the PWA, this reservoir and water system is part of the Los Angeles water-supply network.

FIGURE 5. The PWA increased the Hetch Hetchy Reservoir in Tuolumne County, California, by expanding the O'Shaughnessy Dam from 226 feet to 312 feet.

FIGURE 6. The PWA enlarged the Port of Oakland, California, increasing wharf space and the outer harbor terminal.

FIGURE 7. The state capitol building in Salem, Oregon, is one of 4,287 public building projects built by the PWA. The WPA built almost 40,000 such public buildings.

FIGURE 8. One of five coastal bridges built in Oregon by the PWA, this project helped provide an uninterrupted highway along the West Coast between the Columbia River and California.

FIGURE 9. The Pierre S. DuPont High School, in Wilmington, Delaware, is one of 7,488 school projects built by the PWA. The WPA built 6,000 schools, modernized 31,000 more, and constructed additions at 2,170 schools.

FIGURE 10. This surgical hospital building, part of the State Tuberculosis Sanitarium in Hopemont, West Virginia, is one of 822 hospital projects built by the PWA. The WPA built over 225 hospital projects.

FIGURE 11. This overseas highway in the Florida Keys, built by the PWA, connected Key West to Miami.

FIGURE 12. The city of Mobile, Alabama, built this cold storage plant on its docks with a PWA loan and grant, to facilitate the shipping of fruit and other products.

FIGURE 13. The administration building, constructed at the municipal airport in Fort Worth, Texas, is part of the 342 airport-related projects built by the PWA. The WPA built 480 airports and improved 470 others.

FIGURE 14. Built by the PWA, the Davidson County Courthouse, in Nashville, Tennessee, took up an entire city block. It contains all of the county and municipal offices, four courtrooms, and the county jail.

FIGURE 15. This armory in Minneapolis, Minnesota, is another example of the 4,287 public buildings built by the PWA.

FIGURE 16. Built by the PWA, the Allegheny County Bridge connects Pittsburgh and Homestead, Pennsylvania, across the Monongahela River.

FIGURE 17. The Central Fire Station in Louisville, Kentucky, was built with a grant from the PWA.

FIGURE 18. Built by the PWA, the surgical operating and ward building, Boston City Hospital, contains beds for 300 patients and 20 different operating rooms.

FIGURE 19. The De Pere, Wisconsin, public library is one of 105 public libraries built by the PWA. The WPA built or improved over 1,000 public libraries.

FIGURE 20. This grade school was built in Parco, Wyoming, by the PWA. By July 1936, the PWA had built schools in 47 percent of all counties in the United States.

FIGURE 21. The Williamsburg Houses, built in Brooklyn, New York, with funds from the PWA, provided homes for over 1,600 families.

FIGURE 22. The PWA built the U.S.S. *Yorktown*, which launched in 1936. Other PWA defense-related projects include 16 destroyers, 4 heavy destroyers, and over 130 combat airplanes.

FIGURE 23. PWA funds built the Federal Trade Commission Building in Washington, D.C., part of a larger set of New Deal public works projects that transformed the nation's capital.

FIGURE 24. The U.S. Bullion Depository at Fort Knox, Kentucky, was built using PWA funds under the supervision of the Treasury Department's Procurement Division.

5

"Boondoggling" and the Welfare State

The welfare state built during the New Deal, measured as a percentage both of gross national product and of total government spending, surpassed contemporaneous efforts by all major industrial countries, including Germany, the United Kingdom, France, and Sweden. After 1935, the core of this welfare state was represented by the Works Progress Administration. In building its public works projects, the WPA provoked two kinds of hostile responses: The first consisted of charges that its projects were wasteful "boondoggles" and the second of accusations that the agency was injecting politics into the business of providing relief to the unemployed. Republican Alf Landon joined these critiques into a unified attack in his 1936 campaign against President Roosevelt. The nation's budget would be balanced under a Landon administration, he declared, "by cutting out waste and extravagance; by putting an end to the use of public funds for political purposes; by restoring hard-working, painstaking, commonsense administration." These themes of attack, however, led to varying outcomes.[1]

While accusations of boondoggling and "politics in relief" generated a colorful discourse about the inability of government to produce useful accomplishments, during Roosevelt's first term in office they did not give the New Deal's opponents much political traction. FDR and the Democratic Party enjoyed great success at the ballot box, particularly in 1934 and 1936. Even though Congress grew more conservative after 1938,

---

[1] Edwin Amenta, *Bold Relief: Institutional Politics and the Origins of Modern American Social Policy* (Princeton: Princeton University Press, 1998), 5; Landon quoted in Donald R. McCoy, *Landon of Kansas* (Lincoln: University of Nebraska Press, 1966), 314.

opponents of the New Deal made no effort to earmark appropriations for WPA projects, leaving the final decisions about what to build (and where to build it) to the agency's administrators. Throughout the WPA's existence, governmental bodies at the county, city, township, and village level planned and proposed the bulk of the projects funded by the WPA. State and local governments also contributed public moneys to these projects, voting their own dollars in favor of the WPA's presence in their communities. One survey indicated that 93 percent of communities found the WPA's projects were "badly needed and of benefit."[2]

Indeed, while construction changed the landscape and made a physical argument for the WPA's contribution to communities, New Dealers, inspired in part by economist John Maynard Keynes, developed the intellectual scaffolding to justify the federal government's investment in public works. In their view, public works spending was the critical policy lever to be pulled in order to move the economy out of a depression. Drawing in differing degrees on Keynes's work, Americans like Stuart Chase, Lauchlin Currie, Marriner Eccles, and Mordecai Ezekiel also relied on home-grown precedents, such as William Trufant Foster and Waddill Catchings's *The Road to Plenty*, to advance the argument that deficit spending could stimulate increased consumption. From the perspective of these aggregated views of the economy and the state, it did not matter too much how New Deal money was allocated as long as it was spent. Keynes himself captured this notion in a memorable passage in his *General Theory of Employment, Interest, and Money*:

If the Treasury were to fill old bottles with banknotes, bury them at suitable depths in disused coalmines which are then filled up to the surface with town rubbish, and leave it to private enterprise on well-tried principles of laissez-faire to dig the notes up again ... there need be no more unemployment.... It would, indeed be more sensible to build houses and the like; but if there are political and practical difficulties in the way of this, the above would be better than nothing.

Keynes illustrated his thinking in more graphic fashion when he traveled to Washington, D.C., in 1934 and stayed at the Mayflower Hotel. When a visiting New Deal economist carefully took a single towel from a

---

[2] Federal Works Agency, *Final Report on the WPA Program 1935–1943* (Washington, D.C.: U.S. Government Printing Office, 1947), 9; and *U.S. Community Improvement Appraisal: A Report on the Work Program of the Works Progress Administration* (Washington, D.C.: National Appraisal Committee, 1939), 7. Of course, a number of factors account for the success of the Democratic party and FDR during this period; see especially John M. Allswang, *The New Deal and American Politics: A Study in Political Change* (New York: John Wiley & Sons, Inc., 1978).

large stack in Keynes's bathroom, so as not to be wasteful, Keynes reacted by overturning the entire stack with one grand gesture. His method, Keynes argued, would generate more work and thus better stimulate the overall economy. Mordecai Ezekiel echoed this notion when he suggested "virtually scattering money from airplanes" in order to inject government funds into circulation.[3]

FDR himself undertook a defense of the WPA's public works against charges that they produced boondoggles. In the course of making some informal remarks to the New Jersey State Emergency Council, Roosevelt commented, "If we can 'boondoggle' ourselves out of this depression, that word is going to be enshrined in the hearts of the American people for many years to come." On another occasion, while dedicating a new stadium built with federal money in Detroit, FDR declared, "Some people in this country have called it 'boondoggling' for us to build stadiums and parks and forests and to improve the recreational facilities of the Nation. My friends, if this stadium can be called boondoggling, then I am for boondoggling, and so are you." Republicans like Landon, however, rejected the arguments of New Dealers in their entirety and completely dismissed Keynes's theory. Landon scorned Keynes's thinking as "amazing," and argued that what the New Dealers had really decided was that "if $400 million a month of useful projects would be good medicine, $600 million a month thrown around at random would be even better."[4]

Although accusations of boondoggling failed to generate immediate political results, a second set of arguments was more successful. In charting the rise and fall of the WPA's fortunes, the issue of politics and patronage at the local level provides a surer guide to the power and limits of the WPA and the New Deal state. Linking the previous chapter's focus on the variety, scale, and distribution of public works projects across the nation with the next chapter's emphasis on the political consequences of economic development, I will examine in this chapter the difficulties and challenges that confronted the WPA. Activities at the WPA's project sites ultimately led Congress in 1939 to pass the Hatch Act – a measure

[3] John Maynard Keynes, *The General Theory of Employment, Interest, and Money* (New York: Harcourt Brace Jovanovich, 1964), 129; Alan Brinkley, *The End of Reform: New Deal Liberalism in Recession and War* (New York: Alfred A. Knopf, 1995), 65–85; Jordan A. Schwarz, *The New Dealers: Power Politics in the Age of Roosevelt* (New York: Alfred A. Knopf, 1993), 186; for Keynes's behavior, see Robert Skidelsky, *John Maynard Keynes: The Economist as Savior, 1920–1937* (New York: Penguin, 1992), 505.
[4] Samuel I. Rosenman, ed., *The Public Papers and Addresses of Franklin D. Roosevelt* (New York: Russell & Russell, 1938), 5:58; 59; 495; and McCoy, *Landon of Kansas*, 314–15.

designed to prevent "pernicious political activities" – but no legislator ever proposed an "Anti-Boondoggling Act."

The WPA relied on its division of investigation to keep a close eye on project sites. Representing an expanded version of the division of special inquiry of the Federal Emergency Relief Administration (FERA), this section of the WPA relied on both the Public Works Administration's investigators and the Federal Bureau of Investigation to train roughly half of its personnel. Nicknamed the "W–Men," WPA investigators looked into allegations of fraud, corruption, and the misuse of WPA funds and equipment. Over the course of eight years, they generated reports on 17,352 complaints. Of this total, 8,811 complaints were validated by investigators; 2,215 cases were handed over to the attorney general; and 4,496 people were dismissed, demoted, reprimanded, or suspended from the WPA. These investigators, along with the other administrative personnel employed by the New Deal, were so active that they provoked the Republican Party to include a plank in its 1936 platform charging that the New Deal "has created a vast multitude of new offices, filled them with its favorites, set up a centralized bureaucracy, and sent out swarms of inspectors to harass our people."[5] While the reports issuing from these investigations focus on the implementation of policy at the local level, when taken as a whole they provide a detailed account of how public works programs literally built the New Deal across the United States, county by county, precinct by precinct.

THE WPA: THE VIEW FROM WASHINGTON, D.C.

As the Works Progress Administration swung into action, its importance to FDR and his advisers could not be overrated. Postmaster General and head of the Democratic National Committee, James Farley, noted the mood in Roosevelt's inner circle. Farley recorded this cautionary note in his diary: "The Work Relief Program, if handled advantageously, will of course bring fine results, but if placed in the hands of those who are not in sympathy with the President's program, the results will of course be detrimental. I am satisfied that the President realizes the importance of this. I know that he has instructed Frank Walker, Harry Hopkins and Secretary Ickes about the political features involved." Farley thought that the

[5] Charles, *Minister of Relief*, 136–37; *Final Report on the WPA*, 81–83; and Arthur W. MacMahon, John D. Millett, and Gladys Ogden, *The Administration of Federal Work Relief* (Chicago: Public Administration Service, 1941), 212; 236–38.

fate of FDR's reelection depended both on the strength of the Democratic Party's organization and the ability of the WPA to augment the party. The president's political future, he wrote, "will depend upon the proper handling of the Work Relief Program and the clearing up of existing conditions which cause the failure of our political organizations to properly function."[6]

In June 1935, after dining at the White House with an intimate group that included Felix Frankfurter, Joseph P. Kennedy, pollster Emil Hurja, and Harry Hopkins, FDR and company relaxed by watching three reels of movies shot of WPA activities in and around Los Angeles. This footage, Farley noted, "showed the splendid opportunity for propaganda of this kind," and the group debated the advantages of circulating the cinematic material. Farley, Hurja, and FDR adjourned to pore over the latest polling figures and discussed how the WPA could be "correctly handled" so as to help the administration's political prospects.[7]

Farley regularly consulted on a range of issues with Hopkins and his WPA assistants, including Aubrey Williams and Colonel Lawrence Westbrook. Westbrook, Farley noted, "understands the political side of the situation [and] will render, I am sure, a real service to Hopkins and the Administration." Farley clarified what he meant by "the political side" when he recorded his assessment of Hopkins in his diary. "I don't mean that he should be guided by a political basis only, but I mean he should not do anything to antagonize those who are instrumental in the success of the party."[8] Farley went off the record at a press conference in order to answer questions about the WPA in New York State, where he thought the supervisory personnel on WPA projects, such as foremen and time-keepers, could be counted on to help the Democratic Party. While some of these workers were, as Farley noted, "peeved" because they thought they were underpaid, he pointed out that "if it wasn't for the WPA they wouldn't have a job."[9]

The attitude he displayed toward the WPA led conservative newspaper columnist Frank Kent to nickname him "Jobmaster Farley," and, for similar reasons, to give Pennsylvania Senator Joseph Guffey the moniker

[6] James A. Farley diary, May 15, 1935, "Private File 1935 May–June" folder, box 38, James A. Farley Papers, LC.

[7] Farley diary, June 18, 1935, in ibid.

[8] Farley diary, July 23, 1935, "Private File 1935 July 19–31" folder, box 38, Farley Papers, LC.

[9] Press Conference minutes, October 10, 1936, "Subject File Pres. Campaigns 1936. Press Conferences 1936 Sept. 26–Oct. 10" folder, box 55, Farley Papers, LC.

"WPA Guffey." Although Guffey felt that roughly 70 to 80 percent of the WPA workforce could be counted on to vote for FDR and the Democratic Party, some party officials urged Farley to become even more active on behalf of the program. One wrote from Springfield, Illinois, to Farley, commenting, "Quietly, I think the WPA should intensify their political activity the last two weeks of the [1936] campaign amongst their non-relief workers because we are getting the blame for the WPA being in politics, anyway." Other Democrats, such as Chester Atkinson, the mayor of Troy, New York, stressed that FDR needed to make his case to WPA employees, since "WPA workers, I have found, are inclined to be chronically discontented and, while accepting the work relief, are apt to lay all their real or imagined grievances to the Federal Government and it is only with argument that they become aware that they would be a lot worse off without President Roosevelt."[10]

The political impact of Hopkins's Works Progress Administration and Harold Ickes's Public Works Administration far exceeded their possible advantages to the Democratic Party's organizational capabilities, however. Farley himself noted, as the 1936 election approached, that Ickes would be able to "go in every state and point with pride to the accomplishments of his Department." The tangible results of the public works programs – the projects themselves – were physical advertisements for the New Deal, just as explicitly as the signs posted next to the projects that proclaimed "Built by the WPA" or "Built by the PWA." Indeed, FDR's 1936 campaign schedule was designed to showcase the president before a number of the New Deal's public works projects. One of FDR's trips, for example, took the president to a dam in Vermont, federal buildings in New Hampshire, and public works projects in New York City.

Farley's thoughts about Connecticut were extrapolated across the country: The administration believed that "there isn't a county in the state where the PWA, the WPA, etc., haven't done a great deal of good, and that the people should be made to realize this." Farley thought these achievements gave traditionally Republican voters a reason to vote for FDR, too. As he told a group of journalists, at one campaign stop a man came up to tell him that he was going to vote for FDR because he was able

[10] Guffey quoted in Press Conference minutes, October 14, 1936, 3 p.m., "Subject File Pres. Campaigns 1936 Press Conferences 1936 October 11–25" folder; and John Stelle to Farley, September 26, 1936, "Subject File Pres. Campaigns 1936 State Reports Del.–Ill. (Emil Hurja Papers)" folder; both in box 55, Farley Papers, LC; and Chester J. Atkinson to Farley, no date [early October 1936], "Subject File Pres. Campaigns 1936 State Reports New Mex–New York (Emil Hurja Papers)" folder, box 56, Farley Papers, LC.

to refinance the mortgage on his home, thanks to the Home Owners' Loan Corporation, and his community was building a new school, thanks to the WPA.[11] As the 1936 election grew closer, Farley increasingly emphasized the importance of the infrastructure built by the New Deal's public works programs, going so far as to tell Hopkins, "I thought it was a mistake to do much talking on relief." Farley preferred Ickes – and infrastructure – to be the public face of the administration when it came to the subject of public works.[12]

THE POLITICS OF "BOONDOGGLING"

Local papers across the country were filled with tributes to the useful infrastructure built by the WPA. In Decatur, Illinois, one paper opined, "Few persons... seem to know about the astonishing permanent benefits this city, and county, are gaining through the operation of WPA. The uninformed continued to talk about 'boondoggling,' the supposed squandering of public funds, the idleness of men employed upon federal projects." In Decatur, however, "property owners and taxpayers for years to come will receive dividends upon the work done this year by the men and women who are happy to work for the relief they receive." The proof? "As a starting point, to check the statement for yourself, drive to the far eastern sections of the city, or to the far western sections adjacent to Grand avenue. In either locality will be found miles of streets – formerly mud lanes, rutted and unsightly, impassable during much of the year and always a discouragement to civic pride – now made over into well-graded streets, curbed, drained and cindered for year-around use."[13]

The Kentucky *Courier Journal* noted that "in the casual public eye" the WPA has been "the most maligned New Deal organization," the only one "to acquire a standard joke of its own – the joke about WPA told in a million sets of circumstances." However, the paper continued, "WPA has done a job of slugging that would have worn private enterprise to a

[11] Farley diary, March 24, 1936, and June 1, 1936, both in "Private File 1936 March" folder, box 38, Farley Papers, LC; Farley diary, August 12, 1936, "Private File 1936 August 1–15" folder, box 38, Farley Papers, LC; and Press Conference minutes, October 10, 1936, "Subject File Pres. Campaigns 1936. Press Conferences 1936 Sept. 26–Oct. 10" folder, box 55, Farley Papers, LC.

[12] Farley diary, August 22, 1936, "Private File 1936 August 16–31" folder, box 38, Farley Papers, LC.

[13] "Value Received," clipping from the *Decatur Sunday Herald*, May 24, 1936, "610 Illinois March 1, 1936" folder, box 1182, "Work Projects Administration. Central Files: State 1935–1944. Illinois 610 Special Litigation," Record Group 69, Records of the Works Progress Administration, National Archives, Washington, D.C.

frazzle. Spending billions distributed in every corner of the Nation, WPA has never had an appreciable scandal. Local sore spots have been treated promptly." Indeed, "they can laugh at the WPA joke, but the WPA record speaks for itself!"[14]

With the coming of war, the WPA's utility was praised with renewed vigor, and from unlikely corners. Even the staunchly conservative *Boston Herald*, for example, conceded that while the WPA "has been the butt of many jokes and the subject of considerable criticism" in the past, "during the past year or even during the past few months, however, the situation, in this state at any rate, has changed markedly. It would be difficult, indeed, to prove any substantial charges of 'boondoggling' today."[15]

One New York paper also compared the stereotype of the WPA with its actual achievements. "The cruel, grossly unjust myth of the Great Shovel-Leaner has stuck" to the image of the WPA worker "like mud, despite the accumulating evidence of his first-rate contributions to the betterment of American life." The paper ticked off some of the WPA's triumphs: building and improving one-fifth of the nation's road mileage; constructing 30,000 public buildings and improving or enlarging 50,000 more; building the schools that allowed one million kids to learn; building 73,000 new bridges and viaducts and rebuilding 44,000 others; installing over 35,000 miles of water and sewer lines; and building, improving, or expanding 875 civilian and military airports. General George C. Marshall himself offered praise, stating: "In the great task of preparing for national defense the WPA has proved itself an invaluable aid."[16]

The WPA's increased focus on national security and defense public works produced notable achievements. But these triumphs were hard won. What looked good in 1943 did not appear as clear-cut in 1935, when the debates over the utility of WPA infrastructure first unfolded. At stake was the political power of the New Deal, itself. Critics, including Republicans, organizations such as the American Liberty League, and newspapers

[14] Richard Renneisen, "WPA Has Done Its Job Well," clipping from the Kentucky *Courier Journal*, February 16, 1942, "Ky. 610 Jan 1941, Jan 1942" folder, box 1377, "Work Projects Administration. Central Files: State 1935–1944. Kentucky 610 Special Litigation," RG 69, NA.

[15] "WPA in Time of War," clipping from *Boston Herald*, April 30, 1942, "610 Mass. 1942" folder, box 1494, "Work Projects Administration. Central Files: State 1935–1944. Massachusetts 610 Special Litigation," RG 69, NA.

[16] Albert Deutsch, "WPA's Record as an Investment is Better than Its Reputation," clipping from unidentified New York newspaper, November 9, 1941, "610 Mass. 1940–1941" folder, box 1493, "Work Projects Administration. Central Files: State 1935–1944. Massachusetts 610 Special Litigation," RG 69, NA.

such as the *New York Sun* tried to undermine public approval of the program. They accused the WPA of waste and graft, and tarred it with the term "boondoggle." The *New York Sun* made particularly effective use of this notion, publishing a daily column decrying "Today's Boon-Doggle." This term merits close scrutiny. Not only did it carry heavy ideological freight for the opponents of the New Deal; it has also shaped the historical legacy of the WPA. The WPA's division of information kept close track of these charges, assigning a WPA employee, Amy MacMaster, to research each allegation. The *Sun's* column was especially troubling to the WPA, as it was picked up immediately by the program's opponents and recycled into many pamphlets, speeches, and articles that attacked the WPA.

The *Sun* relied on a common formula in its columns on boondoggling. By putting forth the assumption that all projects approved by the WPA would go into operation immediately, the paper could claim that a huge number of projects were being built in isolated areas. The WPA's policy of approving large numbers of projects reflected instead its desire to create a reserve (or, as WPA officials put it, a "reservoir") of projects ready to be constructed if unemployment shot up in a particular area. The *Sun's* columnists emphasized projects proposed for sparsely populated areas in order to portray the New Deal as spending an extraordinarily large amount of money when viewed on a per capita basis. This strategy had the added benefit of depicting even obviously useful projects (roads, dams, and the like) as ludicrous, since they were seemingly being built in the "middle of nowhere." The *Sun* also regularly ignored the locality's contribution to the project, thus eliminating evidence that a city or town wanted (and, indeed, had proposed) the project that was being built with WPA funds.

In short, MacMaster declared, "The New York Sun has been knocking down a series of straw men." To illustrate her conclusion, she examined a column that appeared in the *Sun* on March 13, 1936, taking as its subject the WPA projects planned for Clayton, New Mexico (population 2,512):

[Clayton] is served by two railroads, has an express agency, a post office, a bank, a telegraph station and even an airport.... Yet President Roosevelt has approved the following WPA projects for Clayton: Construct farm-to-market road, $121,408; construct farm-to-market road to Hayden (a road linking Hayden and Clayton already exists), $16,337; construct road, $42,218; construct farm-to-market road, $26,788; improve three farm-to-market roads, $142,354; improve roadway and move fence, $26,486; improve state road No. 58, $29,458; improve streets, $15,783; construct culverts, spillways and drains, $20,629; move bridge, $6,753; replace water service lines, $24,890; improve distribution system, $24,937; improve park, $1,050; construct five school buildings, $12,252; and construct community center, $12,555.

The total authorized expenditure is $522,893, or $209 per inhabitant. The question arises how the citizens of this little metropolis managed to eke out an existence prior to the advent of Harry Hopkins and the adoption of boon-doggling as a national pastime.[17]

In response to this array of charges, MacMaster assembled what she simply termed "The Facts." MacMaster argued that the list reflected projects that were approved, but were not necessarily being built. "Everyone conversant with the workings of the WPA knows that more projects have been approved than will be operated. It is essential that a reservoir of approved projects be available at all times to be placed in operation as unemployment conditions demand." She next quoted the Clayton city manager, who stated that the actual per capita expenditure on WPA projects currently being built was less than $22, not $209, as the *Sun* had claimed. Further, the farm-to-market roads would benefit all of Union County (population 11,036), not simply Clayton's 2,512 inhabitants. In fact, less than one-sixth of the projects the *Sun* itemized would take place inside Clayton's city limits. The entire county needed these projects, as the area was "a part of the 'dust bowl' and many of the inhabitants can do nothing but wait for a return of enough rain to irrigate their lands. For the present they are on relief." Indeed, the *Clayton News* attacked the *Sun*'s charges:

The *Sun* is merely trying to make the citizens of the East believe that the citizens of the West and Union County in particular, at least in this one editorial, are trying to profit at government expense when the truth is that the very projects they are deploring are not only worthwhile but are the only means of feeding more than a thousand families suffering not from depression but drouth [sic].[18]

MacMaster performed a similar analysis of projects attacked by the *Sun* in Phoenix, Arizona; Hardin, Montana; Eufaula, Oklahoma; Grand Forks, North Dakota; Boulder, Colorado; Arcadia, Missouri; and Adelino, New Mexico.

The Republican National Committee and the American Liberty League kept up the barrage of boondoggling charges. In addition to questioning

---

[17] Amy MacMaster, "Analysis of New York Sun 'Today's Boon-Doggle' Column," "36-5-16–Wright–Boondoggling" folder, box 2, entry 732, "Division of Information. Records Relating to Boondoggling Charges, ('Attacks on WPA'), 1936–1939," RG 69, NA.
[18] Ibid.

a project's utility or location, these critics also took on the easy target of the WPA's white-collar projects. One such project, employing out-of-work professionals to work as library aides, was the subject of the following broadside:

Pressing on to new pinnacles of paternalism, the Roosevelt administration has decided to guide the untutored minds of the residents of Stockton, California, in the selection of reading matter. From its $1,700,000,000 boondoggling fund the WPA has decided to spend $1,300 to maintain a corps of literary advisers in the Stockton Public Library to help the patrons select "appropriate material for reading." Thus far, however, the Brains Trusters have overlooked the opportunity of allocating additional funds to psychoanalyze the readers in order to determine accurately what books will or will not be appropriate to their particular needs.[19]

In fact, the WPA spent $924 and Stockton put up $384 to employ a graduate of the University of California Library School to compile bibliographies of library materials. "Without the WPA contributions this work could not be done, one less person would have a job, and the citizens of Stockton would get that much less service at their library at a time when it is especially needed because of the greater attendance occasioned by enforced leisure," one WPA official observed.[20]

The WPA's anti-boondoggle campaign responded to these attacks on several fronts, including funneling its interpretation of the accusations directly to its political friends. The majority leader in the Senate, Arkansas's Joseph T. Robinson, drew directly on this ammunition when he took to the Senate floor in March 1936. The "gentlemen in the opposition party," he declared of the Republicans, "have a new talking point which they hope to build up into a big national issue. They are loosing a terrific national campaign against what they call 'waste and inefficiency' in the work-relief fund."[21] Robinson turned to the campaign's calling card, noting that "those who are seeking to make this a national issue have discovered a word pronounced 'boondoggling.' By distorting its meaning they hope to perform a feat of political magic and by constant repetition of the word to distract the attention of the American people from

[19] WPA notes on Stockton Public Library project, no date [probably February 1936], "Republican Committee Attacks, California" folder, box 1, entry 732, "Division of Information. Records Relating to Boondoggling Charges ('Attack on WPA'), 1936–1939," RG 69, NA.

[20] Frank Y. McLaughlin to Harry Hopkins, May 1, 1936, "Republican Committee Attacks, California" folder, box 1, in ibid.

[21] Clipping of *Congressional Record*, March 10, 1936, "Boondoggling Interpretation and Defence" [sic] folder, box 2, entry 732, "Division of Information. Records Relating to Boondoggling Charges ('Attacks on WPA'), 1936–1939," RG 69, NA.

the real picture of the Works Progress Administration."[22] Robinson read from a press release issued by the National Republican Congressional Committee:

"Boondoggling" is a comparatively new word on the American tongue. It is "frankly destructive" – Roosevelt's pet way of wasting money. It turns the so-called New Deal into an ordeal. "Boondoggle" means gadget. In that respect, it is synonymous with the New Deal. It was born of it. It may well die with it; in fact, its demise is certain. Sheer waste is killing it.[23]

Robinson, drawing on information supplied by the WPA, presented a different etymology: "The word 'boondoggle' means a useful work, and it had its origin in the name of that sturdy American woodsman, Daniel Boone, who certainly knew as much about practical, useful things as the advertising writers now employed by the Republican National Committee and the miscalled American Liberty League." Boone had apparently made a "toggle" out of leather straps in order to tie his rifle on his head when swimming across a stream, thus keeping his gunpowder dry.

Robinson then scrutinized the specific charges of boondoggling, noting that the Liberty League and the RNC had isolated 100 projects from a possible 170,000, or, as he put it, "just one-seventeenth of 1 percent." Second, Robinson noted that charges of boondoggling relied on brief and partial descriptions of WPA projects. "These Republican spokesmen and Liberty Leaguers," Robinson said, "go about the country crying over what they call the break-down of local responsibility and local self-government. As a matter of fact, this report [of the WPA] shows that every project undertaken by the Works Progress Administration was first sponsored by local authorities."[24]

Like Robinson, FDR also realized that the way to rebut the opponents of the WPA on this point was to establish localities' enthusiasm for WPA projects. Early in 1936, FDR asked Harry Hopkins to compile examples of conservative newspapers that decried boondoggles but demanded that the government pay for projects in their own locality.[25] The WPA found that roughly 79 percent of all WPA projects, in terms of value, were

---

[22] Ibid.
[23] Quoted in ibid.
[24] Ibid.
[25] FDR to Harry Hopkins, January 21, 1936, "Chamber of Commerce" folder, box 2, entry 732, "Division of Information. Records Relating to Boondoggling Charges ('Attacks on WPA'), 1936–1939," RG 69, NA.

sponsored by municipalities, townships, or counties; 18 percent by state governments; and 3 percent by various federal governmental agencies.[26] The strategy of defending the WPA by noting its local support culminated in the U.S. Community Improvement Appraisal. This national survey of the WPA's accomplishments found that 90 percent of the responding communities (the Appraisal assessed 42 states and included 2,101 rural communities, 1,201 small cities, 266 mid-size cities, and 154 large cities) declared that the WPA's work "was of permanent value."[27]

Perhaps the most sensational boondoggle charge that Robinson tackled in his speech on the Senate floor was a $25,000 dog pound built by the WPA in Memphis, Tennessee. As Michigan Senator Arthur Vandenberg dryly observed, this project "put the 'dog' in 'boondoggling.'"[28] The *New York Times* was the first to publicize the project, printing, across three columns, an architect's rendering of the dog pound's facade, with the following caption: "A $25,000 boondoggling dog pound for Memphis. An architect's drawing of the building under construction as a WPA project. It will be equipped with shower baths, outside exercise runways, and pens supplied with fresh straw bedding daily for the dogs. A sealed gas chamber will be used to execute all unclaimed animals after three days."[29]

Responding, the mayor of Memphis complained to the *Times* that the city needed the dog pound: Over the previous 3 years, 827 Pasteur treatments had been administered to those (mostly children) bitten by "mad dogs." More than 1,500 people had been bitten by dogs; 362 of the dogs involved had rabies; and at least 6 people had died of rabies during the previous three years.[30] Senator Robinson, noting these facts, proclaimed, "Can one imagine the haunting fear of the people of Memphis over such conditions? Can one imagine any better way to expend Federal funds." Robinson's defense, however, paled against the terrific image of waste and corruption the dog pound provided the WPA's critics. One Republican congressman teased, "I certainly wish I could live in as handsome a building as the Memphis dogs will occupy. The dogs will have individual pens with fresh bedding every day, exercise runways, shower baths, and

[26] WPA press release, January 12, 1938, "Press Releases January thru February, 1938" folder, box 3, entry 740, "Division of Information. Press Releases, 1936–1942, with gaps," RG 69, NA.
[27] *U.S. Community Improvement Appraisal*, 7.
[28] *Congressional Record* 80, pt. 3 (March 10, 1936), p. 3498.
[29] *New York Times*, February 7, 1936, p. 3.
[30] *New York Times*, February 10, 1936, p. 16.

every imaginable comfort of home." Although joking, the congressman was on to something important. Much New Deal architecture was, like the Memphis dog pound, a remarkable combination of solidity and tradition, on the one hand, and of novelty and modernity, on the other. This architectural language, rich in dignity, dramatically announced the New Deal's presence in communities around the country. In the dog pound's case, though, the dignified structure was intended to house animals. This awkward juxtaposition may have added to the controversy the dog pound provoked.[31]

The *New York Sun* hopped on the dog-pound bandwagon, predicting, "If the WPA keeps up its present rate of pound building, every dog will have his shelter as well as his day. The idea of a $25,000 Federal aided refuge for stray curs in Yonkers has been approved by regional authorities, so Memphis, with its fine dog hotel, needn't be so snooty." While plans for the Yonkers pound had not yet been drafted, "undoubtedly they'll include showers, like those in the model in the South."[32] In response to critics' fascination with the dog showers – a topic that was repeated for more than five months after the *New York Times* first ran its picture of the Memphis dog pound – the WPA's Amy MacMaster observed, by way of defense, "In regard to the 'special shower baths,' it should be noted that washing dogs by shower bath is very much cheaper and more sanitary than washing them by hand; and if the dogs happen to have rabies, it is much safer for the person that does the washing."[33]

By the end of 1938, though, the WPA had finally shifted to the offensive in its battle with its critics. "Seldom is the word 'boondoggle' heard these days with respect to projects of the Works Progress Administration," the WPA declared. "This catchy phrase, quickly seized upon and taken out

[31] Clipping of *Congressional Record*, March 10, 1936, "Boondoggling Interpretation and Defence" [sic] folder, box 2, entry 732, "Division of Information. Records Relating to Boondoggling Charges ('Attacks on WPA'), 1936–1939," RG 69, NA. For more on the architectural rhetoric of the New Deal, see Phoebe Cutler, *The Public Landscape of the New Deal* (New Haven: Yale University Press, 1985); Diane Ghirardo, *Building New Communities: New Deal America and Fascist Italy* (Princeton: Princeton University Press, 1989); and Lois A. Craig, *The Federal Presence: Architecture, Politics, and Symbols in United States Government Building* (Cambridge: MIT Press, 1978).

[32] *New York Sun*, February 18, 1936, in "New York" folder, box 1, entry 730, "Division of Information. Statements and Related Papers Relating to Boondoggling Charges and Answers ('Attacks on WPA'), 1935–1936. Alabama–Wisconsin," RG 69, NA.

[33] Amy MacMaster, "Boondoggling: Answer to Charges in *South Jersey Independent*," June 5, 1936, "Greatest Show on Earth now in Fourth Year in this Country (South Jersey Independence)" folder, box 2, entry 732, "Division of Information. Records Relating to Boondoggling Charges ('Attacks on WPA'), 1936–1939," RG 69, NA.

of the testimony of a Scoutmaster in New York under the Civil Works Administration early in 1934, had a rather remarkable run for many months."

Distinguished lexicographers stayed awake nights seeking its origin; two large national organizations, both amply financed into the hundreds of thousands, got out booklets describing in sarcastic language many alleged individual boondoggles of the WPA; the United States Senate had at least one memorable debate on the subject of alleged WPA boondoggles; one metropolitan newspaper ran daily a short two column head entitled "Today's Boondoggle"; and even President Roosevelt used the word in one of his speeches.[34]

What had happened? The principal explanation, the WPA asserted, was that "many projects called boondoggles by hostile critics, when completed, turned out to be the reverse; they were found to have been sound, sensible projects, fully warranted both because of the primary employment opportunities they offered and because their operation at this time goes on entirely unquestioned by anyone." Revisiting the most famous of boondoggles, the Memphis dog pound, the WPA noted that since the pound opened, the number of persons bitten and the number of people treated for rabies had dropped dramatically.[35]

Despite the contempt they heaped on projects like the Memphis dog pound, opponents of the New Deal were not able to convince the public that all of the New Deal's projects were worthless. Their failure was due, in part, to the national scope of the New Deal public works programs. As the U.S. Community Improvement Appraisal survey indicated, localities wanted their WPA projects. An examination of how the WPA functioned at the level of the project site, however, demonstrates how New Deal public works became a politically controversial issue. Opponents of the New Deal were able to mount an effective argument against the WPA by charging that the program was being used by politicians to win votes.

"POLITICS IN RELIEF"

The political implications of spending federal funds on public works projects became a central factor in the public's perception of the WPA.

[34] "Boondoggle's Puppies," December 2, 1938, "1938 Material on Boondoggling" folder, box 2, entry 732, "Division of Information. Records Relating to Boondoggling Charges ('Attacks on WPA'), 1936–1939," RG 69, NA.
[35] Ibid.

The issue of "politics in relief," as it was often termed, culminated in the debate and passage of the 1939 Hatch Act, an event that will be explored more fully in Chapter 6. The chain of events that led to the Hatch Act, however, was complicated. WPA administrators, local and state politicians, interested businessmen and citizens, the unemployed, and those employed on public works projects confronted with increasing frequency the politicization of the WPA.

The politicization of the WPA reflects the messy way that it worked across the country, in urban and rural locations. These activities, however, were not new; nor were they exclusive to the WPA. Indeed, the Federal Emergency Relief Administration (FERA), run by Harry Hopkins from 1933 until it was phased out in 1935, confronted similar incidents of graft. In Kentucky, for example, a county judge, a mayor, and members of the local relief committee misappropriated $122,500 in federal funds; state FERA personnel were regularly selected via patronage instead of by professional qualifications; and often federal funds were spent on projects that benefited businessmen and politicians rather than the poor and unemployed.[36]

Paul Kellogg, the well-known editor of *Survey*, reflected on what was at stake in such an environment for supporters of the WPA. In a speech entitled "Social Workers in a Campaign Year," given to the New York State Conference of Social Work, Kellogg argued that when public welfare "is drawn into politics we must follow it there, and stand for the right as we see it and the well-being of those concerned." During an election year, Kellogg noted, "there is the huge bulk of grouching" about the "partisan manipulation" of government spending. "With so much smoke these days along the political horizon, far be it from me to say there are not running fires under the smoke," Kellogg acknowledged. However, he thought, "if we look closely, we see that for the most part [these fires] run where civil service standards are lax locally, where the natural order of political machines is still to live on spoils – and this holds for cities, counties, states." While Kellogg and other liberals objected to politics entering into the selection of WPA administrative personnel, the real opportunity for political maneuvering in the operation of the WPA was at the level of the project site. Foremen and timekeepers, as

---

[36] "Kentucky Investigation Final Report of Special Investigations," no date [probably after November 19, 1934], "Kentucky" folder, entry PC-37, 23, "Work Projects Administration. Records of the Division of Investigation, 1934–43. Work Projects Administration. Miscellaneous State File ("New File"). Iowa–Kentucky," RG 69, NA.

politicians like Jim Farley were well aware, were the key players in these stratagems.[37]

For example, in 1936 the WPA received complaints that WPA foremen in Hart County, Kentucky, had been urging their workers to vote Republican in the 1936 election. Stokes A. Baird, the chairman of the Democratic Party in Hart County, wrote to George Goodman, the state director of the WPA in Kentucky, that he suspected 7 WPA foremen in his county of coercing WPA workers to vote the Republican ticket. These foremen supervised about 200 workers on WPA farm-to-market road projects in Hart County. Even though the WPA investigating agent interviewed more than 100 WPA workers, he could not find one who would confirm that his foreman had tried to influence his vote while he was on the job site. Ten citizens of Hart County, however, did submit affidavits stating that they thought the Republican foremen were responsible for decreasing the Democratic majority from 1,400 votes in 1932 to 194 in 1936. Although the Republican foremen avoided influencing their workers at the project sites, they did use their cars to take them to the polling places on election day.[38]

In Clinton County, Illinois, Delmont Schaeffer, the chair of the county's Democratic Committee, and Clarence Beckemeyer, the WPA engineer in charge of the county, formed a WPA "social club." Schaeffer and Beckemeyer then proceeded to threaten WPA employees with dismissal if they failed to support Democratic candidates for political office. One WPA laborer, Irvin Chester Moffatt, told investigators what happened as he worked on a countywide road improvement project sponsored by the WPA.

About February, 1939, Dan Dermody, WPA foreman, came to me on the said project and told me that Delmont Schaffer [sic], Cashier of the Farmers Bank, Trenton, Illinois, and Clinton County Democratic Chairman, wanted the WPA project workers to form a political club under the guise of a social club and that he, Dermody, was to be president of that club and that he wanted me to act as its secretary. I refused to accede to that request until I had further information. Accordingly, I went and talked to Delmont Schaffer at the Farmers Bank and

---

[37] Paul Kellogg, "Social Workers in a Campaign Year," no date [October 1938], in "610 N.Y. Political Coercion A–Z" folder, box 2003, "Work Projects Administration. Central Files: State 1935–1944. New York City 610 Special Litigation," RG 69, NA.

[38] WPA investigation report, January 26, 1937, "2-KY-97 Kentucky Hart Corr. File" folder, box 380; and see also the WPA investigation reports in "5-KY-98 Kentucky Johnson Corr. File" folder, box 380; and "1-KY-223 Kentucky Union Corr. File" folder, box 383; all in entry PC-37, 23, "Work Projects Administration. Records of the Division of Investigation, 1934–43. Work Projects Administration Investigative Cases. Kentucky," RG 69, NA.

he advised me that Dermody's statements were correct and that I should do as Dermody requested if I wanted to retain my WPA job. He said that the proposed club was to be political and that if I would help him he would help me; that the Township offices must be kept within the Democratic ranks and that whomever he endorsed he would expect the members of the said club to support.[39]

At the first club meeting Moffatt and Dermody collected fifty cents in dues from the WPA workers who attended, using the money to purchase beer and other refreshments.

While a number of WPA workers attended the club, six workers refused. Moffatt recalled what happened next:

Delmont Schaffer [sic] did not attend any meetings of the said club but he discussed the meetings with me and on one occasion told me that he had heard that several of the WPA employees refused to join the club or to support his candidate for election. I told him that there were a few who had not joined the club and he requested that I submit their names to him; he said that he would call Clarence Beckemeyer and have those men dismissed from WPA employment. I refused to divulge the names of these men and evaded Schaffer's request.[40]

At Schaeffer's urging, however, Moffatt and Dermody mobilized WPA workers to vote for J. H. "Zip" Quitmeyer for Township Road Commissioner:

On instructions of Delmont [sic] Schaffer and under his threats of having us dismissed from WPA employment, Dan Dermody and I made short political speeches to the WPA workers at the meetings of the WPA Social Club, and we advised the membership to vote at the said township election for "Zip" Quitmeyer, and a straight Democratic ticket, or lose their WPA jobs. The election was duly held and J. H. "Zip" Quitmeyer was elected by a majority of about one hundred twenty-five votes (125); the WPA Social Club had a membership of about forty (40) WPA project workers at the time of the said election, most of whom were married men with families.[41]

These sorts of cases were often uncovered in WPA investigations. WPA investigators, however, realized that a remedy was not entirely clear, outside of discharging the personnel in question. As one investigator wrote to the director of investigations for the WPA regarding this WPA "social

---

[39] Statement of Irvin Chester Moffatt, October 4, 1939, "7-IL-1136" folder, box 342, entry PC-37, 23, "Work Projects Administration Investigative Cases. Records of the Division of Investigation, 1934–43. Work Projects Administration. Illinois," RG 69, NA.
[40] Ibid.
[41] Ibid.

club," "Past experience has indicated the difficulty of obtaining convictions in cases of this nature."[42]

In states like Pennsylvania, the WPA's upper tier of administrators was all too aware of the extent that political forces permeated the WPA at the local level. As late as 1940, Howard Hunter, who had served in the New Deal since the early days of FERA, advised Hopkins's successor as head of the WPA, Colonel Francis Harrington, that the WPA needed to be cautious when deciding what activities merited investigation. "We could conceivably have the entire Division of Investigation in just the state of Pennsylvania," Hunter cautioned, "if we formalized all the charges which are likely to come in."[43]

Indeed, opponents of the New Deal in Pennsylvania sought to capitalize on the resentment WPA workers might feel toward the foreman or time-keeper who subjected them to political pressure. One group, identifying itself only as the "Americanism Committee," mailed one-cent postcards during the 1938 campaign with the following message:

WPA OR PROJECT WORKER, READ THIS:
You are at work right now, but after Election, WHAT? Until now you have been like a slave – pleading and begging to Foremen, Timekeepers, Inspectors, Bosses; then when you were placed, you were assessed and maced for a big part of your scanty wage, to pay for Sign Boards, Graft and Lying Propaganda. Under Little New Deal Rule the same thing is before you for some years, if you can ever get a job at all. New Deal Rule has driven many Industries, big and little, out of the State and that is why you can get no real Man's job. On November 8th is your one and only chance to win back your American Freedom, by voting STRAIGHT REPUBLICAN. The sure and sacred promise of the REPUBLICAN candidates is that you get real jobs, and be FREE MEN again. Do not fear that your Bosses will know how you vote – they have no way of finding out; so VOTE AGAINST LITTLE NEW DEAL SLAVERY.[44]

Although the 1930s are remembered today as the Age of Roosevelt, Democrats by no means monopolized control of the WPA at the local level. In fact, the WPA was flooded with complaints about the politicization of

[42] WPA investigation report, January 8, 1940; Statement of Irvin Chester Moffatt, October 4, 1939; and Richard Thompson to Roger J. Bounds, July 10, 1940; all in "7-IL-1136" folder, box 342, in ibid.
[43] Howard O. Hunter to Colonee Francis Harrington, April 3, 1940, "610.3 PA. K-Mc" folder, box 2395, "Work Projects Administration. Central Files: State 1935–1944. Pa. 610 Special Litigation," RG 69, NA.
[44] Americanism Committee to Edwin B. Zeiser, November 4, 1938, in "610 PA. Charges of Sen. Davis (P.C.)" folder, box 2388, "Work Projects Administration. Central Files: State 1935–1944. Pa. 610 Special Litigation," RG 69, NA.

the WPA in Republican-controlled areas of the country. One WPA worker, Frank Bukowski of Momence, Illinois, wrote to Harry Hopkins to complain that "before the WPA went into effect here this county of Kankakee was 85 percent Democratic, and now it is 85 percent Republican." The reason for this shift? Bukowski thought it simple: "[T]he foremen on these WPA jobs tell the laborers that if they dont [sic] vote the Republican ticket they will lose their jobs. And they do vote the Republican ticket because they are working under Republican foremen."[45]

Timekeepers and foremen were not the only people who solicited political support from their workers: WPA supervisory personnel were themselves subject to coercion from their superiors. In 1939, William R. Garrison, a WPA superintendent in Joplin, Missouri, met with about fifty WPA timekeepers and foremen at the county courthouse and collected one-half of a month's pay from them in order to pay the debts of the Democratic Central Committee of Newton County. Ruth Williamson, the treasurer of the Democratic Central Committee, received the money and was told that it was given by the "boys down at the courthouse." Williamson added that the chairman of the committee, Phil Graves, told her that if she served as treasurer she would receive employment supervising a WPA sewing project.[46]

John Harris, a WPA timekeeper, showed investigators a letter from Graves advising him that he had been "assessed" for political funds for the committee. Graves's letter read in part:

You are now working because the Democratic Party is in power. It is your Party and you owe your present job to YOUR PARTY. The time has come when your financial help is needed. We must have money to conduct a successful campaign. That money must come from those who are receiving the benefit of jobs.[47]

Graves acknowledged that WPA employees were sent letters under his signature, but he accused his secretary of using a list of addresses of WPA employees and sending the letters out on her own. Graves's secretary, however, produced the list – in Graves's handwriting – and stated that he instructed her to use it. Although Garrison was fired from his

45 Frank Bukowski to Harry Hopkins, June 28, 1938, "Illinois 610 Political Coercion A-L" folder, box 1181, "Work Projects Administration. Central Files: State 1935–1944. Illinois 610 Special Litigation," RG 69, NA.

46 WPA investigation report, May 6, 1939, "5-MO-305 Missouri Newton Corr. File" folder, box 480, entry PC-37, 23, "Work Projects Administration. Records of the Division of Investigation, 1934–43. Work Projects Administration Investigative Cases. Missouri," RG 69, NA.

47 Philip H. Graves to John Harris, September 30, 1938, in ibid.

WPA position as supervisor, the case languished in the judicial arena for nearly three years, demonstrating what one WPA administrator termed "a shining example of the lack of cooperation we have received in a number of cases on the part of United States Attorneys."[48]

In Montana, the WPA's administrative and project supervisory personnel mustered the organization's employees to back Congressman Jerry O'Connell's 1938 reelection campaign. WPA foremen lined up their workers and distributed O'Connell's campaign literature to them, promising that WPA workers could make up hours lost campaigning on the project site. Projects were "over-loaded" with rodmen, foremen, and project clerks just before the election (195 of 222 rodmen, foremen, and clerks were laid off right after the election); WPA workers were forced to listen to radio broadcasts made by O'Connell during project working hours; and WPA telephone and stenographic equipment was used in O'Connell's campaign. Several WPA supervisors who opposed O'Connell were called into the state WPA administrator's office and falsely accused of working against O'Connell. WPA investigators, however, concluded that there was not enough tangible evidence to warrant prosecution, recommending only the dismissal of four WPA supervisors, the demotion of one WPA foreman, and issuance of a reprimand against another.[49]

Sometimes the corruption uncovered by the WPA was not linked to party politics at all. The WPA's division of investigation often found incidents of local and state WPA administrators working with local politicians and businesses to provide infrastructure that benefited private industry. For example, in 1940 the WPA and Washington's Skagit County worked together to build an access road between an established county road and the Pacific Nickel Company's mine. Over 75 percent of the road, however, was constructed on Pacific Nickel's property. Although the WPA's district director and project engineer objected to the road being built, the project was nevertheless approved by the WPA's state planning engineer. WPA investigators came to a clear conclusion: "The circumstances surrounding the transaction reflect a clear-cut and well-planned scheme to evade regulations and defraud the Government through the cooperation of the company and county officials with at least the tacit assent or obeisance on the

[48] WPA investigation report, May 6, 1939; Leo Simonton to Frank Bukowski, February 12, 1942; both in ibid.
[49] WPA investigation report, August 17, 1939, "1-MT-146 Montana Silver Bow Corr. File" folder, box 490, entry PC-37, 23, "Work Projects Administration. Records of the Division of Investigation, 1934–43. Work Projects Administration Investigative Cases. Montana," RG 69, NA.

part of Ralph O. Robinson, Director of Operations Washington WPA."
Without any evidence of money changing hands, however, the WPA agents
did not recommend criminal prosecution. Rather, they advised the WPA
to seek financial reimbursement from Pacific Nickel for the $3,156.74
spent by the WPA on the road.[50]

Such difficulties in pinning down allegations were evident near Chicago
as well. In the last half of 1938, the WPA built over half a million dollars
worth of sewer pipes in an unincorporated part of Niles, Illinois. Although
WPA investigators were unable to figure out how this odd state of affairs
came to be, they suspected that a group of developers had manipulated
the WPA into building a sewer system on their tract, making it easier to
sell and develop the lots on the property. When one WPA investigator and
engineer visited the site in October 1939, they encountered the following
situation:

The evidence of recent sewer work is still quite visible; we walked along a number
of the ridges left by the backfill of this sewer construction. It was noted that in
addition to installing the main sewers down what would be the center of streets,
if there were any streets in the area, WPA has constructed a great many 6-inch
and 8-inch stubs, so that the sewer system now extends up to the property line of
many of the unoccupied and uninhabited lots in the area. There are a number of
signs posted on these premises advertising lots for sale and indicating that FHA
terms are available.[51]

The foreman on the project testified as to the undeveloped state of the
area. "The area in which the men working under me laid these stubs and
catch basins was a prairie in which there were no houses, no sidewalks,
no streets and no water connections."[52] The 155-acre tract was owned by
three trustees of the West Rogers Park Realty Trust, which stonewalled
WPA requests for information. "There seems to be no logical explanation
for this attitude on the part of the Trustees and members of the Board of
the West Rogers Park Realty Trust unless they may have something which
they desire to conceal," wrote one WPA investigator. "Their refusal to
furnish any information as to the extent of their sales of property tends to

[50] WPA investigation report, April 15, 1941, "1-WA-328 Washington Skagit Corr. File" folder, box 766, entry PC-37, 23, "Work Projects Administration. Records of the Division of Investigation, 1934–43. Work Projects Administration Investigative Cases. Washington," RG 69 NA.

[51] Richard Thompson to Roger J. Bounds, October 26, 1939, "3-IL-1221" folder, box 344, entry PC-37, 23, "Work Projects Administration Investigative Cases. Records of the Division of Investigation, 1934–43. Work Projects Administration. Illinois," RG 69 NA.

[52] Thompson to Bounds, February 14, 1940, in ibid.

support the theory that some lots may have been given or at least promised to those who arranged to secure WPA work in this area," he speculated.[53]

The investigator also suspected that the WPA's services were procured through the influence of several officials: Thomas Bowler, a former Chicago alderman and the clerk of the Criminal Court of Chicago; William Link, who worked for Chicago's Board of Improvements; and William Cowhey, alderman for Chicago's forty-first ward. Although WPA agents conducted an extensive investigation, they were unable to pin down a solid connection. Rather, they concluded, several factors coincided: Pressure on the WPA to generate employment, a lack of available projects, and interest on the part of landowners to promote the sewer project all came together "to result in the submission, approval and operation of a series of projects [the sewer construction] which undoubtedly are ineligible."[54]

In other instances, even when the WPA found partisan politics shaping corruption, the politicization of the WPA did not always occur along Democratic–Republican lines. At times, Democrats split over the patronage potential of the public works program. In 1936, in Sedalia, Missouri, a factional dispute broke out between two candidates for the Democratic congressional nomination, Henry C. Salveter and Reuben T. Wood. Investigators for the WPA found several instances of local WPA officials using the power of their positions to back Wood. Several people told investigators that they heard Frank Monroe, the district director for the WPA, proclaim, "You know this [the WPA] is a Truman–Wood set up," declaring that the organization was backing Harry Truman for Senate and Reuben Wood for Congress. Although investigators were unable to prove any illegal activities, they recommended that Monroe be reprimanded and ordered to cease any political activities.[55]

Owners of heavy equipment used on WPA projects were often grateful for the work. This gratitude, however, was at times exploited by WPA employees. In Los Angeles, Byron G. Karn, a heavy-equipment owner, was told by a group of WPA equipment inspectors that he needed to "kick thru with some money" in order to keep his steam shovels employed on the project site. Eventually, these inspectors were charged with extorting $200 from Karn. At the time, even the conservative *Los Angeles Times*

[53] Ibid.
[54] Thompson to Bounds, April 6, 1940, in ibid.
[55] WPA investigation report, August 19, 1936, "4-MO-78 Missouri Pettis Corr. File" folder, box 473, entry PC-37, 23, "Work Projects Administration. Records of the Division of Investigation, 1934–43. Work Projects Administration Investigative Cases. Missouri," RG 69, NA.

praised the efficiency of the WPA in clearing up this incident. While "the local organization of WPA appears to have clean hands in the matter," the *Times* opined, "the development of such scandals is an almost inevitable concomitant of such circumstances as, in general, surround the lavish expenditure of public funds with more attention to giving employment than to getting full value for the money laid out. A dozen eastern States have already furnished examples of the tendency of this free and easy money to stick to various fingers in transit; it would be a miracle of human nature if it were otherwise." Indeed, the WPA found itself investigating issues entailing the use of heavy equipment and kickbacks in a number of states, including Illinois, New York, Pennsylvania, and Missouri.[56]

Congress also took steps to regulate the operation of the WPA, at times adding more specific language to the legislation governing the WPA's appropriations. Reflecting a growing concern with national security, the 1940 Emergency Relief Appropriation Act banned Communists and Nazis from the WPA's rolls and required that WPA employees swear their loyalty to the United States. As a result, the WPA's investigation division began to concentrate more on the politics of individual workers. Often, WPA investigators found Communists on the Federal Writers Project and Theater Project, and supporters of the Nazi regime (musicians of German descent) employed on the Federal Music Project.[57]

Although the term "boondoggle" has remained in the American political vocabulary, between 1935 and 1938 New Dealers were able to counter effectively critics who charged that the New Deal's public works projects

[56] WPA investigation report, June 11, 1936; *Los Angeles Times* editorial clipping, May 26, 1936; both in "11-CA-58 California Los Angeles Correspondence File" folder, box 235, entry PC-37, 23, "Work Projects Administration. Records of the Division of Investigation, 1934–43. Work Projects Administration Investigative Cases. California," RG 69, NA. For Illinois, see WPA investigation report, June 30, 1937, "2-IL-437 Illinois Cook Correspondence File" folder, box 328, entry PC-37, 23, "Work Projects Administration Investigative Cases. Records of the Division of Investigation, 1934–43. Work Projects Administration. Illinois"; for New York, see "WPA Press Digest," February 20, 1936, "100 Dec 35–Feb 36" folder, box 68, "Central Files: General 1935–1944. 100 Administration"; for Pennsylvania, see Aubrey Williams to Senator James J. Davis, February 14, 1938, no folder, box 2388, "Central Files: State 1935–1944. Pa. 610 Special Litigation"; for Missouri, see WPA investigation report, September 11, 1937, "1-MO-151 Missouri Clinton Correspondence File" folder, box 475, entry PC-37, 23, "Work Projects Administration. Records of the Division of Investigation, 1934–1943. Work Projects Administration Investigative Cases. Missouri"; all in RG 69, NA.

[57] The WPA regularly conducted extensive investigations into the political affiliations of the most low-level of WPA employees, prefiguring, in many ways, the focus on loyalty more commonly associated with the post–World War II national security state. For an

were wasteful and inefficient. Despite their emphasis on projects like the Memphis dog pound, opponents of the New Deal were not able to convince the public that all the New Deal's projects were worthless. This was due, in part, to the national scope of the New Deal public works programs. As the U.S. Community Appraisal and other measures taken by the WPA indicated, localities wanted their WPA projects. When viewed from the perspective of the local communities, the boondoggles were always "somewhere else." An examination of how the WPA functioned at the level of the project site, however, demonstrates how New Deal public works became a controversial political issue. Opponents of the New Deal were able to mount an effective argument against the WPA by charging that the program was being used by politicians to win votes. The criticism of the WPA that eventually came to stick in the public mind was that the initials "WPA" stood for the "Wild Politics Administration." [58]

example of these continuities, see Ellen Schrecker, *Many Are the Crimes: McCarthyism in America* (Boston: Little, Brown, 1998), 86–115; for examples of the WPA's investigations, see boxes 347–53, entry PC-37, 23, "Work Projects Administration Investigative Cases. Records of the Division of Investigation, 1934–43. Work Projects Administration. Illinois"; boxes 383–84, entry PC-37, 23, "Work Projects Administration. Records of the Division of Investigation, 1934–43. Work Projects Administration Investigative Cases. Kentucky"; boxes 715–17, entry PC-37, 23, "Work Projects Administration. Records of the Division of Investigation, 1934–43. Work Projects Administration Investigative Cases. Pennsylvania"; and boxes 766–67, entry PC-37, 23, "Work Projects Administration. Records of the Division of Investigation, 1934–43. Work Projects Administration Investigative Cases. Washington," all in RG 69, NA. Of course, this is not to imply that everyone working for the Federal Writers Project, for example, was a Communist; rather, it is to state that WPA investigators generally found more Communists working for the FWP than, say, on construction projects such as road work.

[58] WPA Press Digest, February 20, 1936, "100 Dec 35–Feb 36" folder, box 68, "Central Files: General 1935–1944. 100 Administration," RG 69, NA.

6

Party Building and "Pernicious Political Activities"

The Road to the Hatch Act

As the New Deal entered its sixth year, Americans ranked the Works Progress Administration both as its "greatest accomplishment" and as the "worst thing the Roosevelt administration has done." This dramatic polarization of public opinion only begins to indicate the tremendous presence the WPA had assumed in the social and political life of the country. One WPA official outlined the program's broader significance:

> [It is] more than 3,000,000 workers earning . . . wages and their 10,000,000 dependents, it is another 3,000,000 workers who have been on WPA rolls, but have gone on to other work. It is also 125,000 engineers, social workers, accountants, superintendents, foremen and timekeepers scattered in every state and community. It is in part all the public officials of all the sponsoring bodies in all the communities of the United States. It is in part 800,000 storekeepers who get most of the money paid to WPA workers. . . . It touches intimately the lives of more than fifty million people.[1]

Just how the organization that gathered in this wide assortment of workers, professionals and small business people came to symbolize both the "greatest achievement" and the "worst thing" about the New Deal is a

---

[1] Donald S. Howard, *The WPA and Federal Relief Policy* (New York: Russell Sage Foundation, 1943), 105; and "Work Relief or the Dole?" WPA Press Release, September 8, 1938, quoted in Howard, *WPA and Federal Relief Policy*, 105–6. The most recent argument for the central place of the WPA in the New Deal state is made by Edwin Amenta; see his *Bold Relief: Institutional Politics and the Origins of Modern American Social Policy* (Princeton: Princeton University Press, 1998); and Amenta, Ellen Benoit, Chris Bonasitia, Nancy K. Cauthen, and Drew Halfmann, "Bring Back the WPA: Work, Relief, and the Origins of American Social Policy in Welfare Reform," *Studies in American Political Development* 12 (Spring 1998): 1–56.

complex matter. Of course, historians have long pointed to the persistent strength of an antistatist political culture in the United States as part of the explanation for opposition to the expansion of the federal government.[2] To explain the vehemence of the antagonism toward the WPA, however, we must look beyond arguments based solely on culture and consider the complementary role of politics. The connection between the WPA and the volatile issue of "politics in relief" at state and local levels of government was a critical factor in the federal administration of public works. Opposition to the WPA was less the product of a transhistoric cultural mistrust of the national state than it was the concrete outcome of specific political decisions and institutional developments.

I explore these decisions and developments through a case study of Kentucky's 1938 primary election. This seemingly unremarkable event merits extended notice for several reasons. The 1938 electoral cycle, although not featuring a presidential race, attracted national attention as FDR, with the support and advice of New Dealers like Harold Ickes, Harry Hopkins, and Thomas Corcoran (informally known as the "elimination committee"), sought to expel conservative elements from the Democratic Party. Domestic critics, prompted by the conduct of Joseph Stalin in Russia, quickly labeled this a party "purge." What might otherwise have been a comparatively uneventful series of midterm elections became a referendum on the Democratic Party, the New Deal, and FDR himself. While Roosevelt campaigned vigorously in several states against conservative Democratic candidates – most notably, in Georgia, South Carolina, Maryland, and New York – the stakes in Kentucky were higher for FDR.[3]

This campaign pitted the new Democratic Senate Majority Leader Alben Barkley against the state's Democratic Governor Al "Happy" Chandler. Because of Barkley's stature in the Senate – he had become

---

[2] Particularly useful on this cultural strain are Barry D. Karl, *The Uneasy State: The United States from 1915 to 1945* (Chicago: University of Chicago Press, 1984); David T. Beito, *Taxpayers in Revolt: Tax Resistance during the Great Depression* (Chapel Hill: University of North Carolina Press, 1989); Leo P. Ribuffo, *The Old Christian Right* (Philadelphia: Temple University Press, 1989); Alan Brinkley, *Voices of Protest: Huey Long, Father Coughlin and the Great Depression* (New York: Vintage, 1983); and James Holt, "The New Deal and the American Anti-Statist Tradition," in John Braeman, Robert H. Bremner, and David Brody, eds., *The New Deal: The National Level* (Columbus: Ohio State University Press, 1975), 27–49.

[3] William E. Leuchtenburg, *Franklin D. Roosevelt and the New Deal* (New York: Harper & Row, 1963), 266–74; Anthony J. Badger, *The New Deal: The Depression Years, 1933–1939* (New York: Hill and Wang, 1989), 268–71; and James T. Patterson, *Congressional Conservatism and the New Deal: The Growth of the Conservative Coalition in Congress, 1933–1939* (Louisville: University of Kentucky Press, 1967), 250–87.

majority leader in 1937, selected with FDR's backing – his fate was a barometer of the New Deal's fortunes. Would the people of Kentucky return Roosevelt's hand-picked majority leader to the Senate? Like political campaigns in other states, the Kentucky contest featured charges against each candidate of attempting to use public funds to build a political machine: in Barkley's case, through the WPA, and in Chandler's, with state highway funds. This particular aspect of the Kentucky race commanded nationwide attention after a series of newspaper stories written by a committed New Dealer, syndicated columnist Thomas Stokes, exposed the role of the WPA in the campaign. Stokes won a Pulitzer Prize for his reporting, and his stories led to an extensive investigation of the WPA by both the Senate and the House.

Stokes was not the only person to propel the WPA into the spotlight, however. In this task he was ably assisted by WPA head Harry Hopkins. During the 1938 campaigns, Hopkins made a particularly ill-timed remark about the political philosophy of the New Deal while relaxing at the race track: "We shall tax and tax, spend and spend, and elect and elect," he reportedly declared when asked to define the New Deal. Most historians have concluded that this story was apocryphal, basing their refutation on Hopkins confidant Robert Sherwood's account in *Roosevelt and Hopkins*.[4] I take the statement at face value, however, and I will give my reasons for believing that Hopkins did say this and demonstrate that it was a striking (if instrumentalist) expression of how the New Deal's public works programs not only succeeded in generating infrastructure and providing employment but were also effective politics.[5]

Hopkins's statement, coupled with the activities of the public works programs, made a robust case for what is now derisively referred to as "tax and spend liberalism." Continuing to deny that Hopkins connected the taxing and spending functions of government with a politics based on government-sponsored economic development and employment makes it difficult to understand how New Deal liberalism was at once so effective and so filled with conflict. If we take Hopkins at his word, we can begin

---

[4] For example, David Kennedy terms Sherwood's book the "definitive account of what Hopkins did not say." David M. Kennedy, *Freedom from Fear: The American People in Depression and War, 1929–1945* (New York: Oxford University Press, 1999), 349, n. 53; and Robert Sherwood, *Roosevelt and Hopkins: An Intimate History*, rev. ed. (New York: Grosset & Dunlap, 1948), 102–4.

[5] For a classic study that argues for the importance of viewing the New Deal as a political project, see Ellis W. Hawley, *The New Deal and the Problem of Monopoly: A Study in Economic Ambivalence* (Princeton: Princeton University Press, 1966).

to recapture the power, appeal, and controversial place of the New Deal in American political history.

Portrayals of the late New Deal as a time of the Supreme Court–packing debacle, the "Roosevelt Recession" of 1937–38, FDR's decreasing popularity and political effectiveness, and the abandonment of statist reform for Keynesian economic expansion, are incomplete. In contrast, this chapter draws attention to how broad concern over the role of public works programs – the New Deal featured the largest number of federal government employees who owed their jobs purely to patronage (i.e., they were exempt from civil service) in history – grew after the Kentucky primary and the concomitant government investigations, leading Congress to write (and FDR reluctantly to approve) the Hatch Act.[6] This measure, intended to prevent "pernicious political activities," curtailed the federal government's control over a striking feature of the New Deal order: the political use of public works projects at the state and local levels. The Hatch Act reflects several important and overlapping developments in the late New Deal: the growing strength of conservative opposition, the often blurry line between the "political" and the "economic" in the public works programs, and the long tradition of what historian Barry Karl has termed the "uneasy state" of American attitudes toward a powerful federal government.[7]

"IN OLD KENTUCKY": PARTY BUILDING AND THE NEW DEAL

In June 1938, Democrat Carl Hatch of New Mexico rose on the floor of the Senate to put forward an amendment to a relief-and-recovery appropriation bill, proposing that the government forbid employees of New Deal relief programs from standing as candidates or "interfering" in any primary or general election. Hatch, a supporter of the New Deal, had firsthand experience with the issue of politics in relief. Over the previous year, New Mexico's other senator, Dennis Chavez, was embroiled in a WPA scandal that eventually resulted in seventy-three people – including several of Chavez's relatives – being indicted for conspiracy to use the WPA in state politics.[8] Hatch's desire to clean up New Mexican politics

---

[6] Ronald N. Johnson and Gary D. Libecap, *The Federal Civil Service System and the Problem of Bureaucracy: The Economics and Politics of Institutional Change* (Chicago: University of Chicago Press, 1994), 70.

[7] Karl, *Uneasy State.*

[8] Roy Lujan, "Dennis Chavez and the Roosevelt Era, 1933–1945" (Ph.D. diss., University of New Mexico, 1987), 219–90.

meshed with a broader desire to apply moral codes of conduct to public life.[9]

Opposing Hatch's amendment, though, was the Senate's majority leader, Kentucky's Alben Barkley, who made what political commentator Raymond Clapper called an "impassioned speech against this proposal to take WPA out of politics." Clapper, who located himself on the political spectrum as a progressive Republican or a "seventy-five percent New Dealer," generally supported the aims of Roosevelt and the New Deal.[10] He did not, however, agree with Barkley's objections:

[Barkley] explained that it wasn't fair to hog-tie WPA workers this way when state highway employees were free to play politics. "We all know," Barkley said, "that there is not a state in the Union in which the political organization which is in control of the state does not prostitute for its own political purposes the employment of men and women on the highway, and within the offices constructing and conducting the highways." . . . "They are at liberty," Barkley said, "to roam around at their will, or at the will of their boss or their organization, and indulge in politics to their heart's content; but we are proposing that anybody connected with a job under WPA or PWA, or CCC or the AAA, or any other activity for which we appropriate money in this joint resolution, shall be tied with a rope to a tree so that he is helpless and cannot even speak, unless he can whisper in the ear of somebody what his convictions are, while all these others who draw pay out of the Treasury of the United States are free to roam at will and play the political game to their heart's content."[11]

Barkley thought that since state-level politicians had ready access to patronage through state highway offices, New Dealers could not afford to disarm unilaterally.[12] Hatch's amendment failed to win enough backers in three separate roll-call votes. It was supported, generally, by Republicans, anti–New Deal Democrats, and long-time progressive Republicans, such as George Norris and Robert La Follette; and opposed by New Deal supporters.[13] Despite this defeat, most Republicans quickly perceived that the

9 David Porter, "Senator Carl Hatch and the Hatch Act of 1939," *New Mexico Historical Review* 48 (April 1973): 152.
10 *New York Times*, February 4, 1944, p. 3.
11 Raymond Clapper, "A Disturbing Speech," June 6, 1938, "Clapper Columns," vol. 1, scrapbook, box 60, Raymond Clapper Papers, LC *New York Times*, June 3, 1938, p. 1; June 4, 1938, p. 1; and June 5, 1938, p. 3.
12 The connection between state highway spending and patronage was widespread and long-standing; see, e.g., T. Harry Williams, *Huey Long* (New York: Vintage, 1981 [1969]), 486–88.
13 Raymond Clapper, "A Disturbing Speech," June 6, 1938; and "Relief Minus Politics," April 26, 1938; both in "Clapper Columns," vol. 1, scrapbook, box 60, Clapper Papers, LC.

issue of "keeping politics out of relief" could prove to be a very good issue
for the Republican party, with the potential even to outstrip the issue of
"boondoggling." Senator Charles McNary, the minority leader, immediately stated, "The implication" of the Barkley-led Democratic opposition
to Hatch's measure "is clear: . . . that a portion of these relief funds will be
used for political purposes, thereby depriving those in need of relief from a
free exercise of their opinions."[14] McNary's theory would be tested soon.

Investigating the contest between Barkley and Governor Chandler for
the 1938 Senate nomination, journalist Thomas Stokes took a winding,
1,400-mile tour through the state of Kentucky and reported his findings
in an eight-part series of articles. Stokes was not a conservative hack. In
fact, the WPA's own investigations confirmed much of what Stokes uncovered, while disagreeing with his conclusions about the WPA's responsibility. Exploring what he described as "a grand political racket in which
the taxpayer is the victim," Stokes traveled from the bluegrass country of
Lexington to the Tennessee-Kentucky border, visiting the mining region
of Harlan County, the eastern Appalachians, and the western tobacco-
growing part of the state. "Through the WPA organization, which is loyal
to the President and therefore interested in his Senate floor leader," Stokes
reported, "there exists a political consciousness which is expressing itself
actively." Stokes found that this political activism was most evident among
the local directors and project foremen who lived in southern and eastern
Kentucky. "WPA foremen are passing out Barkley buttons, instructing
their workers that they must vote for the Senator, and, in numerous cases,
making support of him a prerequisite for jobs." Workers who favored
Chandler were dismissed from their WPA jobs, in several cases, and workers who were registered Republicans (perhaps more than 300) had been
"induced" by WPA officials to reregister as Democrats. While low-level
WPA officials were clearly engaged in this type of coercive activity, Stokes
ventured onto shakier ground when he reasoned that "the trail leads back
from the bottom to higher-ups in such a way as to indicate that the local
officials and bosses directly involved have received the 'go' sign from those
above to whom they are responsible." Stokes inferred that the absence
of opposition to political activity by the head of the WPA in Kentucky,
former newspaperman George H. Goodman, meant that Goodman sanc-
tioned this behavior. "Testimony on all sides," reported Stokes, "is to the
effect that the WPA under Mr. Goodman has kept its hands off politics in

[14] *New York Times*, June 6, 1938, p. 2.

previous elections, which leads to the assumption, common in Kentucky, that word has come from still higher up than the state director – from Washington."[15]

Stokes gathered affidavits from WPA supervisors, timekeepers, and project foremen, documenting the incursion of politics into the works program. This interference took place in a variety of ways, including "lecturing WPA workers about support of the Senator, threatening them with dismissal, actual firing in some few cases that have come to light, discrimination in type of work, and promoting re-registration of Republican WPA workers as Democratic so they can vote for the Senator in the primary." E. T. Rich, a sixty-five-year-old foreman, swore in his statement that he was dismissed from the WPA because he would not recruit other workers for Barkley. About a week after he was fired, Rich spoke with Zack Taylor, the WPA engineer for Pulaski and Russell counties. Rich recalled that "he asked me if I wasn't pretty mad at him for firing me, but I said I wasn't mad because he fired me but I didn't like it because he didn't have the nerve to come up and tell me why he did it. Then he said I haven't a thing in this world against you personally or nothing against your work, and I said Zack what made you fire me and he said I fired you because you was for Happy Chandler and I had to do it to save my job." In Russell County, Alvin Flanagan, who had worked for the WPA for three years, stated, "Before I was laid off the foreman called me off and said that I have a paper here that I would like for you to sign pledging your support to Sen. Barkley, and I told him that I would rather not sign a petition supporting anyone. I refused to sign the paper pledging my support to Sen. Barkley, and I was dismissed from the payroll. I honestly believe that my refusal to support Sen. Barkley was the cause of my dismissal from the WPA."[16]

Distributed by the Scripps-Howard news service, Stokes's stories appeared in the nation's capital in the *Washington Daily News* and generated a buzz in the Senate, which had just rejected Hatch's amendment banning this kind of pressure based on threat. As Stokes later recalled, "To me it was another job of reporting . . . one that I did not particularly relish when I discovered the facts, for it was a keen disappointment to find that the WPA was being exploited for politics and to ponder the ultimate

[15] Thomas L. Stokes, "WPA & Politicians Victimize Taxpayer in Kentucky Battle," *Washington Daily News* clipping, no date, "Reference File Kentucky 1938" folder, box 160, Clapper Papers, LC.

[16] Thomas L. Stokes, "Fired for Refusal to Back Barkley, Say WPA Workers," *Washington Daily News* clipping, June 9, 1938, ibid.

effects to our Democracy if such a large group, dependent upon the administration in power, should be hereafter utilized and organized politically." Hopkins and the WPA did not react to Stokes's stories immediately, however. As Stokes remembered, it took the interest of the Senate to prod Hopkins and the WPA into releasing a fifteen-page, point-by-point rebuttal of his stories.[17] By late May 1938, Eleanor Roosevelt had also taken an interest in the Kentucky situation, asking her friend, deputy WPA administrator Aubrey Williams, if he could arrange "an unbiased investigation," as she had "been told that in Harlem [sic] [County] there is a great deal of graft in the WPA. A great many people are taking WPA checks and paying the people who gave them a certain percentage and, at the same time, they are holding [non-WPA] jobs." Williams declined to act, though, asking if Mrs. Roosevelt had more specific information for him. "As you know," he wrote to the First Lady, "it is pretty difficult to get at this sort of thing without some fairly definite leads to start on."[18]

More details had been provided to the WPA, however, by Brady M. Stewart, Chandler's campaign manager. During the last week of May 1938, Stewart released to the press his letter informing FDR that "it has become common talk among our people that the State Administrator of the Works Progress Administration in Kentucky has openly and boldly stated that he and his organization will leave nothing undone to achieve the re-election of Senator Barkley; and, accordingly, every federal relief agency in Kentucky, is frankly and brazenly operating upon a political basis." Stewart charged that WPA administrators issued "definite instructions" that "no one should be placed on federal relief except upon the advice of Senator Barkley's campaign managers in the respective counties" and that WPA workers had been tapped for donations to the Barkley campaign, after being "sharply informed that if they did not give the amounts demanded, they would be discharged immediately from their job." Workers were also given groceries in paper bags, which were stamped with the helpful reminder, "Paper Bags Donated by Friend of Sen. Alben W. Barkley." Stewart, no doubt with an eye toward a broader audience, concluded, "The Works Progress Administration in Kentucky

[17] Thomas L. Stokes, *Chip Off My Shoulder* (Princeton: Princeton University Press, 1940), 535–37.

[18] Eleanor Roosevelt to Aubrey Williams, no date; Aubrey Williams to Eleanor Roosevelt, May 31, 1938; both in "Kentucky 610 (Political Coercion) (Adm) (June–July 1938)" folder, box 1377, entry "Work Projects Administration. Central Files: State 1935–1944. Kentucky 610 Special Litigation," Records of the Works Projects Administration, Record Group 69, National Archives, Washington, D.C.

has been converted into an out-and-out political machine dedicated, over and above all other considerations, to re-electing Senator Barkley. Those with starving mouths to feed are forced to surrender their one remaining privilege of choosing for whom they shall vote, otherwise they and their dependents must go hungry and naked."[19] A more complete account of these charges, including photos of the "paper bag of groceries," soon appeared in the national press.[20]

Republicans also saw these missteps as a political opportunity. In a speech delivered over CBS radio, entitled "Pumping the Primaries," Ohio representative Dudley A. White seized on the spending proposal put forth by FDR and his advisers as a solution to the 1937–38 "Roosevelt Recession." With the beginning of the election season, White declaimed:

A different type of visitor began to descend upon Mr. Roosevelt, visitors interested not in relief but in *votes*. First one at a time and then in groups the wily political henchmen of the world's greatest vote getting machine sat down in the White House study, bit off the ends of their cigars, and told President Roosevelt that if the depression continued, New Deal voting strength would slip badly next November. At last the warm humanitarian heart of our Chief Executive was touched. "We cannot let this continue," he cried, and sent for his brain trust.[21]

Soon after, White related, the administration called for government to spend where business would not. "Roosevelt and his advisers knew exactly what they were doing. They were not priming the business pump. They were PUMPING THE PRIMARIES. The $6 billion were not intended to revive business – they were intended to revive New Deal majorities and to punish any man who was not subservient to White House dictators."[22] Referring to Barkley's speech against the Hatch amendment, White charged, "Even the Democratic floor leader of the Senate now confesses to the perversion of Federal relief for political purposes."

Although political opportunism fueled White's rhetoric, Hopkins and the WPA still had to deal with the substance of Stokes's findings. Hopkins and the WPA were forced to acknowledge directly the veracity of two of Stokes's most serious allegations. Regarding a WPA supervisor in

[19] Brady M. Stewart to FDR, May 23, 1938, in ibid.; and see *New York Times*, May 26, 1938, p. 5.
[20] See, e.g., Walter Davenport, "Happy Couldn't Wait," *Collier's*, July 16, 1938, p. 50, in "Reference File Kentucky 1938," box 160, Clapper Papers, LC; for Hopkins's denial of WPA involvement, see *New York Times*, July 10, 1938, p. 2.
[21] Dudley A. White, "Pumping the Primaries," June 7, 1938, "Reference File Work Relief" folder, box 256, Clapper Papers, LC. Emphasis in original.
[22] Ibid.

Edmonson County who was compiling detailed registration lists of all voters, Hopkins announced, "We have taken steps to see that this man minds his own business. He was told that 'any such activity on his part in the future would result in his being fired.'" Second, with respect to Stokes's report of a WPA project foreman, Cleve Keeney, who allegedly said that "the fellows on the job were going to have to support Barkley if they stayed on the WPA," Hopkins and his investigators at the WPA found the remark to have been true. "We regard this remark by Mr. Keeney as reprehensible," Hopkins stated, "and State Administrator Goodman has been instructed to take the necessary punitive action."[23] While Hopkins conceded that "in a far-flung organization" such as the WPA, "covering the 3,300 counties in America, with 64,000 projects and 2,700,000 workers, there will occur indiscretions by overzealous partisans in the midst of heated campaigns." He argued that "that is a vastly different thing from a planned and organized political campaign on the part of the responsible heads of any government agency."[24]

Subsequently, during Senate hearings on his nomination to be secretary of commerce, Hopkins was more frank about the Barkley–Chandler contest. "A political campaign starts, about as hot a political campaign as I have ever seen in America, and it was a hot one, and they threw everything at each other but the kitchen stove," Hopkins told the Senate Commerce Committee, generating laughter. "Now you get down in some of those Kentucky counties, and the local political party fellows started operating on our boys," Hopkins continued, "and our boys caved in. Now that is what happened. Goodman did not like it. I did not like it. But the real heat there was from people not inside of the WPA but outside of the WPA."[25] Dismissing the many affidavits that contradicted his case, Hopkins said that "those affidavits were submitted here by a purely partisan political organization, and I want to repeat that it was one of the toughest political campaigns I have ever seen, and they were dishing them up at – they were a dime a dozen down there." Or as Hopkins put it at another point in the hearings, "After all, one group of investigators might go out and find one

[23] WPA Press Release, June 30, 1938, "Kentucky 610 (Political Coercion) (Adm) (June–July 1938)" folder, box 1377, entry "Work Projects Administration. Central Files: State 1935–1944. Kentucky 610 Special Litigation," RG 69, NA; and *New York Times*, July 1, 1938, p. 6.
[24] Ibid.
[25] Hopkins statement in U.S. Congress, Senate, Committee on Commerce, *Hearings on the Nomination of Harry L. Hopkins to be Secretary of Commerce*, 76th Cong., 1st sess. (Washington, D.C.: U.S. Government Printing Office, 1939), 46.

thing, and another might go out and find another. These things are not always factual. Somebody says something was done; and another man denies it was done. Then a competent investigator makes up his mind who was telling the truth, and he says it was done or it was not done."[26]

THE SENATE INVESTIGATES: THE SHEPPARD COMMITTEE

Despite Hopkins's thorough defense, Stokes's reports on public works sites throughout Kentucky raised more than a few eyebrows in the Senate. Indeed, after Hatch's amendment was defeated, one contemporary authority on congressional power noted that "the upshot of these reversals" would be "a renewed insistence on an investigation" of politics in public works.[27] Surveying the political landscape four days after Hopkins and the WPA released their rebuttal, *New York Times* reporter Turner Catledge observed, "Whatever honest doubt any one might have had of a mixing of Federal relief with politics must have been shaken by the events of the past week." These "undoubtedly have pinned a campaign button on the relief program which will remain there until the smoke clears away from the coming primaries and general election."[28] Adding fuel to the growing surge of indignation was the abrupt announcement from the WPA's Washington headquarters of large pay raises for unskilled WPA workers, especially in Kentucky and Oklahoma (both hotly contested states), and a speech made by the WPA's Aubrey Williams to the union of WPA workers, the Workers Alliance, urging them to vote to "keep our friends in power." In this context, Hopkins's careful parsing of Stokes's many charges was noteworthy only for the acknowledgment that his WPA investigators had confirmed the most serious of Stokes's allegations.

The Senate's Special Committee to Investigate Senatorial Campaign Expenditures and Use of Governmental Funds, chaired by Texas Democrat Morris Sheppard, took on the task of looking into the charges made by Stokes and others. Featuring such conservative Democrats as Mississippi's Pat Harrison, Massachusetts's David Walsh, and Wyoming's Joseph O'Mahoney, the Sheppard Committee was thought by many to herald "another major reverse" for FDR.[29] Of Sheppard himself, however, Drew Pearson and Robert Allen reported, "There were titters in the

---

[26] Senate, *Hearings on the Nomination of Harry L. Hopkins*, 69.

[27] M. Nelson McGeary, *The Development of Congressional Investigative Power* (New York: Columbia University Press, 1940), 19.

[28] *New York Times*, July 3, 1938, p. E3.

[29] Hatcher, "Alben Barkley," 252.

press gallery when Vice President Jack Garner announced the appointment of Senator Morris Sheppard as chairman," since "some of the boys
thought it was a great joke that the gentle, soft-spoken little Texan should
be given the tough job of riding herd on electioneering funds."[30] The
Sheppard Committee, although formed in the final hours of the Seventy-
Fifth Congress, met immediately and passed a resolution that, according
to one reporter at least, "said, in effect, that it took its job seriously."
The Sheppard Committee, the resolution read, "gives warning now to all
candidates for Senatorial office, their friends and aides, that any violation or attempted violation of the laws pertaining to the conduct of the
campaign and the conduct of the election . . . will be fully exposed and
publicized with a view to criminal prosecution . . . [and] that all governmental agencies must keep clear of all primary and election campaigns –
must keep their hands off."[31]

By July 15, the committee sent an investigator, one H. Ralph Burton,
to Kentucky to examine the allegations.[32] Burton later would work on
an investigation of the WPA by a House committee that was labeled at
the time a "pretty crummy lot" of investigators.[33] Burton's competence
notwithstanding, two weeks after he returned from Kentucky the committee rushed to publish a preliminary public report before the primary
election occurred on August 6. The report stated that both Chandler and
Barkley shared responsibility for a "deplorable situation," which "should
arouse the conscience of the country." The actions of the WPA officials,
the committee argued, "imperil the right of the people to a free and unpol-
luted ballot."[34] Despite the timing of this report, Barkley managed to win
the primary with 56 percent of the vote. Throughout the summer and
fall of 1938, however, the Sheppard Committee continued its work. One
Kentucky politician wrote to the committee, praising its efforts in these
words: "When voters are purchased as slaves with public funds or taxpayers' money out of Federal and state treasuries, and driven like dumb

---

[30] Pearson and Allen quoted in Escal Franklin Duke, "The Political Career of Morris
Sheppard, 1875–1941" (Ph.D. diss., University of Texas, 1958), 463.

[31] *New York Times*, June 18, 1938, p. 1.

[32] Davis, *Alben W. Barkley*, 62; *New York Times*, July 16, 1938, p. 1.

[33] WPA official (possibly F. C. Harrington) to Harry Hopkins, personal, April 23, 1939,
"Works Progress Administration (WPA) Investigation – April 1939" folder, box 80, Harry
L. Hopkins Papers, FDL.

[34] *New York Times*, August 3, 1938, p. 10; U.S. Congress, Senate, *Report of the Special
Committee to Investigate Senatorial Campaign Expenditures and Use of Government
Funds in 1938*, Senate Report No. 1, Part 2, 76th Cong., 1st sess. (Washington, D.C.:
U.S. Government Printing Office, 1939), 68.

cattle to vote and perpetuate a political aristocracy, that is sapping the life blood of the Republic."[35] Worries about the corrupting influence of centralized power on the body politic are, of course, as old as the nation itself. For opponents of the New Deal, defining federal spending on public works programs as "corruption" constituted a broad characterization of the New Deal that could be deployed on the campaign trail or in drafting the Hatch Act.[36]

By October 1938, the committee was ready to report on its findings in Kentucky. While it determined that private parties were responsible for soliciting campaign funds from WPA workers, it also accused WPA officials themselves of exerting pressure on workers, and it declared them exclusively responsible for the "systematic canvassing of the WPA employees as to preference in the race for the Democratic senatorial nomination." The committee concluded that Stokes was correct "in a majority of the charges" made in his series of reports, and that Hopkins was justified in his objections "in four instances." In comparing the Barkley and Chandler campaigns, though, the committee found that Barkley had raised $24,000 from WPA employees, while Chandler had raised about $70,000 from employees who were paid in part or in full by federal funds.[37] This wide disparity in funds strengthened New Dealers' arguments against the political restrictions on public works spending that had been proposed by Senator Carl Hatch.

In making its recommendations, the Sheppard Committee focused directly on the intersection of public works, politics, and money, recalling the substance of Hatch's failed amendment and presaging the 1939 Hatch Act against "pernicious political activities." The committee urged legislation prohibiting any recipient of federal relief funds from making political contributions and advocated placing limits on campaign contributions to candidates for federal office. Similarly, the committee recommended expanding the prohibition on solicitation of political contributions in any federal office building to include requests made by letter and by telephone. In addition to urging that candidates for the Senate be required to disclose their contributions and expenditures, the committee even went so far as to advocate the prohibition of "any contribution by any national bank, any corporation organized by authority of any law of Congress, or by

---

[35] G. Tom Hawkins to the Senate Investigation Committee, August 15, 1938, in Senate, *Report of the Special Committee*, Part 2, p. 70–71.
[36] For the history of republicanism, see Daniel T. Rodgers, "Republicanism: The Career of a Concept," *Journal of American History* 79 (June 1992): 11–38; an effective treatment of its persistence during the New Deal is Brinkley, *Voices of Protest*, 143–68.
[37] Senate, *Report of the Special Committee*, Part 1, p. 11–12.

any corporation engaged in interstate or foreign commerce of the United States, in connection with any primary or general election." Regarding public works programs, the committee stated that candidates should be prohibited "from promising work, employment, money, or other benefits in connection with public relief."[38]

Although the Sheppard Committee concluded that there was no evidence indicating that Barkley knew of the actions of WPA employees and officials in Kentucky, correspondence and memoranda in Barkley's collected papers do suggest, in the opinion of Barkley's biographer, that "the senator did have knowledge of political activity in his behalf within the WPA and other federal agencies." However, Barkley argued that out of the 69,000 people employed by WPA in Kentucky, he probably received only 10,000 votes. Barkley estimated that 50 percent of WPA employees were Democrats, and, of them, only half were registered to vote. Furthermore, he claimed that Chandler's recent successful campaign for the governorship meant that many county-level officials in the state (who often had influence over who was certified for relief) had backed Chandler in the Senate primary.[39] Hopkins, though, when asked by a journalist what percentage of WPA workers would vote for FDR without any active recruiting by politicians, responded, "Oh, at least 90 percent. Why not? What other outfit have got any program that would be of any interest to people who are at a disadvantage or to the people with incomes like ourselves. I just think that is so obvious." Hopkins hedged a bit when asked about how Roosevelt's appeal translated to Barkley's chances with voters employed by the WPA, responding, "Do you mean right now in Kentucky? I think that is a little different situation; a Democratic primary, two Democrats running against each other. I don't think you can tell them how to vote. I think that is a lot of whitewash. You don't tell people how to vote. People vote because they think it is to their interest to vote, one way or another."[40]

Jim Farley, however, recorded a rather different analysis of the WPA's impact on the 1938 elections in his diary, drawing on a survey he had just made of Democratic Party county chairmen and, of course, benefiting

---

[38] Senate, *Report of the Special Committee*, Part 1, p. 39–41; and *New York Times*, January 4, 1939, p. 1.

[39] Davis, *Alben W. Barkley*, 64–65; 70, n. 80. The best authority on this Kentucky election remains Jasper Shannon; he concluded that the farmer-labor vote and urban voters were more responsible than the WPA for electing Barkley. Shannon, "Presidential Politics in the South," 169–70.

[40] Harry Hopkins press conference, July 21, 1938, no folder, box 6, entry 737, "Division of Information. Administrative Speeches, 1933–1942," RG 69, NA.

from hindsight. Farley speculated that WPA workers were "voting against the ticket, and I wouldn't be surprised if this included 50 percent of them, because they were dissatisfied with their rate of pay." Further trouble was caused, Farley thought, when "feeling developed against the WPA by interested tax payers and citizens who feel the WPA makes jobs for ne'er-do-wells, making it possible for them to receive an income they could never earn in industry and never did earn even in good times."[41] Farley had discussed his opinions on these factors with FDR at the close of 1938.[42]

In his study of this question, however, political scientist Wesley C. Clark found that there was "no evidence to support the hypothesis that the President's popularity varies directly with the amounts of money spent on relief," finding instead that the performance of the economy was a better predictor of presidential standing.[43] While it remains difficult to characterize the relation between the WPA and the electoral fortunes of FDR and the Democratic Party, it is clear that people across the political spectrum – from Democrats such as Hopkins and Farley to Republicans such as Charles McNary and Robert A. Taft, Jr., – thought that a great deal was at stake in these debates.

While FDR and other Democrats were troubled by the controversy surrounding the WPA, in the spring of 1939 a dismissed WPA employee, Ernest Rowe, released to the press correspondence between himself and George Goodman, the state director of the WPA in Kentucky. In these documents, Goodman outlined how WPA employees were to be solicited for campaign contributions for Barkley's campaign, instructing Rowe to keep records of the donations. Goodman suggested that workers contribute 2 percent of their salaries, but stipulated that there was to be "no discrimination against any employee who, because of home expenses or other reasons, does not feel able to assist financially in the campaign."[44] Four days later, on the same day that the Sheppard Committee had been authorized to begin its investigation, Goodman wrote to Rowe, ordering him

---

[41] Farley diary, January 10, 1939, "Private File 1939 January–April" folder, box 43, Farley Papers, LC.

[42] Farley diary, December 28, 1938, "Private File 1938 December" folder, box 43, Farley Papers, LC. Farley drew on this section of his diary in his book, *Jim Farley's Story* (New York: McGraw-Hill, 1948), 160.

[43] Wesley C. Clark, "Economic Aspects of a President's Popularity" (Ph.D. diss., University of Pennsylvania, 1943), 53.

[44] George H. Goodman to Ernest Rowe, May 23, 1938, quoted in Searle, *Minister of Relief*, 197.

to dispose of all correspondence regarding political matters that "carries a meaning which would subject us to criticism by the wrong interpretation."[45]

Despite all this bad press, Barkley's successful renomination pleased and relieved New Deal Democrats. "Immediately," reporter Thomas Stokes noted, "the inside group of New Dealers who have been active in the party 'purge' hope it will have the effect of stimulating the President to renewed vigor for the second phase of the 'purge' program, the attempt to defeat Senator George of Georgia and Senator Tydings of Maryland, conservatives who have bucked much of the New Deal." The victory also put Barkley into the mix of prospective Democratic presidential candidates for 1940. However, "in the opinion of observers," Stokes wrote, Barkley "did not add to his prestige by the type of campaign conducted on his behalf and by him personally, especially his concluding plea: 'If you want to swap all you're getting now from the Federal Government for a set of balanced budget Government books down in Washington, then vote for Happy Chandler, but if you want to keep on getting what you're getting and get some more, then vote to keep me in the Senate.'"[46] While Barkley's frankness had helped him to achieve reelection, Harry Hopkins's variation on Barkley's maxim attracted far more controversy.

TAX, SPEND, AND ELECT: HARRY HOPKINS AND
NEW DEAL LIBERALISM

Near the end of July 1938, during the high point of the Barkley-Chandler campaign and the start of the Sheppard Committee's investigation, Harry Hopkins joined some of his friends and acquaintances for a diverting afternoon spent wagering at a New York racetrack. Among those present were theater producer Max Gordon, newspaper columnist Heywood Broun, and transportation expert Daniel Arnstein. There, several journalists later claimed, he regaled his party with an acerbic assessment of the New Deal's political formula for success, reportedly saying, "We shall tax and tax, spend and spend, and elect and elect." In a single phrase, Hopkins had encapsulated the tangible benefits at the ballot box that the New Dealers derived from spending government revenues on public works

---

[45] George H. Goodman to Ernest Rowe, May 27, 1938, quoted in Searle, *Minister of Relief*, 197–98.
[46] Thomas Stokes clipping, August 8, 1938, "Reference File Kentucky 1938" folder, box 160, Clapper Papers, LC.

programs. However, according to his friend Robert Sherwood, Hopkins "stated categorically that he had said no such thing." He emphasized this by announcing, "I deny the whole works and the whole implication of it." Coming on the heels of Stokes's investigation of the WPA's political activities in Kentucky, though, reports of this incident generated immediate controversy. Subsequent historians, however, have generally accepted Sherwood's assessment that the statement was apocryphal.[47] These "eggs of canards," as Sherwood termed the reports, are "happily hatched out by presumably reputable journalists and, when they have taken wing, the denials seldom catch up with them. This particular one created a great deal of trouble for Hopkins and produced considerable wear and tear on his frazzled nervous system, but it did not greatly affect the course of events."[48]

Sherwood, though, was wrong. While Hopkins's apocryphal statement may not have affected the course of events, it marked an important point in the history of the New Deal. The controversy holds the potential for a more coherent understanding of the salience of phrases like "tax and spend liberal," which have continued as themes in American politics since 1938. The WPA was the centerpiece of the New Deal's welfare state but, as Hopkins's statement makes clear, it also represented very practical politics.[49]

Arthur Krock, one of the journalists who reported Hopkins's remarks, recalled in his memoirs that he had at first hesitated to mention the incident. He had learned of Hopkins's statement upon reading conservative commentator Frank R. Kent's political column in the *Baltimore Sun*. "I was impressed with the aptness of this capsule of the technique of the regime in power," Krock wrote, "but I made no reference to it until it was repeated in a column by Joseph Alsop."[50] At that point, Krock asked Kent for his sources, contacted them and satisfied himself as to their veracity, and reported the story for the Sunday *New York Times*. The day the story ran, Krock ate lunch in Virginia with Hopkins and

---

[47] See, e.g., Kennedy, *Freedom From Fear*, 349, n. 43.

[48] Sherwood, *Roosevelt and Hopkins*, 103–04.

[49] Amenta, *Bold Relief*.

[50] Alsop, a New Deal liberal, was a good friend of Hopkins. For more on their relationship, see Robert W. Merry, *Taking on the World: Joseph and Stewart Alsop – Guardians of the American Century* (New York: Viking Penguin, 1996), 88; Alsop touches briefly on the "tax, spend, and elect" incident in Joseph W. Alsop with Adam Platt, *"I've Seen the Best of It": Memoirs* (New York: W.W. Norton & Company, 1992), 120; 128.

several others. "Not only did he make no mention of the article, he gave no indication of any diminishment in our friendly relationship," Krock recalled of Hopkins's behavior. As Krock remembered it, a couple of days later the *New York Times* received a letter from Hopkins, denying the story and claiming that Krock had not tried to verify it. "It was all quite belated," Krock said. "Someone had told him this story was injuring the administration and probably would interfere with his confirmation as Secretary of Commerce," he speculated. A few nights later, a delighted Harold Ickes – no friend of Hopkins, or of Krock, for that matter – joked with Krock at a dinner party, "I see you have Harry by the short hairs."[51] Privately, Krock also told Jim Farley that Hopkins had indeed made his statement, to which Farley replied, "I said I thought Hopkins was foolish to get into any controversy with [Krock] on that subject."[52]

"But he did say it," Krock later claimed of Hopkins, "and he would always have stuck by it because he was a *cynic* in politics, except that it became a burden politically to the administration who wanted him confirmed as Secretary of Commerce. That would have been in his way had he admitted it, so he just said he had never made the statement, which I could understand perfectly, because I understand politicians. But there is no doubt at all he said it."[53] Indeed, Krock praised Hopkins's savvy. "That was the magic formula," Krock said of taxing, spending, and electing. Hopkins had "proved it, and it kept working."[54]

In fact, in an interview Hopkins gave to journalist Raymond Clapper three months before he visited the racetrack, the picture Hopkins outlined then did not differ much from the sentiments he expressed in his disputed

[51] Arthur Krock, *Memoirs: Sixty Years on the Firing Line* (New York: Funk & Wagnalls, 1968), 216–17; and "The Reminiscences of Arthur Krock," Columbia University Oral History Project, 68.

[52] Farley diary, November 24, 1938, "Private File 1938 October" folder, box 43, Farley Papers, LC.

[53] Krock also took issue with Sherwood's account of events in *Roosevelt and Hopkins*: "In connection with the Hopkins story about 'Tax and tax, spend and spend, elect and elect,' Sherwood used the word 'perjury' in connection with me," Krock wrote, referring to his testimony about the incident during Hopkins's Commerce Department confirmation hearings. "He conceded later that the word he meant was *injury* – not 'perjury' at all." Krock also threatened legal action regarding Sherwood's description of Krock's "malevolent venality," forcing him to back down and change the wording in the book. "The Reminiscences of Arthur Krock," Columbia University Oral History Project, 61, emphasis in original.

[54] "The Reminiscences of Arthur Krock," 65.

"tax, spend, and elect" statement. Clapper's raw notes, preserved in his personal papers, give a vivid sense of Hopkins's political realism:

Re politics. Hopkins says two angles, long range and petty political interference. Re long range – he says that he is conscious that WPA and other developments have far reaching political implications. Government checks of one kind or another are going into about 20,000,000 homes – which with relatives and friends creates vast group of beneficiaries, political group. Says been history in Europe that these benefits are never reduced but on contrary tend to enlarge. Politicians run for election on issue of giving more benefits – used to be tariff or abstract issues but now issue is how large a check will you give me. Few years ago were not ten men in cgs [Congress] who favored social security, now not a one would vote against it.[55]

It was in this sort of political universe that Hopkins located the WPA. As Clapper recorded:

Coming down to more detail, Hopkins thinks that on the whole his show is clean and reason he does is that when there is anything sour they hear about it instantly, so many people have to be in on anything crooked that someone will always squeal. . . . Hopkins says politicians wont stop at anything to get vote lined up and have no regard for WPA or anything except winning elections. Politicians plant workers just off project site and canvass men, give them slips to sign and turn in at party clubhouse, etc., and in all sort of ways intimate and hint that they better vote right or they might lost jobs etc. Hold meetings just as workmen are leaving project, call on them at their homes, etc., and thus exert pressure which WPA has difficulty in stopping.[56]

This interview formed the basis of Clapper's published analysis of the WPA's problems with politics, reinforcing his conclusion that "Hopkins can and does crack down whenever politicians actually get into his territory, but the most insidious attempts to gain political advantage out of WPA are beyond his reach, and can be broken up most effectively by local exposure."[57] In his interview with Clapper, Hopkins emphasized the ability of government spending to generate new political coalitions, an ability that the "tax, spend, and elect" remark would seem to have encapsulated nicely.

[55] Raymond Clapper diary, May 3, 1938, "RC Diaries 1938 2" folder, box 8, Clapper Papers, LC.
[56] Ibid.
[57] Raymond Clapper, "Hopkins Fights Politics," May 9, 1938, "Clapper Columns" vol. 1, scrapbook, box 60, Clapper Papers, LC.

Perhaps New Dealer-turned-columnist Hugh S. Johnson best captured the dilemma that has vexed those who have pondered Hopkins's "tax, spend, and elect" statement. While Johnson believed that the anonymous witnesses of Hopkins's remarks were not lying, he also professed his conviction that Hopkins would not lie. "My belief might be something like the aged and doting Kentucky Colonel who accused his young fiancée of embracing a handsome stranger," wrote Johnson. "She indignantly denied it. He protested he had seen it in broad daylight at three yards distance," but the young woman "convinced his fond heart by saying, 'Do yo' believe your honey, or do yo' believe yo' eyes?' " Indeed, Johnson argued, anyone at the racetrack with Hopkins "could have thought he said what they said he said because it is consistent with everything the Third New Deal has recently done – and inconsistent with nothing Mr. Hopkins has said or ever done.... For that reason it doesn't make the slightest difference whether he said it or not. The actions to which the misunderstood (?) words seemed to apply say it so much more eloquently than even these quaintly characteristic Hopkinsesque words, the words are wholly unimportant."[58]

The day before Johnson's column appeared, the *Washington Daily News* ran a cartoon that confirmed Johnson's reasoning about the unimportance of words at this point. Entitled "WPA Project Number One!" the cartoon featured a frantic Hopkins, running but unable to escape a tin can rattling on the ground behind him, as this can has been tethered to the bottom of his coat. Hopkins specifies the content of "WPA project number one," crying out, "Quick Somebody – Git that off my tail!" On the can, of course, was the label, "We will spend and spend, and tax and tax, and elect and elect!"[59] Johnson concluded, "Because the saying, whether spoken or not, so aptly and so accurately describes what the Administration and especially WPA has been doing, the denial falls dead and the words become a catch phrase that will haunt Hopkins for years."[60] This catch phrase has also continued to haunt historians of the New Deal, who have slighted the potential for the WPA to remake the electoral map and have chosen to concentrate instead on seconding Hopkins's denials. While we may never know with complete certainty exactly what Hopkins

---

[58] Hugh S. Johnson clipping from the *Philadelphia Inquirer*, November 30, 1938, p. 17, "November 30, 1938. Press Clippings. Division of Press Information Room 210" folder, box 30, Hopkins Papers, FDRL.
[59] Cartoon clipping from the *Washington Daily News*, November 29, 1938, p. 16, in ibid.
[60] Johnson column, cited above.

said, a brief examination of the passage of the Hatch Act indicates that the debate surrounding Hopkins's denials transcended the particulars of his original statement.

POLITICAL BACKLASH: "AN ACT TO PREVENT PERNICIOUS POLITICAL ACTIVITIES"

Although Senator Carl Hatch's amendment to a public works appropriation was voted down in the spring of 1938, he did not abandon the idea of preventing the political use of public works. Hatch revived his amendment, and in 1939 he presented it separately as "an Act to prevent pernicious political activities." Hatch's bill was intended to prevent solicitation of money from relief recipients and to keep the WPA from denying assistance to people because of their political views. More extreme, however, was Section 9(a) of Hatch's proposed law, which declared, "No officer or employee in the executive branch of the Federal Government, or any agency or department thereof, shall take any active part in political management or in political campaigns."[61]

This section of the proposed law attracted little attention or opposition at first. After the Senate approved it unanimously, though, the Roosevelt administration began to study the measure more closely. One New Dealer warned FDR's press secretary, Steve Early, that the Hatch measure was meant "to hit the President himself," keeping FDR, cabinet officials, and Congress from campaigning.[62] Alarmed, FDR and his advisers arranged for the House to delay debate on the Hatch bill until this huge loophole could be addressed. Hatch finally agreed to the rewrite of Section 9(a), acknowledging that the terms "officer" and "employee" did not include the president, vice president, or cabinet secretaries.[63]

Even with this problem addressed, FDR was uncertain about whether to sign the Hatch bill into law. Illinois congressman Kent Keller notified FDR that Democrats had taken to calling it "the HATCHET bill," referring to what they considered a direct assault on the New Deal.[64] These sentiments were echoed by Charles M. Shreve, the executive secretary of the Young Democrats of America, who argued, "There is no justification

[61] James R. Eccles, *The Hatch Act and the American Bureaucracy* (New York: Vantage, 1981), 298.
[62] Quoted in Porter, "Hatch Act of 1939," 155.
[63] Eccles, *Hatch Act*, 298–99.
[64] Kent Keller to FDR, August 1, 1939, "OF 252a Permitting Government Employees to Hold Elective Office" folder, OF 252-A, FDR Papers, FDRL.

for making political eunuchs of the future statesmen and leaders of our Democracy. It should suffice to point out that every Republican member of the House present for the vote voted for the Hatch Bill, together with every avowed Democratic enemy of the New Deal."[65]

Longtime progressive Republican George W. Norris, however, urged FDR to resist pressure to veto the Hatch bill. "I believe this bill is a great step towards the purification of politics and Government," Norris wrote. "To veto it would be the greatest mistake of your career – the full effects of which you could never overcome." Roosevelt quickly reassured Norris, firing back a note, "Wait until you see what I say about the Hatch Bill!"[66] Despite his bravado, however, Roosevelt was not at all sure of what his message would be. While relaxing at his Hyde Park estate, Roosevelt conferred with Jim Farley about the implications of the bill. Farley urged FDR to persuade Attorney General Frank Murphy to render an opinion about its legality – particularly Sections 5 and 9, which dealt with the assessment of relief employees and freedom of political speech for the Executive Branch – and they discussed the possibility of vetoing it. Murphy ventured the opinion that the Hatch bill was constitutional. Annoyed, FDR retorted that the legislation should have never reached his desk.[67]

Roosevelt faced a difficult decision. In an effort to preempt the "politics and relief" issue, he could sign the measure into law. However, he was undecided. Part of him wanted to follow the counsel of advisers – chiefly Thomas Corcoran and Ben Cohen – and veto the measure. In fact, Corcoran and Cohen teamed up with Murphy to draft a detailed message for FDR to deliver as he vetoed the Hatch Act. Corcoran argued that he and his two colleagues had developed "a line of approach which is outside of any speculation in the newspapers, and which seems to us to offer a real chance to turn the tables" on the Hatch bill's supporters. They would argue that since the Constitution permits the Congress to regulate elections, FDR could claim that the Hatch Act did not go far enough,

[65] Shreve quoted in Sidney M. Milkis, "New Deal Party Politics, Administrative Reform, and the Transformation of the American Constitution," in Robert Eden, ed., *The New Deal and its Legacy: Critique and Reappraisal* (Westport, CT: Greenwood Press, 1989), 143.

[66] George W. Norris to FDR, July 26, 1939; FDR to Norris, July 28, 1939; both in "Subject File. Hatch Bill: 1939" folder, box 137, President's Secretary's File, FDR Papers, FDRL.

[67] Farley Diary, July 23, 1939, "James A. Farley Private File 1939 July" folder, box 44, Farley Papers, LC; and Farley to Missy LeHand, July 25, 1939, "OF 252a Permitting Government Employees to Hold Elective Office" folder, OF 252-A, FDR Papers, FDRL.

as it did not ban state and local officeholders from influencing political campaigns.[68]

Harold Ickes later recalled that "the Cohen draft, in the preparation of which Tom Corcoran had helped, seemed to me to be a brilliant piece of work." Ickes elaborated:

The theory of it was that the Hatch bill should be vetoed and that a much more comprehensive bill should be passed, one which would keep out of active Federal political participation not only Federal but state and county employees. The theory further was that the power of money should be taken out of politics, and so this draft advocated an appropriation by Congress to cover the campaign expenses of all political parties. No other contributions would be allowed.[69]

That Ickes would term this set of steps "brilliant" takes on greater significance after examining the text of the veto message, as well as Cohen's private and frank assessments of how this veto would benefit the administration. Cohen's message opened with FDR acknowledging that the Hatch Act sought to "free federal elections from the subversive use of money" and "to free federal elections from the subversive use of the administrative personnel of government for purposes of party organizations and the manipulations of elections." In other words, "the objectives [were] to take money out of politics and take politics out of government." Roosevelt would then heartily agree with such sentiments and offer this rationale: "Of the practical devotion of this Administration to the broad objectives of this bill therefore there can be no doubt." FDR would then point to his government reorganization plans, which "continually and consistently I have urged upon the Congress" as "the only real remedy for the spoils system which compels government officeholders to act as parts of a political machine, i.e., the extension upward, downward, and outward of the principles of Civil Service."[70] With these bona fides presented, Roosevelt would announce that he was nevertheless vetoing the Hatch Act, "because in its present form it is so poorly drawn that it not only fails to carry out those objectives but actually interferes with the progress already made toward them."

---

[68] Thomas Corcoran to FDR, July 30, 1939, "Benjamin V. Cohen. Subject File. Hatch Act, 1939–56 and undated" folder, box 9, Benjamin V. Cohen Papers, LC; and copy in "Subject File. Hatch Bill: 1939" folder, box 137, PSF, FDR Papers, FDRL.

[69] Harold L. Ickes, *The Secret Diary of Harold L. Ickes* (New York: Simon & Schuster, 1954), 2:689–90.

[70] Proposed veto message, no date, "Special Files. New Deal Era. Subject File. Hatch Act, 1939" folder, box 253, Corcoran Papers, LC.

While presenting this objection in the name of good government, Cohen and Corcoran were political realists. They were well aware that the Hatch Act would damage the administration, as the brief memo they attached to their proposed veto message indicates. They summed up the fundamental principles backing their approach: By "demanding that all state officials and employees be included (as they constitutionally certainly can) the resistance of members of Congress under pressure from state political machines may very well be increased to the point where there will be no bill passed at all." And in the event that a revised bill incorporating these new regulations was somehow passed by Congress, Cohen and Corcoran predicted frankly, "If state officials are included in a revision of the bill the political situation will become so mixed up that it cannot help but result to advantage" for the New Dealers.[71]

Cohen's final strategy in his proposed veto message was for FDR to request greater federal participation in campaign financing, addressing "the growing concern of all decent citizens over the use of money in political campaigns with the great increase of concentrated wealth in this country – and the unmistakable indications that in the coming campaign the power of wealth will be abused as never before." However, president Roosevelt would argue, "I am convinced that any realistic treatment of the abuse of political funds must reach the disparity between the amount of campaign contributions openly or secretly available to contending political parties."

His argument can be summed up as follows: Just as it is counterproductive to increase the political influence of state and local machines by imposing upon federal officeholders restrictions that do not equally apply to state and municipal officeholders, so may it also be counterproductive to strengthen, in effect, the influence of those who contribute to political campaigns in the hope of securing economic advantages and privileges by imposing restrictions on those who contribute to political campaigns in the hope of securing political jobs.

On the basis of this line of reasoning, Roosevelt would call for Congress to incorporate a system for public funding of elections and would announce, "It has always seemed to me unimportant whether the political faction with the wrong candidate and the wrong platform had *too much* money to spend, provided the party with the right candidate and the right platform had *enough* to spend to put its case fairly before the

---

[71] Untitled memo with penciled notation, "Hatch Bill," no date, "Special Files. New Deal Era. Subject File. Hatch Act, 1939" folder, box 253, Corcoran Papers, LC.

country. Given a decent advocacy to delineate the issues the American people can be trusted to find the truth." Therefore, FDR called for Congress to appropriate $5 million to each of the two major parties for the 1940 election, basing this figure on spending during the 1936 campaign. Any "substantial" third party would receive "proportionate sums." While "the entire plan might cost the federal treasury $15 million, one-sixth of the cost of a battleship," this money "would save the American people hundreds of millions of dollars in eliminating trails of corruption in public life which are almost impossible to trace." Likening the American political system to "a seamless web," Roosevelt would conclude by arguing: "You cannot change the pattern of part of it without considering the effect upon all of it." Thus the Hatch Act "in its present form ... only creates greater evils than it seeks to cure, [but] it can be effectively revised along the lines that I have indicated to do a really effective job of reshaping our political technique to the interest of an enduring democracy."[72]

This proposal to pay for electoral campaigns with public funds, Cohen acknowledged, was not well thought out. However, it was a chance to introduce into the political debate "for the first time a note which should recur from now on – warning about the use of money by the other side." While government funding of election campaigns "may be sound – depending on circumstances, i.e., by whom it is to be spent, national committee officials or otherwise, and where the control of such officials will lie," Cohen's view was that this vague and far-reaching proposal "will provide so much discussion that it will red-herring any headlines about the vetoing of the bill." By proposing a bold measure, Cohen argued that FDR could simultaneously claim the mantle of democracy while distracting the press and the public from the fact that he had vetoed the Hatch Act.[73]

FDR, however, was not persuaded by Corcoran and Cohen. The President received their veto draft while spending the weekend on his yacht *Potomac* with Harry Hopkins and loyal Democratic operative Frank Walker. "These were not the best men to be with him at a time when he was considering such an important matter," Harold Ickes wrote in his diary. "Frank Walker," Ickes's former nemesis when he was head of the Advisory Committee on Allotments in 1935, "has no fight in him and doesn't know any politics," while Hopkins "is more or less licked, especially on the subject of WPA, and the Hatch bill was an outgrowth

---

[72] Proposed veto message, cited above. Emphasis in original.
[73] Untitled memo with penciled notation, "Hatch Bill," cited above.

from WPA."[74] Although FDR's decision to sign the Hatch Act into law most likely was finalized during this weekend vacation with Hopkins and Walker, it makes more sense to view this step in the context of the previous year's controversy over relief in politics, FDR's attempted purge of the Democratic Party, and the growing strength of conservative elements in Congress. Indeed, the striking differences between Corcoran and Cohen's proposed veto and the message that FDR sent to Congress upon signing the Hatch Act – on the very last day before it would become law without his signature – capture this turn of events.

Seeking to dispel the "many misrepresentations, some unpremeditated, some deliberate, in regard to the attitude of the Executive Branch" to the Hatch Act, FDR set out in his message to Congress to write a new history of the Hatch Act and his administration's relationship to it. He portrayed the Hatch Act not as a bill that originated from conservative Democrats frustrated with FDR's attempts to expel them from their own party, but rather as Congress's just response to Roosevelt's own call for greater regulation of politics in relief. Quoting from an earlier message he had sent to Congress requesting more money for the WPA, Roosevelt reiterated, "It is my belief that improper political practices can be eliminated only by the imposition of rigid statutory regulations and penalties by the Congress, and that this should be done." Further, Congress should levy these penalties "not only upon persons within the administrative organization of the Works Progress Administration, but also upon outsiders who have in fact in many instances been the principal offenders in this regard." FDR's only caution was that "no legislation should be enacted which will in any way deprive workers on the Works Progress Administration program of the civil rights to which they are entitled in common with other citizens." This said, Roosevelt welcomed the Hatch Act, remarking, "It is well known that I have consistently advocated the objectives of the present bill," and claiming that he was not worried by assertions that "partisan political reasons have entered largely into the passage of the bill," because "it is my hope that if properly administered the measure can be made an effective instrument of good Government."[75]

To this end, FDR turned in the remainder of his message to explicating his attorney general's assessment of the rights of those who were

[74] Ickes, *Secret Diary*, 2:689. For Walker's opinion of Ickes, see Robert H. Ferrell, ed., *FDR's Quiet Confidant: The Autobiography of Frank C. Walker* (Niwot: University Press of Colorado, 1997), 99.
[75] Samuel I. Rosenman, ed., *The Public Papers and Addresses of Franklin D. Roosevelt* (New York: Russell & Russell, 1939), 8:410.

covered by the Hatch Act. FDR reassured federal employees that they still had the right to attend political meetings, make voluntary campaign contributions to political parties and candidates, and express their political opinions and preferences publicly, so long as it was not part of a formal campaign. Indeed, FDR had secured reassurance from Hatch himself on these questions three days before signing the bill into law.[76] Going further, Roosevelt also clarified that citizens who received government loans were not subject to the bill, and neither were government employees who were members of political parties or labor unions, veterans who received government benefits, or recipients of unemployment insurance or old-age pensions.[77]

FDR further noted that while the Hatch Act did not cover members of Congress or their employees, it was unclear whether the president, vice president, and cabinet officials were the only members of the executive branch who could speak freely. Drawing on the rhetoric of patriotism, Roosevelt argued:

It can hardly be maintained that it is an American way of doing things to allow newspapers, magazines, radio broadcasters, members and employees of the Senate and House of Representatives and all kinds of candidates for public office and their friends to make any form of charge, misrepresentation, falsification or vituperation against the acts of any individual or group of individuals employed in the Executive Branch of the Federal Government with complete immunity against reply except by a handful of high executive officials. That, I repeat, would be un-American because it would be unfair, and the great mass of Americans like fair play and insist on it. They do not stand for any gag act.[78]

FDR then declared that under the counsel of the attorney general he was of the opinion that all federal employees could respond to attacks.

Only in the second-to-last paragraph of his message did FDR get around to discussing a central feature of the Cohen and Corcoran veto draft: "the fact that the bill does not in any way cover the multitude of State and local employees who greatly outnumber Federal employees and who may continue to take part in elections in which there are candidates of Federal office on the same ballot with candidates for State and local office." FDR suggested that Congress, in a future session, consider extending the Hatch Act so as to cover state and local government employees,

---

[76] Porter, "Hatch Act of 1939," 160.
[77] Rosenman, ed., *The Public Papers and Addresses of FDR*, 8:411–12.
[78] Ibid., 413–14.

and he concluded, "It is because for so many years I have striven in public life and in private life for decency in political campaigns, both on the part of Government servants, of candidates, of newspapers, of corporations and of individuals, that I regard this new legislation as at least a step in the right direction."[79]

While Congress did take up FDR's proposal in passing a second Hatch Act in 1940, the Hatch Act of 1939 troubled many New Dealers. Senator Key Pittman, for example, complained to Jim Farley that Pittman's fellow Nevada Democrats were deeply concerned about the Hatch Act. In fact, at their annual Jackson Day Dinner held in Carson City, Nevada, federal employees made their contributions to the Jackson Day Committee over the signatures of their wives or sisters, while others did not attend at all. The presiding officer asked the state employees to take a bow, but then said that because of the Hatch Act he would not ask the federal employees present to stand and be recognized. "This further emphasizes the necessity for a definite interpretation of the Hatch Act," Pittman complained. "If our Federal employees have got to have their wives contribute to the Jackson Day Dinner it would probably be better for some of us if the Republicans had the Federal employees. When the Republicans get into power they won't permit anything like the Hatch Act to break up their organization."[80]

While some Democrats echoed Pittman's complaints, others explored the possibility of legal action. Democratic lawyer Ernest Cuneo corresponded with the American Civil Liberties Union about bringing a test case of the Hatch Act's constitutionality. The ACLU's head, Roger Baldwin, wrote to Cuneo, saying that the organization could not decide whether this course of action was worth pursuing: "The presentation of your project of having a [WPA] employee make a speech and then sue out a writ to restrain his superior from firing him did not seem enough to go on." Baldwin asked Cuneo for more information, noting that the ACLU "would like to see an outline of actually how you propose to test the law, and what points you would rely on, before we can indicate whether we could take charge of such proceedings."[81] The Hatch Act, however, was not reviewed by the courts until after World War II, when

[79] Ibid., 415.

[80] Key Pittman to James A. Farley, January 15, 1940, "Hatch Act" folder, box 13, Key Pittman Papers, LC.

[81] Roger Baldwin to Ernest Cuneo, August 29, 1939; and see also Jerome M. Britchey to Ernest Cuneo c/o Drew Pearson, August 18, 1939; both in "Hatch Act" folder, box 25, Ernest Cuneo Papers, FDRL.

the Supreme Court upheld it by a margin of four to three in *United Public Workers* v. *Mitchell* and *Oklahoma* v. *U.S. Civil Service Commission.*[82]

The debate over the Hatch Act went to the core of questions about the political significance and viability of the WPA specifically and the New Deal in general. An Irish American foreman on a Boston WPA project realized this when he called together the one hundred workers under his supervision at the close of a work day. "I want to warn ye fellers against political activity," he said. "There is a bird named Hatch who comes from Texas [sic] and is a Member of Congress. While the other Congressmen were not looking he put through a law that makes it a crime for you or me to talk politics, attend political rallies, wear the button of any candidate or even mention the name of any candidate." If you do any of these things, he warned them, "you not only lose your job but you may go to prison and I'm telling yer to watch out." However, the foreman concluded, "Just one more word before dismissing you, if any of you birds come back to work Election Day without having voted for a lame man, well – it will be just too bad."[83]

While the Hatch Act ultimately did not keep that "lame man" from getting elected to two more terms as president, it did signal the growing unpopularity and political liability of public works programs, and it provided a common point of reference both for future liberals and for conservatives who looked to expand or roll back the welfare state. As historian Anthony Badger has observed, the strength of conservative stereotypes about the WPA can in part explain Lyndon Johnson's refusal to bring back the program as part of the War on Poverty. Johnson, who had run the National Youth Administration in Texas for another southern New Dealer, Aubrey Williams, knew firsthand the political costs and benefits of works programs. Ironically, another president with a less developed sense of history, whose father had led the WPA in Dixon, Illinois, had a rather different view of the WPA. "Now a lot of people remember it as boondoggles and raking leaves," observed Ronald Reagan. "Maybe in some places it was. Maybe in the city machines or something. But I can

[82] Ferrel Heady, "The Hatch Act Decisions," *American Political Science Review* 61 (August 1947): 687–99; and L.V. Howard, "Federal Restrictions on the Political Activity of Government Employees," *American Political Science Review* 35 (June 1941): 470–89. The 4–3 margin was because Justice Robert Jackson was prosecuting the Nuremburg Trials and Justice Frank Murphy recused himself, as he had previously decided the Hatch Act was constitutional while serving as Attorney General.
[83] William H. O'Brien to Margaret LeHand, September 20, 1940, "OF 252a Permitting Government Employees to Hold Elective Office" folder, OF 252-A, FDR Papers, FDRL.

take you to our town and show you things, like a river front that I used to hike through once that was a swamp and is now a beautiful park place built by WPA."[84]

The passage of the Hatch Act signaled a political backlash against the demonstrable impact that New Deal public works programs had on politics at the state and local levels. While the scale of this public works spending was new, changing the political map of the country while developing the national estate, in many ways this moment represents the endpoint of what has been labeled the distributive "party period" in American politics.[85] Harry Hopkins's assertion that the state's taxing and spending powers could be used to forge an electoral coalition clarifies the importance of public works programs to the state built by New Dealers. Although conservatives supported the Hatch Act in order to curtail the power of the New Deal state, New Dealers would attempt to recover from this setback. With the coming of world war, these reformers pushed to carve out a more secure place for public works programs in the American state.

[84] Badger, *New Deal: The Depression Years*, 215. For more on the connection between LBJ and New Deal liberalism, see Schwarz, *New Dealers*, 264–84; and Anthony J. Badger, "Whatever Happened to Roosevelt's New Generation of Southerners?," in Robert A. Garson and Stuart S. Kidd, eds., *The Roosevelt Years: New Perspectives on American History, 1933–1945* (Edinburgh: Edinburgh University Press, 1999), 122–38.

[85] Richard L. McCormick, *The Party Period and Public Policy: American Politics From the Age of Jackson to the Progressive Era* (New York: Oxford University Press, 1986).

7

Public Works and New Deal Liberalism in Reorganization and War

During the 1930s, New Dealers radically expanded the power of the federal government and deployed it in new ways. These structural changes in the American state were not, however, matched by a corresponding revolution in the nation's constitutional structure. As legal historians such as Bruce Ackerman and Lawrence Friedman have noted, no constitutional amendments were passed to codify the New Deal's reforms. Searching for a way to direct the rapidly growing federal government, New Dealers turned not to the task of amending the Constitution, but rather to the arena of administration and management. Here, within seemingly endless stacks of organizational charts, budget tables, and memoranda, a fierce fight for the New Deal's survival took place.[1]

Proposals in 1937 and 1938 to reorganize the executive branch of government quickly drew concern from an increasingly conservative Congress. Set against the backdrop of the Supreme Court–packing debacle and the "Roosevelt Recession" of 1937–38, this concern flowered into a debate over whether too much power was being concentrated in the

---

[1] Bruce Ackerman, *We the People: Transformations* (Cambridge: Harvard University Press, 1998); and Lawrence M. Friedman, *American Law in the Twentieth Century* (New Haven: Yale University Press, 2002). For the importance of organization and administration in government and in business, Erwin C. Hargrove, *Prisoners of Myth: The Leadership of the Tennessee Valley Authority, 1933–1990* (Knoxville: University of Tennessee Press, 2001); Chester Barnard, *The Functions of the Executive* (Cambridge: Harvard University Press, 1938); and see also Louis Galambos, "The Emerging Organizational Synthesis in Modern American History," *Business History Review* 44 (Autumn 1970): 279–90; and Brian Balogh, "Reorganizing the Organizational Synthesis: Federal-Professional Relations in Modern America," *Studies in American Political Development* 5 (Spring 1991): 119–72.

hands of a dictatorial, king-like president. After the 1938 defeat of an initial reorganization plan, presented by the President's Committee on Administrative Management, a more limited measure made it through Congress in 1939 and was signed into law. While much of the reorganization controversy revolved around apparently neutral topics, such as how best to consolidate budget and account planning in the executive branch, surprisingly, the fate of the controversial public works programs was not the subject of serious discussions.[2]

In 1939 the federal government consolidated its public works construction functions within one umbrella agency, justifying the move as being "in the interests of economy and efficiency." This new organization, christened the Federal Works Agency (FWA), contained the newly renamed Work Projects Administration (formerly Works Progress Administration), the Public Works Administration (PWA), the Public Buildings Administration (formerly part of the Treasury Department), the Public Roads Administration (transferred from the Agriculture Department), and the United States Housing Authority.[3]

Unpacking the high stakes hidden within the phrase "in the interests of economy and efficiency," this chapter revisits the consolidation of these New Deal agencies. Covering the period beginning in 1938 and continuing through World War II, it locates this institutional history in the changing political trajectory of the New Deal during wartime. Previous chronicles of the fortunes of New Deal liberalism in war often focus on FDR's claim that it was time for "Dr. Win-the-War" to replace "Dr. New Deal."[4] This line of interpretation has resulted in various accounts that document how the war distracted FDR from continuing the New Deal, for example lamenting the "honorable discharge" he issued to the WPA in 1943. While this reading of history accurately reflects the sensibilities of contemporary New Deal notables like Harold Ickes, Eleanor Roosevelt, and Leon Henderson, it is seriously incomplete, as it neglects the many wartime activities

---

[2] Barry Dean Karl, *Executive Reorganization and Reform in the New Deal: The Genesis of Administrative Management, 1900–1939* (Cambridge: Harvard University Press, 1963); and Richard Polenberg, *Reorganizing Roosevelt's Government, 1936–1939: The Controversy over Executive Reorganization* (Cambridge: Harvard University Press, 1966).

[3] Floyd Dell, draft of "Federal Works Agency" entry for *Encyclopaedia Americana*, December 5, 1939, "Federal Works Agency" folder, box 1, entry 746, "Division of Information. Publications of the Federal Works Agency and Subordinate Agencies, 1936–1942," Record Group 69, Records of the Work Projects Administration, National Archives, Washington, D.C.

[4] Transcript of December 28, 1943, press conference, in *The Press Conferences of Franklin D. Roosevelt* (Hyde Park, NY: Franklin D. Roosevelt Library, 1957), reel 11.

carried out by the New Deal's central enterprise, the public works programs.[5]

Rather than quietly accept that war and a more conservative Congress meant the curtailment of public works, various New Dealers successfully combined the emergency presented by the approach of war with their desire to use public works projects to reduce unemployment and develop the nation's infrastructure. They quickly realized that justifying these projects as necessary wartime spending provided a powerful rationale for continuing to fund programs that were becoming unpopular. This reorientation was much more than a mere rhetorical move or political gambit; instead, it directly drew upon the New Deal's long engagement with building infrastructure. Indeed, since 1933, the New Dealers had responded to the crisis of the Great Depression by embracing public construction.

As the 1930s drew to a close, however, New Dealers no longer had to rely upon the "analogue" of war when making their case for further reforms. They could now point to war itself. During the early 1940s, in the name of wartime necessity, the public works programs produced substantial infrastructure throughout the nation, building hundreds of airports, erecting housing for defense workers, and improving miles of roads, to name but several of their endeavors. For the first time, they even provided job training for the unemployed, a step that organized labor had long opposed.[6] The American wartime state was constructed on the deep and vital foundations that had been laid down by the New

[5] The most important recent treatment of New Deal social policy follows this interpretive tradition; see Edwin Amenta, *Bold Relief: Institutional Politics and the Origins of Modern American Social Policy* (Princeton: Princeton University Press, 1998). Synthetic treatments of the New Deal – such as William E. Leuchtenburg's *Franklin D. Roosevelt and the New Deal, 1932–1940* (New York: Harper & Row, 1963) – generally end in 1940, thus avoiding this question. The many biographies of FDR, Eleanor Roosevelt, and prominent New Dealers such as WPA head Harry Hopkins and PWA head Harold Ickes, however, generally cleave to this theme.

[6] For the classic account of the widespread use of wartime metaphors by New Dealers, see William Leuchtenburg's essay, "The New Deal and the Analogue of War," revised and reprinted in William E. Leuchtenburg, *The FDR Years: On Roosevelt and His Legacy* (New York: Columbia University Press, 1995), 35–75. An insightful and often-overlooked analysis of the place of World War II in New Dealer arguments for the continuation of reform is found in Richard Polenberg, "The Decline of the New Deal, 1937–1940," in John Braeman, Robert H. Bremner, and David Brody, eds., *The New Deal: The National Level* (Columbus: Ohio State University Press, 1975), 246–66; esp. 262–63.

Deal, and the public works programs created state capacities essential to the preparedness effort.[7] During these years, New Deal public works programs returned to the heavier construction and emphasis on efficiency that was first epitomized by Harold Ickes's PWA.

In an effort to highlight the potential for a "third" New Deal to advance the cause of reform, some historians have posited an alternative to Roosevelt's "Dr. Win-the-War–Dr. New Deal" dichotomy, arguing that the late 1930s, not the wartime years, were the critical testing ground for the New Deal. In this scheme, New Dealers continued to make critical advances in their policies after the "second" New Deal of 1935, passing the 1937 Wagner–Steagall Housing Act and the 1938 Fair Labor Standards Act and scoring an important victory by expanding the administrative capacity of the American state, a feat they accomplished by reorganizing the executive branch of the federal government.[8] Presenting a less optimistic variation on this interpretive theme, historian Alan Brinkley has likewise argued that the pivotal moment for New Deal liberalism was not wartime. Rather, following Herbert Stein's argument in *The Fiscal Revolution in America,* Brinkley considers the 1937–38 recession to have been a key turning point. The New Deal's embrace of expansionary fiscal policy at the expense of a strong regulatory state – the end of reform, in other words – marked this historical moment. While alerting us to a significant reorientation within New Deal liberalism, these interpretations ignore the multifaceted and longstanding relationship between New Deal liberalism and its public works programs, failing to consider their role either as producers of state-financed infrastructure or as providers of employment. For public works programs, reform was far from at an end. War did

---

[7] Over twenty years following the beginning of World War II, Alice O'Connor has argued, precisely the reverse arrangement occurred. Instead of welfare programs providing state capacities to the military, in the 1960s the military provided important state capacities to the government programs fighting the War on Poverty. Alice O'Connor, "Neither Charity Nor Relief: The War on Poverty and the Effort to Redefine the Basis of Social Provision," in Donald T. Critchlow and Charles H. Parker, eds., *With Us Always: A History of Private Charity and Public Welfare* (New York: Rowman & Littlefield Publishers, 1998), 191–210; especially 196–99.

[8] Barry Dean Karl, *The Uneasy State: The United States from 1915 to 1945* (Chicago: University of Chicago Press, 1983); John W. Jeffries, "A 'Third New Deal'? Liberal Policy and the American State, 1937–1945," *Journal of Policy History* 8 (1996): 387–409; Jeffries, "The 'New' New Deal: FDR and American Liberalism, 1937–1945," *Political Science Quarterly* 105 (fall 1990): 397–418; and see also Jeffries, *Wartime America: The World War II Home Front* (Chicago: Ivan R. Dee, 1996), 145–69.

not replace the New Deal so much as it enhanced and strengthened its defense-related programs.[9]

While the reorganized New Deal public works programs succeeded in using the war to justify their continued existence, the victory came with a high price. This chapter measures this cost via an examination of the fate of the most socially progressive of the New Deal's works programs, the WPA. With private industry finally ending the Depression's crisis of mass unemployment, the WPA worked to find a new mission. As it turned to building wartime public works, the WPA increasingly discarded its primary method of construction – "force account," whereby people were put to work directly in order to reduce unemployment – in favor of cost-plus contracting, which emphasized timely production and increasingly turned to private contractors in order to get the job done. More notably, New Dealers within the WPA demonstrated the extent of their willingness to embrace the wartime emergency when they participated in carrying out the internment of Japanese Americans in relocation camps on the West Coast. This event remains an indelible stain on American history. Yet it continues to deserve close scrutiny, encapsulating as it did the consequences of reorganizing and executing public works programs "in the interests of economy and efficiency."

Both the WPA and the PWA faced significant changes in leadership as executive reorganization became a reality. By the end of 1938, Harry Hopkins resigned from the WPA and was nominated by FDR to become secretary of commerce. (As Eric Goldman once noted, Hopkins, in addition to his sincere concern for the poor, also possessed "a highly developed ability to confuse advancing mankind with advancing Harry Hopkins.")[10] However, Hopkins was not succeeded at the WPA by his assistant and fellow New Dealer, Aubrey Williams. Williams, also head of the National Youth Administration (NYA) and a good friend of Eleanor Roosevelt, was too controversial a choice for FDR. Before the 1938 elections, Williams, a progressive Southerner, had told a Workers Alliance meeting of WPA workers, "Just judge the folk who come and ask for your support by the

9 Herbert Stein, *The Fiscal Revolution in America* (Chicago: University of Chicago Press, 1969); and Alan Brinkley, *The End of Reform: New Deal Liberalism in Recession and War* (New York: Alfred A. Knopf, 1995).

10 Eric F. Goldman, *Rendezvous with Destiny: A History of Modern American Reform*, rev. ed. (New York: Vintage, 1977), 257.

crowd they run with. Vote to keep our friends in power."[11] Press reports
of this statement caused a firestorm of criticism. Williams was portrayed
as blatantly encouraging the Workers Alliance to vote as FDR instructed
them in order to preserve their government paychecks. Williams wrote to
Senator Morris Sheppard, the conservative Texas Democrat who was leading the Senate's investigation into politics in the public works programs,
defending his statement. Claiming that he was misquoted, Williams wrote
that he simply "pointed out to them [the WPA workers] that in a democracy it was important for them to keep in office those who had their
point of view just as their opponents think it important to remove from
office those who have their point of view. There was nothing political
in what I said nor were any political implications intended." However,
Williams continued, "It does so happen... that there are a few people so
steeped in partisan politics that they read insidious political motives into
every statement of a public official."[12] Williams's protest did not stop the
bleeding. Williams later recalled that FDR told him, "I can't appoint you
to succeed Harry. The situation on the Hill is such that I can't do it." FDR
instead named Army Colonel Francis P. Harrington, who had worked with
Hopkins since 1935, to head the WPA. Disappointed, Williams resigned
his WPA position in order to concentrate his efforts at the NYA.[13]

Born in Bristol, Virginia, in 1887, Francis Harrington was a young man
when the United States acquired France's rights to the Panama Canal in
1904. Inspired by this awesome project, he later recalled, he decided to
attend West Point and join the Army Corps of Engineers. He graduated
second in his class in 1909, and by 1924 was working at the Panama
Canal himself as chief engineer, gaining experience in supervising labor
on a large scale. In 1935 he was assigned to the WPA for three months
to help plan its organization. He stayed on as a permanent addition to
Hopkins's staff and was named WPA chief engineer in October 1935.
Hopkins, who was at first "cool" to the notion of using military personnel
in the WPA, soon warmed to the political advantages that an "apolitical"
army engineer could provide. Harrington, who liked to boast that he had
never voted, provided a reassuring counterweight to brash New Dealers

[11] John A. Salmond, *A Southern Rebel: The Life and Times of Aubrey Willis Williams, 1890–1965* (Chapel Hill: University of North Carolina Press, 1983), 97–98.
[12] Aubrey Williams to Morris Sheppard, June 28, 1938, "310 Cong. Campaign Expendi-
ture Investigating Committee" folder, box 661, "Central Files: General 1935–1944. 310
General Correspondence," RG 69, NA.
[13] Salmond, *A Southern Rebel*, 102.

like Williams. A tall man with distinguished gray hair, Harrington – nicknamed "Pink" because of his ruddy complexion – prided himself on his efficient administrative style. Harrington's lack of experience as a business executive led some members of the House to call for a three-man panel to run the WPA, but congressional opposition to his appointment was minimal.[14]

Liberal supporters of the WPA, however, were concerned by Harrington's appointment. The Workers Alliance and its executive secretary, David Lasser, reacted cautiously to the change in WPA leadership. Lasser, reported the *New York City Herald-Tribune,* "not only refrained from attacking Colonel Harrington, other than as the 'Army type' to be avoided in civilian office, but accepted the President's dilemma which forced the compromise for political reasons, and promised peace with the new WPA administrator." The *Washington Herald Times,* on the other hand, gleefully reported that Harrington's appointment "came as a horrid discovery to Messrs. Lasser and Benjamin, the patroons of the Workers Alliance, that he [Harrington] could say no even to them, who had never heard the word before in their presence."[15]

At his first press conference as head of the WPA, Harrington addressed two major issues. First, he responded to concerns that his military background might push the WPA toward playing a greater role in national defense. Harrington's reply was noncommittal, indicating that the WPA's projects would continue to provide for the national defense only to the extent that they had previously done so. "I don't think we are going to be building artillery or anything like that. There are certain phases of things

---

[14] My portrait of Harrington draws on newspaper clippings from *New York Herald-Tribune,* December 31, 1938; *Herald Times,* March 3, 1939; *Washington Herald Times,* January 1, 1939; *Washington Post,* October 1, 1940; and ibid., October 2, 1940; *Washington Herald Times,* October 2, 1940; WPA memorandum from Roscoe Wright to Gilfond, August 7, 1939; and "Colonel Harrington" profile, November 16, 1939; all in "Colonel F. C. Harrington Administrator" folder, box 1, entry 736, "Division of Information. Photographs and Biographical Information about WPA Officials, 1933–1942," RG 69, NA; Lawrence Westbrook to Robert Sherwood, "H.L.H. and the Army Engineers," October 13, 1947, "Westbrook, Lawrence" folder, box 94, Isador Lubin Papers, FDRL; and Sherwood, *Roosevelt and Hopkins,* 75–76; 106. See also Alfred F. Beiter to Harold L. Ickes, June 12, 1939, "Public Works 40) 1939 May–Dec." folder, box 255, Harold L. Ickes Papers, LC; "Proceedings Work Project Administrators. National Meeting. Sevens Hotel, July 12–13, 1939. Chicago, Illinois," "100 Administrative July–Sept 35" folder, box 71, "Central Files: General 1935–1944. 100 Administration," RG 69, NA.

[15] *New York Herald Tribune,* December 31, 1938; and *Washington Herald Times,* January 1, 1939; cited above.

that we have been doing all the time, perhaps the airport program more particularly than any other one," he declared. Second, the press queried Harrington about the problem that had long dogged the WPA: the intersection of public works programs with politics. Harrington answered this question at some length. "That question has got so many implications that I don't want to give a categorical answer. I told you what I think, that the money should go where it belongs. That obviously means the fellow who is unemployed, whether he is a Democrat or a Republican or whatever he may be."[16]

While Harrington's air of apolitical military efficiency quieted critics of the agency's involvement with local politics, a number of WPA administrators were troubled that Hopkins was not replaced by a like-minded New Dealer. Six months after Harrington assumed his post, several African American WPA administrators approached him directly with their concerns about the WPA's treatment of blacks after the program was reorganized into the FWA. "There is too little opportunity," they wrote, "for skilled employment on construction projects and for foremen and supervisors on such projects." The authors continued: "In our judgment we need [administrative] machinery, both to get more Negroes on projects, particularly of the professional and service type, and also to assist in evaluating and reducing complaints of racial discrimination." To accomplish this, they proposed reorganizing and expanding the small race-relations unit of the WPA, thus enabling it to handle complaints or project matters that concerned African Americans, and they urged that the WPA promote the employment of African Americans in currently segregated state organizations.[17] While there is no record of Harrington's response to this appeal, the problems raised by these African American administrators were not new. With Hopkins's departure and with executive reorganization changing the shape of the government, African American administrators were clearly concerned about Harrington's position on discrimination and race. For FDR, however, Harrington had filled a pressing need: His military training and engineering expertise helped insulate the WPA from its conservative critics.

[16] Colonel Francis P. Harrington Press Conference, December 23, 1938, "Col. Harrington Press Conferences" folder, box 3, entry 737, "Division of Information. Administrative Speeches, 1933–1942," RG 69, NA.
[17] Alfred Edgar Smith, T. Arnold Hill, James A. Atkins, Sterling Brown, Dutton Ferguson, Eugene Holmes, and John W. Whitten to F. C. Harrington, June 23, 1939, "1939 Letters To: A–Z" folder, box 1, entry 725, "Division of Information. Office File of Dutton Ferguson, 1938–1939. Correspondence and Reports," RG 69, NA.

SCIENTIFIC MANAGEMENT AND PUBLIC WORKS: JOHN CARMODY
AND THE FEDERAL WORKS AGENCY

Soon after Harrington took over the Work Projects Administration, the New Deal's oldest public works program, the Public Works Administration, also witnessed a change in leadership. The story of how John Carmody, the head of the Rural Electrification Administration (and former engineer with Harry Hopkins's short-lived Civil Works Administration) became Federal Works Administrator, thereby gaining authority over the WPA, PWA, the Public Buildings Administration, the Public Roads Administration, and the U.S. Housing Authority and dislodging Harold Ickes from the helm of the PWA, is complicated. High stakes were attached to Carmody's appointment, since FDR chose him to supervise all the public construction functions of the federal government. Consolidating these functions within one agency offered the opportunity for the New Deal to ensure that its emergency public works programs became permanent fixtures within the American state.

An advocate of the principles of scientific management and Taylorism, Carmody also traced his intellectual roots to the great University of Wisconsin labor economist John R. Commons. On one occasion, he even asserted, "I was among the first to advocate public employment offices in the United States."[18] Carmody gained a glowing reputation at the Rural Electrification Administration (REA) as an efficient and progressive-minded administrator. FDR offered Carmody a position first as head of the Federal Communications Commission, and after he declined that offer, FDR nominated him as chair of the Federal Power Commission. As Carmody later recalled, "I said, 'Mr. President, what I really want is the Administration of Federal Works.'" FDR replied that he had already turned Ickes down for the job but was considering filling the position with Ickes's assistant, Oscar Chapman. Carmody interrupted FDR, telling him, "Oscar is a lawyer. Federal Works is a big construction operation; I'm a construction man." FDR evidently agreed, and Carmody got the job.[19]

[18] "Proceedings of the National Meeting of the Works Progress Administration," July 2–3, 1941, "100 Appropriations (Material from Dort) Various Drafts" folder, box 75, "Central Files: General 1935–1944. 100 Administration," RG 69, NA.
[19] John M. Carmody to Colette Cummiskey, September 12, 1958, "Carmody Book Notes by Catherine from past correspondence. Federal Works Agency" folder, box 261, John M. Carmody Papers, FDRL; Carmody marginalia on John B. Haggerty to John M. Carmody, July 3, 1939, "Congratulatory letters 700a (acknowledgments)" folder, box 120, Carmody Papers, FDRL; "Biographical Sketch" of Carmody, no date, "John M. Carmody" folder, box 1, entry 736, "Division of Information. Photographs and Biographical

Public reaction to Carmody's appointment was positive. Columnists Joseph Alsop and Robert Kitner portrayed the move as part of a broader agenda to position the Democratic Party for the 1940 electoral campaign. While FDR pleased conservative Democrats by choosing Reconstruction Finance Corporation (RFC) head Jesse Jones, a Texan, to direct the Federal Loan Agency, he appointed Carmody for the FWA because Carmody was "a member of the New Deal group, friendly with the leaders and especially known for his enthusiasm for the New Deal policy." Alsop and Kitner concluded that Carmody is "a 'safe man' from the New Dealers' standpoint, just as Jones is not." Indeed, as evidence of Carmody's New Dealer credentials, the columnists pointed not only to Carmody's work with Hopkins's Federal Emergency Relief Administration (FERA) and Civil Works Administration (CWA) and to Carmody's tenure at the REA, but also to the fact that Ickes had recently "signified the New Dealers' faith in Carmody by offering him the place of administrator of the Bonneville dam project."[20]

While Alsop and Kitner touted Carmody's appeal to New Dealers, other journalists noted how his career as a businessman and an engineer, committed to the principles of scientific management, neutralized opposition from conservatives. "When utility executives and labor leaders join with members of the Dies committee on un-American activities and the La Follette civil liberties committee," wrote one scribe "in praise of John Michael Carmody, whom President Roosevelt has placed in charge of the new federal works agency, that is news." Newspapers played up his gregarious personality, running headlines such as "Powerhouse John Carmody Gets Job of Handling U.S. Spending: Big and Irish, He's Practical."[21]

Ickes deeply resented his removal from the PWA and did his part to ensure that Carmody's tenure at the Federal Works Agency got off to a rocky start. A visit from columnist (and former NRA head) Hugh

Information about WPA Officials, 1933–1942," RG 69, NA; and Columbia University Oral History Project, "The Reminiscences of John Michael Carmody," 572–75.

[20] Clipping of Joseph Alsop and Robert Kitner's column from the *Washington Star*, June 29, 1939, untitled folder, box 111, Carmody Papers, FDRL; for Carmody's response to Ickes, declining his offer of the Bonneville Project, see John M. Carmody to Harold L. Ickes, March 29, 1939, "I" folder, box 67, Carmody Papers, FDRL.

[21] My portrait of Carmody draws on the Carmody Oral History, especially 296–315; and Bonnie Fox Schwartz, *The Civil Works Administration, 1933–1934: The Business of Emergency Employment in the New Deal* (Princeton: Princeton University Press, 1984), 54–56; clipping from the *Louisville Courier-Journal*, June 26, 1939; and clipping from the *Boston Globe*, July 18 [?], 1939; both in untitled folder, box 111, Carmody Papers, FDRL.

Johnson led Ickes to conclude that "Johnson is going to express him-self on the Carmody appointment in vigorous terms."[22] Indeed, Johnson did just that. On June 26, 1939, in his nationally syndicated newspa-per column, Johnson bluntly posed the question, "Who the hell is Mr. Carmody?" and answered it himself, writing, "That question alone con-demns this appointment." Carmody, Johnson argued, achieved his posi-tion only because "he is now the best hand-shaker and oiliest yes-man toward the New Deal Gamorra that Washington has known."[23] Ickes probably drew on his relationship with journalist Drew Pearson, coau-thor, with Robert Allen, of the popular and influential newspaper column "Washington Merry-Go-Round," to leak additional unflattering stories about Carmody. Thus, between October 1939 and January 1940, Pearson and Allen wrote stories of Carmody's firing Hugh Johnson's brother-in-law from the PWA as payback for Johnson's harsh public attack, of his promising a trip to Hawaii for the PWA executive who could eliminate the most staff, and of his self-promotion as a potential presidential can-didate by "delivering PWA checks in person" at project sites "to the tune of clicking cameras and radio broadcasts."[24] This was a marked change from the duo's earlier treatment of Carmody when he ran the REA; then Carmody was glowingly portrayed by Pearson and Allen as "a husky, two-fisted Irishman," "one of Roosevelt's chief troubleshooters," "famous for his colorful forthrightness" to his friends and colleagues, blessed with "a fighting man's voice and temper," and "the champion red tape-cutter of the New Deal."[25]

Although embattled, as the head of the FWA Carmody made the case for the federal government's role in constructing public works, relying on his engineering expertise and knowledge of scientific management. First, Carmody stressed the deep historical roots of this use of government, at one point even going so far as to declare that "there is some reason to suppose that the heritage of Greece is almost entirely made up of WPA projects, such as the Parthenon." Second, Carmody argued that federal

[22] *Secret Diary of Harold L. Ickes*, 2:663.
[23] Clipping of Hugh Johnson's column from the *New York City World-Telegram*, June 26, 1939, untitled folder, box 111, Carmody Papers, FDRL.
[24] See, respectively, "Washington Merry-Go-Round" clippings for October 5, 1939; Octo-ber 9, 1939; October 11, 1939; and January 4, 1940; and John M. Carmody to Drew Pearson, October 5, 1939; October 7, 1939; October 12, 1939; and M. E. Gilmore to John M. Carmody, January 11, 1940; all in untitled folder, box 112, Carmody Papers, FDRL.
[25] Clipping of the "Washington Merry-Go-Round," undated [1937], "REA – Morris L. Cooke Administration" folder, box 95, Carmody Papers, FDRL.

public works were essential for the nation's defense.[26] Third, uniting these first two points, was Carmody's sense that the reorganization of the works programs into the FWA "represents not at all the expression of any new governmental policy, but is simply a normal and obvious step taken in the interests of administrative economy and efficiency." In his opinion, it had only been "the shock of actual practice" that caused public works to be perceived as "to some extent a political issue." A federal public works program, he argued, was "in practice just as much as in theory, non-political in its essential nature." Indeed, Carmody felt that with executive reorganization in place, the FWA "constitutes, as we can see by looking around at other nations, the most fully perfected instrumentality of its kind possessed by any nation in the world."[27]

On another occasion, Carmody put his point in terms he thought the average American could understand. "When you re-design an automobile or an airplane wing to cut down wind resistance," he declared, "that's streamlining! When you re-design the mechanism of government – that's re-organization! The purpose is the same... to promote efficiency... to get greater economy, faster, more effective public service, better operating results." In Carmody's opinion, the "coordination" between works agencies allowed by executive reorganization "is just a fancy word for common sense procedures that make for real economy. Coordination simply makes it possible to get greater results from every dollar expended for a given job, and that's the essence of economy – of thrift in business, or government or in private life."[28] By stressing the FWA's commitment to economy and efficiency, Carmody hoped to avoid the sort of charges of involvement in state and local politics that had been leveled earlier against the WPA.

To this end, Carmody also strongly supported focusing federal public works on defense-oriented projects. In August 1939, shortly after he took his position at FWA, Carmody conferred with FDR on this issue and publicized the work of the WPA in building public works for defense. In debating with Senator Robert A. Taft, Jr., the question, "Shall relief administration be returned to the states?" Carmody pointed out that the

[26] John M. Carmody speech to the Commonwealth Club of San Francisco, California, April 19, 1940, "FWA Speeches April 1940" folder, box 127, Carmody Papers, FDRL.
[27] John M. Carmody speech to the North Carolina League of Municipalities, August 19, 1939, "Federal Works Agency Speech File July 1939" folder, box 126, Carmody Papers, FDRL.
[28] "Interview. John M. Carmody, Administrator. Federal Works Agency," no date [probably August 1939], "Federal Works Agency Speech File August 1939" folder, box 126, Carmody Papers, FDRL.

WPA had spent nearly half a billion dollars for defense purposes, building facilities for the Army, Navy, Coast Guard, and National Guard, as well as public airports. "The War and Navy Departments," Carmody told the nation, "have found that because WPA is federally controlled, is organized in almost every county in the nation, is experienced and flexible, it can execute many types of important work in the preparedness program."[29]

Carmody cautioned the business community not to expect too swift a return to prosperity with the coming of war. "Instead of dreaming of the benefits of a second World War," Carmody said to them, "we ought to be considering how to protect ourselves from such disastrous consequences as followed the first World War." Carmody argued for patience: "[L]et us not expect too much in the way of war purchases from a Europe that is now on the verge of bankruptcy.... Let us not be tempted to exchange the solid benefits of our own American program of peace and progress for imaginary profits from European miseries.... Let us not exchange the substance for the shadow."[30] Carmody's sense of caution was only reinforced by WPA chief economist Arthur E. Burns, who in 1939 estimated that $18 to $20 billion of public and private money would need to be spent each year to restore employment to pre-1929 levels. While the effects of war in Europe were difficult to forecast, Burns noted that a works program twice the size of the consolidated FWA would not have been enough to bring combined public and private investment to $20 billion.[31] With federal spending on public works so far below this estimate, Carmody increasingly leaned on national defense to justify as much spending as possible.

In December 1940, a hint of Carmody's evolving stance on public works emerged at a conference held by the Bureau of the Budget and the National Resources Planning Board. There, economist Gardiner Means, who had written the landmark book, *The Modern Corporation and*

[29] John M. Carmody to FDR, August 31, 1939, President's Personal File 7086, FDR Papers, FDRL; John M. Carmody untitled radio transcription, September 12, 1940, and John M. Carmody radio transcription, September 25, 1940; both in "FWA Speeches September 1940" folder, box 127, Carmody Papers, FDRL. For more on the attitude of the WPA and FWA to the question of returning relief to the states, see John M. Carmody and Howard O. Hunter to FDR, no date [probably July 1940], "1940 Misc No Dates" folder, box 5, PPF 1820, FDR Papers, FDRL.
[30] John M. Carmody, "Business and Relief," September 9, 1939, no folder, box 1, entry 737, "Division of Information. Administrative Speeches, 1933–1942," RG 69, NA.
[31] Arthur E. Burns to John M. Carmody, September 30, 1939, "FWA–Defense (Memos from Arthur E. Burns)" folder, box 110, Carmody Papers, FDRL.

Private Property with Adolf A. Berle, was struck by Carmody's remarks. While Frank W. Herring of the American Public Works Association "talks of *Public* Works," Means wrote, Carmody spoke "of *Works* including WPA," envisioning a lesser role for this agency. The WPA would perform the "same work" that was "done by business employees but using socially employable but not businessly [*sic*] employable" people, concentrating on older workers.[32] Just a few days before this conference, in fact, Carmody had discussed the fate of the WPA with WPA labor relations expert Nels Anderson. "I believe the time has come," Anderson told Carmody, "for salvaging WPA and perhaps some of the other member agencies into a united work program which would be the Federal Works Agency," adding, "I can see little place in the Federal Works Agency for several subordinate agencies, each operating under special laws and each operating as if it had an identity apart from the mother agency."[33] By shifting focus toward the unified goal of national defense, the New Deal's public works programs were making strides toward even further administrative consolidation.

THE WPA AND NATIONAL DEFENSE

With this reorientation toward national defense underway, the threat of war appeared to many liberals to offer the possibility of recharging and strengthening the reforming impulse of the New Deal. Particularly important to New Dealers involved in this effort were the statements made by the Army chief of staff, General George Marshall. Marshall went out of his way to praise the defense work done by both the WPA and PWA since their inception. Vermont Senator Warren Austin, the ranking minority member of the military affairs committee, told the *New York Times* that, in testimony before Congress, Marshall dispelled the notion that $7 billion had been "poured down a rathole" of public works spending without obtaining returns in national defense. Austin, for one, the *Times* reported, "was convinced that the money had been well spent, after listening to General Marshall." Marshall, who was adept at making political and bureaucratic allies, took pains to provide the WPA with good press. His

---

[32] Gardiner Means marginalia on Conference Agenda, "Bureau of the Budget and National Resources Planning Board. Conference on Public Works – Work Relief Program," December 4, 1940, "Works Program Conference, 12/4/40" folder, box 14, Gardiner Means Papers, FDRL, emphasis in original.

[33] Nels Anderson to John M. Carmody, November 18, 1940, "FWA–WPA" folder, box 115, Carmody Papers, FDRL.

participation in remaking the WPA's public image extended beyond the occasional statement of support before Congress. Marshall also spoke in radio broadcasts, such as the "Symposium on National Defense" that was broadcast over NBC radio on October 29, 1940. Marshall, along with acting commissioner of the WPA Howard Hunter, coordinator of national defense purchases Donald M. Nelson, economist Stuart Chase, and manufacturer Henry Dennison, discussed the role of the WPA in defending America.[34]

"In the great task of preparing for national defense," Marshall proclaimed, "the Work Projects Administration . . . has proved itself to be an invaluable aid. Already in the field, it has been carrying out work for the Army and Navy for the last five years, and its services in this direction have been rapidly expanded." The WPA was busy building and repairing army facilities, such as rifle ranges, storage buildings, and barracks, as well as constructing and expanding airports. By July 1, 1940, Hunter bragged, "the WPA has already done a half a billion dollars' worth of work on primary national defense projects and an additional billion dollars' worth on projects of secondary military importance." Nelson backed up Hunter's boast, adding, "The work program has indeed been a good business proposition, paying dividends both in economic recovery and in social betterment." Nelson also noted "the valuable services that the army of WPA workers has been able to perform in disaster emergencies – floods, hurricanes, droughts – when help is needed and needed quickly. Today, too, in our great emergency of national defense, the WPA is repeating its record for quick emergency services. As everybody knows, the great problem in national defense is to get things done in a hurry." The WPA, Nelson claimed, could shift its workforce to defense tasks more quickly and efficiently than private firms and the labor market could reallocate employees to such work.[35]

[34] Clipping from *New York Times*, May 19, 1940, "Defense Construction" folder, box 4, entry 768, "Records of the Works Projects Administration. Division of Information. Records Concerning National Defense Projects, 1939–1942," RG 69, NA; for more on Marshall's ability to forge bureaucratic alliances in government, see Frank J. Rader, "Harry L. Hopkins: The Works Progress Administration and National Defense, 1935–1940," (Ph.D. diss., University of Delaware, 1973), ch. 5.
[35] Marshall, Hunter, and Nelson's statements from transcription of "Symposium on National Defense," October 29, 1940, "Interview Program (transcribed)" folder, box 1, entry 706, "Division of Information. Correspondence, Scripts, and Other Records Relating to Special Transcribed Programs, 1940–1941," RG 69, NA. Marshall's praise was often touted by the WPA; see, for example, WPA Press Release, January 15, 1941, "Press Releases 1941" folder, box 1, entry 740, "Division of Information. Press Releases,

Stuart Chase made the most comprehensive case for defense public works. "During the last five years," Chase argued, "the WPA has constructed and improved many thousands of miles of roads, hundreds of airports, and thousands of public buildings. It would be good bookkeeping to set a fair value on these public improvements, and, with due allowance for amortization, credit ourselves with the net gain in national wealth." Dennison, who had been a member of the unemployment council set up by President Harding, and was currently serving on the National Resources Planning Board's advisory committee, agreed with Chase, noting that in addition to providing employment, the WPA "has literally changed the face of the nation" through its construction projects and was now "training tens of thousands of its workers in mechanical skills needed in the defense industries."[36] Howard Hunter summed up the themes that connected the remarks made by Marshall, Chase, and Dennison when he declared, "There was a time when thoughtless people made idle jokes about 'shovel-leaning' and 'boondoggling,'" but now, "in the light of these requirements for total defense, we can all look back upon the five years of WPA work with the feeling that the *entire* program has been a program of national defense."[37]

While army officers like Marshall were quick to capitalize on the mutual advantage of collaborating with the public works programs, other military officials voiced skepticism. One army officer worried that all road projects suddenly will be deemed "defense related," that small streams "will be named as navigable rivers in the guise of national defense," and politicians will push for every "pet project" to be sheltered beneath the "petticoat of national defense." By 1940, about 20 percent of WPA projects were "defense activities." The war and navy secretaries certified specific projects, including airports, access roads for military bases,

---

1936–1942, with gaps," RG 69, NA; and "The WPA and Private Contractors," March 17, 1941, "Fellows" folder, box 2, entry 737, "Division of Information. Administrative Speeches, 1933–1942," RG 69, NA.

[36] Transcription of "Symposium on National Defense," ibid. For more on Chase's vision of political economy, see Robert B. Westbrook, "Tribune of the Technostructure: The Popular Economics of Stuart Chase," *American Quarterly* 32 (fall 1980): 387–408; for more on Dennison's career, see Patrick D. Reagan, *Designing a New America: The Origins of New Deal Planning, 1890–1943* (Amherst: University of Massachusetts Press, 1999), 111–39.

[37] Transcription of "Symposium on National Defense," October 29, 1940, "Interview Program (transcribed)" folder, box 1, entry 706, "Division of Information. Correspondence, Scripts, and Other Records Relating to Special Transcribed Programs, 1940–1941," RG 69, NA. Emphasis in original.

national guard and ROTC facilities, and "strategic" highways, in order to give them priority status, thus exempting them from WPA rules regarding wages, hours, and the use of relief labor.[38]

Roads and airports were two types of defense projects favored by the WPA, because of their ability to put large numbers of unskilled workers to work quickly. WPA chief engineer Perry Fellows observed that the organization of the WPA, "which extends into almost every county in the nation, its flexibility, and its immediately available labor supply, adapt it particularly to do certain phases of this vital road building job." Assistant Secretary of War Robert Patterson echoed Fellows's point, noting, "Because the WPA is organized in almost every county in the nation, because of its experience and flexibility, it can execute almost every type of work in the preparedness program." While defense road building accounted for about 36 percent of WPA employment on highway and other road projects, it was not always visible to the public as defense work per se. Or, as Howard Hunter once put it, "We've been seeing WPA national defense work somewhat as one sees an iceberg. The part we have not seen is so much greater than the part we have seen."[39]

With this increasing emphasis on defense, though, the WPA also began to shift away from putting people to work directly on "force account" construction and relied increasingly upon private contracting. This marked a dramatic shift in philosophy, departing from the WPA's explicit commitment to employ as many people as possible on its projects. WPA chief engineer Fellows summarized the reception accorded the WPA's previous approach by contractors. Speaking to the American Road Builders Association, Fellows remarked that when the WPA was created in 1935, "one might imagine that the Federal Government had not only confiscated the businesses of all the contractors but had transported the contractors themselves to Alaska for forced labor." However, Fellows stated, "We all wake up from such nightmare imaginings and realize that we are still living in the United States, under a government whose prime purpose is to encourage private enterprise and to keep government economic activity

---

[38] Major Arthur Wilson quoted in Rader "Harry L. Hopkins," 164–65; and see WPA Press Release, November 11, 1940; October 31, 1940; both in "Defense Construction. 1940 Material. N.W." folder, box 2, entry 768, "Division of Information. Records Concerning National Defense Projects, 1939–1942," RG 69, NA.

[39] Perry Fellows, "WPA Defense Road Construction Program," December 20, 1940, "Defense Construction. 1940 Material. N.W." folder, box 2, ibid., RG 69, NA; Federal Works Agency, *Final Report on the WPA Program, 1935–1943* (Washington, D.C.: U.S. Government Printing Office, 1947), 85; and "WPA National Defense Broadcast Columbia Broadcasting System," August 28, 1940, ibid.

at a minimum." By January 1941, the WPA was turning to contractors at an unprecedented rate. While still carrying out force-account work on occasion, the WPA, Fellows announced, "is leaning backwards trying to turn over as much of its work as possible to contractors." While some contractors saw this development as "an indication that the WPA is an octopus that reaches out into everything, even into the sacred work of national defense, which [the contractors] take for granted should be handled entirely by private contract, and which they think would be handled by private contract if the WPA did not exist," Fellows argued that the WPA was only using force-account construction to provide employment to the permanently jobless and was turning over the bulk of its defense work to private contractors. [40]

By March 1941 the WPA was putting about half a million people to work on defense projects, particularly on access roads for military bases and airports, and it was constructing buildings at army and navy bases. [41] Soon afterward, John Carmody indicated the "hopeful possibility" that relief labor could be employed on vast public works such as interregional highways. Speaking at the first meeting of the National Interregional Highway Committee to fellow committee members, including Rexford Tugwell, Frederic A. Delano, and the head of the Bureau of Public Roads, Thomas H. MacDonald, Carmody argued that the WPA's project to assemble a "shelf" of public works projects, sponsored by the National Resources Planning Board and the FWA, might form a basis for future decision making by the Interregional Highway Committee. [42] Out of these efforts came the report, *Highways for the National Defense*, prepared by the Public Roads Administration, the FWA, the Advisory Commission to the Council of National Defense, and the War and Navy Departments, which emphasized upgrading the strength of bridges, widening strategic roads, ensuring adequate access to larger cities, and servicing current and proposed populations at army, naval, and air bases. [43]

Between 1935 and 1939, the WPA had spent about $66 million dollars to improve 169 of the 191 regular airline stops in 47 states, expenditures that the organization characterized as critical to national

---

[40] Perry A. Fellows, "Contracting in WPA Operations," January 27–31, 1941, "221 American A–Z" folder, box 559, Central Files – 221 Roads, RG 69, NA.

[41] "The WPA Week in National Defense," March 12, 1941, "Defense Construction 1941 Material" folder, box 2, ibid.

[42] Minutes of the National Interregional Highway Committee, June 24, 1941, "National Interregional Highway Committee" folder, box 16, Rexford G. Tugwell Papers, FDRL.

[43] "Highways for the National Defense," February 1, 1941; "OF 1e Bureau of Public Roads 1939–1941" folder, box 11, Official File 1e, FDR Papers, FDRL.

defense.[44] Colonel Harrington, weeks after taking over the WPA, noted that while the WPA's "largest airport operations have been on the commercially important fields of many of the nation's largest cities, including the present airports of New York, Chicago, Cleveland, San Francisco, and Newark," it had also built up facilities that linked the east and west coasts of the country, such as "the Salt Lake City municipal field, where five lines of travel intersect, and five [air] fields in Tennessee cities, key points in the airline map of the east and south."[45] Between July 1940 and June 1943, the WPA built 215 airports and retrofitted 160 more; since 1935 the WPA had built over 480 airports while improving or expanding more than 470 other sites.[46]

New Dealers Aubrey Williams and Corrington Gill joined Harrington in touting WPA airport construction. Williams, in a press release titled "WPA Aids Aviation," noted the advantages airport projects offered in relieving unemployment. "Many unskilled workers, the class which constitutes two-thirds of all those on WPA rolls, can be quickly and usefully employed in developing airports and airways," Williams wrote. "Because of this fact and because of the importance of airport development, the Works Progress Administration and earlier federal work-relief agencies have spent more than a hundred million dollars on such work." In addition to putting people to work in an effective fashion, though, airport projects also did vital work in modernizing the nation's infrastructure. "Airplanes are becoming larger, heavier and faster every year," observed Williams. "To accommodate such craft our airports and other aviation facilities must be correspondingly developed." Williams continued, making an argument that resonated with engineers like Carmody: "To attempt to fly 1938 planes from war-time [i.e., 1918] airports would be as foolish and dangerous as to attempt to drive modern automobiles at full speed along the narrow, winding and bumpy roads which were adequate for horse-and-buggy traffic."[47]

The WPA airport program garnered positive support in government and from the public. Young Texas Congressman Lyndon B. Johnson

44 WPA Press Release, December 4, 1938, "1/Defense Construction" folder, box 1, entry 768, "Division of Information. Records Concerning National Defense Projects, 1939–1942," RG 69, NA; and see *Final Report on the WPA Program*, 85.
45 WPA Press Release, March 15, 1939, ibid.
46 *Final Report on the WPA Program*, 85.
47 WPA Press Release, January 24, 1938, and the text of the Gill articles, both in "1/Defense Construction" folder, box 1, entry 768, "Division of Information. Records Concerning National Defense Projects, 1939–1942," RG 69, NA.

worked hard to assure his state's place in the expansion of the nation's airport facilities, pushing for the establishment of a naval air station at Corpus Christi and touting what one army officer referred to as the "unusually fine climate" for air travel that existed in his state. LBJ had, in the words of historian Jordan Schwarz, "seen the future of American politics... public works projects could help elect congressmen, but defense contracts had become public works."[48] While politicians like Johnson had seen the future, others viewed the WPA's airport program as a turning point in the history of American aviation.[49] Edgar S. Gorrell, president of the Airport Transport Association of America, declared, "When the history of civil aeronautics during its formative era is finally written, there will be a chapter on the activities of WPA which will be unstinted in its praise."[50] Henry Stimson, the conservative secretary of war, wrote to Howard Hunter to thank Florida's WPA for its important contribution to national defense, noting that by late 1940, of the seventeen civilian airport improvements in Florida that the War Department had requested, fourteen were well underway.[51] Army Chief of Staff George Marshall concurred with Stimson's assessment of the key role played by airports, noting that "the construction or improvement of a total of thirty airports in Maine is important for military purposes [because] the New England area and Maine in particular is a very strategic location from the standpoint of the possible concentration of large numbers of military

[48] Major General H. H. Arnold to Lyndon B. Johnson, June 3, 1940; and see also FDR to Lyndon B. Johnson, June 3, 1940; Rear Admiral J. H. Towers to Lyndon B. Johnson, June 3, 1940; and John M. Carmody to Lyndon B. Johnson, June 12, 1940; all in "White House – General Correspondence – January thru August 1940" folder, box 1, entry 4, "Correspondence of Administrators. Correspondence of Administrators with the House, 1939–1942. White House (General Correspondence, August–June, 1939) to White House 9/1/41–12/31/42," General Records of the Federal Works Agency, Record Group 162, National Archives, Washington, D.C.; and Schwarz, *New Dealers*, 281.

[49] For the impact of these airports on the growth and development of cities, generally, see Douglas Karsner, "Aviation and Airports: The Impact on the Economic and Geographic Structure of American Cities, 1940s–1980s," *Journal of Urban History* 23 (May 1997): 406–36; and Jon C. Teaford, *The Rough Road to Renaissance: Urban Revitalization in America, 1940–1985* (Baltimore: Johns Hopkins University Press, 1990), 93–105.

[50] WPA Press Release, April 3, 1940, in "Defense Construction. 1940 Material. N.W." folder, box 2, entry 768, "Division of Information. Records Concerning National Defense Projects, 1939–1942," RG 69, NA.

[51] Henry L. Stimson to Howard O. Hunter, no date [prob. Nov. 1940], "100 Appropriations (Material from Dort) Various Drafts" folder, box 75, "Central Files: General 1935–1944," RG 69, NA. For a brief assessment of Stimson's lengthy career, see Alan Brinkley, "Icons of the American Establishment," in Brinkley, *Liberalism and Its Discontents* (Cambridge: Harvard University Press, 1998), 164–209.

aircraft."[52] Further south, the WPA administrator for Georgia declared, "Cancel out the work of the WPA in the past six years and, I assure you, it would seem that Hitler's *Luftwaffe* had suddenly visited us in the night."[53] By April 1941, the WPA was even running a small program for airport ground personnel, under the sponsorship of the Advisory Commission for National Defense and the Civil Aeronautics Administration, that trained 5,750 airport workers.[54]

As we have seen, with the coming of war, the WPA stepped up its involvement in national preparedness, building defense-related roads, improving military bases, constructing airports, and maintaining the skills of the unemployed by providing meaningful work. At the same time, the WPA was beginning to abandon its cardinal principle of putting the unemployed to work directly, instead resorting to private contracting and the labor market. The WPA's increased involvement in the heavier construction required by defense public works projects represented a reordering of internal priorities, demonstrated in the shift from providing employment to carrying out timely construction in the name of wartime efficiency and economy. In many ways, war allowed New Dealers to achieve new landmarks, not only in construction but also in the field of worker training.

WPA WORKER TRAINING FOR DEFENSE

In addition to its defense-related construction, as part of its preparedness campaign, the WPA began to train workers for the first time in its history, helping them find employment in the growing defense-related industries. The relationship between worker training and New Deal works programs, such as the WPA, the Civilian Conservation Corps (CCC), and the NYA, had long been controversial. Organized labor had consistently opposed government training for the unemployed, fearful that this would create too much competition for skilled union craftsmen. FDR himself famously had accompanied AFL president William Green on a tour of the CCC's first camp, taking the opportunity to be photographed reassuring Green (and, by extension, the labor movement he represented) that not one of the

---

[52] George C. Marshall to Guy Gannett, November 9, 1940, in ibid.

[53] "Information Exchange Letter No. 12," January 21, 1942, no folder, box 1, entry 13 [unidentified entry], "Information Service Letters, 1938–1941. Administrative Division," Records of the Public Works Administration, Record Group 135, National Archives, Washington, D.C.

[54] "045 Special Folder airports Servicemen's Training Program (Corres. from Ms. Peter)" folder, box 64, "Central Files: General 1935–1944. 045 Defense Training Program, 1940–43," RG 69, NA.

workers on relief was learning anything that would enable him to supplant a union member on the job. Indeed, to reassure further organized labor, Robert Fechner, the head of the AFL machinists, was put in charge of running the CCC.[55]

Of course, WPA officials realized, the attitude of organized labor toward worker training varied from union to union. Industrial unions, in the steel, auto, and mining industries, for example, "have either been friendly or indifferent toward the program," one WPA official noted. The autoworkers expressed their solidarity with the relief workers by forming a WPA department within their union that publicized the WPA's projects, pushed for more to be added, and demanded higher wages and better working conditions for WPA work. Construction unions, however, consistently opposed the WPA, uniting with contractors to object to a works program that often bypassed private construction firms and skilled union labor. The building-trades unions argued that this work ought to be done at union wages and under union-supervised and approved conditions. For building-trades unions, though, the defense program of public works represented a more favorable alternative to typical WPA practices, as nearly all of these projects were built under closed-shop conditions that predominantly employed union workers.[56]

Despite the strong opposition from building-trades unions toward government sponsored worker training, the WPA had previously considered the idea on several occasions. As early as 1937, Harrington reported to a conference of WPA state administrators that the WPA was debating "whether we should go in general into a vocational training program." He added, "As you all know, we can't go into the training of apprentices in the organized crafts and building trades." By 1940, however, Harrington was of a different mind. With the WPA now explicitly authorized by Congress to train workers, Harrington took to the radio. Two rationales supported the WPA's new training program and its participation in national defense, announced Harrington. "First, to provide the trained workers which industry will need; and secondly, to endeavor to

[55] For more on organized labor's opposition to government training programs, see Howard, *The WPA and Federal Relief Policy*, 237–38; and Richard J. Jensen, "The Causes and Cures of Unemployment in the Great Depression," *Journal of Interdisciplinary History* 19 (Spring 1989): 576–77; for the CCC see John A. Salmond, *The Civilian Conservation Corps , 1933–1942: A New Deal Case Study* (Durham, N.C.; Duke University Press, 1967), 30–45.

[56] For the WPA's perspective, see "Attitude of the Labor Unions toward the WPA Work Program," May 13, 1942, "100 May 1942" folder, box 77, "Central Files: General 1935–1944. 100 Administration," RG 69, NA.

assure WPA workers of an opportunity to secure a share of the increased employment which will result from our preparedness effort." Although "the primary responsibility of WPA is still to provide work and wages for the needy unemployed," Harrington asserted that "to the greatest degree possible, the energies of WPA will be devoted to furthering national defense."[57]

Harrington's death in September 1940, scarcely two years after Hopkins had stepped away from the WPA, threatened to leave the program without an experienced administrator at the helm. While the consensus inside the WPA was that FDR would place another army officer in charge of the program, Howard Hunter was kept on as acting commissioner of the WPA, a post he had assumed when Harrington fell ill. A good friend of Harry Hopkins's since the early days of the New Deal, Hunter was born in Georgia and attended Louisiana State University, graduating in 1917 and serving with a Tulane University medical unit in France during World War I. After the war he worked in Michigan's relief and welfare department, did Community Chest work in Connecticut, Michigan, and New York City, and served as New England director under Herbert Hoover for the President's Organization on Unemployment Relief (POUR) in 1931. Hunter then supervised FERA's and the WPA's efforts in the Midwest; after Hopkins and Aubrey Williams left the WPA, Hunter was appointed deputy administrator and served directly under Harrington.[58]

Looking to solidify the WPA's standing in this increasingly uncertain political landscape, Hunter addressed a July 1941 conference of WPA administrators on the state of the program. Noting the favorable impression the defense training program had made on the Congress, Hunter said he was of the opinion that Congress thought it "was the most important project that the WPA had been operating" and asserted that Congress had given "almost mandatory instructions to the WPA to not only continue that project, but to expand it." By 1941, the WPA formally established a new Training and Reemployment Division, headed by Fred Rauch. Rauch

[57] "Proceedings Conference of State Administrators. Works Progress Administration," February 12–13, 1937; "100 Jan–Feb 37" folder, box 69, "Central Files: General 1935–1944. 100 Administration," RG 69, NA; and WPA Press Release, July 1, 1940, "Press Releases, 1938–1940" folder, box 3, entry 740, "Division of Information. Press Releases, 1936–1942, with gaps," RG 69, NA.
[58] "Biographical Sketch Howard O. Hunter," no date, "Howard O. Hunter" folder, box 2, entry 736, "Division of Information. Photographs and Biographical Information about WPA Officials, 1933–1942," RG 69, NA.

had previously worked as an engineer and as an executive in the construction and manufacturing fields, as well as for the CWA, before joining the WPA's administrative staff in 1935.[59]

Speaking frankly to his fellow administrators, Rauch reported that the WPA avoided interfering with employer-employee relations in the day-to-day running of its training program. By confining its training to the "learner period" that most union contracts provided for new hires, Rauch reported that "so far we haven't had the slightest bit of difficulty with the unions," and, for their part, employers "have all agreed that the program is very acceptable." During the training period, which was not to surpass 160 hours or 4 weeks, the WPA paid the wages of the trainees, who had been interviewed and selected by the companies' own personnel departments. In addition to training men at 375 plants, the WPA gave the approval for 12 plants to train women for defense work. With the rapid increases in defense-related orders, trained workers were essential to speeding up production. Despite continued objections by the AFL Building and Construction Trades Department to the use of WPA labor on defense-related projects, the WPA declared it would not change its policy.[60]

That the WPA information division did not stint in its promotion of the defense training program is apparent in the script it prepared for the radio program, "Trainees in Defense Jobs." Over sound effects meant to bring to mind acetylene torch welding, riveting, and engine production, various workers related their invariably triumphant experiences of being trained by the WPA. It was, of course, no accident, that these stories were uniformly positive. The director of the WPA's information division, Earl Minderman, instructed his staff to "round up four or five WPA workers here in the District of Columbia who are taking the training course and

[59] "Proceedings of the National Meeting of the Works Progress Administration," July 2–3, 1941, "100 Appropriations (Material from Dort) Various Drafts" folder, box 75, "Central Files: General 1935–1944. 100 Administration," RG 69, NA.
[60] "Proceedings of the National Meeting of the Works Progress Administration," July 2–3, 1941, ibid.; "Biographical Sketch Fred R. Rauch," June 1941, "Fred R. Rauch" folder, box 3, entry 736, "Division of Information. Photographs and Biographical Information about WPA Officials, 1933–1942," RG 69, NA; Fred R. Rauch, "Training for Defense Industry," October 21, 1941, "Vocational Training and Other White Collar" folder, box 3, entry 768, "Division of Information. Records Concerning National Defense Projects, 1939–1942," RG 69, NA; "The WPA Week in National Defense," Sept. 10, 1941, "Vocational Training and Other White Collar" folder, box 3, ibid.; and F. H. Dryden to Sidney Hillman, July 25, 1941, "Labor Agreement" folder, box 8, entry 5, "Correspondence of Administrators. Correspondence of General Philip B. Fleming, 1942–1949," RG 162, NA.

arrange to have them meet in the recording studio in the North Interior Building so we can make transcriptions of their personal experiences." He added, "Of course you will have to write the statements." Minderman thought "it would be a good idea to have one person who has graduated from our course and is now holding down a lucrative job far beyond the dreams of avarice." The WPA announcer would establish "that these men are typical of thousands of WPA workers all over the United States who are being enabled by the WPA to take training and fit themselves for better jobs in our defense industries."[61]

The press, for the most part, gave the WPA's defense training program positive marks. The *New York Times* editorialized that while the WPA had previously been "an obstacle to defense" with its "system of inventing projects, the overwhelming majority of them of a nondefense nature, to 'make work,'" the defense training program, in contrast, "is the rare type of plan, in short, that, properly administered, could help the men directly concerned, Government economy, and defense, all at the same time." The *New York City Herald-Tribune* concurred, writing that the program "seems the most sensible and practical program yet undertaken for the unemployed."[62]

This public perception of the effectiveness of the WPA's defense training, however, was countered by misgivings within the WPA. Bruce Uthus, a WPA regional administrator, worried about what he termed the "definite administrative deficiencies, of both a general and particular nature" of the program. The lack of consistent record-keeping was an obstacle to reaching an accurate assessment of the WPA's impact on the labor market. In addition to encouraging better coordination between the WPA, the USES (United States Employment Service), and the states, Uthus advised WPA officials in Washington that "really substantial gains in meeting defense industries' future needs and contemporary reductions in WPA rolls can best be attained by regional planning for basic [job] training." Uthus projected that new shipyards, aircraft plants, and aluminum plants would

---

[61] "Trainees in Defense Jobs," no date [Sept. 1941?]; and Earl Minderman to Floyd Dell, October 2, 1940; both in "Training Course Sept. 1941" folder, box 2, entry 706, "Division of Information. Correspondence, Scripts, and Other Records Relating to Special Transcribed Programs, 1940–1941," RG 69, NA.

[62] Clippings from *New York Times*, August 20, 1941; *New York City Herald-Tribune*, August 20, 1941; and see also the assorted clippings in "045 Newspaper Clippings on the Training and Reemployment Program – From Various Newspapers in the Country, 1941" folder, box 64, "Central Files: General 1935–1944. 045 Defense Training Program, 1940–43," RG 69, NA.

immediately generate 65,000 new jobs, disrupting existing patterns in the labor market. Assuming that semiskilled workers would be able to move up into skilled labor positions, Uthus argued that the WPA ought to concentrate on providing "basic training" to help the unskilled to fill the resulting openings in semiskilled positions. WPA social worker Hilda Worthington Smith echoed this assessment, adding that the WPA also needed to address the loss of its own management personnel to defense industries. For growing numbers of experienced WPA engineers, administrators, and economists, leaving government service for lucrative private employment was turning into a realistic option.[63]

By 1942, this turmoil had reached the top of the WPA's division of training and reemployment, as Fred Rauch left the WPA to take a job with a group of utility companies near Cincinnati. Rauch was replaced by Lieutenant Colonel John J. McDonough, a trained lawyer and labor relations expert, who had previously served as the chief WPA state administrator in Massachusetts. Reviewing his division's accomplishments through May 19, 1942, McDonough noted that about 205,000 trainees had finished their training. Of these, 73 percent had found jobs in industry. By June 9, approximately 35,000 workers were still in training. The most notable feature of the first half of 1942, however, was the special attention the WPA gave to training women for defense work. While only 661 women were enrolled in defense training at the beginning of the year, by May this number had increased by over 500 percent. Women were registering for training in machine-shop courses, aviation services, and sheet-metal work. The WPA also began to train and employ older workers.[64]

Although employment had generally been going up – in May 1942, 48 percent more workers were leaving WPA rolls than had exited in May 1941 – McDonough observed that the WPA could not take full credit for this development. Indeed, the impact of the Pearl Harbor bombing and entry of the United States into the war made it difficult for the WPA to assess accurately the effectiveness of their training and reemployment

---

[63] Bruce Uthus to H. J. McCormack, January 24, 1941, "045 AAAA Jan–Oct 1941" folder, box 64, "Central Files: General 1935–1944. 045 Defense Training Program, 1940–43," RG 69, NA; Hilda W. Smith, "General Impression of the WPA Program," February 1941, "FWA–WPA" folder, box 115, Carmody Papers, FDRL; and see also Corrington Gill to John M. Carmody, April 28, 1941, "1941 Corrington Gill" folder, box 62, entry "PC-37, 21, Records of the Office of the WPA Commissioner (Formerly Administrator), 1935–1943," RG 69, NA.

[64] My profile of McDonough draws on the "Works Progress Bulletin – Massachusetts" newsletter, December 2, 1936, in "610 Mass. Oct. 1936–Jan. 1937" folder, box 1493, "Central Files: State 1935–1944. Massachusetts 610 Special Litigation," RG 69, NA.

measures. Despite difficulties in running the program and in precisely measuring its success, the WPA concluded that its worker-training program had reached over 330,000 workers while it was in operation. It contributed to readying the nation's defenses while assisting older workers, unskilled workers, and women workers, groups most often ignored by private employers. Although the WPA had waited for many years before launching a formal worker-training program, once it began to gear up, the agency was able to expand the program quickly and to meet the needs and requirements of both the unemployed and industry. The WPA succeeded not only in placing the out-of-work in jobs but also in stimulating private demand for the skills and abilities of WPA administrators. The addition of this key reform to the WPA program did not occur during the Great Depression. Instead, it was the coming of war that created a political opportunity for the WPA, and it was New Dealers like Fred Rauch, Bruce Uthus, and John McDonough who seized it.[65]

NATIONAL DEFENSE AND THE NEW DEAL

While the WPA increased its contributions to the preparedness effort as war approached, the PWA's engagement with national defense commenced at the outset of the New Deal. For the PWA, Dr. Win-the-War and Dr. New Deal were both present as early as 1933. In an unpublished article drafted for Harold Ickes by his Interior Department staff, entitled "Thank God for PWA! Where would we have been today without it?" Ickes applauded his agency's handiwork while making the broader point that via the PWA over $1 billion was "diverted" ("and I use the word advisedly and boastfully," wrote Ickes) to national defense, dating back to the $237 million appropriated in 1933 by the NIRA for the Navy. The PWA bankrolled the building of 74,000 miles of strategic highway for the Army; the renovation and modernization of munitions and ordnance; the improvement of 32 army posts (housing about 12 percent of enlisted soldiers); the purchase of cars, motorcycles, trucks, and tractors; and the construction of over 50 military airports. Further, the PWA gave

[65] "State Administrators Meeting in Chicago, July 7 and 8. John J. McDonough. Director, Division of Training and Reemployment," July 7–8, 1942, "Speeches of John J. McDonough 1942" folder, box 5, entry PC-37, 25, "Records of the Division of Training and Reemployment, 1940–1943"; and WPA Press Release, May 3, 1942, in "Vocational Training and Other White Collar" folder, box 3, entry 768, "Division of Information. Records Concerning National Defense Projects, 1939–1942"; all in RG 69, NA; and *Final Report on the WPA Program*, 91.

the Army Air Corps the funds to purchase more than 100 airplanes; the navy received funding for 2 aircraft carriers (the *Yorktown* and the *Enterprise*), 16 destroyers, 4 heavy destroyers, 4 submarines, 2 gunboats, and more than 130 combat airplanes. In addition to citing this direct spending on the military, Ickes noted carefully the import of the great hydroelectric projects built by the PWA, singling out the dams at Grand Coulee and Bonneville. By 1940, the PWA had spent over $314 million on the Navy and over $155 million on the War Department.[66]

In 1940, the FWA made its case to the public, issuing *Millions for Defense* a thinly disguised electoral pamphlet designed to tout the long-run contributions of the New Deal works programs to the nation's preparedness. "Over a billion dollars of emergency funds has been spent for direct national defense purposes in the past 7 years," the FWA proudly declared. Billions more had gone to roads, bridges, railroad modernization, power plants, warehouses, and dock facilities. The army's chief of military history concurred with this assessment, declaring that "it was the WPA worker who saved many Army posts and Naval stations from literal obsolescence" during the 1930s, when the armed forces' budgets were so small.[67]

Building on this range of pre-1940 activity, the centerpiece of the new defense public works effort was the construction of wartime housing under the Community Facilities Act, passed in October 1940 in response to a growing consensus that an emergency shortage of housing for defense workers had to be addressed. Sponsored by Texas Congressman Fritz

[66] Harold L. Ickes, "Thank God for PWA! Where would we have been today without it?" [1942], "Articles: Miscellaneous 'PWA Spent a Billion for Defense!' 'Thank God for the PWA! ca. 1942?" folder, box 119, Ickes Papers, LC; and Harold L. Ickes to Briggs, October 5, 1942, "Articles Miscellaneous Re: PWA and National Defense ca. 1942," ibid. For Ickes's use of ghostwriters, generally, see Watkins, *Righteous Pilgrim*, 760–65; for the role of hydroelectric power and importance of New Deal public works to defense, see Schwarz, *New Dealers*, 280–84; 297–324; Philip J. Funigiello, "Kilowatts for Defense: The New Deal and the Coming of the Second World War," *Journal of American History* 56 (December 1969): 604–20; and Funigiello, *Toward a National Power Policy: The New Deal and the Electric Utility Industry, 1933–1941* (Pittsburgh: University of Pittsburgh Press, 1973), 226–54; for totals for PWA military spending, see Oscar Chapman to Samuel I. Rosenman, November 14, 1944, "OF 466b PWA 1940–1945" folder, box 16, OF 466b, FDR Papers, FDRL.

[67] Federal Works Agency, *Millions for Defense: Emergency Expenditures for National Defense, 1933–1940* (Washington, D.C.: U.S. Government Printing Office, 1940), unpaginated; the Army's Chief of Military History quoted in Hugh Conway and James E. Toth, "Building Victory's Foundation: Infrastructure," in Alan Gropman, ed., *The Big "L": American Logistics in World War II* (Washington, D.C.: National Defense University Press, 1997), 197.

Lanham, this act was commonly known as the Lanham Act. Under its authority, the FWA could fund the construction of housing and other structures, such as schools, child-care centers, and hospitals, that were deemed necessary for the war effort. Indeed, the 1943 WPA appropriation legislation specified $6 million to be spent on nursery schools and day care for children of working mothers. By the summer of 1941 the FWA was building more than 5,000 houses per month; by November a total of 44,000 homes had been built.[68]

The defense housing effort drew on a wide variety of expertise, including stalwart advocates of public housing Catherine Bauer and Edith Wood. Despite this reliance on expert advice, however, the complex diffusion of bureaucratic responsibility for defense housing – John Carmody at FWA, Nathan Straus at the United States Housing Authority, and Charles F. Palmer, the defense housing coordinator – only bred conflict between the administrators. "I am so deeply disturbed about the conduct of the defense housing program," Straus complained to presidential aide Isador Lubin. "Defense housing under the Lanham Act is producing neither an adequate number of homes for workers in National Defense today, nor is it building up the local housing Authorities for usefulness when the defense emergency is over." By the end of 1941, Straus had gone public with his criticism, openly criticizing Carmody and Palmer. As one FWA official protested to FDR's press secretary, Marvin MacIntyre, "Mr. Straus is violating the ethics of his organizational relationship to the Federal Works Administrator, and is doing it in such a way as to create a mistaken impression of serious disharmony and inefficiency."[69] Whether a

[68] For an example of the consensus on the housing shortage, see the Twentieth Century Fund volume, *Housing for Defense: A Review of the Role of Housing in Relation to America's Defense and a Program for Action* (New York: The Twentieth Century Fund, 1940). For more on WPA defense spending on child care, see transcript of "Broadcast on War Nurseries and Day Care of Children through the Evening Star Forum over Station WMAL and the Blue Network," November 4, 1942, "Broadcast on War Nurseries and Day Care of Children – Evening Star Forum, November 4, 1942" folder, box 1, entry 38, "Information Records. Records Relating to Child Care in World War II, 1943–46," RG 162, NA; and Sonya Michel, *Children's Interests/Mothers' Rights: The Shaping of America's Child Care Policy* (New Haven: Yale University Press, 1999), 118–49. For the Lanham Act, see Philip J. Funigiello, *The Challenge to Urban Liberalism: Federal-City Relations during World War II* (Knoxville: University of Tennessee Press, 1978), 44–45. The correct date of the Lanham Act's passage can be found in the FWA's *Second Annual Report* (Washington, D.C.: U.S. Government Printing Office, 1941), 26; 54.
[69] Minutes of "Conference on Management Policy of Defense Housing Projects," January 7, 1941, no folder, box 3, entry 23, "Minutes and Reports of Conferences of the PWA,

mistaken impression or not, this dispute helped to curtail both Straus's and Carmody's influence and stature. Straus was forced to resign his position, a victim, he thought, of "the real estate lobby." FDR eased Carmody out of his post by nominating him to fill a vacancy on the Maritime Commission. Carmody, citing his dangerously high blood pressure and the advice of three doctors to slow down, accepted Roosevelt's decision and submitted his formal resignation from the FWA.[70]

John Carmody had faced a number of obstacles during his tenure as head of the Federal Works Agency. Resented by many in the WPA and the PWA, beleaguered by a skeptical press corps, and confronted with a hostile Congress, Carmody attempted to consolidate the New Deal's public works programs within the American state. While he did not ultimately succeed at this task, he did preside over the notable public works achievements in construction and wartime preparation made by the New Deal during his administration. After Carmody's departure, it was rumored that FDR was considering appointing General Brehon Somervell to take over the post. A member of the Army Corps of Engineers since 1914, Somervell had run the important New York City branch of the WPA since August 1936, supervising one out of every seven dollars spent nationally by the WPA. Somervell had established a strong record in New York, maintaining good relations with the Workers Alliance and with Mayor Fiorello La Guardia. FDR, however, punctured the notion of Somervell's being promoted as head of the FWA, writing to New York politician Edward J. "Boss" Flynn, "There is no truth in the rumor about General Somervell." Although passed over for that assignment, Somervell would go on to supervise the building of the Pentagon and would play a key role in supplying American troops during World War II.[71]

1934–1941," RG 135, NA; Nathan Straus to Isador Lubin, January 16, 1941, "Straus, Nathan" folder, box 88, Isador Lubin Papers, FDRL; John N. Edy to Marvin MacIntyre, November 7, 1941, "FWA – Defense Housing USHA" folder, box 119, Carmody Papers, FDRL; this letter is also found in "White House 9/1/41–12/31/42" folder, box 1, entry 4, "Correspondence of Administrators. Correspondence of Administrators with the House, 1939–1942. White House (General Correspondence, August–June, 1939) to White House 9/1/41–12/31/42," RG 162, NA.

70 Roger Biles, "Nathan Straus and the Failure of U.S. Public Housing, 1937–1942," *The Historian* 52 (Autumn 1990): 33–46; Funigiello, *Challenge to Urban Liberalism*, 102–106; Columbia University Oral History Project, "The Reminiscences of Nathan Straus," 103–104; FDR to John M. Carmody, October 1, 1941; and Carmody to FDR, October 7, 1941; both in "Roosevelt, F.D." folder, box 76, Carmody Papers, FDRL.

71 Excerpts from L. D. Dunbar, "Profiles – Army Man at Work," *The New Yorker*, February 10, 1940, "Lt. Col. Brehon Burke Somervell New York City" folder, box 3, entry 736, "Division of Information. Photographs and Biographical Information about WPA

Roosevelt instead chose another army engineer with strong New Deal credentials, General Philip B. Fleming. Fleming had worked in Ickes's PWA before being put in charge of administering the Fair Labor Standards Act in 1939. Labor Secretary Frances Perkins thought highly of Fleming's success in enforcing wage and hour standards. Fleming's position, she wrote to Helene P. Gans of the National Consumers' League, "requires not only administrative ability of the highest order but also immunity to pressures and courage to make such changes in personnel, structure and procedures as are necessary to accomplish the objectives of the act." Fleming, Perkins continued, "had demonstrated his ability to meet comparable requirements both in the PWA and in other federal agencies established during the Roosevelt administration. . . . Those of us who are directly concerned with the administration of the act feel that we are most fortunate in having secured his services for this important task." When Fleming was tapped to fill Carmody's job, Perkins told him she had fought hard to retain him on her staff because he was such a valuable administrator, and she complained to FDR about his propensity to reassign her administrators. Roosevelt, however, did not let Perkins's complaints keep him from appointing Fleming head of the FWA on December 10, 1941.[72]

Approximately four months later, however, Fleming fell ill, causing FDR to reconsider his decision. However, it was not Fleming's illness alone that led to FDR's misgivings. Howard Hunter, who had run the WPA since October 1940, met with Roosevelt in the middle of March 1942 to

Officials, 1933–1942," RG 69, NA; Edward J. Flynn to FDR, November 1, 1941; and FDR to Edward J. Flynn, November 6, 1941; both in "OF 3710 Federal Works Agency Sept.–Dec. 1941" folder, box 2, OF 3710, FDR Papers, FDRL; Barbara Blumberg, *The New Deal and the Unemployed: The View from New York City* (Lewisburg, PA: Bucknell University Press, 1979), 99–123; and John Kennedy Ohl, *Supplying the Troops: General Somervell and American Logistics in WWII* (DeKalb: Northern Illinois University Press, 1994).

72 Frances Perkins to Helene P. Gans, December 1, 1939; and Frances Perkins to Philip B. Fleming, October 24, 1941; both in "Wage and Hour" folder, box 103, entry 20, "Office of the Secretary. Secretary Frances Perkins. General Subject File, 1933–1941," Record Group 174, General Records of the Department of Labor, NA–College Park. For more on the opinion of the National Consumers' League on Fleming, see Landon R. Y. Storrs, *Civilizing Capitalism: The National Consumers' League, Women's Activism, and Labor Standards in the New Deal Era* (Chapel Hill: University of North Carolina Press, 2000), 202–5. For Fleming's appointment, see FWA Press Release, December 10, 1941, "Federal Works Agency" folder, box 1, entry 746, "Division of Information. Publications of the Federal Works Agency and Subordinate Agencies, 1936–1946," RG 69, NA.

protest what he later termed "the incompetence of the active officials of the Federal Works Agency, and their interference with the operations of the WPA." Hunter indicated that he would resign effective May 1, 1942, if FDR would agree to let him go. This meeting prompted FDR to confide in budget director Harold D. Smith, "I think something must be done about my very good friend, Colonel Phil Fleming. We simply cannot go along with his continued illness. How should I get word to him that I am putting in Howard Hunter as Acting Federal Works Administrator, with the understanding that as soon as Phil Fleming is ready to resume work he would replace him or would go to active war duty, whichever he prefers?" For his part, Fleming complained to FDR about the "spirit of competition existing between employees of the Federal Works Agency engaged in war public works and the regional offices of the Works [*sic*] Projects Administration." In his opinion, both agencies "should be amalgamated so that in the creation of public works the Federal Government appeared only as the Federal Works Agency." Fleming's assistant told an FDR aide that the FWA had "been consolidating over here to get a line organization which operates similarly to the Corps of Engineers of the Army."[73]

In this contest between Hunter and Fleming, Fleming emerged as the decisive victor. Hunter left the government in April 1942. The Associated Press reported that "it was a personal matter between him and Mr. Roosevelt [and thus] he was not at liberty to discuss it." By July, Fleming who later became renowned for his "natural flair for diplomacy" (in fact, after World War II he became a diplomat, serving as ambassador to Costa Rica), added the title of acting WPA commissioner to his responsibilities as head of the FWA.[74] Fleming would continue to supervise the FWA and its constituent agencies until 1949, presiding over the institutional unification of New Deal public works. Under Fleming, the FWA continued to prosecute public construction based on the philosophy of efficiency and

[73] Howard O. Hunter to FDR, March 16, 1942; and FDR to Harold D. Smith, March 21, 1942; both in "OF 3710 Federal Works Agency – Jan.–June 1942" folder, box 2, OF 3710; and see Howard O. Hunter to Grace Tully, March 16, 1942, "1942 Jan–Nov" folder, box 6, PPF 1820; both in FDR Papers, FDRL. Philip B. Fleming to FDR, March 23, 1942, and Baird Snyder to Edwin M. Watson, March 23, 1942, both in "White House (Confidential) File," folder, box 1, entry 6, "Correspondence of Administrators. Correspondence of Administrator with the White House, 1942–1949," RG 162, NA.

[74] *New York Times*, April 28, 1942, p. 23; ibid., July 10, 1942, p. 5; and Philip B. Fleming to all state WPA administrators, July 13, 1942, "100 May 1942" folder, box 77, "Central Files: General 1935–1944. 100 Administration," RG 69, NA. See also Fleming's obituary in the *New York Times*, October 7, 1955, p. 25.

economy, reviving the approach first tried by Harold Ickes and the PWA in 1933.

When Franklin Roosevelt called for the liquidation of the WPA in late 1942, he paid tribute to the agency's ability to accomplish "almost immeasurable kinds and quantities of service." The WPA was responsible for "reaching a creative hand into every county of the nation," the President declared.[75] Since 1935, the WPA had served as the central agency of the New Deal state, employing eight million people, building public works projects across the nation, and providing work for a wide variety of unemployed Americans, including artists, writers, and musicians. What Roosevelt's "honorable discharge" did not acknowledge, however, was the immeasurable kind of service rendered by the WPA after the bombing of Pearl Harbor.

The wide scope of New Deal public works programs during wartime was epitomized by the WPA's part in carrying out the relocation and internment of Japanese Americans in the western United States. During the Depression, New Dealers such as Harry Hopkins and Harold Ickes had built extensive bureaucracies for constructing public works and providing employment. During the war, the resultant expertise and bureaucracies were deployed in a way no one had foreseen during the dark days of the early 1930s. Eager to justify the continued existence of a shrinking unemployment relief program in the face of growing private demand for workers, WPA administrators looked for other ways to contribute to the domestic war effort.

Between March and November 1942, the WPA, led by its assistant commissioner Rex L. Nicholson, organized and staffed the "assembly centers" and "relocation camps" that had been built to house approximately 120,000 Japanese Americans. During these months, Nicholson and the WPA administered the "reception and induction" division of the newly created Wartime Civilian Control Administration (WCCA), spending more money on internment during this period than did the Army itself. At the Army's request, the WPA used its own procurement and disbursement systems to supply and maintain the internment camps. As War

---

75 Franklin D. Roosevelt to Major General Philip B. Fleming, December 4, 1942, in *Final Report on the WPA Program*, v.

Relocation Authority (WRA) officials noted, Nicholson had declared, in essence, "You formulate the policies and WPA will carry them out."[76]

As we have seen, the WPA tried to adapt to the approach of war by training workers for defense-industry work and ramping up the production of public works to aid the war effort. Despite these achievements, the decline in unemployment and an increasingly conservative Congress signaled that the agency's days were numbered. It is reasonable to assume that WPA administrators made their decisions to participate in Japanese American internment within this political context. This point is worth emphasizing not to excuse the actions of these officials, but to understand better the historical moment they faced. Since few people (outside of the Japanese Americans themselves) voiced opposition to internment as it was taking place, it should not be surprising to find that the people who ran the WPA, whether they were motivated by a desire to shore up support for an agency confronting political opposition, by a xenophobic sense of patriotism, or by a misguided sense that they could somehow "help" Japanese Americans, were willing to participate in such an active fashion.

As relocation and internment got under way, Hopkins was aware of the WPA's role in the process and apprised the President of its work. Although he had left his post as head of the WPA at the end of 1938 to become commerce secretary, Hopkins kept in contact with his many friends and associates in the agency, including Howard Hunter, its acting commissioner during the first months of 1942. The day after construction of the camp at Manzanar began, and about a week before the first Japanese Americans arrived in the arid Owens Valley, Hopkins wrote to Roosevelt, praising Hunter's work on internment. Hopkins assured the President that Hunter and the WPA were "handling all the building of those camps for the War Department for the Japanese evacuees on the West Coast" and "doing it with great promptness." No doubt aware of Hunter's feud with Fleming, Hopkins suggested to FDR that Hunter's work merited a promotion, and he urged him to put Hunter in charge of the entire FWA. "I don't think you are going to find anybody better," Hopkins wrote. Hunter, he insisted, "has a lot of steam, he acts very quickly and is thoroughly loyal

[76] E. R. Fryer, WRA regional director, and Lieutenant Colonel Cress, WRA deputy director, "Memorandum for the files," April 20, 1942, Japanese American Evacuation and Resettlement Records (hereafter cited as JERS), BANC MSS 67/14 c, Bancroft Library, University of California, Berkeley, reel 22. For a more detailed account of this episode, see Jason Scott Smith, "New Deal Public Works at War: The WPA and Japanese American Internment," *Pacific Historical Review* 72 (February 2003): 63–92.

to you."[77] Although army engineers and private contractors were largely responsible for constructing the camps for the Wartime Civilian Control Administration, the agency created by the army to handle internment, Hopkins was correct in stating that the WPA played an important part in the internment and relocation effort.

Not only did the WPA run the internment bureaucracy for the WCCA; it also helped supervise the preparation and staffing of fifteen assembly centers.[78] Japanese Americans were held in these assembly centers until the internment camps were ready to receive them. One of these WPA-run assembly centers, at Manzanar, was simply converted into one of ten internment camps, or "relocation centers," as they were called. While the WCCA was superseded by the WRA by the end of 1942 as relocation centers replaced the assembly centers, WPA staff remained in place to administer the camps.

In fact, between March and the end of November 1942 the WPA spent approximately $4.47 million on relocation and internment, more than any of the other civilian agencies involved in internment, and slightly more than the Army itself. The Office for Emergency Management, for example, spent only about $986,000 (funding the operating expenses of the WCCA), and the Federal Security Agency spent slightly over half that amount, about $533,000. During these months, by comparison, the military spent approximately $4.43 million on internment.[79] Of course, this does not mean that the WPA was solely responsible for the decision making behind internment. As historian Roger Daniels has argued, many groups deserve blame for advocating the relocation of Japanese Americans

---

[77] Hopkins to Franklin D. Roosevelt, March 19, 1942, "OF 3710 Federal Works Agency Jan.–June 1942" folder, OF 3710, OF, FDRL. For a detailed history of Manzanar, see Harlan D. Unrau, *The Evacuation and Relocation of Persons of Japanese Ancestry during World War II: A Historical Study of the Manzanar War Relocation Center* (2 vols., n.p., 1996).

[78] "Nicholson, Rex Lee," *National Cyclopaedia of American Biography* (New York, 1964), suppl. vol. J.

[79] U.S. Army, *Final Report: Japanese Evacuation from the West Coast 1942* (Washington, D.C.: U.S. Government Printing Office, 1943), 350. Other key expenses include the construction of the assembly centers ($10.7 million) and relocation projects ($56.5 million), which were charged to the U.S. Army Corps of Engineers, and $4.1 million in crop loans issued by the Farm Security Administration. In addition to drawing on WPA personnel, the internment effort relied on a number of federal agencies, including the Federal Security Agency, the Office of Emergency Management, and the Bureau of Indian Affairs. Department of Justice Press Release, January 29, 1942, in Roger Daniels, ed., *American Concentration Camps: A Documentary History of the Relocation and Incarceration of Japanese Americans, 1942–1945*, 9 vols. (New York, 1989), 1: unpaginated.

following the bombing of Pearl Harbor. These include military officials such as Lieutenant General John L. DeWitt and Secretary of War Henry L. Stimson, politicians such as Culbert Olson, governor of California, State Attorney General Earl Warren, and Senator Hiram Johnson, and influential newspaper columnists such as Westbrook Pegler and Walter Lippmann, as well as local California elites motivated by fear and racism.[80] Nonetheless, the WPA's role was significant. On March 12, 1942, Colonel Karl R. Bendetsen, the army officer in charge of the WCCA, asked Rex L. Nicholson, the assistant WPA commissioner based at Salt Lake City, to take charge of the management of the first thirteen reception and assembly centers.[81] Nicholson, who had participated in a number of informal pre-evacuation planning meetings, agreed to carry out the job, with the understanding that while he and his personnel would report to DeWitt, they would remain salaried employees of the WPA. "General plans and policies for the operation of Reception Centers and Assembly points," DeWitt wrote Nicholson, "will be worked out by you with my Assistant Chief of Staff, Civil Affairs Division [Colonel Bendetsen], and subject to his final approval. The actual administration and management of the Assembly Points and Reception Centers will be the responsibility of your agency."[82]

Nicholson kept his WPA position and was named chief of the WCCA "reception and induction" division. Born into a Texas cattle-ranching family, Nicholson had forged his own career as a structural engineer. In 1933 he took a leave from a promising position in a Washington state construction company to work for the CWA during the winter of 1933–34. In 1936, he once again left private employment, this time to become acting state administrator for the WPA in Washington. By late 1937, he was promoted to director of employment and labor relations for the WPA in the western United States (including Alaska and Hawaii). Nicholson's star continued to rise in the WPA, attributable in part to his successful direction of an investigation into graft in New Mexico's WPA, which led to the federal prosecution of 121 people. Following this victory, Nicholson took charge of the WPA's war construction in the western United States and

---

[80] Roger Daniels, *Concentration Camps: North America–Japanese in the United States and Canada during World War II*, rev. ed. (Malabar: Robert E. Krieger Publishing Company, Inc., 1981), 70–73.

[81] U.S. Army, *Final Report*, 46. Eventually sixteen assembly centers and ten relocation centers were built. Roger Daniels, *Prisoners Without Trial: Japanese Americans in World War II* (New York: Hill and Wang, 1993), 55.

[82] Lieutenant General John DeWitt to Rex L. Nicholson, March 28, 1942, reprinted in U.S. Army, *Final Report*, 47.

Pacific islands, supervising the building of 110 airports and over 200,000 miles of military highways and roads. To undertake the imprisonment of approximately 120,000 people, the army turned to Nicholson and the WPA for expertise and efficiency. Nicholson and the WPA delivered.[83]

As the internment process began, WPA officials in Southern California briefed Earl Minderman, director of the WPA's division of information in Washington, D.C., on the specific accomplishments of the agency. "Ten days after the assignment was made," reported the WPA's Southern California state information officer to Minderman, "we opened the first [camp site] at Manzanar in Owens Valley under the management of Clayton L. Triggs, one of our regional men." Henry Amory, the WPA administrator in charge of Southern California, became camp manager at the Santa Anita assembly center, a location the WPA referred to as "our baby." "The rest of the staff," the report continued, "both here and at Manzanar, have been drafted from WPA." A third center, at the Pomona Fairgrounds, also managed by a WPA official, was projected to be ready within another ten days.[84] Conditions at these assembly centers were terrible, as Stanford history professor Yamato Ichihashi testified. The Santa Anita center was "mentally and morally depressive." "Thousands are housed in stables which retain smells of animals. A stable which housed a horse now houses 5 to 6 humans.... There is no privacy of any kind. In short the general conditions are bad without any exaggeration; we are fast being converted into veritable Okies."[85] Conditions were so unsanitary that government bureaucrats were surprised that there were not more outbreaks of illness.[86] Despite the WPA's claims that they had created a livable environment, the testimony of Ichihashi, along with the eloquent recollections of many other "evacuees," indicates how severely the WPA fell short of this goal.

Robert L. Brown, the reports officer and the assistant project director at Manzanar, recalled that Triggs, his boss, drew directly on what he had earlier learned firsthand about camp administration while running camps for workers hired to construct roads by the WPA. After the

[83] "Nicholson, Rex Lee," *National Cyclopaedia of American Biography*, and *San Francisco Chronicle*, March 27, 1951, p. 7.

[84] L. W. Feader to Earl Minderman, April 8, 1942, "Japanese Evacuation (N. California S. California)" folder, box 2, entry 687, "Division of Information. General Correspondence of the Field Relations Section, 1937–1942," RG 69, NA.

[85] Yamato Ichihashi quoted in David M. Kennedy, *Freedom From Fear: The American People in Depression and War, 1929–1945* (New York: Oxford University Press 1999), 753–4.

[86] Daniels, *Concentration Camps*, 89.

war, Brown applied his own experience working in the internment camps to the requirements of a position with the United Nations Relief and Rehabilitation Administration, which entailed handling camps of refugees in Europe. "A lot of the people that came to Manzanar to start with," Brown remembered of his fellow camp staffers, "were fellows that [Triggs] picked up from his WPA experience, and were people he knew."[87] Triggs, however, was able to come up with variations on his WPA experience while running Manzanar. Indeed, Triggs requested Nicholson's approval for the installation of some of the most restrictive elements of the camp: barbed-wire fencing, guard towers, and spotlights.[88] Nicholson, at the request of Colonel Bendetsen, also ordered camp administrators to post notices of Civilian Restrictive Order No. 1, erecting signs that instructed evacuees to remain inside the fences of the camp.[89]

The WPA also lent its procurement and disbursement systems directly to the Army in order to supply the camps and conduct maintenance and repairs.[90] Indeed, the very first administrative order of the WCCA placed Nicholson and the WPA in charge of "the location, planning, construction, [and] equipping of Reception Centers."[91] The Army's reliance on the WPA to perform these basic functions illustrates not only the breadth and capability of the WPA but also the reluctance of the military to undertake such tasks. Neglected during the isolationist climate of the interwar years, the Army declined to commit potentially large numbers of men and supplies to running such an open-ended program.[92] While the Army had worked with the Labor, Interior, and Agriculture Departments between 1933 and 1942 to administer the Civilian Conservation Corps (CCC), that collaborative assignment was different from administering internment.

---

[87] "An Interview with Robert L. Brown conducted by Arthur A. Hansen on December 13, 1973, and February 20, 1974, for the California State University, Fullerton Oral History Program Japanese American Project," in Arthur A. Hansen, ed., *Japanese American World War II Evacuation Oral History Project*, 5 vols. (Westport, Conn., Greenwood Press: 1991), 2: 100; 105.

[88] Clayton E. Triggs and Harry L. Black to Rex L. Nicholson, May 12, 1942, JERS, reel 148.

[89] Colonel Karl R. Bendetsen to All Assembly Center Managers (Through Mr. R. L. Nicholson, Chief Reception Center Division), May 22, 1942, JERS, reel 148.

[90] "Ruth McKee Notes. Interview with E. R. Fryer," February 18, 1943, JERS, reel 22; and U.S. Army, *Final Report*, 74, 222.

[91] WCCA Administrative Order #1, March 16, 1942, JERS, reel 12.

[92] For more on the weaknesses of the U.S. Army during this period, see Mark Skinner Watson, *The United States Army in World War II: The War Department: Chief of Staff: Prewar Plans and Preparations* (Washington, D.C., 1950), 15–56; and D. Clayton James and Anne Sharp Wells, *From Pearl Harbor to V-J Day: The American Armed Forces in World War II* (Chicago, 1995), 5–15.

Most obviously, the unemployed had voluntarily enrolled in the CCC. Supervising Roosevelt's "tree army" as it performed light forestry work was not equivalent to overseeing the confinement of Japanese Americans behind barbed wire. Two or three Army officers supervised each CCC camp, consulting with several of the enrollees on aspects of running the facility. The army viewed this as a useful opportunity to provide on-the-ground command training for its officers.[93] By 1942, however, the Army's central priority was to modernize and prepare for war, not to deploy its limited resources in the internment effort. Even if the Army had wanted to become more involved in that undertaking, Attorney General Francis Biddle and Secretary of War Stimson told Roosevelt at the end of February 1942 that "the difficulties [of internment and relocation] were practical, i.e., the Army did not have enough men to evacuate or guard any very large number of Japanese at this time."[94] The strength of the New Deal state filled this void.

As the Army completed its delivery of Japanese Americans into the assembly centers and prepared to shift the administration of the internment program from the WCCA to the WRA, the WRA began to consider hiring WPA administrators to run its organization. Two WRA officials arranged a meeting with Nicholson to discuss the availability of his personnel. The minutes of the meeting show these officials saying that the WRA "is finding it nearly impossible to locate suitable administrative service personnel" and registering their opinion that the WPA "had an excess of available personnel in administrative services." Nicholson, in turn, argued that the WPA was capable of running the entire internment program. "Obviously," the WRA officials noted in the record, "what Mr. Nicholson had in mind was to take over the WRA function as applied to project management," the euphemistic phrase used to describe how the centers and camps were run. Nicholson said "he would take over all functions except that of policy making. He said, in effect – you formulate the policies and WPA will carry them out."[95]

Lieutenant General DeWitt's control over the internment bureaucracy, however, stymied the efforts of WPA officials to make political capital out

[93] Salmond, *Civilian Conservation Corps*, 30–45.

[94] Francis Biddle, Notes on Cabinet Meeting, February 27, 1942, "Cabinet Meeting, Jan–Jun. 1942" folder, box 1, Francis Biddle Papers, FDRL, microfilmed as part of the "Papers of the U.S. Commission on Wartime Relocation and Internment of Civilians. Part 1. Numerical File Archive" (Frederick, Md., 1983), reel 3.

[95] E. R. Fryer, WRA regional director, and Lieutenant Colonel Cress, WRA deputy director, "Memorandum for the files," April 20, 1942, JERS, reel 22.

of their role in uprooting approximately 120,000 people and removing them from their homes and businesses. One frustrated WPA administrator wrote, "The moving of these japs is one of the biggest tasks of its type ever attempted[;] we should get credit." He complained, "A complete report on the extent of our participation...would enable us to write a good story for periodicals." Even in recent newsreel footage, this official continued to grumble, "the WPA is getting no credit for this work."[96] Indeed, Minderman sent several urgent letters and telegrams to Amory, pressing him for more details so that he could showcase the WPA's achievements to a broader audience. Although "I had the impression," Minderman wrote Amory, "that nothing was to be said about this activity publicly," he requested that Amory's state information officer, L. W. Feader, "write me how much of the WPA's part in this program is being made public."[97]

Several months after internment began, it was clear that Nicholson was not making allies in this new bureaucratic world. Leland Barrows, an aide to WRA solicitor Philip Glick, told University of California, Berkeley, sociologist Morton Grodzins that friction between Nicholson and WCCA head Bendetsen and WRA head Milton Eisenhower caused Nicholson's downfall. Barrows called Nicholson "the worst goddamned political dealer I ever saw." Nicholson, Barrows told Grodzins, "wanted to be made Deputy Director and to let his own gang run the Centers. When Eisenhower said no, Nicholson walked out in a huff."[98] E. R. Fryer, regional director of the WRA in San Francisco, confirmed to WRA historian Ruth McKee that "Nicholson, Regional Director of the Western area of WPA put a cog in the works by refusing to release WPA men except on a condition. The condition which he put up to Eisenhower was that Eisenhower make him an assistant director.... Eisenhower got very mad and kicked him out."[99]

Nicholson's and the WPA's role in internment has remained unknown for many years. After leaving the WPA, Nicholson moved to Berkeley, California, and ran his own businesses, selling tractors and farm

---

[96] H.W. to Jim [Branson?], undated [probably April 1942], "Japanese Evacuation (N. California S. California)," folder, box 2, entry 687, "Division of Information. General Correspondence of the Field Relations Section, 1937–1942," RG 69, NA.

[97] Earl Minderman to Henry R. Amory, April 14, 1942; and see Earl Minderman to Henry R. Amory, April 17, 1942; and Earl Minderman to Henry R. Amory, April 22, 1942; all in ibid.

[98] Morton Grodzins, "Interview with Leland Barrows," October 4, 1943, JERS, reel 22.

[99] "Ruth McKee Notes. Interview with E. R. Fryer," February 18, 1943, JERS, reel 22.

equipment. In 1946 Nicholson was asked by President Truman to plan the reorganization of all federally owned lands under the Department of Interior.[100] In 1952 Nicholson became the California head of Adlai Stevenson's presidential campaign and was active in the state's Democratic Party.[101] When Edmund G. Brown declared that he would not run for governor in 1954 but instead would run for reelection as the state's attorney general, one journalist reported that "some Southern California Democratic bigwigs are talking of attempting to build up Rex Nicholson of Berkeley" as the party's gubernatorial candidate.[102] Nicholson was also mentioned as a potential candidate for the Senate. When he died in 1974, his role in interning Japanese Americans was largely forgotten.

In carrying out its work, the War Relocation Authority drew on a variety of New Deal precedents and government agencies. WRA administrator Milton Eisenhower had served in the Department of Agriculture. His successor, Dillon Myer, had administered the Agricultural Adjustment Act and after the war had run Federal Public Housing and the Bureau of Indian Affairs. University of California, Berkeley, sociologist Dorothy Swaine Thomas was among the first to identify the significance of the New Deal's contribution to the WRA, however, when she recorded her impressions of Myer and his staff in 1944. "WRA is a typical, New Deal, idealistic agency," she wrote.

I worked for FERA for quite a period under Harry Hopkins and observed exactly the same phenomena. They carry the torch for the Japanese people, but always in abstract, idealistic terms without much understanding of the problems that are being faced in the projects, or of what the people themselves really want. Policies are formed partly on an opportunistic basis (which is really necessary) but partly in terms of this abstract idealism ... but almost never in terms of concrete problems met by actual individuals.[103]

While Thomas's criticisms of the WRA were accurate, they were based on the assumption that the agency's job was to do what the Japanese Americans wanted. The WRA and the WPA, however, were not primarily

---

[100] *San Francisco Chronicle*, March 27, 1951, p. 7; and *National Cyclopaedia of American Biography*, suppl. vol. J, s.v. "Nicholson, Rex Lee."
[101] *San Francisco Chronicle*, August 28, 1952, p. 7.
[102] *San Francisco Chronicle*, December 2, 1953, p. 1.
[103] Dorothy Swaine Thomas notes, "High Points in Conversation between DST and Dillon Myer, Tozier, Glick and Barrows," January 20, 1944, JERS, reel 92.

occupied with assisting Japanese Americans; they were concerned with efficiently carrying out Executive Order 9066.

The role of the WPA in Japanese American internment, viewed broadly, was a consequence of the reorganization and execution of New Deal public works programs under the twin goals of economy and efficiency. In the face of growing opposition from a conservative Congress, New Dealers had managed to maintain the increasingly unpopular works programs during the late 1930s and early years of World War II, building housing, roads, and airports, and providing worker training. However, the WPA – the program that to many New Dealers epitomized the potential of the welfare state to level inequalities – eventually played a key part in carrying out the largest forced relocation of people in U.S. history since Indian removal. This use of the capacities of the state to shape society casts serious doubts on the notion that a weakened New Deal state was reenergized by the advent of World War II and transformed into a vigorous wartime regime. Rather, the multifaceted role played by the public works programs in readying the country for war indicates that this wartime state drew upon deep and vital roots in the state structure built by the New Deal, simultaneously illustrating the considerable strengths of New Deal liberalism and calling into question its social democratic potential.

8

Public Works and the Postwar World

The postwar legacy of the New Deal's public works programs is complex and far reaching, spanning the entire nation with projects ranging from military bases to national highways. During the years between the end of the Work Projects Administration in 1943 and the passage of the Federal-Aid Highway Act in 1956, the federal government turned away from a rationale for public works based on social welfare and returned to an ideology of efficiency and economy. Public works projects, such as dams, airports, and especially, highways, became central aims of the American state. New national security and defense programs, such as the Manhattan Project, relied directly on the infrastructure built by the New Deal. This transition in public works philosophy marked less an end of reform, however, than a restoration of the approach epitomized by the Hoover Administration and continued and expanded by Harold Ickes's Public Works Administration throughout the New Deal. The character of this transitional moment emerges most clearly through examination of several key areas of public policy and debate: the relationship between the New Deal state and planning; the postwar reorganization of the executive branch of government; and the influence of New Deal public works on the development of federal highway construction, culminating in the passage of the 1956 Federal-Aid Highway Act.[1]

[1] Alan Brinkley, *The End of Reform: New Deal Liberalism in Recession and War* (New York: Alfred A. Knopf, 1995). The fate of what historian Nelson Lichtenstein terms "labor liberalism" also pivots around a shift in liberalism's fortunes during and after World War II. Nelson Lichtenstein, *Walter Reuther: The Most Dangerous Man in Detroit* (Urbana: University of Illinois Press, 1995), 155–57; and see also the accounts in Kevin Boyle, *The UAW and the Heyday of American Liberalism, 1945–1968* (Ithaca: Cornell

Although individual New Deal public works programs were eliminated by a conservative Congress during the war, the Federal Works Agency continued to function until 1949, supervising such organizations as the Public Roads Administration, the Public Buildings Administration, and the Public Works Administration. In 1949, the federal government again reorganized its public works functions. Under the direction of a commission headed by a retired president, Herbert Hoover, the federal government folded the responsibilities of the Federal Works Agency into a new agency, the General Services Administration. The creation of the GSA formalized the return of federal public works to an ideal of efficiency and economy.[2]

This bureaucratic story of reorganization and reduction was at odds with what was happening to public works spending by the American state. In a period marked by a growing cold war between the Soviet Union and the United States, the federal government justified renewed spending on public works projects in the name of national security. As the infrastructure of what President Dwight Eisenhower would term the military-industrial complex spread across the nation, the southern and western regions of the United States became home to military bases, a comprehensive highway network, and new and improved airports. Private construction firms, such as Bechtel and Brown & Root (today a subsidiary of Halliburton), went into business overseas, drawing on the knowledge and capacities they had acquired while building public works for the New Deal state. Politicians like Lyndon Johnson eventually came to believe in exporting New Deal–inspired economic development to Southeast Asia, recommending, for example, the establishment of a Tennessee Valley Authority on the Mekong Delta. While efforts during the last half of the twentieth century to improve the federal government's involvement in social welfare programs are notable for their lack of connection

University Press, 1995); Robert H. Zieger, *The CIO, 1935–1955* (Chapel Hill: University of North Carolina Press, 1995); and David L. Stebenne, *Arthur J. Goldberg: New Deal Liberal* (New York: Oxford University Press, 1996). For an important study that questions the notion of a postwar retreat from reform by liberals at the local level, see Guian A. McKee, "Philadelphia Liberals and the Problem of Jobs, 1951–1980" (Ph.D. diss., University of California, Berkeley, 2002). On the Manhattan Project, see Thomas P. Hughes, *American Genesis: A Century of Invention and Technological Enthusiasm, 1870–1970* (New York: Viking Press, 1989), 353–442; Peter Bacon Hales, *Atomic Spaces: Living on the Manhattan Project* (Urbana: University of Illinois Press, 1997); and Richard Rhodes, *The Making of the Atomic Bomb* (New York: Simon & Schuster, 1986).
² Peri E. Arnold, *Making the Managerial Presidency: Comprehensive Reorganization Planning, 1905–1996*, 2d ed., rev. (Lawrence: University Press of Kansas, 1998), 118–59.

to New Deal programs like the WPA, liberal and conservative politicians
continued to rely on the New Deal's legacy of fostering economic development through public works construction in formulating both foreign
and domestic policy.[3]

THE FEDERAL WORKS AGENCY, 1939–1949: PLANNING
FOR POSTWAR PUBLIC WORKS

Created in 1939, the Federal Works Agency consolidated within one
agency the potential for the New Deal to establish its emergency public works programs on a permanent basis within the American state.
The FWA contained the newly renamed Work Projects Administration
(formerly Works Progress Administration), the Public Works Administration (PWA), the Public Buildings Administration (formerly in the
Treasury Department), the Public Roads Administration (transferred from
the Agriculture Department), and the United States Housing Authority.
The Federal Works Agency maintained its hold on these functions until
1949.[4]

   The FWA was run by New Dealer John Carmody for a brief period
(1939–41), before being taken over by Major General Philip B. Fleming.
Fleming, who had worked closely with Harold Ickes during the first years
of the PWA, drew on his years of experience with the Army Corps of
Engineers in charting the FWA's course. In addition to such wartime
public works activities as road and highway building, worker training,
and wartime housing construction, the FWA, along with the National
Resources Planning Board, began to plan for the postwar period.[5] Specifically, the two organizations sponsored a Public Work Reserve project,

[3] Jordan A. Schwarz, *The New Dealers: Power Politics in the Age of Roosevelt* (New York:
Alfred A. Knopf, 1993); Bruce J. Schulman, *From Cotton Belt to Sunbelt: Federal Policy,
Economic Development, and the Transformation of the South, 1938–1980* (Durham:
Duke University Press, 1994); Roger Lotchin, *Fortress California: From Warfare to
Welfare* (New York: Oxford University Press, 1992); Lloyd C. Gardner, *Pay Any Price:
Lyndon Johnson and the Wars for Vietnam* (Chicago: Ivan R. Dee, 1995), especially 185–
200; and Alice O'Connor, *Poverty Knowledge: Social Science, Social Policy, and the Poor
in Twentieth-Century U.S. History* (Princeton: Princeton University Press, 2001).
[4] Floyd Dell, draft of "Federal Works Agency" entry for *Encyclopaedia Americana*, December 5, 1939, "Federal Works Agency" folder, box 1, entry 746, "Division of Information. Publications of the Federal Works Agency and Subordinate Agencies, 1936–1942,"
RG 69, Records of the Work Projects Administration, NA; and see Federal Works Agency,
Annual Report (Washington, D.C.: U.S. Government Printing Office, 1940–1949).
[5] For a fuller profile of Fleming and a review of the wartime activities of the FWA, see
Chapter 7.

using funds from the WPA.[6] This effort to assemble a "shelf" of public works plans that could be activated at the first signs of an economic downturn was an outgrowth of earlier work by the NRPB's Public Works Committee to develop a six-year program of public works. Indeed, the concept of a prepared "shelf" of plans dated back to Progressive Era arguments for public works construction.[7] Anticipating the challenge of reconverting to a peacetime economy, New Dealers thought that public works could alleviate unemployment, stabilize the economy, and enhance national security.

The Public Works Committee included a range of personnel from the worlds of public works, labor, and construction. Chaired by a former PWA official and vice president of the American Society of Civil Engineers, Colonel Henry Waite, the committee's members included Frank W. Herring of the American Public Works Association, F. E. Schmitt of the *Engineering News–Record*, long-time public works advocate Otto T. Mallery of the Pennsylvania State Planning Board, William Stanley Parker of the Construction League of America, Frederick J. Lawton of the Bureau of the Budget, Corrington Gill of the WPA, the PWA's Fred Schnepfe, and representatives of the departments of Labor and Commerce.[8]

In drawing upon earlier planning by the PWA and the NRPB, the Public Work Reserve project also built on the Hoover-era heritage of public works. This heritage was evident in its concerns for economy and efficiency and in its very legislative history. In 1939, the NRPB's Public Works Committee declared that all its recommendations for future construction were made in the service of "economy and efficiency in federal

[6] Philip B. Fleming to Frederic A. Delano, September 22, 1942, "National Resources Planning Board" folder, box 9, entry 5, "Correspondence of Administrators. Correspondence of General Philip B. Fleming, 1942–1949," Records of the Federal Works Agency, RG 162, NA. For more on the NRPB, see Marion Clawson, *New Deal Planning: The National Resources Planning Board* (Baltimore: Johns Hopkins University Press, 1981) and Patrick D. Reagan, *Designing a New America: The Origins of New Deal Planning, 1890–1943* (Amherst: University of Massachusetts Press, 1999).

[7] Otto T. Mallery, "The Long-Range Planning of Public Works," in *Business Cycles and Unemployment*, ch. 14 (New York: National Bureau of Economic Research, 1923); and V. A. Mund, "Prosperity Reserves of Public Works," *Annals of the American Academy of Political and Social Science* 149, Part II (May 1930): 1–9. For a historical treatment, see Udo Sautter, *Three Cheers for the Unemployed: Government and Unemployment before the New Deal* (Cambridge: Cambridge University Press, 1991), 94–110.

[8] F. E. Schmitt to H. M. Waite and Fred E. Schnepfe, October 6, 1939, "Subcommittee I – Public Works Comm. of NRC" folder, box 2, entry 33, "File of Fred E. Schnepfe Relating to the 6-Year Planning Program of the National Resources Committee, 1936–1940," Records of the Public Works Administration, Record Group 135, National Archives.

public works construction."⁹ In another progress report, the committee described its origins and methods, noting for the record that it was planning in six-year periods because this was the time span adopted by the Federal Employment Stabilization Board created under the Employment Stabilization Act of 1931.¹⁰

The Public Work Reserve focused on assembling a range of projects "designed to develop the resources, services and facilities of the Nation and through them, to provide employment." These projects, the Federal Works Agency declared, would be "undertaken by local, state, and federal agencies after the reduction of defense activities." John Carmody, FWA head when the Public Work Reserve was announced, argued that the Reserve presented "two distinct advantages – it is undertaken definitely and deliberately at a time when the nation's resources are being heavily taxed in order to be prepared as never before to cushion the economic and industrial shock that follows war preparation effort." Second, Carmody said, was that the Reserve would enlist "the best efforts of planning bodies everywhere – local, state, and national – in the preparation of a sound, well rounded out program that will be related not only to public needs but to the plans of private industry for readjustment and future expansion." Ultimately, in Carmody's view, "Our aim is to utilize the full potentialities of the nation to provide needed public service and facilities rather than the limited concept of public work merely as a means of providing employment."¹¹ In other words, infrastructure as well as employment were the chief aims of New Deal public works projects.

Although the Public Works Reserve was a short-lived entity, this notion of public works as a government-supervised effort to provide the construction of necessary infrastructure would increasingly animate debate over federal spending on public works during the postwar period. By July 20, 1942, the PWR came to an end, a victim of budget cutbacks and the wartime reorientation of the works programs. FWA head Philip B. Fleming explained these circumstances to NRPB chair Frederic A. Delano, writing,

---

⁹ "Report of Public Works Committee of the National Resources Planning Board on *Federal Six-Year Program of Public Works for 1941–1946*," September 1, 1939, "Executive Order – NRC" folder, box 2, in ibid.

¹⁰ "Appendix C – Origins and Methods of Six-Year Programming of Federal Public Works," February 27, 1939, "Subcommittee I – Public Works Comm. of NRC" folder, in ibid.

¹¹ Federal Works Agency Press Release #106, June 23, 1941, "Public Works Reserve" folder, box 2, entry 746, "Division of Information. Publications of the Federal Works Agency and Subordinate Agencies, 1936–1942," RG 69, NA.

"I do not feel that it will be possible for us to continue with post-war planning until our authority to do so has been clearly expressed." However, Fleming continued, "The President has asked me to give continued study to the whole subject in an effort to find some way, if possible, to permit a resumption of the work, and, if necessary, to draft a proposal for possible submission to the Congress."[12]

Fleming continued to champion the cause of public works planning throughout his career as head of the FWA. In 1943, Fleming went before the House Committee on Public Buildings and Grounds to testify on the importance of planning. The committee's chair, Texas congressman Fritz Lanham, wanted to gather a range of opinions on the part that public works could play in postwar reconversion. Seeking to capitalize on a recent Gallup poll finding that a main topic of concern to the American people was the issue of postwar employment, Fleming argued that public works could address the problem of providing work for demobilized soldiers and for people employed in war-related industries. If depression strikes the postwar economy, Fleming cautioned that "America cannot expect to make her voice effective in the world if she is hampered by disillusionment, conflict, and disunity here at home. If we are to speak effectively in the councils of the world we must have the unity which has at its base a rising standard of living and a wide diffusion of the means of reasonable comfort and peace of mind."[13]

Several weeks after Fleming testified, National Resources Planning Board member Beardsley Ruml went before the Committee on Public Buildings and Grounds. Ruml, a registered Republican, treasurer for the R. H. Macy department store, philanthropist, and University of Chicago professor, was described by *The New Yorker* magazine as a man whose "career is almost geological in its mixed stratification of science, public affairs, and private business."[14] Like Fleming, Ruml believed in the importance of a planned public works policy for the postwar period. Ruml, however, had a more limited and focused goal in mind. As part of a nine-point proposal for a postwar fiscal program, Ruml urged, "Let us

[12] Philip B. Fleming to Frederic A. Delano, September 22, 1942, "National Resources Planning Board" folder, box 9, entry 5, "Correspondence of Administrators. Correspondence of General Philip B. Fleming, 1942–1949," RG 162, NA.

[13] "Statement of Major General Philip B. Fleming, Administrator, Federal Works Agency, before the Committee on Public Buildings and Grounds of the House of Representatives," November 23, 1943, "Post-War" folder, box 1, entry 23, "Administrative Records. Records Concerning Plans for Postwar Public Works, 1941–1944," RG 162, NA.

[14] Quoted in Reagan, *Designing a New America*, 143.

plan our public works, not to balance the whole economy, but to help toward stabilizing the construction industry." It was not realistic, Ruml thought, to expect public works to work as "a general cure-all for the business cycle." Rather, "the most we can expect, and this is no small gain, is that public works can be planned and undertaken in such a way as to even out the activities of the construction industry itself, thereby providing a reasonable level of construction throughout the year and year after year." Along with readying a shelf of useful public works projects, Ruml urged Congress to establish an inquiry into the needs of the construction industry, and he stressed the importance of obtaining accurate budget estimates before permitting the use of government "to accomplish our national purposes."[15]

The chair of the AFL's committee on housing, Harry C. Bates, also testified before the House Committee on Public Buildings and Grounds. "Building trades have played a leading part in the launching of war mobilization," Bates proclaimed, "acting as the advance guard which build the initial defense projects of the Army and the Navy and erected cantonments for the training of our troops." To ease the readjustment to peacetime, Bates called for a "double-barreled public works program," consisting of a combination of short-term construction projects, which are "dictated by the most essential requirements of local community welfare," and of long-term projects, "which can extend over a period of years and which could also be contracted and expanded to counterbalance the effect of the business cycle upon employment."[16]

The American Society of Civil Engineers joined the AFL and the FWA in stumping for the cause of postwar public works planning, publishing a program entitled "Postwar Construction: Planning Now Will Safeguard National Economy in Critical Transition Period."[17] If the nation neglected the responsibility to plan for the return to a peacetime economy, the engineers opined, it would run the risk of contributing to widespread unemployment, lead "into another dole or so-called work relief period," and, in

---

[15] "Testimony of Beardsley Ruml Before the Committee of the House of Representatives on Public Buildings and Grounds," January 19, 1944, "Post War Planning – 1944" folder, box 10, entry 5, "Correspondence of Administrators. Correspondence of General Philip B. Fleming, 1942–1949," RG 162, NA.

[16] American Federation of Labor Information and Publicity Service Press Release, February 10, 1944, "Post-War" folder, box 1, entry 23, "Administrative Records. Records Concerning Plans for Postwar Public Works, 1941–1944," RG 162, NA.

[17] American Society of Civil Engineers, "Postwar Construction: Planning Now Will Safeguard National Economy in Critical Transition Period," July 29, 1943, in ibid.

general, "add to the economic ills that may befall the country." To avoid such a disaster, the engineers urged a program of privately contracted public works construction. "The construction industry," the society argued, "consists not only of engineers and architects but also of contractors. By training and experience this group is most competent to plan, supervise, and execute construction projects with economy and dispatch, and to secure the maximum return for the dollar invested."[18] The engineers proposed a short-term roster of necessary projects as the most practical solution to the problem of postwar planning. "Many of these projects are of the self-liquidating type that can be financed by revenue bonds to be retired by the beneficiaries on a 'pay-as-you-use' basis," they declared, recalling the approach favored by Ickes and the PWA.[19]

While Congress heard from many different parties, Fleming traveled around the country to promote public works planning. In 1944, he spoke to a gathering of civic organizations in New Orleans. Fleming made the case for thinking of public works planning as simply an extension of the sorts of planning people do in their everyday lives, for business or pleasure. "As to our planning of public works construction for the post-war period," Fleming argued, "the great trouble, I think, is that too many people are trying to make it seem harder than it needs to be." Who were these people, wondered Fleming? "I think that the tremendous anxiety all of us entertain as to the future of our country, of our cities, and of our individual affairs has spawned a new breed of experts, some of whom – but of course, not all – are among the star-gazers and medicine men who despise the commonplace and obvious, and look instead to the esoteric and the occult for their inspiration." Against these unrealistic dreamers and their schemes, Fleming proposed that public works planning be thought of as "a truly national program...[that] would give us the best guarantee that post-war projects will be socially useful and of value in themselves."[20]

Fleming's assistant, George Field, also traveled to promote the cause of public works planning. Field, like many New Dealers, viewed the establishment of public works programs as a policy measure, whereby government planning would use the private market in order to strengthen capitalism. He argued that an extensively planned public works program would not only prevent the return of a WPA-like agency to minister to

[18] Ibid.
[19] Ibid.
[20] "Address of Major General Philip B. Fleming, Administrator, Federal Works Agency, at a Luncheon Meeting of Representatives of Civic Organizations," February 8, 1944, in ibid.

the unemployed. It would also generate "the public works that will be required as accessory facilities for the great expansion of industry and business which must take place if we are to have full peace-time employ-ment."[21] Although the FWA leaders were willing to abandon the WPA and its direct methods of employing the out-of-work, in this way they still remained interested in linking their agency and its public works projects to the cause of full employment.

Indeed, Fleming testified for the FWA before Senator Robert Wagner's Full Employment Subcommittee in support of the Full Employment Act of 1945. Fleming viewed the bill, which called for the federal government to make economic policy in order to generate "the highest feasible levels of employment opportunities through private . . . investment and expen-diture," as operating "in the old-time American tradition."[22] If planned carefully, public works projects, he assured the Senate, could help to sta-bilize the economy. They "do not compete with private industry; rather they tend to supplement and stimulate private industry":

Extension of streets and water and sewer lines create new opportunities for home building. Good highways promote the speedy and cheaper dissemination of agri-cultural and manufactured products. Much manufacturing requires for its efficient operations an abundant supply of uncontaminated water and adequate sewerage for the disposal of industrial wastes. It is no exaggeration to say that the expansion of production which will be needed to assure a continuing high level of national income and to provide abundant jobs will be contingent upon a like expansion of the social overhead.[23]

Fleming informed FDR of his many speaking engagements before civic, labor, and business groups on behalf of the FWA and public works plan-ning, and he kept the President apprised of the different arguments he was developing in support of public works.[24] While he agreed with Field

[21] Ibid.
[22] The Full Employment Act of 1945 quoted in J. Joseph Huthmacher, *Senator Robert F. Wagner and the Rise of Urban Liberalism* (New York: Atheneum, 1968), 297; for Fleming's testimony see Congress, Senate, Subcommittee of the Committee on Banking and Currency, *Full Employment Act of 1945*, 79th Cong., 1st sess., July 30, 31, August 21, 22, 23, 24, 28, 29, 30, 31, and September 1, 1945, p. 863.
[23] Congress, Senate, Subcommittee of the Committee on Banking and Currency, *Full Employment Act of 1945*, 79th Cong., 1st sess., July 30, 31, August 21, 22, 23, 24, 28, 29, 30, 31, and September 1, 1945, p. 868.
[24] Philip B. Fleming to Franklin D. Roosevelt, July 30, 1943, in "Federal Works Agency June–Dec. 1943" folder, box 3, OF 3710, FDR Papers, FDRL; and in "White House 1943" folder, box 1, entry 6, "Correspondence of Administrators. Correspondence of Administrator with the White House, 1942–1949," RG 162, NA.

on the need to avoid the return of the WPA, Fleming also tried to portray government construction as inherently apolitical. Speaking to a joint
meeting of labor officials, businessmen, and local politicians in St. Paul,
Minnesota, Fleming declared, "Public works do not involve economic or
political ideologies at all...whether a bridge is to be used by Jews or
Gentiles, Republicans or Democrats, the techniques used in constructing
it are the same."[25] To the American Road Builders Association in Chicago,
Fleming declared, "To paraphrase Thomas Jefferson, I believe that, after
the experience of the last twelve or thirteen years, we now hold these truths
to be self-evident.... That worth-while [sic] public works require months
for advance preparation – for engineering surveys, the preparation for
plans and specifications, and the acquisition of land."[26] Also in Chicago,
Fleming spoke before assembled members of the Associated General Contractors, suggesting that public works planning was as sensible as home-
owners' insurance. "It is far better that we should be prepared at all times
than that we should stagger from one crisis to another, trying to 'get by'
on hastily improvised plans that, precisely because of hasty preparation,
are so often ill-advised and wasteful of public funds."[27] These efforts to
portray government-sponsored economic development as free of ideological content foreshadowed discussions of how to export American-style
development overseas.

Private enterprise, Fleming reasoned, was a necessary but not sufficient factor in the reconversion process. To a group of municipal officials
in Florida, Fleming stated, "Much of America's greatness is due to the
private enterprise system, and we are all agreed, I think, that we want
to keep that system." However, Fleming assured the New York AFL, "I
do not personally feel that we can leave it all to private business" to
assure postwar prosperity. Fleming noted that even the Chamber of Commerce had endorsed a comprehensive program of public works projects
to ensure employment after the war's end. Fleming made the case for the
federal government's role before a number of organizations, placing the
FWA's activities in a long history of federal actions that benefited business. Addressing the Associated Equipment Distributors, Fleming made
the following argument:

One might suppose that there is something alien and un-American, or even
immoral, in using the Federal power to save the country, including business itself.

[25] Ibid.
[26] Ibid.
[27] Ibid.

The fact is we have been doing it from the very start. We have never hesitated to assist business. We have protected it from competition with prohibitive tariffs. The Reconstruction Finance Corporation has loaned billions to bolster up the sagging economy. We have directed harbors and rivers and built port facilities at public expense to assist business. We have subsidized publishers with low postal rates, and provided the aviation industry with airports at public expense. When we needed transcontinental railroads to open up the West and private capital hesitated to assume the risks we came to the rescue to the tune of a free gift of 20 sections of land and a credit of from $16,000 to $48,000 for every mile of track laid.[28]

Fleming issued this reminder to his audience: "Business needs to remember that a large part of it will be heading the procession to the bankruptcy court if, because of inertia, we permit this war to taper off into another Great Depression."[29]

After the war had ended, Fleming traveled to the American Road Builders Association meeting in Chicago in early 1946. Although he was speaking to a group of contractors who were suspicious of government's role in the economy, Fleming presented a robust case for federal involvement in the construction industry. "We need a well-stocked shelf of plans available at all times to throw into the breach when needed," Fleming told the road builders. "Only in that way can public works construction be made to pull its full weight and to help stabilize the construction industry which historically has been subject to nearly ruinous fluctuations." Arguing that public works had "a two-fold role to play in the overall economy," Fleming asserted that, first of all, public construction delivered "the facilities and services which the people need," and, secondly, that it provided "useful employment when needed to supplement the jobs available in private industry."[30]

Later that year, Fleming spoke to the National Institute of Governmental Purchasing on the subject of "Tomorrow's Public Works." Noting that states, counties, and municipalities were constructing very few public works, Fleming worried that "the public and professional attitudes toward public works have changed so drastically within the last few years that they amount almost to a revolution.... [W]e will do little building hereafter in yesterday's tradition." Rather, Fleming proposed, "We will

[28] Ibid.
[29] Ibid.
[30] "Address of Major General Philip B. Fleming, Administrator, Federal Works Agency, before the American Road Builders Association," January 14, 1946, "Addresses by General Fleming 1946" folder, box 5, entry 32, "Information Records. Speeches of FWA Administrators, 1939–49," RG 162, NA.

build in the social, political, and economic context of tomorrow."[31] Perhaps most controversially, Fleming asserted that planning "should lift orderly public works development from the realm of political controversy." The more the American public thought of public works planning as an everyday occurrence, Fleming thought, the less it would seem like a foreign intrusion into the economy.[32] Fleming's skepticism was well judged. Although he continued to lead the FWA effectively – testifying before Congress from 1947 through 1949 on such issues as planning, the need to develop Alaska with public works projects, and the ability of the FWA to coordinate emergency disaster relief – he was unable to make a successful case for the continued existence of the Federal Works Agency.[33] When the subject of the reorganization of the executive branch again arose in 1947, New Deal public works at last faced bureaucratic extinction.

HOOVER REDUX: GOVERNMENT REORGANIZATION AND PUBLIC WORKS

In July 1947 Congress again took up the topic of reorganizing the executive branch, calling for a commission to make recommendations on how to reduce and streamline the federal government. Of the commission's twelve members, six came from each party: Four were selected by President Harry Truman, four by Speaker of the House Joseph Martin, and four by the president of the Senate, Arthur Vandenberg. But who would head such a body? Truman and the Congress turned to a retired, yet still active, former president: Herbert Hoover. Hoover was pleased to accept the position, announcing that the Commission on Organization of the Executive Branch of the Government would strive to reduce the costs of government to the taxpayer, in the name of "efficiency and economy."[34] Joining Hoover on the commission were Dean Acheson, James Forrestal,

[31] "Address of Major General Philip B. Fleming, Administrator, Federal Works Agency, before the National Institute of Governmental Purchasing," August 19, 1946, in ibid.

[32] Ibid.

[33] See Fleming's testimony in Congress, Senate, Subcommittee of the Committee on Public Works, *State Planning for Public Works*, 80th Cong., 1st sess., July 11, 1947; Congress, Senate, Subcommittee of the Committee on Public Works, *Alaska Public Works*, 81st Cong., 1st sess., April 28 and May 17, 1949; and Congress, Senate, Subcommittee of the Committee on Public Works, *Coordinating Emergency Activities of Federal Agencies in Disaster Areas*, 80th Cong., 2d sess., June 14, 1948.

[34] Gary Dean Best, *Herbert Hoover: The Postpresidential Years, 1933–1964* (Stanford: Hoover Institution Press, 1983), 2:312–13.

Arthur S. Flemming, and George H. Mead (appointed by Truman), along with Joseph P. Kennedy, Senator George Aiken, Senator John McClellan, and Professor James Pollock (appointed by Vandenberg). Speaker Martin named Hoover, James Rowe, Jr., Representative Clarence Brown, and Representative Carter Manasco.[35]

Hoover's private view of the commission's power was rather more explicit than his public pronouncements about undertaking reorganization in order to achieve greater efficiency and economy. Truman's tenuous popular support led Hoover to view his role leading the commission as an opportunity to take advantage of Thomas Dewey's 1948 Republican presidential campaign. As one historian has noted, Hoover "clearly envisioned that the [commission's] report would be issued after the election of Dewey to the presidency, and that with a friendly, GOP-dominated Congress the report could be used to roll back much of the New Deal."[36] Hoover's friend, Julius Klein, informed Hoover of Commissioner Clarence Brown's plans:

> Brown plans to get into the matter very aggressively and asked me to pass along the word to you in strict confidence that he put in the provision that the Commission should report *after* November 1948...so as to lay the groundwork for the expected complete housekeeping that will be necessary at that time.[37]

By scheduling publication of the report after the election, the commission could claim the mantle of bipartisanship for its findings. Hoover himself wanted the staff for the commission to reflect his views, however. "The first thing we need is a good counsel," Hoover wrote, "preferably someone who has had experience in the departments and who is surely not a New Dealer." The Republican Conference in the Senate was even more direct in voicing its hopes: The commission would undertake "a major operation on the sprawling, tax-eating, patchwork bureaucracy bequeathed to us by the New Deal."[38]

While the central recommendations issued by the commission dealt directly with the public works bureaucracies built by the New Dealers, these proposals were not as explicitly anti–New Deal as one might have

---

[35] Arnold, *Making the Managerial Presidency*, 122–23; and Ferrel Heady, "A New Approach to Federal Executive Reorganization," *American Political Science Review* 41 (December 1947): 1118–26.

[36] Best, *Herbert Hoover*, 2:325.

[37] Julius Klein quoted in Arnold, *Making the Managerial Presidency*, 122–23.

[38] Hoover quoted in William E. Pemberton, "Struggle For the New Deal: Truman and the Hoover Commission," *Presidential Studies Quarterly* 16 (Summer 1986): 516; the Senate Republican Conference quoted in ibid., 517.

expected. Truman and his appointees to the commission were able to thwart a broad-based conservative assault against the New Deal by working with the commission to shape its recommendations. Hoover's own assessment of the New Dealers on the commission was more blunt:

The major worries of the New Dealers were: the total abolition of political appointment in civil servants; the entire subjection of the military to the civilian arm; forms of budgeting and accounting which would expose the concealed expenditures and subsidies in the Government; the exposure of the extent to which socialism had run; and, especially, they disliked the estimates of $2.5 billion annual savings at a time when they were trying to add $4 billion taxes for their socialist-fascist program.[39]

In their impact, however, the commission's findings on the issue of public works programs delivered less a full-scale rollback of these agencies than a codification of the dismantling of the programs that had begun during World War II.

New York public works czar Robert Moses, the head of the Hoover Commission task force on public works, had originally recommended to Hoover that the federal government create a new Department of Public Works, a position that both Hoover and Truman supported. Faced with opposition from entrenched interests – especially the Army Corps of Engineers – however, Hoover and the commission did not follow Moses' plan.[40] The commission recommended instead that the Federal Works Agency be dissolved. Its public building functions would be replaced by a new Office of General Services, or, as it was eventually called, the General Services Administration. A public works bureaucracy that, during the New Deal, supervised public works construction across the nation was to be replaced by a far less powerful agency that would be in charge of the "housekeeping" functions of the federal government, including such tasks as record storage and courthouse maintenance. The other public works functions of the federal government would be shifted to the Interior Department.[41]

One-time head of the Federal Works Agency John Carmody kept a close eye on the recommendations of the Hoover Commission. Indeed,

---

[39] Hoover Commission Memoir, April 13, 1949, in Timothy Walch and Dwight M. Miller, eds., *Herbert Hoover and Harry S. Truman: A Documentary History* (Worland, Wyoming: High Plains Publishing Company, 1992), 159.

[40] For Moses' account, see Robert Moses, *Public Works: A Dangerous Trade* (New York: McGraw-Hill, 1970), 711–32.

[41] *The Hoover Commission Report on Organization of the Executive Branch of the Government* (New York: McGraw-Hill, no date), 75–83; 263–95.

Carmody served briefly as an adviser to the reorganization effort, recalling later that, of all his different experiences in twenty-five years of government service, "none was more unsatisfactory nor more fantastic than
my brief period with the Hoover Commission." Carmody observed that
"a more reactionary group could not well have been gathered to destroy
liberal gains that had been made, legislatively and administratively, during
the previous twenty years." His colleagues on the commission, however,
were just as uneasy with Carmody as he was with them. Carmody concluded, "It was a mistake to invite me to help with the kind of reorganization of government operations Mr. Hoover and his colleagues, largely
presidents of large corporations, had in mind and it was a mistake for me
to accept."[42] Carmody went so far as to organize a "Citizens Committee
against the Hoover Report" to counter the Hoover-inspired body, Citizens
Committee for the Hoover Report, by lobbying against the commission's
recommendations.[43]

Carmody's personal files and correspondence reflect the active interest
he took in following the trajectories of the two major New Deal agencies
he had been involved in: the Rural Electrification Administration and the
FWA. He saw the Hoover Commission as an explicit attempt by Hoover
"to kill public power in the United States, including the Tennessee Valley
Authority."[44] Carmody's suspicions were not unfounded. Hoover supposedly remarked to Senator Barry Goldwater, "I would sell the TVA if I
could only get a dollar for it."[45]

As the years passed, Carmody watched the growth of the General Ser-
vices Administration with deep misgivings. Reading a 1955 letter from
Alan Johnstone, who had been Carmody's general counsel at the FWA,
Carmody marked up this passage:

As to our Federal Works days, the outfit which we started with such devotion and
care has been converted by the book-keepers in the Budget from a Works Department into an old woman's knitting bag containing varicolored bits of yarn, while
the Government's construction personnel is scattered all over the lot in futile competitive enterprises. To that extent the advances of the Roosevelt Administration

[42] July 31, 1958, "Hoover Commission – 1954: Reminiscences of John M. Carmody," in
    "Hoover Commission – Reminiscences of JMC," box 156, John M. Carmody Papers,
    FDRL.
[43] "Citizens Committee against the Hoover Reports," typed notes, no date, "Hoover,
    Herbert. John" folder, box 227, Carmody Papers, FDRL.
[44] Columbia University Oral History Project, "The Reminiscences of John Michael
    Carmody," 448.
[45] Joan Hoff Wilson, *Herbert Hoover: Forgotten Progressive* (Prospect Heights, IL:
    Waveland Press, 1992), 227.

which proposed to used [sic] public work and the development of the public domain as a stimulant to the enterprise of the people has been, at least, shunted aside.[46]

Johnstone and Carmody both resented the trajectory taken by the FWA as it was absorbed by the General Services Administration. The GSA's first head was not a New Dealer; instead, Truman appointed the head of the War Assets Administration, Jess Larson. While Larson was in charge of the WAA, he had supervised the disposal of about $8 billion in government property. Under Larson, the structure of the GSA became decentralized, with ten regional offices distributed throughout the country. As Larson put it, the GSA's purpose was "performing the housekeeping operations of the Government."[47]

Larson's administration of the GSA was far from smooth, however. He became a central figure in two influence-peddling scandals, involving (unproved) allegations of favoritism in awarding government contracts for supplies.[48] Larson's administration of the GSA drew derision from Johnstone, who viewed Larson as only the most recent example in a series of missteps that made up public works policy:

And I hold it against certain of our friends that they induced Roosevelt and Truman to throw the switches the wrong way when you left Federal Works. Then the "great liquidation" began, as I warned [General Philip B.] Fleming – to be completed by [Jess] Larsen [sic] when he replaced competent men by the ambitious but inept War Assets boys.[49]

The GSA even attracted the attention of *Fortune* magazine, which, six years after the agency's founding, labeled it "Washington's Most Durable Mess."[50]

Reflecting further on the place of public works policy within the reorganization of the federal government, Johnstone remarked, "It has always seemed inconceivable to me that we can agree to establish a Department of

[46] Alan Johnstone to John M. Carmody, October 29, 1955, untitled folder, box 115, Carmody Papers, FDRL.

[47] Jess Larson to Senator John L. McClellan, August 22, 1949 [draft], "Hoover Commission" folder, box 1, entry 30, "Administrative Records. Records Relating to the Organization of the General Services Administration, 1949–50," RG 162, NA.

[48] Eleanora W. Schoenebaum, ed., *Political Profiles: The Truman Years* (New York: Facts on File, 1978), s.v. "Larson, Jess." For more on the War Assets Administration, see Gerald T. White, *Billions for Defense: Government Financing by the Defense Plant Corporation during World War II* (University, AL: University of Alabama Press, 1980), 98–112.

[49] Johnstone to Carmody, October 29, 1955, untitled folder, box 115, Carmody Papers, FDRL.

[50] Herbert Solow, "GSA: Washington's Most Durable Mess," *Fortune*, August 1955, p. 76.

Education, Health and Welfare, which is doing dam [sic] little education, no health and only scant welfare, but are unwilling to have a Department of Public Works which could replenish the fountain to refresh the whole private enterprise system which supports the whole." Johnstone argued that public works were more beneficial for the economy than the social security program. He wrote to Carmody, "I am sure that it must have occurred to you that Social Security which is based on payroll taxes is a depressant, because it takes money out of pay checks which make up buying power, while public works, the public jobs aside, makes the bed for more jobs since it puts the public facilities, including the hiterto [sic] undeveloped public resources, to the service of all the people on equal terms."[51]

In looking for the continued legacy of the New Deal's public works programs within a specific department of the federal government, however, Johnstone was searching in the wrong place. New Dealers had watched silently while the FWA was absorbed into the newly created General Services Administration in 1949. This stance, in part, reflected the tight links between the works programs' accomplishments and limitations. Perhaps it also indicated the broader reluctance of many Americans to view public works as a vital part of a larger political project. While the creation of the GSA marked the eclipse of the New Deal's public works bureaucracy, government construction by no means disappeared. Rather, with the advent of the Cold War, public works took on different forms. During these years, the heavier construction that was a hallmark of the New Deal quietly became a central focus of the federal government. While federal funds paid for the infrastructure that comprised the nation's highway system, network of military bases, and airports, the influence of New Deal public works traveled overseas.[52]

PUBLIC WORKS AND THE COLD WAR

The legacy of the New Deal's public works influenced a number of Cold War programs, particularly Truman's Point Four program. In his 1949 inaugural address, Truman announced four major foreign policy points

[51] Johnstone to Carmody, October 29, 1955, untitled folder, box 115, Carmody Papers, FDRL; for an evaluation of social security's origins, see Mark H. Leff, "Taxing the 'Forgotten Man': The Politics of Social Security Finance in the New Deal," *Journal of American History* 70 (September 1983): 359–81.
[52] On the "apolitical" character of technological innovation, generally, see Hughes, *American Genesis*; and for the tendency of public works to be overlooked, see Jon C. Teaford, *The Unheralded Triumph: City Government in America, 1870–1900* (Baltimore, 1984).

for his administration: The first three were continued support of the United Nations, the Marshall Plan, and plans for the North Atlantic Treaty Organization. As his fourth proposal, Truman announced a "bold new program" that would draw on American science and resources to aid underdeveloped nations. The *Washington Post* termed Point Four a "'Fair Deal' Plan for the World."[53]

As the Truman administration tried to flesh out the substance behind Truman's address, Thomas Corcoran turned to the man who had led the Public Works Administration, Harold Ickes. Corcoran wrote to Ickes that he had been "working like hell on the Point IV business." Although Ickes had fallen out with Truman and had resigned his post as interior secretary in 1946, Corcoran wondered if Ickes was interested in returning to public service. Point Four, Corcoran declared, had the potential to use public works and economic development as the carrot to containment's stick. "The usefulness for you" was what "intrigues me most," Corcoran wrote. "Point IV has to be the affirmative hope-side of our foreign policy to balance the negative military policy of keeping strong and being tough." If Ickes was interested, and if Truman could be persuaded to appoint him, Corcoran proposed that, "your appointment will mean that the program takes on the character of an international PWA as distinguished from a boondoggling WPA."[54]

Ickes was interested but skeptical. "Your suggestion, as to how the money appropriated in support of Point Four should be used, is another of your inspirations," he wrote Corcoran. "By all means, an international PWA should be set up." Ickes, however, did not think that Corcoran would be able to persuade Secretary of State Dean Acheson or President Truman to consider him for any role in Point Four. "I suspect that you had better give up trying to do anything with this particular lame duck," Ickes concluded.[55] Despite meager funding, during the 1950s the Point Four program made important strides, building much needed highways and airports in Afghanistan, Jordan, Saudi Arabia, Thailand, and Vietnam, among other places.[56]

[53] David McCullough, *Truman* (New York: Simon & Schuster, 1992), 730–31.
[54] Thomas Corcoran to Harold L. Ickes, September 6, 1950, "Harold L. Ickes. General Correspondence, 1946–52. Corcoran, Thomas, 1946–51" folder, box 53, Harold L. Ickes Papers, LC. Emphasis in original.
[55] Ickes to Corcoran, September 11, 1950, in ibid.
[56] Schwarz, *New Dealers*, 340. For more on the links between Point Four and the New Deal's rural rehabilitation programs, see Sarah T. Phillips, "Acres Fit and Unfit: Conservation and Rural Rehabilitation in the New Deal Era" (Ph.D. diss., Boston University, 2004), ch. 5.

This exporting of the New Deal created unexpected results. American policy makers often overlooked the potential for overseas development programs to go awry. They were so impressed by the undeniable success of programs like the TVA at home – for example, the cost of electricity produced by the TVA declined, uninterrupted, for over three decades – that they failed to take account of different circumstances abroad. Drawing on the social scientific framework of modernization theory, many policy makers (and their intellectual advisers) simply assumed, as historian Nils Gilman has observed, that the United States demonstrated "an apparently universalizable American model of development." Economists, in particular, fresh from their success in guiding the nation's mobilization during World War II, reinforced this assumption. This intellectual scaffolding, when combined with the impressive track record of the New Deal's public works programs in developing the United States, presented a potent and heady combination for liberals during the postwar years. As Arthur Schlesinger, Jr., argued, "Our engineers can transform arid plains or poverty-stricken river valleys into wonderlands of vegetation and power.... The Tennessee Valley Authority is a weapon which, if properly employed, might outbid all the social ruthlessness of the Communists for support of the people of Asia." While the New Deal failed to remake the world's political economy in the ways that it so emphatically did for the domestic United States, the achievements of the public works programs profoundly shaped how America interacted with the rest of the planet.[57]

While Point Four encapsulated the notion of exporting New Deal public works abroad during the first years of the Cold War in order to fight Communism and aid the developing world, the program that most explicitly drew upon the legacy of New Deal public works at home was the

[57] Nils Gilman, *Mandarins of the Future: Modernization Theory in Cold War America* (Baltimore: Johns Hopkins University Press, 2003), 39; and Arthur M. Schlesinger, Jr., *The Vital Center: The Politics of Freedom* (Boston: Houghton Mifflin Company, 1949), 233. See also Nick Cullather, "Damming Afghanistan: Modernization in a Buffer State," *Journal of American History* 89 (September 2002): 512–37; the essays collected in David C. Engerman, Nils Gilman, Mark H. Haefele, and Michael E. Latham, eds., *Staging Growth: Modernization, Development, and the Global Cold War* (Amherst: University of Massachusetts Press, 2003); and Michael A. Bernstein, *A Perilous Progress: Economists and Public Purpose in Twentieth-Century America* (Princeton: Princeton University Press, 2001). For the TVA, see Erwin C. Hargrove, *Prisoners of Myth: The Leadership of the Tennessee Valley Authority, 1933–1990* (Princeton: Princeton University Press, 1994); and Thomas K. McCraw, "The Hubris of the Engineers," *Technology and Culture* 36 (October 1995): 1007–14. For a cautionary account of the limitations of "authoritarian high modernism," see James C. Scott, *Seeing Like a State: How Certain Schemes to Improve the Human Condition Have Failed* (New Haven: Yale University Press, 1998).

national highway system. Although the story of the building of the highways has been told, the links between this project and the New Deal public works have been largely neglected.[58] While the Public Works Reserve did not sustain the New Deal's planning capacity, in the case of the highways things were different. Many of the arguments mustered in favor of national highway construction were anticipated by New Deal planners. In April 1941, FDR created the Interregional Highway Committee, directing this group to develop a national road-building policy to be implemented after the war. New Deal planners, state road engineers, as well as political appointees, one historian has observed, "were committed to engineering specifications, traffic flows, and city and regional planning as their form of political expression."[59]

Speaking at the first meeting of the National Interregional Highway Committee to fellow committee members, including Rexford Tugwell, Frederic A. Delano, and longtime head of the Bureau of Public Roads Thomas H. MacDonald, FWA head John Carmody argued that the Public Work Reserve's shelf of projects might form a basis for future decisions made by the committee.[60] Presidential adviser Lauchlin Currie supported Carmody's efforts to cast the FWA as the leader of the wartime road-building program, urging FDR to give "primary responsibility for the highway part of the [transportation] program ... to Carmody." Out of these efforts came the report, "Highways for the National Defense," prepared by the Public Roads Administration, FWA, the Advisory Commission to the Council of National Defense, and the War and Navy departments, which paid particular attention to upgrading the strength of bridges, widening strategic roads, ensuring adequate access to larger cities, and servicing the existing and proposed populations at army, naval, and air bases.[61]

Other New Dealers and reformers weighed in on the importance of highway construction. Public works advocate Otto T. Mallery, for example, was quick to see in national highway building the potential

---

[58] See, for example, Tom Lewis, *Divided Highways: Building the Interstate Highways, Transforming American Life* (New York: Penguin Books, 1997).

[59] Mark H. Rose, *Interstate: Express Highway Politics, 1939–1989*, rev. ed. (Knoxville: University of Tennessee Press, 1990), 19.

[60] Minutes of the National Interregional Highway Committee, June 24, 1941, "National Interregional Highway Committee" folder, box 16, Rexford G. Tugwell Papers, FDRL.

[61] Lauchlin Currie to FDR, June 21, 1940; and "Highways for the National Defense," February 1, 1941; both in "OF 1e Bureau of Public Roads 1939–1941" folder, box 11, OF 1e, FDR Papers, FDRL.

for continuing the work of New Deal public works projects. In 1943, Mallery wrote to Columbia University economist Carter Goodrich and FDR adviser Isador Lubin about the ability of a "Pan American Highway" to stand as a public works project of "international scope and significance."[62] In a study of American highway policy for the Brookings Institution, published during World War II, Charles L. Dearing was struck by the extent that "federal highway policy has been dominated and complicated" since 1933 by New Deal public works programs.[63] While these programs provided employment, Dearing was particularly impressed by the ability of the New Deal's public works to complicate and unsettle established pathways of highway planning and funding. "The injection of emergency considerations into federal road activity created general confusion in the country's highway policy," reported Dearing. "This trend has produced a more complex managerial structure characterized by additional dispersion and overlapping of authority and responsibility among the several levels of government."[64] The FWA tried to resolve this confusion through its planning for the postwar period.

Arguing that federal direction of highway construction was an issue "so vital and fundamental in the economy of this Nation," FWA head Philip Fleming told Congress that World War II should serve as an important lesson. "I do know from our war experience how vital our highway system was to our existence then. Our highways really became a part of our production line."

There were wings and fuselages and turrets and engines moving over our highways to Kansas and Texas and being assembled there in finished airplanes. There were mechanical parts moved up into New Hampshire which became bomb sights. So our highways really were a part of our national effort. Without them I do not know where we would have been in our war effort.[65]

When the Eisenhower administration turned to the task of highway construction, it embraced all the arguments for federal public works put forward by the New Dealers. Public construction would head off rising unemployment and recession; improved highways would help secure

[62] Otto T. Mallery to Carter Goodrich, November 19, 1943, enclosed in Otto T. Mallery to Isador Lubin, November 19, 1943, "Mallery, Otto T." folder, box 65, Isador Lubin Papers, FDRL.
[63] Charles L. Dearing, *American Highway Policy* (Washington, D.C.: The Brookings Institution, 1942), 86.
[64] Dearing, *American Highway Policy*, 89; 99.
[65] Congress, Senate, Subcommittee of the Committee on Public Works, *Federal Aid for Highways*, 80th Cong., 2d sess., February 28, 1948, pp. 153–54.

national defense; and a widespread network of reliable roads would spur economic development throughout the country. It was through the construction of the federal highway program that Eisenhower most notably performed the task of assimilating the political innovations established under the New Deal.[66] Although subsequent conservative Republicans, such as Barry Goldwater, would mock Eisenhower's use of these state capacities as a mere "Dime Store New Deal," the highway program begun in 1956 signaled a public works effort as significant as anything undertaken during FDR's four terms as president.[67]

The New Deal's public works programs did more than establish an important precedent for the economic development carried out by the Federal-Aid Highway Act of 1956; they also provided private firms and politicians with a way of thinking about how the world worked. During the Great Depression, heavy-construction contractors, such as Kaiser, Bechtel, and Brown & Root, all benefited from public works contracts. After World War II, these firms went overseas. Partnering with nations on all seven continents, they helped build projects like Saudi Arabia's petrol infrastructure and refineries, the Channel Tunnel between France and Great Britain, chemical plants in Singapore and India, and numerous others. These firms subsequently reapplied the knowledge they learned in constructing these overseas ventures within the United States, building the Bay Area Rapid Transit (BART) system, Boston's Central Artery/Tunnel project (the "Big Dig"), and other "mega-projects."[68]

No politician drew on the New Deal's public works legacy more extensively than did a former Texas head of the National Youth Administration,

[66] Fred Greenstein, *The Hidden-Hand Presidency: Eisenhower as Leader* (New York: Basic Books, 1982); and the essays collected in Shirley Anne Warshaw, ed., *Reexamining the Eisenhower Presidency* (Westport, Conn.: Greenwood Press, 1993).
[67] Goldwater quoted in James T. Patterson, *Grand Expectations: The United States, 1954–1974* (New York: Oxford University Press, 1996), 271.
[68] Stephen B. Adams, *Mr. Kaiser Goes to Washington: The Rise of a Government Entrepreneur* (Chapel Hill: University of North Carolina Press, 1997); Mark Foster, *Henry J. Kaiser: Builder in the Modern American West* (Austin: University of Texas Press, 1989); Bechtel Corporation, *Building a Century: Bechtel, 1898–1998* (Kansas City: Andrews McMeel, 1998); Laton McCartney, *Friends in High Places: The Bechtel Story: The Most Secret Corporation and How It Engineered the World* (New York: Simon and Schuster, 1988); Christopher James Tassava, "Multiples of Six: The Six Companies and West Coast Industrialization, 1930–1945," *Enterprise & Society* 4 (March 2003): 1–27; Geoffrey Jones, *The Evolution of International Business: An Introduction* (London: Routledge, 1996); Thomas P. Hughes, *Rescuing Prometheus* (New York: Pantheon Books, 1998); and Alan Altshuler and David Luberoff, *Mega-Projects: The Changing Politics of Urban Public Investment* (Washington, D.C.: The Brookings Institution Press, 2003).

Lyndon Baines Johnson. Former FWA head John Carmody was quick to notice when Johnson declared his intention to replicate the Tennessee Valley Authority overseas, in Vietnam's Mekong Delta. Carmody tore journalist Drew Pearson's "Washington Merry-Go-Round" column out of the *Washington Post* on May 10, 1965. In this piece, Pearson noted the long-standing connections between Abe Fortas, Arthur "Tex" Goldschmidt, and Johnson. Fortas and Goldschmidt, while working at the PWA, helped advise Johnson on securing a public works loan for a series of dams that were constructed in thirteen Texas counties; by 1965 Fortas was a White House adviser for LBJ, and Goldschmidt had gone to the United Nations, "where," Pearson related, "he has continued building dams all over the world." The result of this association, Pearson reported, was that LBJ "began pushing the idea that a giant series of dams on the Mekong River might bring peace and prosperity to war-torn North and South Viet-Nam."[69] Carmody, who knew Goldschmidt quite well when they both worked for Harry Hopkins's Civil Works Administration, was pleased to see that the philosophical approach behind the New Deal's public works programs was continuing to shape public policy.

Indeed, in presenting the "TVA on the Mekong Delta" plan to LBJ, Goldschmidt made explicit comparisons to the success that New Deal public works programs scored in attacking what FDR called the nation's number one economic problem, the South. "Only economic integration with the nation as a whole," Goldschmidt wrote, "could cure the South and close the North–South gap. And this integration could only be accomplished by Federal action. There is a direct parallel today in the economic development of the former colonial regions of the world."

Economic development is too important to leave to the blind play of economic forces; it can be hastened or hindered by the intervention of policies designed to increase production and promote welfare. And the process is strengthened by outside assistance. The rich nations of the world will have to do for the poor nations what the Federal Government of the U.S. did for the South.[70]

Johnson agreed, replying to Goldschmidt, "We are in a better position to handle some of the problems of the developing countries because of the problems we faced so recently in developing our own."[71] This confidence, expressed through Johnson's Great Society liberalism, in the ability of

---

[69] Drew Pearson, "LBJ's Mekong Project Not New," *Washington Post*, May 10, 1965, in "Johnson, Lyndon B." folder, box 188, Carmody Papers, FDRL.

[70] Goldschmidt quoted in Gardner, *Pay Any Price*, 195.

[71] Johnson quoted in ibid.

government to address broad economic and social concerns, both at home and abroad, stemmed directly from the liberalism fostered by the New Deal.

Perhaps no New Dealer better articulated this confidence and optimism than did TVA director David Lilienthal. In his classic work, *TVA: Democracy on the March,* Lilienthal crafted a manifesto that expressed the scale and scope of New Deal liberalism. The "dreamers with shovels" could use the power of the federal government to spread economic development and democracy across the United States and around the globe. In so doing, Americans could provoke the rest of the world to make a "second discovery" of America, to see the United States as a nation of technologically advanced builders. Lilienthal urged people to "cut through the fog of uncertainty" and grasp the reality in front of them – namely, that institutions created by the New Deal could use the power of government to build "real things" and help "real people."

My purpose is to show, by authentic experience in one American region, that to get such new jobs and factories and fertile farms our choice need not be between extremes of "right" and "left," between overcentralized Big-government and a do-nothing policy, between "private enterprise" and "socialism," between an arrogant red-tape-ridden bureaucracy and domination by a few private monopolies. I have tried in these pages to express my confidence that in tested principles of democracy we have ready at hand a philosophy and a set of working tools that, adapted to this machine age, can guide and sustain us in increasing opportunity for individual freedom and well-being.[72]

In forging this brand of liberalism, New Dealers created a political philosophy that transformed the American economy, landscape, and political system for nearly fifty years.

THE SPIRIT OF THE NEW DEAL

In the years following World War II, the Federal Works Agency was turned into the General Services Administration, the agency that today supervises federal office space. A bureaucracy that once epitomized the ability of the New Deal to put people to work while improving the nation's infrastructure became the agency that, in late 2000, handled such tasks as handing out the keys for the presidential transition offices to Dick Cheney.[73] While

---

[72] David E. Lilienthal, *TVA: Democracy on the March* (New York: Harper & Brothers, 1953), xxi. For the "second discovery" of America, see Hughes, *American Genesis.*

[73] *Washington Post,* December 15, 2000, p. A39.

the consolidation of government agencies marked a formal end of the
New Deal's public works agencies, the these programs heavily influenced
and helped to foster the public works spending that proceeded under the
categories of national defense and federal highways.

Few were as aware of the many changes that New Deal public works
underwent during these years than was FWA head Major General Philip
B. Fleming. Heir to the state capacities initially built by Harold Ickes
and Harry Hopkins and then consolidated under John Carmody, Fleming
paused near the end of his tenure to reflect on the connection between New
Deal liberalism and the federal government's public works programs. In
response to a letter from Richard Wilson of *Look* magazine, Fleming took
stock of the legacy of the New Deal:

> Your recent letter interests me very much and I am glad to give you my thoughts
> on the questions you raise. I do feel, however, my position will be much clearer if
> it is set in a more specific frame of reference than the terms "liberals" and "New
> Deal" imply. These labels carry such different connotations for different people
> and groups that I prefer more direct language. To me as a Government official the
> programs and policies which I have been associated with had a common purpose –
> to make this country a better place to live and work in. As I saw it, that was the
> spirit which animated the "New Deal."[74]

That established, Fleming reviewed his record as a New Dealer. Working as an assistant to Harold Ickes's Public Works Administration from
1933 to 1935, Fleming wrote, gave him "a two year close-up of the com-
pelling need and the difficulties of putting men to work on useful public
projects. It took about eighteen months to employ 100,000 men because
we lacked adequate plans, drawn up in advance." Fleming's subsequent
service on the huge Passamaquoddy dam project in Maine, and his work
directing engineering improvements in the upper Mississippi valley, "convinced [him] more and more of the widespread and continuing need for
planned public works."[75]

Out of all of these projects, though, what was the most important contribution of federally supervised public works programs? Fleming ended
his reflection on New Deal liberalism and public works with the obser-
vation that it was "in the vital matter of highway construction," since
with this program "we are now launched upon a huge program that for

---

74 Philip B. Fleming to Richard L. Wilson, February 26, 1948, "L (General)" folder, box
  8, entry 5, "Correspondence of Administrators. Correspondence of General Philip B.
  Fleming, 1942–1949," RG 162, NA.
75 Ibid.

the first time links the plans and resources of Federal, state, county, and municipal governments." In so doing, Fleming concluded, "Some may not call this the 'spirit of the New Deal,' but whatever name you give it, the spirit is very much alive."[76] Indeed, Fleming was acutely aware that, in developing the more backward regions of the United States, linking the nation through land and air in an integrated market, and providing a basis for thinking about the postwar world, New Deal public works and the highway programs and defense contracts that succeeded them forged an expression of New Deal liberalism in mortar, concrete, and steel.

[76] Ibid.

9

Epilogue

Public Works and the Building of New Deal Liberalism

Above all, the New Dealers were builders. From the Public Works Administration, to the Works Progress Administration, to the Federal Works Agency, New Dealers like Harold Ickes, Harry Hopkins, John Carmody, and Philip Fleming deployed the state capacities of the public works programs across the nation, building in almost every county in the United States. For too long, though, these works programs have been judged unsuccessful because of their inability to solve the most vexing problem of the Great Depression, mass unemployment. Viewing them as the extraordinarily successful economic development measures that they were, however, helps us understand just how dramatically the New Deal transformed the American economy, political system, and physical landscape. As programs like the PWA and WPA demonstrated, government-sponsored economic development was deeply political. From appointing staff to selecting projects, from Washington, D.C., to project work sites across the country, the New Deal public works programs wrought in concrete and steel a tangible representation of a political philosophy, New Deal liberalism. Harry Hopkins encapsulated the power of this approach when he defined the New Deal as a political project that could "tax and tax, spend and spend, and elect and elect." Opponents of the New Deal recognized the genius of Hopkins's statement, spearheading the drive to pass the Hatch Act in 1939. This, in effect, rolled back a striking feature of the New Deal order: the massive expansion of the federal payroll outside of the civil service structure.

This backlash demonstrated that the New Deal's vision of a development-oriented state was more vulnerable on political than on economic grounds. Viewed as producers of infrastructure, it is clear that the public works programs built an astonishing variety of projects: roads, dams, highways, bridges, airports, sewage systems, housing, and military bases, to name but several. With the creation of the Federal Works Agency in 1939, New Dealers were close to carving out a permanent place for their emergency works programs within the American state. They seized World War II as an opportunity to promote government-funded construction for preparedness efforts. In retooling for wartime, these reformers concentrated on projects such as access roads for military bases, temporary housing for war workers, and job-training programs for defense-related industries. This change was most evident in the activities of the WPA, as it shifted more of its projects to private contracting, gradually abandoning the goal of providing direct employment in its public works projects. Most notably, WPA personnel contributed to the war effort by playing a crucial role in the internment of Japanese Americans.

All these achievements raise a central question: How do we evaluate New Deal liberalism when we place the activities of its public works programs at the center?

Viewing these programs from the New Dealers' perspective – as the New Deal's central enterprise – we are reminded of the extremes represented by the New Deal's accomplishments and shortcomings. As historians like Arthur Schlesinger, Jr., have long stressed, the New Deal was truly revolutionary. In terms of public works, this revolution was awesome in both scale and scope. The PWA sponsored a tremendous amount of the New Deal's infrastructure, but the WPA also put its resources behind this cause, devoting 75 percent of its funds and projects to construction. These programs secured the foundations for forging a national market after 1945, spurred dramatic advances in economic productivity, built networks of roads and airports, drew up blueprints for national highways, improved military bases, foreshadowed the rise of the Sunbelt, and gave New Dealers a policy tool that could be used to shape overseas development, from the onset of the Cold War and continuing through the Vietnam War. Facing the problems of the Great Depression, the New Deal and its public works projects saved capitalism.[1]

---

[1] Bruce J. Schulman, *From Cotton Belt to Sunbelt: Federal Policy, Economic Development, and the Transformation of the South, 1938–1980* (Durham: Duke University Press, 1994); Randall M. Miller and George E. Pozzetta, eds., *Shades of the Sunbelt: Essays on Ethnicity, Race, and the Urban South* (Boca Raton: Florida Atlantic University Press, 1989); Ann Markusen et al., *The Rise of the Gunbelt: The Military Remapping of Industrial America* (New York: Oxford University Press, 1991); Jordan A. Schwarz, *The New Dealers: Power Politics in the Age of Roosevelt* (New York: Alfred A. Knopf, 1993);

Bound up with these triumphs, however, were many limitations. Most notable, of course, was the public works programs' failure to end mass unemployment. The New Deal managed, for the most part, simply to employ white men – hardly surprising, given their disproportionate presence in the building trades and construction industry, generally. Yet the New Deal had a remarkable chance to address the crisis of unemployment among African Americans and women. While well-intentioned employment quotas and specialized projects (sewing projects for women, for example) demonstrated a concern for social justice that was comparatively absent immediately before and after the period from 1933 to 1945, the question remains of whether New Dealers fully grasped this opportunity to remake the nation's labor markets.[2] Ultimately, the public works programs reflected the boundaries of New Deal liberalism and the limitations inherent in the New Deal electoral coalition. Public works programs, like New Deal liberalism generally, dealt better with issues of economics and class than with those of race. On the ground, for every instance of a "culture of unity" that brought Americans together to support the New Deal at the ballot box, there was strong evidence that the New Deal coalition was deeply fragmented at its very inception. One need look no further than the vicious race riots in Detroit in 1943, when white members of the United Auto Workers attacked African Americans, at the racial strife that persisted in postwar Chicago public housing, or at the struggles of African Americans in Oakland, California, to gain a sense of how poorly racial concerns were integrated into New Deal liberalism.[3]

John M. Jordan, *Machine-Age Ideology: Social Engineering and American Liberalism, 1911–1939* (Chapel Hill: University of North Carolina Press, 1994); Alexander J. Field, "The Most Technologically Progressive Decade of the Century," *The American Economic Review* 93 (September 2003): 1399–1413; Field, "Uncontrolled Land Development and the Duration of the Depression in the United States," *Journal of Economic History* 52 (December 1992): 785–805; and David C. Mowery and Nathan Rosenberg, "Twentieth Century Technological Change," in Stanley Engerman and Robert Gallman, eds., *The Cambridge Economic History of the United States* (Cambridge: Cambridge University Press, 2000), 3:803–926.

[2] Suzanne Mettler, *Dividing Citizens: Gender and Federalism in New Deal Public Policy* (Ithaca: Cornell University Press, 1998); Nancy E. Rose, *Workfare or Fair Work: Women, Welfare, and Government Work Programs* (New Brunswick: Rutgers University Press, 1995); Jill Quadagno, "From Old-Age Assistance to Supplemental Security Income: The Political Economy of Relief in the South, 1935–1972," in Margaret Weir, Ann Shola Orloff, and Theda Skocpol, eds., *The Politics of Social Policy in the United States* (Princeton: Princeton University Press, 1988), 235–63.

[3] Gary Gerstle, "The Protean Character of American Liberalism," *American Historical Review* 99 (October 1994): 1043–73; Lizabeth Cohen, *Making a New Deal: Industrial Workers in Chicago, 1919–1939* (Cambridge: Cambridge University Press, 1991); Thomas

When the focus is shifted from unemployment and race to consider the environment, the New Deal's shortcomings are likewise apparent. While architectural historians have generally praised the New Deal for creating a more democratic landscape, environmental historians have strongly disagreed. The New Deal spent far too much money on roads and not enough on developing alternative mass-transportation technologies, these historians have argued. They charge that the New Deal's large hydroelectric projects promoted an imperialist view of resources, leaving nature to be exploited by a coercive, undemocratic power elite composed of technically oriented engineers and narrow-minded bureaucrats. Developments like the TVA displaced thousands of people, while the cheap electric power generated by its dams led to increased pollution. The great dams built in the American West failed to create more family farms. The only achievement of the New Deal, in this view, is its role in creating an "asphalt nation." To be sure, the environmental consequences of the New Deal's public works projects were real, if difficult to measure accurately. But to blame New Dealers like Philip Fleming and Harold Ickes for not being environmentalists is to fail to recognize the full historical significance and impact of the New Deal's public works projects.[4]

In setting out to preserve capitalism, New Dealers turned to what they knew. They experimented with various policy measures, strengthened the national state's power to boost the standing of labor and consumers vis-à-vis business, and regulated the nation's labor and financial markets

---

Sugrue, *The Origins of the Urban Crisis: Race and Inequality in Postwar Detroit* (Princeton: Princeton University Press, 1996); Arnold Hirsch, *Making the Second Ghetto: Race and Housing in Chicago, 1940–1960* (Cambridge: Cambridge University Press, 1983); and Robert O. Self, *American Babylon: Race and the Struggle for Postwar Oakland* (Princeton: Princeton University Press, 2003).

[4] For architectural historians, see Phoebe Cutler, *The Public Landscape of the New Deal* (New Haven: Yale University Press, 1985); Diane Ghirardo, *Building New Communities: New Deal America and Fascist Italy* (Princeton: Princeton University Press, 1989); and Lois A. Craig, *The Federal Presence: Architecture, Politics, and Symbols in United States Government Building* (Cambridge: MIT Press, 1978). For environmental historians, see Ted Steinberg, *Down to Earth: Nature's Role in American History* (New York: Oxford University Press, 2002), 212–13; 242; 264–68; Donald J. Pisani, *Water and American Government: The Reclamation Bureau, National Water Policy, and the West, 1902–1935* (Berkeley: University of California Press, 2002); Donald Worster, *Rivers of Empire: Water, Aridity, and the Growth of the American West* (New York: Pantheon Books, 1985); and the classic Samuel P. Hays, *Conservation and the Gospel of Efficiency: The Progressive Conservation Movement, 1890–1920* (Cambridge: Harvard University Press, 1959). For a recent argument that the New Deal advanced the cause of conservation, see Neil M. Maher, "A New Deal Body Politic: Landscape, Labor, and the Civilian Conservation Corps," *Environmental History* 7 (July 2002): 435–61.

to address the greatest economic crisis of the twentieth century. Short-sightedness on their part should be viewed within this broader context: Despite its deficiencies, the New Deal kept the United States from embracing undemocratic political philosophies, such as fascism or communism. Through public works projects, the federal government presented a physical justification of its new presence in the nation's economy. New Dealers compellingly demonstrated that public investment and state-sponsored economic development were essential to a modern society, not only in order to survive the Great Depression but especially in order to lay the structural foundations for a period of postwar economic growth and sustained productivity rarely equaled in world history. Labeling the trajectory of New Deal liberalism as a narrative of declension leading to the "end of reform," as a journey away from the 1933 statist intervention of the NRA's industrial codes to the manipulation of fiscal policy in 1937 and 1938, misses the central significance of the New Deal's commitment to public works throughout these years and afterward. The interpretation that I have presented in the pages of this book, using the lens of political economy, helps us instead to comprehend more fully the New Deal's long-lasting achievements in using public investment to spur economic development during and after the 1930s. The mixed economy constructed by the New Deal eventually helped to foster tremendous economic growth (for example, between 1940 and 1973 American gross domestic product (GDP) grew, in real terms, at an average annual per-capita rate of 3 percent per year).[5]

While the Federal Works Agency was absorbed into the General Services Administration in 1949, the heavier construction that was a hallmark of the New Deal quietly became a central focus of the federal government. Federal funds paid for the infrastructure that made up the national highway system, military bases, and airports. Whereas the New Deal's legacy for economic development has thus remained an important part of the American state since 1956, the social welfare component of its works programs has not. Subsequent welfare measures, such as those undertaken during Lyndon Johnson's Great Society, bypassed the precedent of the WPA. The Great Society had no jobs program

[5] Thomas K. McCraw, "The New Deal and the Mixed Economy," in Harvard Sitkoff, ed., *Fifty Years Later: The New Deal Evaluated* (New York: Alfred A. Knopf, 1985), 37–67; Alan Brinkley, *The End of Reform: New Deal Liberalism in Depression and War* (New York: Alfred A. Knopf, 1995); and see also Brinkley, "The Transformation of New Deal Liberalism: A Response to Michael Brown, Kenneth Finegold, and David Plotke," *Studies in American Political Development* 10 (Fall 1996): 421–25.

that remotely approached the scale of those inaugurated by the New Deal.[6]

When considering the spectrum of New Deal public works activities from 1933 through 1956, the WPA appears less as the centerpiece of federal construction efforts and more as an employment-oriented variation on the theme of infrastructural development. This theme was articulated first by the approach to public works tried under the Hoover administration and the Reconstruction Finance Corporation. It was amplified and expanded by the PWA; and it was recapitulated vigorously during World War II and afterward. Viewing its public works in this fashion alerts us to further limitations of the New Deal. By and large, the New Deal was a political project not centrally concerned with advancing racial equality, redistribution of wealth, or social democratic ideals. It was focused instead on the goals of administering and managing resources efficiently while preserving the social order. These goals were pursued with tremendous energy, but their relatively conservative character reveals the oft-termed "weakness" of the welfare state as it developed in the United States. Put another way, New Deal public works programs led not to the embrace of a "social" Keynesianism, but rather to the adoption of a "commercial" Keynesianism. That this choice supported a comparatively weak welfare state should not surprise: After all, the New Deal's public works programs were more successful in building roads and dams than in employing people. Indeed, many of the staffers of the PWA and the WPA – civil-engineering experts and members of the Army Corps of Engineers, for example – were specialists in planning and constructing public works projects. They were not experts in solving a crisis in unemployment; they were professional builders. The business of the New Deal's public works construction was the focus of this political era, shaping policy debates for many subsequent years.[7]

---

[6] On the "apolitical" character of technological innovation, generally, see Thomas P. Hughes, *American Genesis: A Century of Invention and Technological Enthusiasm, 1870–1970* (New York: Viking, 1989).

[7] Margaret Weir and Theda Skocpol, "State Structures and the Possibilities for 'Keynesian' Responses to the Great Depression in Sweden, Britain, and the United States," in Peter R. Evans, Dietrich Rueschemeyer, and Theda Skocpol, eds., *Bringing the State Back In* (Cambridge: Cambridge University Press, 1985), 107–63. See also Herbert Stein, *The Fiscal Revolution in America* (Chicago: University of Chicago Press, 1969); Sven Steinmo, *Taxation and Democracy: Swedish, British, and American Approaches to Financing the Modern State* (New Haven: Yale University Press, 1993); and Theodore Rosenof, *Economics in the Long Run: New Deal Theorists and Their Legacies, 1933–1993* (Chapel Hill: University of North Carolina Press, 1997).

Debates over federal public works programs in the years since 1956 have diverged into separate considerations of their capacity to provide employment and their ability to develop infrastructure. For example, an important intervention in this debate during the early 1980s, from the infrastructure side, barely acknowledged the WPA in proposing a new agenda for public works. "The WPA model may be very difficult to undertake today because public construction requires a labor force versed in skills that few of the unemployed have acquired," asserted a contributor to *Rebuilding America's Infrastructure*.[8] The volume's editor agreed:

As is so often true of simple solutions to complex problems, a new WPA would not work. It would neither build what needs building nor employ those who most need employment. Rehabilitating public works is not so simple as passing out overalls and paint to people in line for unemployment benefits and pointing them toward a crumbling bridge. For one thing, the federal government keeps no records on the condition of public facilities; thus, it is in a poor position to know where a new WPA army should march.[9]

Even such a harsh and obviously uninformed dismissal of the WPA's history as an employment program, however, had to acknowledge its achievements in building public works. Although "the WPA exerted a trivial impact on the nation's unemployment rate and did nothing to stimulate an overall recovery," this critic thundered, nevertheless "it did, of course, build thousands of public facilities... many of which survive in use today."[10]

Supporters of federal public works projects observed that these programs contributed to overall economic growth, accounting for 20 percent of the increase in national income between 1950 and 1970 by one measure. They remain essential to American prosperity, they argued.

Without a major effort to rebuild America's public works, we jeopardize our ability to sustain an economic recovery, we weaken government's capacity to deliver essential public services, we seriously threaten the quality of the environment, and we pose a major threat to public health and safety. Thus, a crucial first step in rebuilding America's public works is forging a public consensus that infrastructure is as essential to economic recovery as private investments in plant and equipment.[11]

[8] Michael Barker, ed., *Rebuilding America's Infrastructure: An Agenda for the 1980s* (Durham: Duke University Press, 1984), 279.
[9] Ibid., xxv.
[10] Ibid., xxxiii, n. 8.
[11] Ibid., xvii.

Although *Rebuilding America's Infrastructure* garnered substantial public attention upon its publication, its proposals for public works were not well received during the presidencies of Ronald Reagan and George Bush. From the Democratic Party, however, a number of politicians have made serious – albeit unrealized – public works proposals. Bill Clinton's pledge to "invest in infrastructure," while much debated during his 1992 presidential campaign, was not fully redeemed once he took office. Senators, including Illinois's Paul Simon during the 1980s and Oklahoma's David Boren during the early 1990s, have also proposed a revival of federally sponsored public works programs. Outside the political arena, one of the more thoughtful advocates of public works has been social scientist William Julius Wilson. He has called for a revival of a neo–WPA in order to address the problem of systemic urban poverty. In making this proposal, however, Wilson treats the WPA as a welfare measure that happens to produce some useful artifacts. While the WPA's public construction functions continue to be neglected, the PWA's capacities have not gathered much attention either. Although larger "mega-projects," following in the tradition of the PWA, continue to play an important role in the politics of urban development, few have attempted to ground the history of these great undertakings in the legacy of the New Deal.[12]

If the promise of New Deal public works is to be revived, it deserves to be revived in a more intellectually coherent fashion, in a form that New Dealers themselves might recognize. While these reformers were highly imperfect, they did not simply provide employment to help raise morale; they invested in a wide range of public works, building socially necessary projects that raised the standard of living for many Americans. While many have not recognized the public works programs for these accomplishments, the New Dealers were well aware of what they had done. "Today it is builders and technicians that we turn to," declared David Lilienthal, whose Tennessee Valley Authority was begun with a $50 million appropriation from Harold Ickes's PWA.

Men armed not with the ax, rifle, and bowie knife, but with the Diesel engine, the bulldozer, the giant electric shovel, the retort – and most of all, with an emerging

[12] Paul Simon, *Let's Put America Back to Work* (Chicago: Bonus Books, 1987); for more on Boren's proposal see Rose, *Workfare or Fair Work*, 171–72; William Julius Wilson, *When Work Disappears: The World of the New Urban Poor* (New York: Alfred A. Knopf, 1996); and Alan Altshuler and David Luberoff, *Mega-Projects: The Changing Politics of Urban Public Investment* (Washington, D.C.: The Brookings Institution Press, 2003). For an important recent attempt to invoke the New Deal as useful precedent for today, see Mike Wallace, *A New Deal for New York* (New York: Bell & Weiland Publishers, 2002).

kind of skill, a modern knack of organization and execution. When these men have imagination and faith, they can move mountains; out of their skills they can create new jobs, relieve human drudgery, give new life and fruitfulness to worn-out lands, put yokes upon the streams, and transmute the minerals of the earth and the plants of the field into machines of wizardry to spin out the stuff of a way of life new to this world.[13]

The administrative talents, imagination, wit, and faith of the New Dealers led a public works revolution in the United States. Their projects built New Deal liberalism, a political order that spanned most of the twentieth century and continues to illuminate the present.

[13] David E. Lilienthal, *TVA: Democracy on the March* (New York: Harper & Brothers, 1953; 3.

Sources

Manuscript Collections

Franklin D. Roosevelt Library, Hyde Park, New York

Carmody, John M. Papers.
Cuneo, Ernest. Papers.
Hopkins, Harry L. Papers.
Hurja, Emil. Papers.
Lubin, Isador. Papers.
Means, Gardiner. Papers.
Roosevelt, Franklin Delano. Official File. Papers.
Roosevelt, Franklin Delano. President's Personal File. Papers.
Roosevelt, Franklin Delano. President's Secretary's File. Papers.
Tugwell, Rexford G. Papers.

Manuscript Division, Library of Congress, Washington, D.C.

Clapper, Raymond. Papers.
Cohen, Benjamin V. Papers.
Corcoran, Thomas G. Papers.
Cutting, Bronson. Papers.
Farley, James A. Papers.
Frankfurter, Felix. Papers.
Ickes, Harold L. Papers.
Jones, Jesse. Papers.
Pittman, Key. Papers.
Richberg, Donald R. Papers.
Schwellenbach, Lewis B. Papers.

Archival Records

National Archives, Washington, D.C.

RECORD GROUP 69: WORKS PROGRESS ADMINISTRATION

Central Files: General 1935–1944. 045 Defense Training Program, 1940–43.
Central Files: General 1935–1944. 100 Administration.
Central Files: General 1935–1944. 221 Roads.
Central Files: General 1935–1944. 310 General Correspondence.
Central Files: State 1935–1944. Illinois 610 Special Litigation.
Central Files: State 1935–1944. Kentucky 610 Special Litigation.
Central Files: State 1935–1944. Massachusetts 610 Special Litigation.
Central Files: State 1935–1944. New York City 610 Special Litigation.
Central Files: State 1935–1944. Pennsylvania 610 Special Litigation.
Central Files: State 1935–1944. Texas 610 Special Litigation.
Central Files: State 1935–1944. Washington 610 Special Litigation.
Entry PC-37. Entry 21. Records of the Office of the WPA Commissioner (Formerly
     Administrator), 1935–1943.
Entry PC-37. Entry 23. Work Projects Administration Investigative Cases. Records
     of the Division of Investigation, 1934–1943. Work Projects Administration.
     California.
Entry PC-37. Entry 23. Work Projects Administration Investigative Cases. Records
     of the Division of Investigation, 1934–1943. Work Projects Administration.
     Illinois.
Entry PC-37. Entry 23. Work Projects Administration Investigative Cases. Records
     of the Division of Investigation, 1934–1943. Work Projects Administration.
     Kentucky.
Entry PC-37. Entry 23. Work Projects Administration Investigative Cases. Records
     of the Division of Investigation, 1934–1943. Work Projects Administration.
     Missouri.
Entry PC-37. Entry 23. Work Projects Administration Investigative Cases. Records
     of the Division of Investigation, 1934–1943. Work Projects Administration.
     Montana.
Entry PC-37. Entry 23. Work Projects Administration Investigative Cases. Records
     of the Division of Investigation, 1934–1943. Work Projects Administration.
     Pennsylvania.
Entry PC-37. Entry 23. Work Projects Administration Investigative Cases. Records
     of the Division of Investigation, 1934–1943. Work Projects Administration.
     Washington.
Entry PC-37. Entry 25. Records of the Division of Training and Reemployment,
     1940–1943.
Entry 687. Division of Information. General Correspondence of the Field Rela-
     tions Section, 1937–1942.
Entry 706. Division of Information. Correspondence, Scripts, and Other Records
     Relating to Special Transcribed Programs, 1940–1941.
Entry 715. Division of Information, Radio Section. Proposed Scripts of Radio
     Interviews Between the State WPA Administrator and the State Director of
     the National Emergency Council, 1938–1939.

Entry 725. Division of Information. Office File of Dutton Ferguson, 1938–1939. Correspondence and Reports.

Entry 730. Division of Information. Statements and Related Papers Relating to Boondoggling Charges and Answers ("Attacks on WPA"), 1935–1936. Alabama–Wisconsin.

Entry 732. Division of Information. Records Relating to Boondoggling Charges, ("Attacks on WPA"), 1936–1939.

Entry 736. Division of Information. Photographs and Biographical Information about WPA Officials, 1933–1942.

Entry 737. Division of Information. Administrative Speeches, 1933–1942.

Entry 740. Division of Information. Press Releases, 1936–1942, with gaps.

Entry 746. Division of Information. Publications of the Federal Works Agency and Subordinate Agencies, 1936–1942.

Entry 768. Records of the Works Projects Administration. Division of Information. Records Concerning National Defense Projects, 1939–1942.

RECORD GROUP 135: PUBLIC WORKS ADMINISTRATION

Entry 1. Minutes of Meetings of the Special Board for Public Works, 1933–1935.

Entry 6. Materials Prepared for Congressional Hearings on PWA Appropriations, 1936–1941.

Entry 22. Decisions Rendered by the Board of Labor Review, 1934–36.

Entry 23. Minutes and Reports of Conferences of the PWA, 1934–1941.

Entry 24. Press Releases, 1933–1939.

Entry 26. Public Speeches and Statements of Harold L. Ickes, 1934–1939.

Entry 28. Organization Charts, 1933–1934.

Entry 30. Records of the Project Control Division, Subject Files, 1933–1940.

Entry 32. Minutes of Meetings of the Advisory Committee on Allotments, 1935.

Entry 33. File of Fred E. Schnepfe Relating to the 6-Year Planning Program of the National Resources Committee, 1936–1940.

Entry 34. Records of the Projects Control Division. File of Lloyd N. Beeker, Assistant Director of the Projects Control Division, 1936–1941.

Entry 49. Records of the Projects Control Division, Research Materials, 1935–1940.

Entry 50. Publications of the Division, 1936–1939. Projects Control Division.

Entry 51. Miscellaneous Publications, 1936–1941. Projects Control Division.

Entry 61. Statistical Materials Relating to PWA Projects, 1934–1942.

Entry 70. Records of the Engineering Division. Records Relating to Equipment to be Used on Certain PWA Projects, 1935–1938. #1,000–4,999.

Entry 85. Case Files Relating to Investigations of Personnel, 1933–1941.

Entry 91. Correspondence Relating to Criminal Indictments, 1935–1942.

Entry 93. Records Relating to the Investigation of the Engineering Division, 1934.

Entry 95. Records of Projects. Records of the Division of Investigation. Manual of Instructions, 1936.

Entry 103. Miscellaneous Issuances, 1933–1938.

Entry 104. Orders Issued by the Accounting Division, 1935–1939. Records of the
    Accounting Division.
Unidentified Entry 13. Information Service Letters, 1938–1941. Administrative
    Division.
Unidentified Entry 21. Published Reports on Non-Federal Projects, 1934–1941.
    Projects Control Division.
Unidentified Entry 25. Records Relating to Investigation of New York Post Office
    Annex and Courthouse. Division of Investigation.

RECORD GROUP 162: FEDERAL WORKS AGENCY

Entry 4. Correspondence of Administrators. Correspondence of Administrators
    with the House, 1939–1942.
Entry 5. Correspondence of Administrators. Correspondence of General Philip B.
    Fleming, 1942–1949.
Entry 6. Correspondence of Administrators. Correspondence of Administrator
    with the White House, 1942–1949.
Entry 7. Administrative Records. Central Files, 1941–1949.
Entry 21. Administrative Records. Records of the War Public Works Program,
    1941–1949.
Entry 23. Administrative Records. Records Concerning Plans for Postwar Public
    Works, 1941–1944.
Entry 30. Administrative Records. Records Relating to the Organization of the
    General Services Administration, 1949–1950.
Entry 32. Information Records. Speeches of FWA Administrators, 1939–1949.
Entry 38. Information Records. Records Relating to Child Care in World War II,
    1943–1946.

National Archives, College Park, Maryland

RECORD GROUP 44: OFFICE OF GOVERNMENT REPORTS

Entry 10. Minutes of Meetings and Related Records of the Special Industrial
    Recovery Board, 1932–1935.

RECORD GROUP 48: DEPARTMENT OF INTERIOR

Entry 749B. Office of the Secretary. Central Classified Files, 1937–1953.
Entry 766. Records of Interior Department Officials. Records of Secretary Harold
    L. Ickes. General Subject File, 1933–1942.

RECORD GROUP 174: DEPARTMENT OF LABOR

Entry 20. Office of the Secretary. Secretary Frances Perkins. General Subject File,
    1933–1941.

University of California, Berkeley, Bancroft Library

BANC MSS 67/14 C. JAPANESE AMERICAN EVACUATION AND RESETTLEMENT RECORDS

Columbia University Oral History Project

The Reminiscences of Arthur Krock.
The Reminiscences of Nathan Straus.
The Reminiscences of John Michael Carmody.

Published Government Documents

America Builds: The Record of PWA. Washington, D.C.: U.S. Government Print-
   ing Office, 1939.
*The Budget of the United States Government for the Fiscal Year Ending June 30,
   1940*. Washington, D.C.: U.S. Government Printing Office, 1939.
*The Budget of the United States Government for the Fiscal Year Ending June 30,
   1941*. Washington, D.C.: U.S. Government Printing Office, 1940.
Federal Emergency Administration of Public Works. *Circular No. 1. The Purposes,
   Policies, Functioning and Organization of the Emergency Administration.
   The Rules Prescribed by the President*. Washington, D.C.: U.S. Government
   Printing Office, 1933.
Federal Works Agency. *Annual Report*. Washington, D.C.: U.S. Government Print-
   ing Office, 1940–1949.
   *Millions for Defense: Emergency Expenditures for National Defense, 1933–
   1940*. Washington, D.C.: U.S. Government Printing Office, 1940.
   Post-War Public Works. Washington, D.C.: U.S. Government Printing Office,
   1944.
   In collaboration with the Bureau of the Census. *Report of Proposed Post-War
   Public Works: Volume and Status of the Plan Preparation of Post-War Public
   Works Proposed by State and Local Governments*. Washington, D.C.: U.S.
   Government Printing Office, 1944.
   Final Report on the WPA Program, 1935–1943. Washington, D.C.: U.S. Gov-
   ernment Printing Office, 1947.
Galbraith, J. K., assisted by G. G. Johnson, Jr. *The Economic Effects of the Federal
   Public Works Expenditures, 1933–1938*. Washington, D.C.: U.S. Government
   Printing Office, 1940.
Ickes, Harold L. *Not Guilty: An Official Inquiry Into the Charges Made by Glavis
   and Pinchot Against Richard A. Ballinger, Secretary of the Interior, 1909–
   1911*. Washington, D.C.: U.S. Government Printing Office, 1940.
*Papers of the U.S. Commission on Wartime Relocation and Internment of Civil-
   ians. Part I. Numerical File Archive*. Frederick, Maryland: University Publi-
   cations of America, Inc., 1983.
Rosenman, Samuel I., ed. *The Public Papers and Addresses of Franklin D. Roosevelt*. 13 vols. New York: Russell & Russell, 1938–1950.
Short, C. W., and R. Stanley-Brown. *Public Buildings: A Survey of Architecture of
   Projects Constructed by Federal and Other Governmental Bodies Between*

the Years *1933 and 1939 with the Assistance of the Public Works Administration.* Washington, D.C.: U.S. Government Printing Office, 1939.

The Story of PWA in Pictures. Washington, D.C.: U.S. Government Printing
Office, 1936.

U.S. Army. *Final Report: Japanese Evacuation from the West Coast 1942.* Washington, D.C.: U.S. Government Printing Office, 1943.

U.S. *Community Improvement Appraisal: A Report on the Work Program of
the Works Progress Administration.* Washington, D.C.: National Appraisal
Committee, 1939.

U.S. Congress. Senate. *Hearings before the Committee on Public Lands and Surveys on the Nomination of Ebert K. Burlew to be First Assistant Secretary of
the Interior.* Part I. 75th Cong., 3d sess., 1938.

*Report of the Special Committee to Investigate Senatorial Campaign Expen-
ditures and Use of Government Funds in 1938.* Senate Report No. 1, Part 2.
76th Cong., 1st sess., 1939.

Committee on Commerce. *Hearings on the Nomination of Harry L. Hopkins
to be Secretary of Commerce.* 76th Cong., 1st sess., 1939.

Subcommittee of the Committee on Banking and Currency. *Full Employment
Act of 1945.* 79th Cong., 1st sess., 1945.

Subcommittee of the Committee on Public Works. *State Planning for Public
Works.* 80th Cong., 1st sess., 1947.

Subcommittee of the Committee on Public Works. *Coordinating Emergency
Activities of Federal Agencies in Disaster Areas.* 80th Cong., 2d sess., 1948.

Subcommittee of the Committee on Public Works. *Federal Aid for Highways.*
80th Cong., 2d sess., 1948.

Subcommittee of the Committee on Public Works. *Alaska Public Works.* 81st
Cong., 1st sess., 1949.

Wiener, Minnie, comp. *Principal Acts and Executive Orders Pertaining to Public
Works Administration.* Washington, D.C.: U.S. Government Printing Office,
1938.

Index

Acheson, Dean, 243, 249
Ackerman, Bruce, 190
Addams, Jane, 24
Advisory Commission for National Defense, 210
Advisory Commission to the Council of National Defense, 178, 215
Advisory Committee on Allotments (ACA), 102–4, 184
Afghanistan, 249
African Americans, 15, 38, 89, 197, 260
Age of Reform, The, 12
Agricultural Adjustment Act, 29, 230
Agricultural Adjustment Agency (AAA), 118
Aiken, George, 244
Airport Transport Association of America, 209
airports, 2, 11, 22, 28, 87, 113–14, 121, 129, 142, 192, 202, 204–10, 216, 225, 231–3, 242, 248–9, 259, 262
Alabama Power Company, 68
Alice in Wonderland, 65
Allen, Robert, 170, 200
Alsop, Joseph, 176, 199
American Association for Labor Legislation (AALL), 24–7
American Bankers' Association, 104

American Civil Liberties Union, 187
American Farm Bureau Federation, 104
American Federation of Labor (AFL), 29–30, 37–9, 210, 238, 241; building and construction trades department, 213; machinist division, 211
American Liberty League, 142, 144, 146
American Public Works Association, 203, 235
American Road Builders Association, 29, 206, 241–2
American Society of Civil Engineers, 235, 238
Amory, Henry, 226
Anderson, Nels, 203
Andrews, John B., 24
Army, *see* U.S. Army
Army and Navy Register, 114
Army Corps of Engineers, *see* U.S. Army Corps of Engineers
Arnold, Thurman, 12
Arnstein, Daniel, 151
Associated Equipment Distributors, 241
Associated General Contractors (AGC), 41, 241
Austin, Warren, 203

Back to Work, 8, 54
Badger, Anthony, 188
Baker, Jacob, 102
Baldwin, Roger, 187
Ballinger-Pinchot affair, 56, 83
Baltimore Sun, 176
Barkley, Alben, 161–2, 164–9, 171–5
Barrows, Leland, 229
Baruch, Bernard, 26
Bates, Harry, 238
Battle, Turner, 42, 46–8, 63
Bauer, Catherine, 218
Bay Area Rapid Transit system, 253
Bechtel, 19, 233, 253
Bellamy, Edward, 23
Bendetsen, Karl, 225, 227, 229
Berle, Adolf A., 203
Bernstein, Barton, 11, 13
Berry, George, 104
Betters, Paul V., 79
Biddle, Francis, 228
Biggs, James C., 34, 47
Black, Hugo, 38
Blumenberg, Henry, 39
Board of Labor Review, *see* Public Works Administration, Board of Labor Review
Bonneville Dam, 94, 199, 217
boondoggling, 158–9, 165, 188, 205, 249; and politics, 135–8, 141–3; Works Progress Administration's response to charges, 144–9
Boren, David, 265
Boston Herald, 142
Boulay, L.A., 63
Boulder Dam, 2, 34, 41, 46
Bowers, William, 66–7
bridges, 2, 11, 28, 44, 78, 90, 99, 115, 123, 126, 142, 207, 217, 251, 259
Brinkley, Alan, 193–4
Britain, *see* United Kingdom
Brookings Institution, 252
Broun, Heywood, 175
Brown & Root, 19, 233, 253
Brown, Clarence, 244
Brown, Edmund G., 230
Brown, Robert L., 226–7

Brownlow, Louis, 59, 64, 78
Bryan, William Jennings, 6
building trades, 15, 29–30, 37–9, 49, 91, 107, 211, 260
Bureau of Indian Affairs, 230
Bureau of Public Roads, 38, 207, 251
Bureau of Reclamation, 46
Bureau of the Budget, 202, 235
Burlew, E.K., 66, 74, 77
Burns, Arthur E., 202
Burton, H. Ralph, 171
Bush, George, 265
Business Advisory Council, 104
Business Week, 98–9

California Conservation and Water Power Commission, 56
Carmody, John, 207–8, 215, 219–20, 251, 254, 256, 258; appointed head of FWA, 198–203; and defense public works, 218–19; and Hoover Commission, 245–8; and Public Work Reserve, 234, 236
Casper–Alcova project, 46
Catledge, Turner, 170
Catchings, Waddill, 136
Central Artery project ("Big Dig"), 253
Chandler, Al, 161, 165–7, 169, 171–3, 175
Channel Tunnel project, 253
Chapman, Oscar, 65, 198
Chase, Stuart, 136, 204–5
Chavez, Dennis, 163
Cheney, Dick, 255
Chicago Sanitary District, 80–1
Chicago Tribune, 47
Civil Aeronautics Administration, 113–14, 210
Civil Works Administration (CWA), 52, 56, 79–80, 149, 198–9, 213, 225, 254; as precedent for Works Progress Administration, 101–2
Civilian Conservation Corps (CCC), 104, 106, 120, 164, 210–11, 227–8
Clapper, Raymond, 164, 177–8
Clayton News, 144

Clark, Wesley C., 174
Clinton, Bill, 265
Coast Guard, 202
Coefield, John, 37
Cohen, Benjamin, 50; and Hatch Act, 181–6
Cold War, 5, 248, 250
Colorado Association of Highway Contractors, 50
Columbia River project, 46
Commission on Organization of the Executive Branch of the Government, *see* Hoover Commission
Commons, John R., 24, 198
Communists, 158, 250
community centers, 38
Community Facilities Act, *see* Lanham Act
Congress, 18, 24, 29, 34, 47, 51, 54, 118, 135, 137, 157–8, 163, 171–2, 178, 190, 192, 203, 211–12, 219, 223, 231, 233, 237–40, 243–4, 252; and creation of Works Progress Administration, 102–103; and Hatch Act, 180–188; and patronage, 60–1, 71–3; and public works policy before the New Deal, 26–7
conservation projects, 113, 115
construction industry, 15, 22, 28–30, 37, 39, 238–9, 242, 260
Construction League, 36, 235
Corcoran, Thomas, 77, 161; Hatch Act, 181–4, 186; and Point Four program, 249
corruption, 41, 43–4, 57–8, 138, 147, 155, 157, 172, 184; *see also* graft
Costigan, Edward, 10, 27, 29, 61
cost-plus contracting, 19, 194; *see also* private contractors
Coughlin, Charles, 83
Court-packing plan, 163, 190
Cowhey, William, 157
Coxey, Jacob S., 23
Coyle, David Cushman, 99–100
Cummings, Homer, 33, 44

Cuneo, Ernest, 187
Curley, James M., 79
Currie, Lauchlin, 100, 136, 251
Cutting, Bronson, 29, 112

dams, 28, 53, 87, 99, 143, 217, 232, 254, 259, 261, 263
Daniels, Roger, 224
Davies, Joseph E., 101
Deaton, Fred R., 66
Dearing, Charles L., 252
Delano, Frederic A., 64–5, 207, 236, 251
Democratic National Committee, 77, 138
Democratic Party, 18, 26, 54, 60, 74–5, 77, 79–80, 135, 139–40, 151, 154, 161, 173–4, 185, 199, 230, 265
Dennison, Henry, 204
Dern, George, 33, 45, 48
DeWitt, John L., 225, 228
Dewey, Thomas, 244
Division of Application and Information, 102
division of engineering, *see* Public Works Administration, division of engineering
division of information, *see* Works Progress Administration, division of information
division of investigation, *see* Public Works Administration, division of investigation, *and see* Works Progress Administration, division of investigation
Documentary Expression and Thirties America, 87
Douglas, Lewis, 9, 43–4, 50
Douglas, William O., 118
Driscoll and Company, 82

Early, Steve, 180
economic development, 5, 15, 17, 19, 21–2, 37, 51, 103, 119–21, 137, 162, 233, 241, 249, 253–5, 258, 262

Eccles, Marriner, 100, 136
Eisenhower, Dwight, 233, 252–3
Eisenhower, Milton, 229–30
Elbert, Robert, 104
Ely, Richard T., 24
Emergency Relief and Construction
    Act (ERCA), 27–8
Emergency Relief Appropriation; of
    1935, 102, 112; of 1940, 158
employment, direct, 91, 96–7, 106–7,
    112, 259
employment, indirect, 22, 46, 79, 87,
    96–7, 103, 107, 112
Employment Stabilization Act of 1931,
    236
Engineering News-Record, 50, 235
engineering surveys, 113, 115, 241
Enterprise, 217
Executive Order 7034, 101
Executive Order 9066, 19, 231
Ezekiel, Mordecai, 136–7

Fair Labor Standards Act, 193, 220
Farley, James, 60, 65, 74–5, 77,
    82–3, 138–41, 151, 173–4, 177,
    181, 187
Farnam, Henry, 24
Faulkner, William, 118
Fechner, Robert, 211
Federal-Aid Road Act of 1916, 21
Federal-Aid Highway Act of 1956, 19,
    232, 253
Federal Bureau of Investigation, 138
Federal Communications
    Commission, 198
Federal Deposit Insurance
    Corporation, 29
Federal Emergency Agency for Public
    Works, *see* Public Works
    Administration
Federal Emergency Relief
    Administration (FERA), 29, 97,
    101–2, 138, 150, 153, 199, 212,
    230
Federal Employment Stabilization
    Board, 236
Federal Loan Agency, 199

Federal Music Project, 158
Federal Power Commission, 198
Federal Security Agency, 224
Federal Theater Project, 87, 158
Federal Works Agency (FWA), 5,
    18–19, 191, 197, 202–3, 220–1,
    223, 233, 248, 254–6, 258–9, 262;
    creation of, 198–201; and defense
    public works, 207, 217–19; and
    postwar planning, 234, 236–8,
    240–41, 243; and highway
    planning, 250–2; and Hoover
    Commission, 245–7
Federal Writers Project, 87, 158
Fellows, Perry, 113, 206
Field, George, 239
Fiscal Revolution in America, The,
    193
Fleming, Philip B., 223, 247, 252,
    256–8, 261; appointed head of
    FWA, 220–22; and postwar
    planning, 234, 236–7, 239–43
Flemming, Arthur S., 244
Flynn, Edward J., 219
Flynn, John T., 49–50
Foley, E. H., 46
force account construction, 19, 40,
    69, 96, 103, 111, 194, 206
Forrestal, James, 243
Fort Peck project, 46, 94
Fortas, Abe, 254
Fortune, 247
Foster, William Trufant, 136
France, 135, 195, 212, 253
Frank, Jerome, 118–19
Frankfurter, Felix, 50, 56, 61, 77,
    139
Friedman, Lawrence, 190
Fryer, E. R., 229
Full Employment Act of 1945, 240

Galbraith, John Kenneth, 79, 112;
    definition of direct and indirect
    employment, 96–7
Gans, Helene P., 220
Garner, John Nance, 27, 60, 171
Gary, Elbert, H., 24

Gayer, Arthur D., 79
General Builders Supply Company, 82
General Services Administration
    (GSA), 19, 233, 245–8, 255, 262
*General Theory of Employment,
    Interest, and Money, The*, 136
George, Walter, 175
Germany, 119, 135
Gholston, Jabez, G., 72–3
Gill, Corrington, 102, 208, 235
Gilman, Nils, 250
Glass, Carter, 74
Glavis, Louis, 56–8, 68, 81–3
Glick, Philip, 229
Goldman, Eric, 194
Goldschmidt, Arthur, 254
Goldwater, Barry, 246, 253
Goodman, George, 151, 174
Goodrich, Carter, 252
Gordon, Colin, 14
Gordon, Max, 175
Gorrell, Edgar S., 209
graft, 32–3, 40, 44, 52, 57–8, 62, 71,
    99, 143, 150, 167, 225; *see also*
    corruption
Grand Coulee Dam, 94, 217
Grand River Dam, 94
Gray, Richard J., 37
Great Depression, 4–5, 22–3, 84,
    86–7, 192, 216, 242, 253, 258–9,
    262
Great Society, 254, 262
Green, William, 210
Grodzins, Morton, 229
Guffey, Joseph, 139
Gutman, Herbert, 23

Halliburton, 233
Harding, Warren, 25, 205
Harrington, Francis C., 103, 111, 153;
    appointed head of Works Progress
    Administration, 195–8; and defense
    public works, 208; and worker
    training, 211–12
Harrison, Pat, 170
Hatch, Carl, 163–4, 166, 172, 180,
    188

Hatch Act, 18, 137–8, 150, 163, 168,
    172, 180–9, 258
Hawley, Ellis, 30
Hearst, William Randolph, 27, 57
Henderson, Charles, 24
Henderson, Leon, 191
Herring, Frank W., 203, 235
Hetch Hetchy Dam, 94, 125
highways, 22, 50, 87, 89–90, 95, 104,
    108, 119, 164, 206–7, 225, 232,
    240, 249, 251–2, 256, 259
"Highways for the National Defense,"
    207, 251
Hill, Julien, 104
Hiss, Alger, 61
Hoan, Daniel W., 79
Hofstadter, Richard, 11–12
Holcombe, Oscar, 79
Holli, Melvin, 75
Home Owners Loan Corporation, 141
Hoover Commission, 244–6
Hoover Dam, 28
Hoover, Herbert, 17–19, 22, 40, 50,
    53, 85–6, 97, 100, 103, 212, 232–3,
    235, 243–6, 263; and Hoover
    Commission, 243–6; and public
    works policy before the New Deal,
    25–7
Hopkins, Harry, 6, 105–6, 111, 138–9,
    144, 146, 150, 153, 167–70, 172–4,
    189, 198–9, 212, 230, 254; and
    creation of Works Progress
    Administration, 98, 100–2; Ickes
    and, 9–10, 51–2, 56, 60, 80, 84, 86,
    96, 102–3, 107, 115, 121, 138,
    140–1, 161, 177, 184, 256, 258; and
    Japanese American internment,
    222–4; resigns from Works Progress
    Administration, 194–7; "tax and
    tax, spend and spend, and elect and
    elect" controversy, 6, 162, 175–80,
    258
Howe, Louis, 60, 103
Hunt, Henry T., 59, 61
Hunter, Howard, 102, 153, 204–6,
    209, 212, 220–1, 223
Hurja, Emil, 74–7, 139

Ichihashi, Yamato, 226
Ickes, Harold L., 7–8, 22, 31–8, 40–2,
    44–9, 54, 61–70, 73, 79–86, 96–9,
    118, 182, 191, 193, 199–200,
    216–17, 220, 222, 232, 234, 239,
    249, 261, 265; and criticism of
    Public Works Administration,
    49–51; Hopkins and, 9–10, 51–2,
    56, 60, 80, 84, 86, 96, 102–3, 107,
    115, 121, 138, 140–1, 161, 177, 184,
    256, 258; and patronage, 74–8; and
    politicization of expertise, 42–3;
    and Public Works Administration
    division of investigation, 56–9
Imperial hydroelectric project,
    94
India, 253
Interregional Highway Committee,
    207, 251

Jackson, Gardner, 61
James Stewart & Company, 82
Japanese American internment, 19,
    194, 222–31, 259
Johnson, Hiram, 29, 61, 225
Johnson, Hugh, 9, 83, 179, 200
Johnson, Lyndon B. (LBJ), 15, 19,
    188, 208–9, 233, 262; and
    exporting New Deal economic
    development, 254–5
Johnstone, Alan, 102, 246–7
Joint Committee on Unemployment,
    30
Jones, Jesse, 199
Jones, Wesley L., 25
Jordan, 249

Kaiser, 19, 253
Kaw River project, 46
Keller, Kent, 180
Kellogg, Paul, 150
Kennedy, Joseph P., 139, 244
Kent, Frank, 139, 176
Kentucky Courier Journal, 141–2
Kenyon, William S., 25
Kerr, Florence, 102
Keynes, John Maynard, 136–7

Keynesianism, 3, 19, 100, 163, 263;
    see also public investment
Kitner, Robert, 199
Klein, Julius, 244
Krock, Arthur, 176–7

La Follette, Robert, 10, 26–7, 29, 61,
    164, 199
La Guardia, Fiorello, 27, 62, 104, 219
Labor Advisory Board, *see* Public
    Works Administration, Labor
    Advisory Board
Lail, Andrew B., 70–1
Lakey, George H., 37
Landon, Alf, 135, 137
Lanham Act, 218
Lanham, Fritz, 218, 237
Larson, Jess, 247
Lasser, David, 196
Lawton, Frederick J., 235
Leuchtenburg, William E., 10–12
Lilienthal, David, 15, 255, 265
Lippmann, Walter, 225
Long, Huey, 75, 82–3
Look, 256
Looking Backward, 23
Los Angeles Times, 157–8
Lower Colorado River Authority, 72,
    94
Lubin, Isador, 37, 39, 218, 252

MacDonald, Thomas H., 38, 207, 251
MacIntyre, Marvin, 218
MacMaster, Amy, 143–4, 148
Mallery, Otto T., 25, 79, 85, 235,
    251–2
Manasco, Carter, 244
Manzanar, 223–4, 226
Margold, Nathan, 56, 61
Markham, Edward, 107
Maritime Commission, 219
Marshall, George C., 142, 203,
    209–10
Marshall Plan, 249
Martin, Joseph, 243
Maxcy, Charles, 67
McAdoo, William Gibbs, 26

McClellan, John, 244
McDonough, Clarence, 68–9, 71–2, 76–7
McDonough, John, 215–16
McDonough, Michael, 37–9
McEntee, James, 106
McKee, Ruth, 229
McNary, Charles, 165, 174
Mead, Elwood, 46
Mead, George H., 244
Means, Gardiner, 202–3
Mekong Delta, 19, 233, 254
Merriam, Charles, 59, 63–4
military bases, 205, 207, 210, 232–3, 248, 259, 262
Millions for Defense, 217, 271
Minderman, Earl, 213–14, 226, 229
Modern Corporation and Private Property, The, 203
Morgenthau, Henry, 82, 107
Morrison-Knudsen, 19
Moses, Robert, 245
Mumford, Lewis, 50
Murphy, Frank, 181
Muscle Shoals, 56, 68
Myer, Dillon, 230

National Conference of Catholic Charities, 30
National Consumers League, 55, 220
national defense, 47, 49, 142, 196, 202–11, 216–17, 253, 256
National Guard, 202, 206
National Industrial Recovery Act (NIRA), 8, 14, 29–32, 36–7, 98–9, 216; section 203(d), 45–6
National Institute of Governmental Purchasing, 242
National Interregional Highway Committee, 207, 251
National Planning Board (NPB), 63–4, 78
National Recovery Administration (NRA), 9, 13, 30–1, 39, 50, 83, 99, 101, 104, 199, 262

National Resources Planning Board (NRPB), 55, 96, 202, 205, 207, 234–7
National Unemployment League, 26, 30
National Youth Administration (NYA), 102, 104, 188, 194, 210, 253
navy, *see* U.S. Navy
Nazis, 158
Nelson, Donald M., 204
New Deal, 1–20, 22–3, 27–30, 32–3, 37–8, 41, 43, 47–8, 51–5, 59–63, 70, 72, 74–5, 77–8, 80–1, 84–8, 90, 98, 100–1, 105, 112–15, 117–22, 134–8, 140–3, 146, 148–9, 153, 158, 160–4, 168, 172, 175–6, 179–83, 188–94, 198–200, 203, 205, 210–12, 216–17, 219–23, 228, 230–6, 243–6, 248–50, 252–6, 258–63, 265–6; and economic development, 5, 15, 17, 19, 22, 37, 51, 119–21, 137, 162, 233, 249, 253–5, 258, 262; and patronage, 54, 60, 74–5, 77, 80, 137, 163–4; and politics in relief, 135, 161, 163; and postwar world, 255–66; *see also* Public Works Administration; Works Progress Administration
New Deal liberalism, 4, 6, 17, 20, 84, 162, 191, 193, 231, 255–6, 258–60, 262, 266
New Dealers, 3, 7, 9, 15, 17–18, 22, 32–3, 47, 53–4, 60, 85–7, 89, 96, 102–3, 112, 118–21, 136–7, 158, 161, 164, 172, 175, 183, 187, 189–90, 192–5, 199, 203, 208, 210, 216, 222, 231, 234–5, 239, 244–5, 248, 251–2, 255, 258–61, 265–6; and economic development, 15, 17, 22, 103, 119–21, 137, 255, 258; and patronage, 54, 60, 137, 164; and politics in relief, 161; and postwar world, 255–66; *see also* Public Works Administration; Works Progress Administration
New Deals, 14

New Jersey State Emergency Council, 137
New Republic, 49
New York City Herald-Tribune, 196
New York State Conference of Social Work, 150
New York Sun, 143–4, 148
New York Times, 147–8, 170, 176, 203, 214
New Yorker, 237
Nicholson, Rex L., 222, 225–30,
Niles, David K., 102, 106
Norris, George W., 29, 56, 68, 164, 181
North Atlantic Treaty Organization, 249
Nye, Gerald, 60

Office for Emergency Management, 224
Oklahoma v. U.S. Civil Service Commission (1947), 188
Olson, Culbert, 225
O'Mahoney, Joseph, 76, 170
O'Neal, Edward, 104
organized labor, 4, 7, 24, 32, 37–8, 40, 52, 84, 192, 211
Osgood, Irene, 24

Pacific Nickel Company, 155
Palmer, Charles F., 218
Pan American Highway, 252
Panama Canal, 195
Parker, George H., 66
Parker, William Stanley, 235
parks, 22, 87, 108, 114, 119, 137
party building, public works and, 6, 18, 77
Passamaquoddy dam project, 256
patronage, 42, 54, 60, 74–7, 80, 137, 150, 157, 163–4; *see also* politics in relief
Patterson, James T., 10
Patterson, Robert, 206
Pearl Harbor, 215, 222–5
Pearson, Drew, 170, 200, 254
Pegler, Westbrook, 225

Pennsylvania State Planning Board, 235
Peoples, Christian, 49
Perkins, Frances, 10, 30–2, 34, 54, 220
Pittman, Key, 115, 187
Point Four program, 248–50
political economy, 1, 5, 250, 262
politics in relief, 135, 150, 161, 163, 185; *see also* patronage
Pollock, James, 244
Portland Cement Association, 29
ports, 11
Post Office, 48, 82
Potomac, 184
President's Committee on Administrative Management, 191
President's Emergency Committee for Employment (PECE), 26
President's Organization on Unemployment Relief (POUR), 212
private contractors, 2, 17, 32, 40, 56, 69–70, 72, 98, 109–10, 194, 207, 224
public buildings, 2, 22, 28, 34, 49, 78, 87, 89–90, 95, 103, 108, 113–14, 126, 130, 142, 205
Public Buildings Administration, 191, 198, 233–4
Public Health Service, 113
public housing, 12, 89, 218, 260
public investment, 4, 84, 87, 262
Public Roads Administration, 113, 191, 198, 207, 233–4, 251
Public Work Reserve, 234–6, 251
Public Works Administration (PWA), 2, 5, 8–10, 14, 17–18, 22, 28, 30–101, 103–4, 107–12, 115–18, 120–21, 123–34, 138, 140, 164, 191, 193–4, 198–9, 203, 216–17, 219–20, 222, 232–5, 239, 249, 254, 256, 258–9, 263, 265; accounting division, 66–7; board of labor review, 39–40; division of engineering, 67–72; division of investigation, 17, 55–9, 74, 81, 83–4; federal projects, 45, 90, 94, 97, 101; finance division,

62, 66, 69; flood control projects, 34, 44, 48, 95, 104; hospital projects, 11, 28, 38, 87, 94, 114, 119, 218; hydroelectric projects, 46–7, 53, 94, 217, 261; inspection division, 72; labor advisory board, 37, 39, 48; library projects, 87, 114, 132; nonfederal projects, 34, 64, 76, 91, 94–5, 110; projects division, 69; railroad projects, 95, 119, 217; reclamation projects, 44, 89–90, 95; school projects, 89, 127; sewer and water projects, 89; Special Board for Public Works, 32–8, 40–9, 51–4, 62, 70; subcommittee on policy, 35; technical board of review, 70, 99;
Public Works Committee, 235–6
public works revolution, 3, 122, 266

Radosh, Ronald, 11, 13–14
Rauch, Fred, 212–13, 215–16
Rayburn, Sam, 15
Read, Charles L., 37
Reagan, Ronald, 188, 265
Rebuilding America's Infrastructure, 264–5
Reconstruction Finance Corporation (RFC), 17, 19, 22, 27, 32, 59, 76, 85–6, 199, 242, 263
Republican National Committee (RNC), 144, 146
Resettlement Administration, 74, 104
Rifkind, Simon, 31
Richberg, Donald, 31, 66
river and harbor projects, 104
Road to Plenty, The, 136
roads, 11, 21, 28, 36, 78, 90, 95, 99, 104, 115, 121, 143–4, 192, 205, 207–8, 210, 217, 225–6, 231, 251, 253, 259, 261, 263; *see also* streets
Robert, Lawrence, 35, 38, 40, 45, 82
Rockefeller, John D., 24
Robinson, Joseph T., 145–7, 156
Roosevelt and Hopkins, 162
Roosevelt, Eleanor, 167, 191, 194
Roosevelt, Franklin D. (FDR), 6–13, 17–20, 27, 36, 42–6, 49–52, 60–1,

68, 72–73, 75–6, 81–2, 87, 96–7, 101–4, 107, 112, 115, 118, 120, 137–40, 153, 160–4, 167–8, 170, 173–4, 197, 210, 212, 218–23, 228, 240, 247, 254; and boondoggling, 135, 138, 143, 145–6, 149; and creation of Public Works Administration, 28–32; and creation of Works Progress Administration, 101–4; and Hatch Act, 180–7; and highways, 251–3; and reorganization of public works programs, 190–4, 198–201
"Roosevelt Recession" of 1937–1938, 163, 168, 190
Roper, Daniel, 33, 49, 63
ROTC, 206
Rounds, G.L., 73
Rowe, James Jr., 244
Ruml, Beardsley, 237–8
Rural Electrification Administration (REA), 104, 198–200
rural rehabilitation, 104
Russell, Richard, 45

Sabath, Adolph, 80
Santee-Cooper Dam, 94
Saturday Evening Post, 77
Saudi Arabia, 249, 253
Sawyer, Donald, 32, 35
Schechter Poultry v. U.S. (1935), 30
Schlesinger, Arthur, Jr., 8–9, 121, 250, 259
Schmitt, F. E., 235
Schnepfe, Fred, 235
schools, 11, 22, 38, 44, 78, 87, 90, 94–5, 108, 114, 119, 121, 127, 132, 142, 218
Schwarz, Jordan, 15, 117–18, 209
Schwellenbach, Lewis, 120–1
scientific management, 198–200
Seager, Henry Rogers, 24
Securities and Exchange Commission, 29, 118
self-liquidating construction, 28, 32, 45, 59, 85–6, 100–1, 104, 239
Senate Indian Affairs Committee, 56

sewage disposal plants, 44
sewers, 87, 94, 113, 156
Shasta Dam, 94
Sheppard Committee, 170–5
Sheppard, Morris, 170–1, 195
Sherman, A. L., 70
Sherwood, Robert, 162, 176
shipbuilding, 34, 44
Shreve, Charles M., 180
Simon, Paul, 265
Singapore, 253
Slattery, Harry, 61
Smith, Adam, 3
Smith, Harold D., 221
Smith, Hilda Worthington, 15, 215
social security, 178, 248
Social Security Act, 14
Somervell, Brehon, 219
Special Committee to Investigate
    Senatorial Campaign Expenditures
    and Use of Governmental Funds,
    see Sheppard Committee
Stein, Herbert, 96, 193
Stevenson, Adlai, 230
Stimson, Henry, 209, 225, 228
Stokes, Thomas, 162, 165–8, 170,
    172, 175–6
Stott, William, 87
Straus, Nathan, 218–21
streets, 87, 90, 95, 98, 113, 115, 141,
    143, 156, 240; *see also* roads
Stewart, Bady M., 167
Survey, 150
Survey Associates, 51
Sweden, 135

Taft, Robert A. Jr, 174, 201
Taft, William Howard, 56
Tennessee Power Company, 68
Tennessee Valley Authority (TVA), 2,
    19, 36, 55–6, 68, 94, 233, 246, 250,
    254, 265
Thailand, 249
Thomas, Dorothy Swaine, 230
Triggs, Clayton L., 226–7
Truman, Harry, 157, 230, 243–5,
    247–9

Tugwell, Rexford, 30, 32, 38, 40,
    43–4, 54, 57, 62, 74, 207, 251
TVA: Democracy on the March, 255
Tydings, Millard, 175

U.S. Army, 34, 36, 48, 74, 80, 114,
    202–5, 207, 209, 212, 216–17, 220,
    222, 224, 226–8, 251; U.S. Army
    Air Corps, 217
U.S. Army Corps of Engineers, 2, 52,
    56, 67–8, 76, 80, 103–4, 107, 195,
    219, 224, 234, 245, 263
U.S. Community Improvement
    Appraisal, 147, 149, 159
U.S. Conference of Mayors, 42, 51,
    78–9, 104
U.S. Department of Agriculture, 48,
    113, 191, 227, 230, 234
U.S. Department of Commerce, 48,
    235
U.S. Department of Interior, 48, 56–7,
    61, 66, 74, 77, 81, 83, 216, 227,
    230, 245
U.S. Department of Justice, 48, 59
U.S. Department of Labor, 47–8, 227;
    division of public work and
    construction development, 24
U.S. Department of Treasury, 35, 48,
    82, 103, 134, 191, 234
U.S. Department of War, 47–8, 209,
    217, 223
U.S. Employment Service (USES), 37,
    214
U.S. Housing Authority, 191, 198,
    218, 234
U.S. Navy, 34, 36, 48–9, 60, 202, 205,
    207, 216
unemployment, 4, 8–9, 14, 17–20,
    22–5, 30–2, 35, 37–8, 46–9, 78, 87,
    95, 97, 101–2, 104, 119, 136,
    143–4, 186, 192, 194, 202, 205,
    208, 222–3, 235, 238, 252, 258,
    260–1, 263–4; *see also* direct
    employment; indirect employment
United Electrical Workers, 48
United Kingdom, 135
United Nations, 226, 249, 254

United Nations Relief and
  Rehabilitation Administration, 227
United Public Workers v. Mitchell
  (1947), 188
United Relief Program, 30
Upper Mississippi River project, 46
Uthus, Bruce, 214–16
utilities, 28, 67, 72, 87, 108

Vandenberg, Arthur, 147, 243
viaduct projects, 78, 115, 123, 142
Vietnam, 249, 254, 259

Wagner Act, 14
Wagner, Robert, 10, 26–7, 29–31, 240
Wagner-Steagall Housing Act, 193
Waite, Henry M., 60, 65, 235
Walker, Frank C., 102, 107, 138,
  184–5
Wallace, Henry, 38
Walmsley, Seems, 79
Walsh, David, 170
War Assets Administration, 247
War Finance Corporation, 27
War Relocation Authority (WRA),
  223–4, 228–30
Ware, Susan, 15
Warren, Earl, 225
Wartime Civilian Control
  Administration (WCCA), 222,
  224–5, 227–9; reception and
  induction division, 222
Washington Daily News, 166, 179
Washington Herald Times, 196
Washington Post, 249, 254
Washington Star, 47
water works projects, 44, 78
welfare state, 15, 98, 135, 176, 188,
  231, 263
Westbrook, Lawrence, 102, 139
White, Dudley A., 168
White, Sue Shelton, 15
Williams, Aubrey, 102, 139, 167, 170,
  188, 194–5, 208, 212

Williams, J. Kerwin, 39–40
Wilson Dam, 68
Wilson, Richard, 256
Wilson, William Julius, 265
Wilson, Woodrow, 25
Wolman, Leo, 79
women, 15, 38, 60, 104, 141, 164,
  213, 215–16, 260
Wood, Edith, 218
Wood, Robert, 104
Woods, Arthur, 26
Woodward, Ellen S., 15, 102
Work Projects Administration, *see*
  Works Progress Administration
Workers Alliance, 170, 194, 196,
  219
Works Progress Administration
  (WPA), 2, 5, 8–9, 11, 18–19, 56, 84,
  87, 96–8, 101–3, 105–8, 111–18,
  120–3, 126–7, 129, 132, 135–74,
  176, 178–80, 184–5, 187–8, 191,
  194–8, 200–31, 234–5, 239, 241,
  249, 258–9, 262–5; boondoggling
  charges, responses to, 145–9;
  division of information, 143, 226;
  division of investigation, 138, 155;
  division of training and
  reemployment, 212–16; and
  economic development, 5, 19, 103,
  120–21, 137, 162, 241, 249, 258,
  262; and Japanese American
  internment, 19, 194, 222–31, 259;
  and patronage, 137, 150, 157,
  163–4; and politics in relief, 135,
  150, 161, 163, 185
World War I, 21, 24, 27, 58, 74, 212
World War II, 4–6, 18, 53, 101, 187,
  191, 219, 221, 231, 245, 250,
  252–3, 255, 259, 263

Yorktown, 133, 217
Young Democrats of America, 180

Zinn, Howard, 12

CPSIA information can be obtained at www.ICGtesting.com
Printed in the USA
LVOW070902120112

263335LV00002BA/9/P

9 780521 139939